IS THE DEATH PENALTY DYING?

Is the Death Penalty Dying? provides a careful analysis of the historical and political conditions that shaped death penalty practice on both sides of the Atlantic from the end of World War II to the twenty-first century. This book examines and assesses what the United States can learn from the European experience with capital punishment, especially the trajectory of abolition in different European nations. As a comparative sociology and history of the present, the book seeks to illuminate the way death penalty systems and their dissolution work, by means of eleven chapters written by an interdisciplinary group of authors from the United States and Europe. This work will help readers see how close the United States is to ending capital punishment and some of the cultural and institutional barriers that stand in the way of abolition. Yet, more than that, this book shows how the death penalty has helped define the political and cultural identities of both Europe and the United States.

Austin Sarat is William Nelson Cromwell Professor of Jurisprudence and Political Science at Amherst College and Justice Hugo L. Black Visiting Senior Faculty Scholar at the University of Alabama School of Law. He is the author or editor of more than seventy books, including *When the State Kills: Capital Punishment and the American Condition*; *Something to Believe In: Politics, Professionalism, and Cause Lawyers* (with Stuart Scheingold); *The Blackwell Companion to Law and Society*; and most recently *The Road to Abolition?: The Future of Capital Punishment in the United States* (with Charles Ogletree, Jr.). Sarat is editor of the journals *Law, Culture and the Humanities* and *Studies in Law, Politics and Society*. In 2009, he received the Stan Wheeler Award from the Law and Society Association for distinguished teaching and mentoring.

Jürgen Martschukat is a Professor of History at Erfurt University and recipient of the opus magnum fellowship of the German "pro-humanities" foundation (2010–2011). He has published several books, edited volumes, and written numerous articles on the history of violence and the death penalty in Europe and the United States from the seventeenth century to the present. In 2002, he was awarded the David Thelen Prize from the Organization of American Historians for his article on the "Art of Killing by Electricity." In 2007, he was a Fellow at the Woodrow Wilson International Center for Scholars in Washington, DC, working on a project on race and capital punishment.

Is the Death Penalty Dying?

EUROPEAN AND AMERICAN PERSPECTIVES

Edited by

AUSTIN SARAT

Amherst College

JÜRGEN MARTSCHUKAT

Erfurt University

CAMBRIDGE UNIVERSITY PRESS
Cambridge, New York, Melbourne, Madrid, Cape Town,
Singapore, São Paulo, Delhi, Mexico City

Cambridge University Press
32 Avenue of the Americas, New York NY 10013-2473, USA

Published in the United States of America by Cambridge University Press, New York

www.cambridge.org
Information on this title: www.cambridge.org/9781107634275

First published 2011
First paperback edition 2013

A catalogue record for this publication is available from the British Library

Library of Congress Cataloguing in Publication Data

Is the death penalty dying? : European and American perspectives / edited by Austin Sarat,
Jürgen Martschukat.
p. cm.
Includes bibliographical references and index.
ISBN 978-0-521-76351-6 (hardback)
1. Capital punishment – Europe. 2. Capital punishment – United States. I. Sarat, Austin.
II. Martschukat, Jürgen. III. Title.
HV8699.E85I82 2011
364.66094–dc22 2010037115

ISBN 978-0-521-76351-6 Hardback
ISBN 978-1-107-63427-5 Paperback

To Ben, for all the joy you bring (A.S.)

To all those who fight for a death penalty–free world (J.M.)

Contents

Contributors

Colin Dayan, English, Vanderbilt University

Agata Fijalkowski, European Legal Studies and International LLB, Lancaster University Law School

Evi Girling, Research Institute of Law, Politics and Justice, Keele University

Marie Gottschalk, Political Science, University of Pennsylvania

Simon Grivet, History, CNRS, Paris

Andrew Hammel, Law Faculty, Heinrich-Heine University, Düsseldorf

Kathryn A. Heard, Jurisprudence and Social Policy, University of California, Berkeley

Timothy V. Kaufman-Osborn, Politics, Whitman College

Jürgen Martschukat, History, Erfurt University

Austin Sarat, Law, Jurisprudence, and Political Science, Amherst College

Jonathan Simon, Jurisprudence and Social Policy, University of California, Berkeley

Pieter Spierenburg, Historical Criminology, Erasmus University, Rotterdam

Jon Yorke, School of Law, Birmingham City University

Acknowledgments

The chapters in this book were originally presented at a workshop at Amherst College on April 9–10, 2010. We want to thank the contributors for their interest and enthusiastic participation. We thank Megan Estes for her able assistance. We are grateful for financial assistance provided by Amherst College's Corliss Lamont Fund for a Peaceful World and by the Humboldt Foundation.

Introduction: Transatlantic Perspectives on Capital Punishment

National Identity, the Death Penalty, and the Prospects for Abolition

Austin Sarat and Jürgen Martschukat

Is the Death Penalty Dying? offers an analysis of the historical and political conditions that have shaped and continue to shape death penalty practices on both sides of the Atlantic from the end of World War II to the twenty-first century. This book focuses on what we can learn about the American death penalty and the prospects of its abolition by studying the European experience with capital punishment and especially the multifaceted trajectory of abolition in different European nations and the European Union. As a comparative sociology and history of the present, our book seeks to illuminate the way death penalty systems work and the way abolition occurs. It includes eleven chapters, written by an interdisciplinary group of scholars in the fields of law and literature, sociology and criminology, political science, and history from the United States and several European countries. This work shows how the death penalty has helped define the political and cultural identities of both Europe and the United States and will help readers understand the cultural and institutional barriers that stand in the way of abolition of the death penalty in America.

AMERICAN QUANDARIES

The United States is today the only retentionist country among the community of Western democracies.[1] Indeed America finds itself in the company of countries such as China, Iran, Iraq, Pakistan, Saudi Arabia, and Sudan in its continuing use of state killing. Moreover, there is hardly any issue on which Europe and the United States seem as far apart as the death penalty. Whereas most American states authorize capital punishment, since the 1980s Europe has emerged as a bastion of abolitionism and its worldwide advance, with the European Union having made abolition a strict requirement for membership.

[1] Austin Sarat, and Christian Boulanger, eds., *The Cultural Lives of Capital Punishment: Comparative Perspectives* (Stanford, CA: Stanford University Press, 2005).

Yet lately, the perception and politics of the death penalty in the United States have been changing.[2] This change has been driven in part by a large number of exonerations from death row, with 55 occurring in the last decade among a total of 138 since 1973.[3] Americans are increasingly aware of judicial errors and wrongful convictions. The malfunctioning of the death penalty system has also been diagnosed by an array of research studies[4], and it has led to far-reaching and widely noticed decisions by political figures like former Governors George Ryan of Illinois or Parris Glendening of Maryland, both death penalty supporters at one time, who declared moratoria on executions, and in Ryan's case granted clemency to everyone on his state's death row.

With increasing intensity, capital punishment in America has been labelled a broken system. Rising scepticism has also been accompanied by dropping execution numbers, from a high of ninety-eight in 1999 to fifty-two in 2009. Furthermore, even though support for the death penalty among the general population is still substantial, it is nevertheless shrinking. The Gallup Poll's latest national survey of American opinion on the death penalty found that support for capital punishment dropped by five percentage points from the year before, falling from a high of 80 percent in the mid-1990s to 69 percent in 2007 and down to 64 percent in 2008. Today American support for the death penalty is equal to the lowest it has been in the Gallup Polls during the past thirty years.[5]

When asked to choose between the death penalty and life without parole as a punishment for murder, the American public now splits right down the middle. Yet, the American public remains wedded to punitiveness. Thus, as Marie Gottschalk indicates in her contribution to this book, the promotion of life in prison without the possibility of parole (LWOP) by leading death penalty abolitionists appears to have contributed to "the construction of the carceral state in the U.S." by legitimizing the greater use of life sentences, even for noncapital crimes. Prior to the mid-1970s (which is also the time when the death penalty returned in America), LWOP was used sparingly, and in the mid-1990s, only sixteen states had LWOP on the books.

[2] Charles Ogletree, and Austin Sarat, eds., *The Road to Abolition? The Future of Capital Punishment in the United States* (New York: New York University Press, 2009).

[3] "Exonerations by year," http://www.deathpenaltyinfo.org/innocence-and-death-penalty#inn-yr-rc (accessed March 9, 2010).

[4] James S. Liebman, Jeffrey Fagan, and Valerie West, "A Broken System. Error Rates in Capital Cases, 1973–1995," New York 2000, http://www2.law.columbia.edu/instructionalservices/liebman/ (accessed March 9, 2010); James Liebmann et al., "A Broken System, Part II: Why There Is So Much Error in Capital Cases, and What Can Be Done About It," New York 2002, http://www2.law.columbia.edu/brokensystem2/index2.html (accessed March 9, 2010); Raymond Paternoster, and R. Brame, "Reassessing Race Disparities in Maryland Capital Cases," *Criminology* 46, 4 (2008): 971–1008; Paternoster et al., "Justice by Geography and Race: The Administration of the Death Penalty in Maryland, 1978–1999," *Maryland's Law Journal on Race, Religion, Gender and Class* 4 (2004: 1–97).

[5] Lydia Saad, "Americans Hold Firm to Support for Death Penalty. Only 21% say it is applied too often," *Gallup* (November 17, 2008), http://www.gallup.com/poll/111931/Americans-Hold-Firm-Support-Death-Penalty.aspx (accessed March 9, 2010).

That number has risen to forty-nine today.[6] Colin Dayan argues in her chapter that LWOP and solitary confinement are other death penalties that do not draw the same amount of attention and opposition as capital punishment.[7] Gottschalk's, Dayan's, and Jonathan Simon's chapters indicate that the American debate on the death penalty is undergoing a transformation that would cover various forms of "ultimate sanctions."[8]

The larger problem of punitiveness that now inflects the American debate on capital punishment has begun to make its appearance in Europe. Thus Pieter Spierenburg notes that European incarceration rates have grown, too, during recent decades, although not on the same scale as in the United States.[9] Furthermore, a March 9, 2010 decision by the German Federal Court of Justice that lifelong preventive detention of criminals who are deemed dangerous to the general public after the expiration of their sentence does not violate human rights, sparked a massive public debate in Germany. The daily "Süddeutsche Zeitung" commented on the German Federal Court's decision by calling lifelong preventive detention the "German substitute for the death penalty."[10]

Contributing to the unsettled status of capital punishment in the United States today, as it has often done in the modern history of the death penalty, are uncertainties surrounding methods of execution, their appropriateness and "decency" – a fact Timothy Kaufman-Osborn discusses in his chapter which analyzes the Report by the British 'Royal Commission on Capital Punishment' of the 1950s.[11] Though lethal injection mimics a healing and benign intervention into the human body, attention recently has been aroused by a substantial number of botched executions due to unqualified personnel and mismanagement. The Supreme Court's May 2008 decision that Kentucky's lethal injection protocol did not present an "unnecessary risk" of harm to the condemned seems unlikely to end the controversy about lethal injection.[12]

6 See Marie Gottschalk, "The Long Shadow of the Death Penalty: Incarceration, Capital Punishment, and Penal Policy in the United States" in this book; see also Marie Gottschalk, *The Prison and the Gallows: The Politics of Mass Incarceration in America* (Cambridge: Cambridge University Press, 2006).

7 Colin Dayan, "Did Anyone Die Here? Legal Personalities, the Supermax, and the Politics of Abolition" in this book; Colin Dayan, *The Story of Cruel and Unusual* (Boston, MA: MIT Press, 2007).

8 See also Jonathan Simon's contribution to this book: "Capital Punishment as Homeowners Insurance: The Rise of the Homeowner Citizen and the Fate of Ultimate Sanctions in Both Europe and the United States."

9 Pieter Spierenburg, "The Green, Green Grass of Home: Capital Punishment and the Penal System from a Long-Term Perspective," Chapter 1, this volume.

10 Heribert Prantl, "Verdammt in alle Ewigkeit," *Süddeutsche Zeitung* (March 10, 2010): 4.

11 Timothy Kaufman-Osborn, "The Death of Dignity," in this book.

12 *Baze v. Rees*, 553 U.S. 35 (2008). For the recent controversy on lethal injection, see the articles by Deborah Denno, "The Lethal Injection Quandary: How Medicine Has Dismantled the Death Penalty," *Fordham Law Review* 76, 1 (2007): 49–128; Denno, "For Execution Methods Challenges, the Road to Abolition Is Paved with Paradox," in *The Road to Abolition?* ed. Ogletree and Sarat, 183–214; Timothy Kaufman-Osborn, "Perfect Execution. Abolitionism and the Paradox of Lethal Injection," in

An important marker of the changing American landscape of capital punishment occurred in New Jersey where on December 18, 2007, then Governor Jon Corzine signed a bill making his state the first in a generation to abolish capital punishment. Corzine stated that "this is a day of progress for us and for the millions of people across our nation and around the globe who reject the death penalty as a moral or practical response to the grievous, even heinous, crime of murder." Among the reasons he mentioned for the abolition of the death penalty were two issues discussed above, namely the impossibility of devising "a humane technique of execution that is not cruel and unusual, and . . . a foolproof system that precludes the possibility of executing the innocent."[13]

Another factor was the high financial cost of capital punishment: Keeping inmates on death row cost the state $72,602 per year for each prisoner, whereas inmates kept in the general population cost $40,121 per year each to house. The New Jersey corrections department estimated that the repeal would save the state as much as $1.3 million per inmate over his or her lifetime – and that figure did not include the millions spent on inmates' appeals. Beside concerns about the execution technique, the error rate, and the economic cost, Corzine noted that the death penalty "begets violence and undermines our commitment to the sanctity of life. We in New Jersey are proud to be the first state to prohibit the death penalty since it was permitted by the U.S. Supreme Court in 1976, and we are proud to serve as leaders on this profound issue of conscience."[14]

New Jersey abolished capital punishment despite the pleas of some high-profile victims and the fact that, at the time of abolition, New Jersey voters were opposed to ending the death penalty by a margin of 53 percent to 39 percent. This conforms to the European experience that public opinion tends to follow decisions by political elites rather than leading them. Thus, Andrew Hammel labels European abolitionist intellectuals and politicians "civilized rebels" in his contribution to this book.[15] Since American institutions are more "porous" and open to popular demands than European political structures, the path to abolition in the United States is less certain. The more democratic penal policy-making in the United States is prone to be punitive. As one observer put it, "basically, Europe doesn't have the death

The Road to Abolition? ed. Ogletree and Sarat, 215–51; Jürgen Martschukat "'No Improvement Over Electrocution or Even a Bullet:' Lethal Injection and the Meaning of Speed and Reliability in the Modern Execution Process," in *The Road to Abolition?* ed. Ogletree and Sarat, 252–78.

[13] For the full text of Governor Corzine's statement, see "New Jersey Governor Jon S. Corzine – Remarks as Delivered December 17, 2007," found at http://www.allamericanpatriots.com/48739396_new-jersey-governor-corzines-remarks-eliminating-death-penalty-new-jersey (accessed September 2, 2010).

[14] New Jersey State League of Municipalities, "Governor Corzine Signs Legislation Eliminating Death Penalty in New Jersey," http://www.njslom.org/death_penalty_press_release.html (accessed May 13, 2010).

[15] Andrew Hammel, "Civilized Rebels: Death-Penalty Abolition in Europe as Cause, Mark of Distinction, and Political Strategy," Chapter 7, this volume.

penalty because its political systems are less democratic, or at least more insulated from populist impulses, than the U.S. government."[16]

In another sign of the changing situation in the United States, fifteen months after New Jersey, New Mexico also abolished its death penalty. On March 18, 2009, Governor Bill Richardson, formerly a supporter of capital punishment, described replacing execution with life in prison without the possibility of parole as "the most difficult decision of his political life." However, noting that 130 death-row prisoners had been exonerated at that point in time, four of them in New Mexico, Richardson observed that even though he still believed in the death penalty in general, he did not trust the "broken system" enough to sign a death warrant:

> "Regardless of my personal opinion about the death penalty, I do not have confidence in the criminal justice system as it currently operates to be the final arbiter when it comes to who lives and who dies for their crime. Faced with the reality that our system for imposing the death penalty can never be perfect, my conscience compels me to replace the death penalty with a solution that keeps society safe."[17]

Yet paradoxically, perhaps the most telling example of America's current quandary with capital punishment is not an effort at abolition, but at its reintroduction. When in April 2005, then–Massachusetts Governor Mitt Romney, a Republican with a progressive record on social issues, was gearing up for an effort to secure the Republican nomination for President, he was looking for ways to reassure conservatives that he really was one of them. As *The New York Times* put it at the time the Romney death penalty bill was introduced, "Mr. Romney, who is widely believed to have national political ambitions, may intend his death penalty bill for a different audience as well: conservatives outside his state who are pivotal in Republican Party politics."[18]

Yet, the Romney bill itself indicated the power of the growing tide of doubt about the death penalty and was designed to respond to the multilayered criticism of the preceding years. It would have restricted capital punishment to a very limited number of crimes, namely murders that involve terrorism, prolonged torture,

16 Joshua Micah Marshall, "Death in Venice: Europe's Death-penalty Elitism," *The New Republic* (July 31, 2000), here quoted after Andrew Moravcsik, "The New Abolitionism: Why Does the U.S. Practice the Death Penalty While Europe Does Not?" Council for European Studies at Columbia University 2006, http://www.ces.columbia.edu/pub/Moravcsik_sep01.html (accessed March 9, 2010). See also Franklin Zimring, Gordon Hawkins, and Sam Kamin, *Punishment and Democracy: Three Strikes and You're Out in California* (Oxford: Oxford University Press, 2001).

17 "New Mexi-Can and New Mexi-Did Abolish Capital Punishment," ACLU Blog of Rights, March 19 2009, http://www.aclu.org/blog/capital-punishment/new-mexi-can-and-new-mexi-did-abolish-capital-punishment (accessed March 14, 2010).

18 Pam Belluck, "Massachusetts Governor Urges Death Penalty," *New York Times* (April 29, 2005), http://query.nytimes.com/gst/fullpage.html?res=9801E6DC1131F93AA15757C0A9639C8B63&sec=&spon=&pagewanted=all (accessed March 15, 2010).

multiple killings, or the killing of police officers, judges, witnesses, or others involved in the criminal justice system. Defendants who had previously been convicted of first-degree murder or were serving life sentences without parole would also have been eligible. Yet, even more important in the context of the current debate is that the Romney bill included several provisions that had never been tried in any other state. To make the system absolutely foolproof, it would have required "conclusive scientific evidence," like DNA, to link a defendant to a crime. Furthermore, it would have allowed a death penalty to be imposed only if a sentencing jury found that there was "no doubt" about a defendant's guilt, a standard even stricter than "beyond a reasonable doubt." Finally, Romney's bill also included a requirement that defendants in capital cases have two and possibly three lawyers, that scientific evidence be examined by a review board, that every death sentence be reviewed by the state's highest court, and that a special panel be set up to handle complaints.[19]

The Romney bill signals a key difference between American and European perceptions of capital punishment. It expressed the hope that the "broken system" of the death penalty in America might be fixed. The question whether the death penalty was appropriate at all in a democratic state that sees itself in the tradition of the enlightenment was not on the agenda. In Europe, the death penalty is not considered primarily to be an issue of the criminal justice system and its reliability, but instead is seen as an issue of human rights.

ABOLITIONISM AND EUROPEAN UNITY

For several decades, the European position on capital punishment moved in the opposite direction from the American position, with the death penalty a significant influence in shaping a European identity. In this book, Evi Girling and Kathryn Heard focus on differences among European and American perceptions of executions and their implications for identity formations.[20] In the press and to the public, European opposition to capital punishment is often presented as an offspring of the European Enlightenment and secularization since the eighteenth century, whereas American adherence to the death penalty is described as a vestige of a centuries-old frontier mentality.

[19] Drake Bennett, "Reasonable Doubt," *Boston Globe* (May 8, 2005), http://www.boston.com/news/globe/ideas/articles/2005/05/08/reasonable_doubt/ (accessed March 15, 2010).

[20] Evi Girling, "European Identity and the Mission Against the Death Penalty in the United States," in *The Cultural Lives of Capital Punishment*, ed. Sarat and Boulanger, 112–28; see also Girling's chapter in this book, "The Witnessing of Judgement: Between Error, Mercy, and Vindictiveness"; see also Kathryn Heard's contribution in "Unframing the Death Penalty: Transatlantic Discourse on the Possibility of Abolition and the Execution of Saddam Hussein," and Stefano Manacorda, "Restraints on Death Penalty in Europe: A Circular Process," *Journal of International Criminal Justice* 1 (2003): 263–83; Martschukat, "Capital Punishment," in *The Oxford Encyclopedia of the Modern World*, ed. Peter N. Stearns (New York: Oxford University Press, 2008), Vol. 2, 33–8.

This version of a deeply rooted European-American dichotomy is overly simplistic, because the reforms triggered by the Enlightenment initiated transformations of the criminal justice systems in both Europe and the United States. Secondly, with respect to the death penalty, neither in Europe nor America did early reforms mean total abolition, but rather a reduction in the number of capital felonies and a "modernization" of execution procedures.[21] Thirdly, in the United States, cultures and systems of punishment were and remain manifold and diverse, and often enough, northern and midwestern states were pioneers in the transatlantic criminal justice reform movement, whereas southern states were most ardently retentionist.[22] Fourth, until the post–World War II period, Europe was not the abolitionist continent it is today. Indeed, neither the Nazi regime nor the horrors of the Holocaust and World War II changed the dominant public attitude of many European countries that taking a life in the name of the state was acceptable and necessary in particular cases. Significantly, in the years immediately after the war, in addition to Finland, only West Germany, Italy, and Austria – former fascist states and World War II aggressors – abandoned the death penalty. When the parliamentary assembly was set up in West Germany in 1948–1949 to write a new democratic constitution, it finally abolished the death penalty in the so-called *Grundgesetz* (basic law). But many members of the German parliament were not primarily motivated by humanistic reasons. For them, the first priority was to protect from the death penalty war criminals or those who had been loyal to the regime to the very end.[23]

The Council of Europe and the European Convention on Human Rights were established in 1949 and 1950 with the mission of defending humanity, yet their general commitment to the right to life explicitly excluded lawful death sentences. This ambivalent position on capital punishment was reflected in the policies of several influential European countries. Timothy Kaufman-Osborn's chapter describes the intense debate Great Britain had on the death penalty in the early 1950s. Executions in Great Britain continued until 1964. The death penalty was struck down the following year, and abolition was made permanent in 1969. In Spain, the era of the death penalty lasted until three years after the end of the Franco regime in 1975, and France continued to carry out executions until 1977. It did not formally abolish capital punishment until 1981. Particularly (but by far not exclusively) in France, the death penalty was abolished against prevailing public sentiment through "a coup

21 Even though during the nineteenth and twentieth centuries, the drive to modernize the execution procedure was more intense in the United States than in Europe, as for instance Simon Grivet's and Timothy Kaufman-Osborn's contributions to this book show. For the eighteenth and nineteenth centuries, see Louis P. Masur, *Rites of Execution: Capital Punishment and the Transformation of American Culture, 1776–1865* (Oxford/New York: Oxford University Press, 1989); Martschukat, *Inszeniertes Töten. Eine Geschichte der Todesstrafe vom 17. bis zum 19. Jahrhundert* (Cologne: Böhlau, 2000).

22 Stuart Banner, *The Death Penalty: An American History* (Cambridge, MA: Harvard University Press, 2002); Martschukat, *Die Geschichte der Todesstrafe in Nordamerika* (München: Beck, 2002).

23 Richard Evans, *Rituals of Retribution: Capital Punishment in Germany 1600–1987* (Oxford: Oxford University Press, 1996), 739–804.

d'etat by a political and intellectual elite against the clearly established sentiments of the vast majority of the public," as Andrew Hammel puts it in his chapter in this book.[24]

Thus the much-ballyhooed European position with regard to the death penalty is a relatively recent development. A milestone was the March 1985 enactment of Protocol No. 6 to the European Convention on Human Rights. It was the first international treaty to call for the abolition of the death penalty, and since 1994, adoption of the protocol has been a requirement for acceptance of new members to the Council of Europe. Since 1999, the same has been true for the European Union, which has made abolition of the death penalty obligatory for members and declared a worldwide execution moratorium one of the major pillars of its human rights policy. Thus it was not before the late twentieth century that European penal policy was guided by the "firm conviction that capital punishment... has no place in civilized, democratic societies governed by the rule of law," as the Council of Europe's Commissioner of Human Rights, Thomas Hammarberg, stated in 2007.[25] Or as European Court of Human Rights Justice Jan de Meyer argued in 1989, "[capital] punishment is not consistent with the present state of European civilisation."[26]

Coinciding with the period from the mid-1960s, when Great Britain abolished capital punishment, to the early 1980s, when France followed the British example, the United States itself had a de facto moratorium that lasted from June 1967 to January 1977. Yet while the death penalty was found constitutional by the Supreme Court in 1976, returned in a constantly increasing number of U.S. states afterward, and reached its heyday in the 1990s, European abolitionism in the very same decade gained momentum as a unifying force in Europe after the dissolution of the Soviet bloc and the eastward enlargement of the European Union. The dynamics of regional and political integration spurred abolition in Eastern and Southeastern Europe. As Evi Girling has shown in her work, the formal acceptance of an abolitionist position became a defining criterion of "Europeanness."[27] Agata Fijalkowski reminds us in her contribution to this book that most governments in post-Communist countries abolished the death penalty less because of the "human rights appeal" of abolitionism, and more because of anticipated benefits of compliance with European norms. Institutional pressure makes the abolitionist consensus

[24] Hammel, *Civilized Rebels*, quoting Robert A. Nye, "Two Capital Punishment Debates in France: 1908 and 1981," *Historical Reflections/Reflexions Historiques* 29 (2002): 226; Robert Badinter: *One Man's Battle Against the Death Penalty* (Boston: Northeastern University Press, 2008).

[25] Thomas Hammarberg, Commissioner for Human Rights, "We need to educate about the true nature of the Death Penalty" (presentation at the III World Congress Against the Death Penalty in Paris, France, February 1, 2007), https://wcd.coe.int/ViewDoc.jsp?id=1089191&BackColorInternet=FEC65B&BackColorIntranet=FEC65B&BackColorLogged=FFC679 (accessed March 15, 2010).

[26] *Soering v. United Kingdom*, (Series A, No 161; Application No 14038/88), European Court of Human Rights (1989) 11 EHRR 439, July 7, 1989, http://www.worldlii.org/eu/cases/ECHR/1989/14.html (accessed March 15, 2010).

[27] Girling, "European Identity and the Mission Against the Death Penalty."

quite solid in Europe, even though many Eastern European populations are still ambivalent about the death penalty.

EUROPEAN AND AMERICAN PERSPECTIVES ON THE DYING DEATH PENALTY

As we see it, the European-American divide on the death penalty is more complex than it has often been thought to be, and the constellations of forces on both sides of the Atlantic are more ambivalent than they appear at first sight to be. Europe's firm abolitionism has a short history, has often been driven by tangible political and economic interests, and has no steadfast support among populations in several European countries. At the same time, the position of the death penalty in America is weakening, criticism is growing, and its popular support is still strong, but shrinking. Yet as several chapters to this book show, the increasingly relied-on sentences of "life in prison without parole" and the use of solitary confinement are also highly troubling in that they indicate an unbroken punishment sentiment. Thus the scrutiny of the transatlantic situation of capital punishment and punitiveness is, we believe, crucial if we are to understand where America is on the road to abolition and what the European experience has to offer.

OVERVIEW OF THE CHAPTERS

Part I of this book explores the relationship between the death penalty and the broader system of punishment of which it is a part. The main topic of Part II is the ways the meanings of capital punishment are framed in the United States and Europe. Part III puts abolitionist discourses, strategies, and dilemmas in transatlantic perspective.

Pieter Spierenburg opens the book by taking contemporary European abandonment of the death penalty and its traces in contemporary culture as the starting point of his argument. An expert in early modern European history, he takes us back to the fifteenth century and shows that Europeans were not always unfamiliar with capital punishment, and that, seen in the historic long run, Europe and America's history of harsh sanctions are less far apart than today's observers might think. As several other scholars in this volume also show, Spierenburg maintains that the death penalty can only be understood within the larger frame of a society's penal system and a culture's punitiveness, which has also gained momentum in Europe in recent years. By taking up the recent debate in *Punishment & Society* between Darvid Garland, Franklin Zimring, and Charles Whitman,[28] and by relating it to further writings

[28] David Garland, "Capital Punishment and American Culture," *Punishment & Society* 7, 4 (2005): 347–76; Franklin E. Zimring, "Path Dependence, Culture and State-Level Execution Policy: A Reply to David Garland," *Punishment & Society* 7, 4 (2005): 377–84; James Q. Whitman, "Response to Garland," *Punishment & Society* 7, 4 (2005): 389–96.

on the history of the death penalty in Europe and America, Spierenburg highlights similarities as well as peculiarities and separate developments in various European countries and America. Drawing on Norbert Elias's theory of the civilizing process, Spierenburg describes a long history of moderation in "the West," characterizing American society to a lesser extent than European societies and coinciding with a lesser inclination to demand restraints on violent punishments.

Colin Dayan embraces Spierenburg's view that the death penalty has to be analyzed in the larger context of a culture's punitiveness. Abolitionist discourse has often presented "life without the possibility of parole" as a viable alternative to the death penalty. Yet Dayan shows that LWOP, and particularly solitary confinement, should be considered a different type of capital punishment to which ever larger parts of the American population are subject. Whereas not long ago, prisoners in solitary confinement were a rare exception, today it has become a major pillar of penal philosophy.

Between 30,000 and 100,000 of America's 2.3 million prisoners are now confined in so-called "supermaxes." Thus while the outcome of America's debate on the death penalty is more open today than it has been in the last thirty years, "alongside it," Colin Dayan stresses, "we have invented a new form of death penalty, one which needs no judicial decision, carries no decent shame, is not open to scrutiny, and already stands in danger of killing more people than the death penalty." Criticizing the recent jurisprudence of the Eighth Amendment, Dayan shows that it is the suffering of a real person that is at stake constitutionally. In her view, the supermax is the background against which the death penalty and the debate on dying by the hands of the state must be read.

In the last chapter in this section, Jonathan Simon relates European and American punitiveness to homeownership and analyzes ultimate sanctions as "homeowners insurance." By understanding long, possibly terminal prison sentences as "death sentences in disguise," Simon hypothesizes that crime fear and the proclivity to support ultimate sanctions correlates with homeownership and is higher where more people own their homes than rent. In his chapter, he compares highly punitive American states like California, Florida, and Arizona to the most booming residential real estate markets of Western Europe, such as Ireland, Spain, and the Netherlands, which also rank among the top four European countries in terms of penal growth.

Evi Girling begins Part II with a chapter that focuses on acts of judgment and punishment in liberal democracies in a time of global witnessing. Today, translocal cultures transcend the apparently stable structures of the nation-state and make local institutional and punitive practices an issue of global awareness and concern. Global communities of "sentiment" and "judgment" emerge, as we are told by Girling, and new media technologies have created global communities of witnessing by facilitating an "intimate proximity" among widely dispersed observers to geographically distant events.

Girling shows how the European Union, the Council of Europe, and abolitionist organizations have shaped global narratives about the death penalty and particularly about the drama of exoneration and error. The notion that miscarriages of justice are not unusual and that an error-free and foolproof criminal justice and death penalty system are impossible, is becoming more salient in the formation of a European abolitionist identity. As Girling shows, this position and the related European self-conception are reinforced by the European witnessing of the death penalty and its quandaries in the United States.

Kathryn Heard's chapter also examines the global community of witnesses. Focusing on American and European reactions to Saddam Hussein's execution on December 30, 2006, she explores "the ideological divergence between the European Union and the United States on what can rightly be construed as justice." Drawing on Judith Butler's notion of framing and on performance theory, she discusses different meanings produced by Saddam's execution and its photographic representation. Taken by Iraqi witnesses, the images seem to present neither a seemingly carefully controlled modern execution nor a meticulously planned military operation but rather a spectacle of punishment. Yet, comments by President George W. Bush on the one side and European Commissioner for Development and Humanitarian Aid Louis Michel on the other side varied widely. They reflected different views of the meanings of the death penalty on both sides of the Atlantic. While Michel saw the execution as antithetical to democratic ideals, George W. Bush characterized it as a foundational act of an emerging democracy in Iraq.

In the last chapter of Part II, Simon Grivet writes about American and French twentieth-century abolitionist discourse, films, and texts on executions. Grivet stresses similarities in the histories of capital punishment in France and the United States. He notes that it was not before the late 1970s that they began to diverge substantially with the reintroduction of capital punishment in the United States after *Gregg v. Georgia* in 1976 and the last execution in France in 1977. Even while France was executing people, the French public reacted critically to certain American executions, such as those of Julius and Ethel Rosenberg in 1953 or of Caryl Chessman in 1960. As we learn from Grivet, until its abolition, France's capital punishment system was marked by great continuity: French governments regularly used the guillotine for more than two centuries, and they handled executions in a highly secretive manner.

Part III of this book takes up abolitionist strategies. It begins with a chapter by Andrew Hammel, who describes what he sees as the elitist character of the postwar abolitionist movement in Europe. He raises the question of whether American adherence to capital punishment is an effect of the more democratic system in the United States compared to European countries. European abolitionists devised rhetorical and political strategies to promote abolition in the face of popular support for capital punishment. He describes the role of elites in post–World War II abolition processes in Germany, the United Kingdom, and France, and he traces the elitist element in abolitionism using the conceptual frame of Norbert Elias's "civilizing process" and Charles Taylor's history of the modern self.[29] Traditionally, abolitionism signified more civilized and therefore higher personal social standing and aspirations. As Hammel shows, it was only after the end of the death penalty in Europe that a consensus on abolition as a human rights issue gained support among European populations and developed into a feature of "Europeanness."

Timothy Kaufman-Osborn takes up the British Royal Commission on Capital Punishment. The Commission's 1953 report[30] particularly reflected on execution methods, considered lethal injection a quarter-century before it was introduced in the United States, and finally deemed hanging more appropriate. Lethal injection, Kaufman-Osborn notes, was finally rejected by the Royal Commission because it was said to deny the execution candidate the chance to die with dignity. Paralyzed by sedatives, the condemned would not have retained a minimal quantum of agency, self-control, and the possibility of showing a "manly notion of courage" at the moment of death. As Kaufman-Osborn's chapter shows, lethal injection serves to protect the dignity of the state and of the execution apparatus, created to execute cleanly and without any disturbances, rather than the dignity of those put to death.

Jon Yorke draws our attention to a different line of abolitionist arguments. Yorke argues that the death penalty has not only been constantly criticized from an ethical point of view, but also by arguments purporting to show its uselessness. Since Cesare Beccaria in 1764,[31] the penitentiary has been praised as an alternative to the death penalty in part because it was said to be more useful and efficient than executing criminal offenders. At the same time, others have described the penitentiary as even more dreadful and cruel than capital punishment.[32] These early skeptical notes and sharp critiques of the penitentiary resonate loudly in today's debate on the abolition of the death penalty, the rise of supermax prisons, and the ambivalence of ultimate sanctions in general.

Agata Fijalkowski points out how dependent the emergence of a strong European position against the death penalty was on events after the fall of the Berlin Wall and the dissolution of the Soviet empire in 1989–1991. On the one hand, the extension of the European Union gave the abolitionist stance further momentum and made the abolition of the death penalty a significant denominator of a shared European

[29] Norbert Elias, *The Civilizing Process: Sociogenetic and Psychogenetic Investigations* (Oxford: Wiley-Blackwell, 2000); Charles Taylor, *Sources of the Self: The Making of the Modern Identity* (Cambridge: Cambridge University Press, 1989).

[30] Report of the Royal Commission on Capital Punishment, 1949–1953 (London: Her Majesty's Stationery Office, 1953).

[31] Richard Bellamy, ed., *Beccaria: On Crimes and Punishment and Other Writings* (Cambridge: Cambridge University Press, 1995).

[32] Benjamin Rush, *An Enquiry Into the Effects of Public Punishments Upon Criminals and Upon Society* (London: C. Dilly, 1787); Charles Dickens, *American Notes for General Circulation* (London: Chapman and Hall, 1842).

identity and human rights politics. On the other hand, a close analysis of various Eastern European countries shows that the seemingly unified European abolitionist position is fraught with tensions between older and newer members of the European Union. As Fijalkowski argues, the abolition of the death penalty in many Eastern European countries is more an effect of their compliance with Western European norms and the economic and political attractiveness and institutional rigidity of the European Union, than the sign of a firm conviction that capital punishment violates human rights.

The final chapter of our book shifts the focus back to the United States and reminds us that analyses of abolitionist strategies have to be embedded into a broader conceptual approach that examines their impact on broader and more encompassing debates about punishment. Marie Gottschalk argues that the legal framing of the death penalty and the evolving strategies of opponents as well as proponents helped fortify the U.S. penal system. She notes that since the 1930s, skirmishes about the death penalty had been fought on the judicial rather than political terrain in America, a strategy that gained further momentum in the 1960s when the American Civil Liberties Union (ACLU) and the NAACP's Legal Defense Fund (LDF) decided to challenge the overall constitutionality of capital punishment in the courts rather than seek legislative abolition.

Until the early 1970s, she contends, capital punishment was not a high priority among American law-and-order conservatives. Abolitionists missed an opportunity to wage a wider legislative campaign against the death penalty, with possibly more lasting effects. The constitutional strategy resulted in the famous *Furman* decision in 1972. Furman accorded public sentiment a crucial place in the constitutional discussion of the meaning of the Eighth Amendment. After Furman, the passions of the public became a major factor in the formation of penal policy, and the death penalty became "the ultimate form of public victim recognition" in America. Thus, as Marie Gottschalk argues, American efforts to abolish the death penalty had multifaceted and ambivalent effects, and paradoxically, abolitionist efforts contributed to the growth and consolidation of the carceral state.

As we have seen, the European road to abolition was rocky and difficult, and it took until the twenty-first century to make the death penalty disappear from the European continent. It is naïve to forget this and to treat it as a smooth and conflict-free endeavor. If the history and sociology of the present that this book offers provides any insight for American abolitionists, it is precisely the fact that the end of the death penalty is hard to come by – and a political and cultural consensus that would consider its end as a desirable achievement is even harder to attain. Nevertheless, European history also shows that even in the face of inner quandaries, conflicts, and tensions, abolition can be achieved. However, abolition can further consolidate punitiveness. Can this be avoided? If so, how? These are the questions that will mark the American road to abolition.

PART I

What Is a Penalty of Death: Capital Punishment in Context

1

The Green, Green Grass of Home

Capital Punishment and the Penal System from a Long-Term Perspective

Pieter Spierenburg

The swan has been KLM's emblem for a long time. In the late 1990s, the airline ran a commercial on Dutch television that showed this bird landing on water at the sound of Tom Jones singing *The Green, Green Grass of Home*.[1] I was utterly surprised. Although the difference between an execution and a plane crash is obvious, yet the association inescapably caught my mind. Didn't the people at the advertising agency know what the song was about? The combination of "a guard" and "arm in arm we'll walk at daybreak" seemed clear to me, but then I happen to know that executions are often scheduled for the early morning. The phrase in between, that I never heard quite right, turned out to speak of a "sad old padre," which suggests that the dreamer's death row is in Mexico. Perhaps the film makers had not paid sufficient attention to the text, but their ignorance also testifies to something deeper: European unfamiliarity with the death penalty as opposed to its relative familiarity for Americans.

We know it has not always been like that. The Dutch and other Europeans have come a long way from the time that the very term "the green lawn" (*het groene zoodje*) referred to the site of the scaffold, visible every day, to their present unfamiliarity. The lynching of the brothers De Witt, moreover, on The Hague's green lawn in 1672, anticipated the alleged association of U.S. popular justice with capital punishment by two centuries. On the other hand, the United States, like Europe, has witnessed the privatization of legal executions, despite occasional pleas to show them live on television. Can history help us further? Surely, I am not the first person to suggest that. My modest aim in this chapter is to examine the issue anew by (1) critically discussing the views of several scholars who have turned to history in order to tackle the problem under scrutiny; (2) widening the scope of the discussion by taking the penal system as a whole, in particular imprisonment, into consideration; and

[1] See http://www.youtube.com/watch?v=vgd426QrtJQ (accessed Dec. 24, 2009; attempt at access on June 8, 2010 led to the notification that the video was removed).

(3) assessing the evidence with the help of insights developed by Norbert Elias, not only his well-known theory of civilizing processes, but also his notion of long-term diminutions in power differences between social groups.

The second of these strategies, a comparison between the United States and Europe from the perspective of imprisonment, forms a necessary complement to a comparison from the perspective of the death penalty, because the conclusions are radically different. European incarceration rates, too, have risen sharply during the last few decades, although not quite reaching the U.S. level. Europeans today experience themselves as living in a punitive age, as evidenced in the title of the closing conference of the mega-project CRIMPREV.[2] Although the excesses at Guantánamo Bay and Abu Ghraib have cast a shadow over the United States' image during the opening decade of the twenty-first century, in Europe the battle against terrorism equally entails threats to the rule of law. In sum, whereas the United States and Europe diverge with respect to some penal trends, they converge on others. Because the divergence is obvious and the primary focus of this volume, let me introduce an intriguing example of convergence. It concerns the trends in incarceration rates in my own country, the Netherlands, and the United States in the past few decades. In both countries, the number of prisoners per capita began to increase during the 1970s. The Dutch embarked on a prison-building program with the notorious *Bijlmerbajes* as its first milestone. Nowadays the Netherlands, like the United States, boasts several so-called *ebi*'s (supermax prisons) for inmates considered dangerous. More important, by the early twenty-first century, the Dutch incarceration rates had risen to six times the level of 1970.

Although the reader will note that the rates in Figure 1.1. are per 100,000 and per 10,000 respectively, the steepness of the two rising curves is strikingly similar and since the mid-1990s even more pronounced for the Netherlands. It should be added that numbers were somewhat down again in the Netherlands in 2009, which caused the Ministry of Justice to decide to rent prison space to Belgium. It remains to be seen whether this indicates a permanent trend reversal. In any case, it was reported in February 2010 that dozens of Belgian prisoners sued their government in an attempt to prevent their transfer to Tilburg, one of the arguments being that life in Dutch prisons was much harder than in Belgian ones.[3]

A RECENT DEBATE

Returning to the death penalty, we may consider a recent scholarly debate in *Punishment & Society*.[4] It is relevant here because the participants all turned to

[2] Open University, Milton Keynes, UK, 17–19 June 2009. CRIMPREV was a coordinated action under FP6, directed by the GERN.

[3] *Volkskrant*, February 13, 2010.

[4] Garland (David), Capital punishment and American culture. In: Punishment & Society 7, 4 (2005): 347–76; Whitman (James Q.), Response to Garland. In: Punishment & Society 7,4 (2005): 389–96;

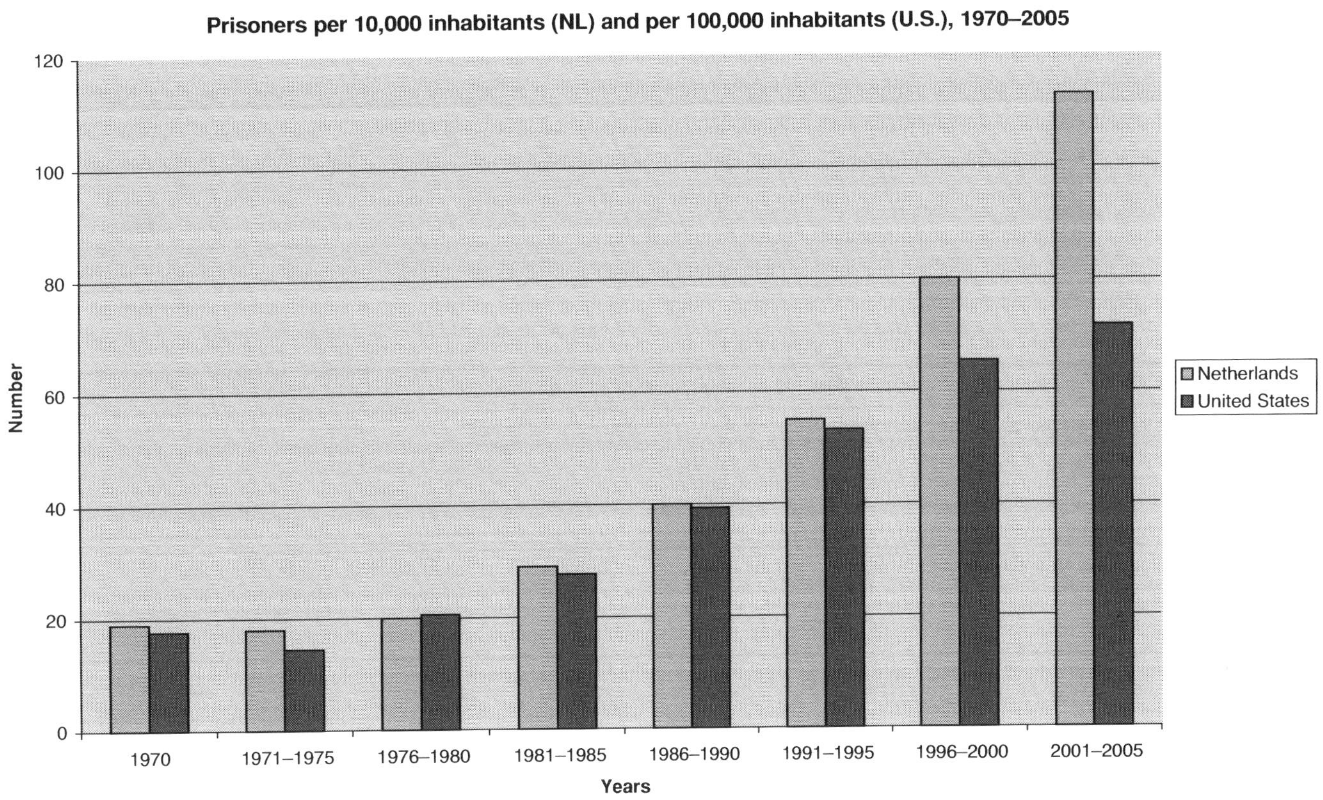

FIGURE 1.1. Prisoners per 10,000 inhabitants (NL) and per 100,000 inhabitants (U.S.), 1970–2005
Source (Netherlands): Downes and van Swaaningen 2007
Source (USA): http://www.angelfire.com/rnb/y/ratesusa.htm#years

history and implicitly or explicitly compared the United States with Europe while placing the issue in a broader context of criminal justice. The debate opens with an essay by David Garland, occasioned by earlier books of two of the other participants, Franklin Zimring and James Q. Whitman.[5] Garland charged them with embracing a theory of exceptionalism. In historiography, such a charge always sounds negative, if only because it is reminiscent of a German scholarly tradition claiming that this country's history had followed a *Sonderweg* (exceptional path). Garland traces the idea of American exceptionalism back to the late nineteenth century, when scholars wondered about the failure of socialism in the United States. He deplores its novel application to capital punishment. According to him, the exceptionalist argument just says that Americans execute because this is part of their culture and has always been that way. Quite to the contrary, he continues, historical trends with respect to the death penalty in the United States and Europe have been basically similar up to the mid-1970s, when the moratorium just failed to turn into total abolition; the divergence exists only since then. The implication is that the United States may once again conform to the general Western trend in the near future and abolish the death penalty. Garland adduces largely ad hoc arguments to explain both the resurgence of executions since the late 1970s and their uneven distribution. He mentions, for example, that especially Southern states assign underpaid and disinterested lawyers to poor defendants, which ensures that a larger number of the accused in the South than elsewhere end up on death row.

Zimring, on the other hand, bases his argument precisely on this uneven distribution. In the debate, he finds no reason to doubt the importance of the statistics presented in his earlier book: There is a significant, if not a total, match between the states with the highest numbers of executions in recent decades and those in which lynchings occurred most frequently at the end of the nineteenth century – and these were mostly Southern states. Zimring considers this as evidence for a firm link between popular justice and legal executions that he subsumes under the heading of vigilante values. His principal shortcoming is that he does not dwell on the question where these values come from, but neither is Garland's counterargument persuasive. He merely tries to restrict the definition of vigilantism.[6] For his part, Whitman equally reasserts the validity of the contrasting long-term developments in America and Europe identified in his earlier book – to which I will return later

Zimring (Franklin E.), Path dependence, culture and state-level execution policy. A reply to David Garland. In: Punishment & Society 7,4 (2005): 377–84. The fourth participant was Eric Monkkonen, who wrote his brief contribution shortly before his death and primarily drew the issue of homicide into the discussion.

5 Zimring (Franklin E.), The contradictions of American capital punishment. New York (Oxford University Press) 2003; Whitman (James Q.), Harsh justice. Criminal punishment and the widening divide between America and Europe. New York (Oxford University Press) 2003.

6 A kind of update of his views in Garland (David), Le processus de civilisation et la peine capitale aux Etats-Unis. In: Vingtième Siècle. Revue d'Histoire 106 (2010): 193–208. There he appears much more sympathetic to Zimring's position.

on. He stresses, among other things, the role of slavery and its influence on thinking about prisons. But he also approaches Garland in denying the heuristic value of exceptionalism. If any continent was exceptional, he adds, it is Europe. According to Whitman, harshness and the wish for revenge are man's natural responses that only Europeans managed to mitigate. Thus, the debate largely resulted in a stalemate.

To take it further, we must start with a few clarifications. For one thing, what is Europe and what is America? Since 1776, the United States has acted externally as a unit of attack and defense. It waged war as a nation. In that respect, the United States is no different from countries such as Denmark or Spain. On the other hand, American states can make their own laws to an extent that is not permitted to Spanish or Danish provinces. As a rule, legal changes such as abolishing the death penalty are made in Europe at the national level only. In 1867, Portugal was the first country to do so, having executed its last death sentence in the 1840s.[7] The Netherlands came second in 1870. Can we put these changes in national law on equal footing with the abolition of capital punishment in Michigan (1846), Rhode Island (1852), and Wisconsin (1853)? I leave this question open for the moment.

A second conspicuous feature of the debate just referred to is that the participants pay no attention, other than in passing, to the major history of American capital punishment by Stuart Banner.[8] Banner confirms that, for a long time, European and American trends were similar. The ceremony of public execution in Colonial America was modeled after that in early modern England, which in its turn resembled the scaffold ritual practiced all over Continental Europe by then. Benjamin Rush, the "American Beccaria," was only seven years younger than his European counterpart. Unease at public executions emerged in the United States a generation later than in the leading European countries, but it translated a little earlier into the removal of capital punishment indoors. Whereas this act of privatization occurred in the major European countries, with the notable exception of France, between 1850 and 1870, in the United States, this was between 1830 and 1860 – that is, only in the Northern states. Subsequently, privatization was only partial. It took about two generations before the liberal provision of entrance tickets to interested citizens was restricted. On this issue, the description by Banner, again only for the Northern United States, is remarkably similar to that by Richard Evans for Germany.[9] Obviously, the question raised earlier, as to how to evaluate the legal autonomy of American states, has repercussions in particular for the North-South divide. During at least one hundred years, each of these regions went its own way. Hence, although

7 Hood gives two different years for the last execution: 1843 (Hood [Roger], Introduction. The importance of abolishing the death penalty. In: The death penalty. Abolition in Europe. Strasbourg [Council of Europe Publishing] 1999: 9–16, see p. 10) and 1849 (Hood [Roger], The death penalty. A worldwide perspective. 3d ed. revised and updated. Oxford [Oxford University Press] 2002: 23).

8 Banner (Stuart), The death penalty. An American history. Cambridge, MA (Harvard University Press) 2002.

9 Evans (Richard J.), Rituals of retribution. Capital punishment in Germany, 1600–1987. Oxford (Oxford University Press) 1996.

Banner confirms Garland up to a certain point, he also provides support for the theses of Zimring and Whitman. The practice of slavery and the North-South division had important repercussions for developments in American criminal justice.

At this point, we can conclude that an exceptionalist thesis is of limited value indeed. It explains nothing simply because we can always find exceptions, as the tradition of referring to German history as a *Sonderweg* already suggested. Thus, whereas for Garland, the period from about 1980 to the present is exceptional in the United States, for Whitman, it is the 1970s. And exceptions can refer to chronology as well as to institutions or situations. In the latter case, it is the existence of slavery and white supremacism within the country that makes the United States exceptional in the Western world.

To finish my discussion of this debate, it should be noted that all participants do not go back in time much further than about 1800. As I have argued elsewhere with reference to homicide, it constitutes a crucial difference that the North American continent moved into the modern world overnight as it were, whereas European societies witnessed an extended development of some five centuries.[10] Consequently, the pre-1800 history does count. The relatively sudden transformation to an urban-industrial society caused Americans, among other things, to remain unaccustomed to being disarmed and distrustful of a state monopoly of force. At first sight, this feature of American societal development would seem to be less consequential for the history of executions and punishment generally. Colonial Americans were certainly accustomed to capital punishment – and didn't I just say that executions there resembled those in Europe at the time? That is true, but by 1600, European societies had already gone through one important transformation: the sacralization of executions.

THE APPEARANCE OF RELIGIOUSLY TAINTED EXECUTIONS

The sacralization of executions is a process only recently discovered whose exact significance has yet to be established. This process was unknown to me when I wrote *The Spectacle of Suffering*, although I did observe that the execution ceremony became more streamlined and elaborate at the beginning of the early modern period.[11] At about the same time, James Sharpe noted that morality plays under English gallows, such as "last dying speeches," were a Tudor innovation.[12] It was the

[10] Spierenburg (Pieter), Democracy came too early: A tentative explanation for the problem of American homicide. In: American Historical Review 111,1 (2006): 104–14, see pp. 106–7. Later in this chapter I come back to the argument presented there.

[11] Spierenburg (Pieter), The spectacle of suffering. Executions and the evolution of repression: From a preindustrial metropolis to the European experience. Cambridge (Cambridge University Press) 1984: 43–5.

[12] Sharpe (J[ames] A.), Last dying speeches. Religion, ideology and public execution in 17th-century England. In: Past and Present 107 (1985): 144–67.

art historian Mitchell Merback and the medievalist Peter Schuster who, independently from each other, brought the sacralization of executions to our full attention (not the concept itself, which I have coined for this occasion).[13] Their observations refer to a broad region of Central Europe encompassing much of Germany, Switzerland, and Northern Italy. Medieval attitudes to executions, Schuster notes, were based on the prohibition for church and clergy to have their hands stained by blood. As is well-known, the Inquisition handed over condemned heretics to the secular authorities to put them at the stake. More generally, church people showed little interest in ordinary executions. This was in line with the attitudes of urban and territorial rulers, who viewed them as completely profane events, something "for us, not for the church." The message that the authorities wished to convey was that capital convicts were totally worthless and less than human. As they would surely face damnation, it was futile to give them the opportunity to confess to a priest.

Gradually, however, church people started to object. They insisted that everyone, even the most hardened criminals, deserved to receive the sacrament of confession. As early as 1312, at the Council of Vienne, Pope Clement V threatened with ecclesiastical sanctions for those magistrates who prevented this from happening, but they were unimpressed yet. The Konstanz authorities did not grant the opportunity for priestly absolution to capital convicts until 1434, and the council of Strasbourg finally complied with the wishes of its bishop as late as 1485. There is some evidence that by the mid-fifteenth century, the ecclesiastical views in this respect found an echo in popular sentiment. The introduction of an elaborate religious ritual at the scaffold by the authorities, however, did not come about until the early sixteenth century. Schuster fixes the breakthrough of the religious embeddedness of executions at 1525. This precise date originates from a detour in his argument, that of the failed hanging. Because the medieval method of hanging was by strangulation, it was not uncommon to find the convict still breathing after the rope had been cut. Other failed hangings simply resulted from the breaking of the rope; also, some criminals sentenced to be drowned did not. As a rule, the spectators as well as the authorities considered such a failure as a sign from above, which induced the magistrates to pardon the convict. Schuster interprets this as a sort of magical custom reminiscent of the earlier ordeals. He connects the new religious view of executions with Lutheranism. This new view symbolically broke through in Nürnberg in 1525: the first time that a German convict whose rope broke was not pardoned but hanged

[13] Merback (Mitchell B.), The thief, the cross and the wheel. Pain and the spectacle of punishment in medieval and Renaissance Europe. Chicago (University of Chicago Press) 1999; Schuster (Peter), Eine Stadt vor Gericht. Recht und Alltag im spätmittelalterlichen Konstanz. Paderborn (Ferdinand Schöningh) 2000; Schuster (Peter), Hinrichtungsritualen in der frühen Neuzeit. Anfragen aus dem Mittelalter. In: Rudolph (Harriet) + Schnabel-Schüle (Helga) (eds.), Justiz = Justice = Justicia. Rahmenbedingungen von Strafjustiz im frühneuzeitlichen Europa. Trierer Historische Forschungen, Band 48. Trier (Kliomedia) 2003: 213–33.

anew. Magical beliefs and practices surrounding executions, it should be added, remained alive in popular culture throughout the early modern period, especially in Germany.[14]

A recent study by Katherine Royer confirms the shift to religiously tainted executions for England. Before 1500, she observes, there was little in execution narratives to imply that any spiritual comfort was offered to the condemned on the scaffold or that they had any hope of salvation.[15] Like Sharpe, Royer considers the last dying speeches as symptomatic for a religious view of executions, adding that these speeches did not become really frequent until the mid-sixteenth century. There were a few medieval precedents, but in the majority of these cases, the convicts, though penitent, denied their guilt. Esther Cohen's study of punishment in late-medieval France does not explicitly refer to the sacralization of executions, but she confirms that they still included various magical elements.[16] Methods of capital punishment that involved total annihilation, for example, were meant to ensure that the convicts in question would not become revenants.

Merback provides evidence for the sacralization of executions from the viewpoint of art history. In particular, he studied the genre of the calvary, a crucifixion in a landscape with a number of people, around 1500. Painters were theologically restricted in the way they could depict Jesus, but they gave free rein to their fantasies in representing his companions, denoted in English as the Two Thieves. Incidentally it was only the evangelist Luke who wrote that one of the two recognized Jesus as savior, whereas according to Mark and Matthew they both mocked him. Many artists modeled their representation of the thieves' tormented bodies on the contemporary punishment of breaking on the wheel. This way of depicting reveals that they associated the crucifixion of Christ with contemporary executions of criminals – a parallel that had already been drawn by medieval theologians like Jean Gerson. This parallel, Merback concludes, ensured that from the late fifteenth century onward – and hence before the Reformation – executions were infused with religious symbolism. The capitally condemned, if they were penitent and acted solemnly, became a kind of martyrs and the execution turned into an act of expiation.[17]

Merback's use of the word 'martyr' is perhaps exaggerated, but his observations provide a clue for the argument about the status of convicts and changing power differentials that I wish to unfold in this article. The sacralization of executions meant a slight rise in the status of capital convicts. From undeserving wretches, bound for hell, they turned into penitent Christians, reflecting Jesus' death on the cross. They were still mostly poor and outside the domain of earthly honor, but

[14] Spierenburg 1984: 87–9; Evans 1996: 86–98.

[15] Royer (Katherine), Dead men talking. Truth, texts and the scaffold in early modern England. In: Devereaux (Simon) + Griffiths (Paul) (eds.), Penal practice and culture, 1500–1900. Punishing the English. Basingstoke (Palgrave Macmillan) 2004: 63–84, see p. 70.

[16] Cohen (Esther), The crossroads of justice. Law and culture in late medieval France. Leiden, etc. 1993.

[17] Merback 1999: 150–7.

God potentially forgave them in heaven. Significantly, in the German-speaking countries, *Armesünder* (poor sinner) became the standard term for a convict bound for and dying on the scaffold. It is highly unlikely that the authorities, or the Church for that matter, consciously wished to raise the status of the condemned. It was an unintended consequence of the interplay between secular customs and ecclesiastical demands or, in Norbert Elias' words, the outcome of a blind process. In this process, the condemned lost something too. They were deprived of their small chance of getting away with it through a failed hanging or drowning, and their raised status only applied if they cooperated, acknowledging their sentence. The condemned were certainly not allowed to deny their guilt. However, this exactly provided them with a measure of power. They were able to (threaten to) spoil the show by being obstinate, announcing their intention to display defiance instead of penitence. This would mean to sabotage the moral play that the authorities intended the spectacle of the scaffold to be. Indeed, when an Amsterdam convict showed this kind of obstinacy, the court dispatched a special deputy-minister to him who exerted every effort to convince him to comply.[18]

This argument implies that early modern authorities were content with the religious element in executions and the morality show that it entailed. Why did the secular rulers and courts of the seventeenth century relish in something that their predecessors had tried to avoid? Neither Schuster nor Merback provides a plausible explanation. It would be too simple to suppose that the secular authorities merely had to yield to powerful pressure by the ecclesiastical ones to let convicts confess to a priest and then tried to make the best of it. An explanation should take account of the various changes in penal practice at the end of the Middle Ages and the beginning of the early modern period and the state formation processes lying behind them. Medieval criminal justice was, for the large part, a justice of arbitration. Most cases were conducted according to the accusatory procedure, in which accuser and accused faced each other as equal parties and the judges acted largely as mediators. In the rare cases that a trial resulted in a death sentence, the accuser usually had the right to execute it. Few jurisdictions had a professional executioner. As a rule, death sentences were relatively infrequent, mainly imposed on rebels or robbers or any other outsiders without a network of support within the community. The infrequency of executions did not stem from any kind of sensitivity against physical retaliation. At times citizens themselves retaliated, because vengeance and feuding were common too and relatively accepted. The coexistence of arbitration justice, private revenge, and a low incidence of executions reflected the relatively low level of monopolization of force during most of the middle ages. In this situation, it made perfect sense to stigmatize the tiny minority of capital convicts as a subhuman set. Unlike vengeance victims, they lacked honor, so why would even God care about them?

[18] Spierenburg 1984: 59.

By 1500, change was visible in various ways. The inquisitorial procedure, which already existed for some time, now became the one most frequently applied in criminal cases. In this procedure, the public prosecutor and the suspect were the principal parties facing each other, with a highly unequal power ratio. Meanwhile, almost all jurisdictions kept a paid executioner, who symbolized the expropriation of private revenge and inherited the infamy of medieval capital convicts. To be sure, the inquisitorial procedure was not necessarily concomitant of legal change, since it remained absent from England. In England as well as continental Europe, however, the incidence of executions markedly increased during the sixteenth century, and they remained at a high level during most of the seventeenth century. Monopolies of force had been established, and those who disposed of these monopolies showed that they had them. Reformation and Counter-Reformation, moreover, brought a heightened moral concern. Despite Schuster's emphasis on Lutheranism, the religious underpinning of the death penalty appears to have been prepared before the Reformation and subsequently strengthened in Protestant as well as Catholic countries. Since the mid-sixteenth century, the representatives of church and state usually cooperated, sharing the same moral outlook and upholding a patriarchal social order that mixed benevolence with sternness. Within this climate, religiously tainted executions easily found their place. As several scholars have noted, early modern executions were not only aimed at deterrence and prevention, but reached out to the whole population by telling them that their own sins might be early symptoms of a career in crime.

It is difficult to determine what it meant for the development of criminal justice in America that this continent never went through a phase of completely profane executions. Perhaps it did not matter at all. The ritual of capital punishment was exported to the colonies on the Atlantic coast from England, and originally from the Dutch Republic and a few other countries as well, at a time when religiously tainted executions were the rule everywhere. Banner discusses the religious element as an integral part of the ceremony. It should be added that all his examples are from New England or Pennsylvania. To Cotton Mather and the likes of him, expiation and the religious atmosphere at executions were so self-evident that they simply could not understand that any convict would refuse salvation. They considered criminals as mere specimens of the sinfulness inherent in all mankind.[19] It would be interesting to know to what extent such an attitude prevailed in Virginia, for example. One conclusion about the different trajectories of European and American criminal justice is obvious. Whereas in Europe, execution ritual, with its religious flavor, underpinned both the power and patriarchalism of the elites in developing states, the white settler communities on the Atlantic coast practiced the same ritual in the absence of a monopoly of force. Significantly, Colonial America knew no professional executioners, and this continued to be the case until the invention of

[19] Banner 2002: 16–22.

the electric chair.[20] This meant that Americans held on to a feature of execution practice that in Europe was characteristic of the Middle Ages, with its arbitration justice and private retaliation. Again, it is difficult to tell what exactly this means for the overall development of American criminal justice.

Whatever overzealous attitude may have characterized Puritan ministers, in Europe, religiously embedded executions were also common in Anglican, Lutheran, and Catholic settings (and perhaps in the world of Eastern Orthodoxy, about which there is less information). I already showed this in my *Spectacle of Suffering*, whereas publications since then provide other examples.[21] Admittedly, it is no big step from the Puritans to Calvin's Geneva, but the city is interesting because it demonstrated that the ritual could be extended to the penalty of drowning. Its court imposed this punishment a number of times, for offenses such as sodomy and infanticide, in the second half of the sixteenth century and the beginning of the seventeenth century. The harbor, at the confluence of the lake and the river Rhône, was the usual location. The convict took off on a boat, with the executioner, of course, but also in the company of several Reformed ministers. They were to provide him or her with spiritual comfort in the last moments of life and to serve as witnesses. The executioner tied the convict's hands and feet together, threw him from the boat and held him under water until he ceased to move. The public prosecutor witnessed all this from the quay, surrounded by an immense audience. Additional spectators watched the scene from boats of their own. Afterward, the convict's body was taken ashore, dragged on a hurdle to the gibbet, and buried there.[22]

The religious element was equally pronounced in Catholic countries. Executions in France traditionally included the ritual of *amende honorable*, in which the condemned knelt down in front of a church with a torch in his hand and asked forgiveness from God and Justice. This could also be required from noncapital convicts. In Seville, Spain's Southern port town, Jesuits were conspicuously present, whereas the capital convict sometimes rode to his fatal destination on a mule, reminiscent of Jesus' ride on a donkey.[23] Throughout the eighteenth century, the *amende* was a frequent feature of capital punishment in Paris. In the French capital, too, the status of the condemned as a penitent sinner did not preclude his infamy. The ceremony of capital or corporal punishment began with the reading of the final sentence. At that point, the criminal not only became infamous, because the executioner came into play, but when the sentence was capital, a priest immediately arrived to hear confession. One of the executioner's first tasks was to dress the convict in a white shirt, so

[20] Banner 2002: 36–9.

[21] According to Devereaux (Devereaux [Simon], Re-casting the theatre of execution. The abolition of the Tyburn ritual. In: Past and Present 202 [2009]: 127–74) even the executions at Tyburn with their notorious processions by the mid-eighteenth century were on average more orderly and solemn than previous historians have assumed.

[22] Rappaz (Sonia Vernhes), La noyade judiciaire dans la République de Genève, 1558–1619. In: Crime, Histoire & Sociétés/ Crime, History & Societies 13,1 (2009): 5–24, see p. 8.

[23] Spierenburg 1984: 51–3.

that he could perform the *amende honorable*. He did this during the procession, in front of a church or at the spot of the crime. The ritual opened with the court clerk summarizing the sentence with emphasis on the convict's evil intentions, which the latter had to repeat on his knees, torch in hand and the executioner standing behind him. At other stops, the clerk read the sentence anew. The cart taking the convict from jail to the place of execution was one of those normally used for the disposal of the city's trash. In contrast to the traditional image, the Place de Grève in front of the town hall was the location of festivities, many in honor of the king, which made it less suitable as a place for capital punishment. In eighteenth-century Paris, only 15 percent of all executions were done at the Place de Grève.[24]

Not surprisingly, modern values such as freedom of religion were absent from the Christian executions of the early modern period. As a rule, the spiritual consolation offered came exclusively from the officially recognized church, whichever it was in the place where the trial was held. Lutheran-born criminals who had wandered to England, for example, were assisted by an Anglican clergyman. When a court in a Calvinist place had condemned a baptized Catholic, he had to be content with a Reformed minister. The presence of a rabbi at the scaffold was unthinkable everywhere. Some of the painters studied by Merback depicted the Two Thieves as ignominious Jews, hanging on their backs with their heads bowed down backwards. Even in Amsterdam, where Jews met with comparably few restrictions, they died on the scaffold alone. In 1746, when Abram Moses Pijpeman was broken on the wheel for murdering his mistress, he refused to pay attention to the Reformed minister. This caused a Christian observer to comment that Abram died as a beast, whereas a Jewish chronicler praised him for remaining true to his faith.[25] The monopoly of the dominant religion in enacting the Christian ritual of executions made sense. Whereas in theory, its function may have been that of spiritual consolation for the condemned, in practice, its primary aim was the edification of the multitude.

As late as 1767, the speech given for another Amsterdam criminal broken on the wheel exemplified the profoundly Christian overtones of capital punishment. Nathaniel Donker and his mistress had murdered his wife to escape from her unwanted attention. At the town hall's inner court, before mounting the scaffold, Donker was admonished that no sins were too grave to be pardoned, if only he would earnestly beg forgiveness. Even if his wife's blood cried for vengeance before God's throne, this sinner should realize that the sacrificial blood of Jesus carried greater weight with his Father.[26] It was a moving speech, but things were about to change.

24 Bastien (Pascal), L'exécution publique à Paris au 18e siècle. Une histoire des rituels judiciaires. Seyssel (Champ Vallon) 2006: 114–42.

25 Spierenburg 1984: 61, 63.

26 Spierenburg (Pieter), Written in blood. Fatal attraction in Enlightenment Amsterdam. Columbus, OH (Ohio State University Press) 2004: 107.

THE ENLIGHTENMENT AND THE DEATH PENALTY

Around the time of Donker's trial, the Enlightenment caused the first breaches in the religious edifice built around capital punishment. As part of his critique of the death penalty, Cesare Beccaria rejected the Christian element in executions. The promise of heaven, he argued, merely eased the convict's fear of death and consequently diminished the audience's fear of committing crimes. Thus, the religious drama subverted capital punishment's ostensible goal of general prevention. This view (not necessarily all his views) found an echo in Hamburg, where the senate decided to remove the religious part of the ceremony indoors for suicidal murderers to avoid the suggestion that absolution earned them heaven.[27] Beccaria's argument that prevention was best served by maximizing a criminal's chances of getting caught and tried is well known. His book was no plea to return to the medieval situation. Although abolitionism remained a minority opinion for quite some time, sensitivity against public physical punishment was clearly visible toward the end of the eighteenth century. It foreshadowed the marginalization of the death penalty and the increasing enthusiasm among lawyers and politicians for the prison.

The end of the Ancien Régime constitutes the chronological starting point of Whitman's book. He does not dwell on the sacralization of executions, even though the status accorded to convicts is the central element in his thesis.[28] This thesis is interesting, nevertheless, if only because it puts the differential developments in Europe and America at center stage. Essentially, he argues that on both continents, punishment became more democratic but in entirely opposite ways. Whereas democratization in Europe meant the extension of dignity to all offenders, in the United States it meant degradation for all. As status differences mattered less in America to begin with, all forms of privileged treatment of individual prisoners were increasingly viewed as unfair. This comparison has definite geographic limits. Europe actually means France and Germany, but Whitman believes that his thesis holds for more countries than just these two. America at first is the Anglo-Saxon world, with the breakdown of status differences in punishment anticipated in eighteenth-century England. After 1776, England disappears from the picture, and it remains unclear whether or not it is supposed to have returned to the European path later.[29] In continental Europe, at least, the central theme is the gradual extension to all offenders of privileges in punishment that originally applied only to high-status offenders.

[27] Martschukat (Jürgen), Inszeniertes Töten. Eine Geschichte der Todesstrafe vom 17. bis zum 19. Jahrhundert. Köln (Böhlau) 2000: 85–90.

[28] Whitman 2003. See also: Whitman (James Q.), The origins of reasonable doubt. Theological roots of the criminal trial. New Haven, London (Yale University Press) 2008. As I have noted in my review of this book (American Historical Review, February 2009: 198), neither does he refer to the sacralization of executions there, even though religious concern in relation to criminal trials is the central issue.

[29] More information on England in Kaufman-Osborn's contribution to this volume.

The first phase of this development is a very French story. In Ancien Régime France, beheading was the honorable mode of capital punishment, reserved for aristocrats; so the Revolution extended the privilege of being beheaded to all capital convicts. This shift is peculiarly French because in prerevolutionary France, hanging, breaking on the wheel, and burning were almost the only modes of capital punishment practiced. Elsewhere, although high-status offenders sentenced to death were indeed beheaded, it was not true that beheading was solely reserved for them. In early modern Amsterdam, for example, this was the standard punishment for manslaughter, unless the condemned faced additional charges such as street robbery. Most decapitated killers were of very humble origin. It is true that the relative honorability of beheading owed much to its noble association, but this honorability simply made it a lighter punishment than hanging. It allowed judges to attune the mode of the death penalty to the type of offense, regardless of the offender's social status. Decapitation, moreover, was not totally honorable. The condemned had to mount a scaffold, an infamous act by itself. The hangman led him there and blindfolded him, unless the condemned had received the privilege of walking alone untouched by the hated official. The honorableness of decapitation was only relative.

The French story revolves around two events, the execution of the brothers Agasse and the introduction of the guillotine. The Agasse brothers were tried just after the beginning of the revolution for falsifying bills of exchange in London two years previously. The Paris court condemned them to death in December and they were hanged on January 21, 1790. Between the sentence and the execution, there was a public outcry about the infamy that the hanging would traditionally cast over the offenders' entire family, which many found contrary to the spirit of the revolution. In protest, the district of Saint Honoré (!) elected an uncle of the brothers as its president. On the day of their execution, Guillotin persuaded the National Assembly to declare that offenses were personal, causing no infamy whatsoever to anyone associated with the condemned. Whitman admits that this implied a shift from collective pollution to individual guilt rather than a step toward dignity, but it helped Guillotin realize his entire program. In March 1792, the French legislature adopted the guillotine as the exclusive mode of capital punishment for all.[30]

But did this mean a dignified death for all? Significantly, Whitman hardly pays attention to the question why, in the Western world, decapitation counts as the most honorable form of capital punishment. He notes that the Chinese have a reversed appreciation, implying that it is just a matter of culture. A brief remark about decapitation's positive "military associations" in European history is tucked away in an endnote.[31] I believe there is more to it, and that the sword is the crucial element. This weapon was the aristocratic attribute *par excellence* and a symbol of

[30] Whitman 2003: 110–13.
[31] Whitman 2003: 243 (note 28).

nobility. In the early modern period, carrying a rapier – a lighter type of sword – was a mark of status, much desired by men to whom it officially was forbidden. Even hangmen tried to raise their infamous status by styling themselves with fancy names such as master of the sharp sword. Successful executioners were proud of their skills in handling the sword, leaving other tasks as much as possible to their servants. The relative honorableness of the penalty of decapitation, then, does not lie in the act of losing one's head but in the instrument used. The guillotine was developed not so much as a machine of honor but as a remedy because many executioners were clumsy rather than skillful. Whitman rightly concludes from the 1789 drawing meant to promote the machine that the executioner was to avert his eyes, but he fails to notice that the drawing has him activate the machine by cutting the rope that holds up the blade with a sword. The sword makes the whole scene honorable, because the guillotine itself is less than honorable. The falling blade is actually an axe, as its German and Dutch names confirm. Moreover, the introduction of the guillotine in Paris did not end the infamous parade of the convict from jail to the place of execution on a dung cart, which lasted until 1832.[32]

To conclude, it is doubtful whether the introduction of the guillotine had much to do with the reduction of the infamy inherent to punishment. Although, as Arasse already showed, this was certainly one of Guillotin's goals, the primary motive was to make capital punishment as painless as possible. That was equally a concern for the machine's opponents, who believed hanging to be most painless.[33] Although France kept the guillotine for nearly two centuries, it was severely compromised during the Terror. In countries occupied by the French, this machine soon became a symbol of the hated foreign invaders. William, within two weeks after his return to the Netherlands as sovereign prince, decided that the death penalty would henceforth be executed with either sword or rope.[34] Although some German states kept the guillotine after the Napoleonic period, the populace as a rule hated it. At about the same time, the majority of German states introduced a new custom: They replaced the sword with a big axe. Obviously, this was a shift from lesser to greater infamy, and the only difference with the guillotine was its handling by a human agent. The introduction of the axe, too, was to prevent unhandy strokes and hence to ensure the convict's painless death. Despite popular sentiment, Hamburg decided in 1842 to re-introduce the guillotine, and when the next person was on trial for a capital crime twelve years later, it was additionally decided to remove the death penalty indoors.[35] Throughout Europe, the main feature of the death penalty's history in the nineteenth century would be its privatization. Although France postponed this

[32] Arasse (Daniel), De machine van de Revolutie. Een geschiedenis van de guillotine. Nijmegen (SUN) 1989: 136–42.

[33] Arasse 1989: 28–32.

[34] Bosch (A.G.), De ontwikkeling van het strafrecht in Nederland van 1795 tot heden. 5th ed. Nijmegen (Ars Aequi Libri) 2008: 32–3. The rope meant hanging for men and garroting for women.

[35] Evans 1996: 215–25; Martschukat 2000: 140–234.

shift, from 1872 onward, the guillotine was placed flatly on the ground, so that only the front rows of spectators could actually see the spectacle.[36]

While Whitman's interpretation of the introduction of the guillotine is one-sided, the death penalty as such plays only a minor role in his account of degradation in the Anglo-Saxon world. For eighteenth-century England, he relies partly on Douglas Hay's classic essay, but he reverses his conclusions.[37] Where Hay saw a hierarchical society in which the criminal law served to maintain the dominance of the ruling classes, Whitman sees the beginnings of an egalitarian disregard for status. Hay considered minor concessions to fair trial or the occasional hanging of an aristocrat such as Lord Ferrers as mere tokens, meant to divert the populace's eyes from criminal justice's real purpose of keeping the lower orders in line. For Whitman, Ferrers' execution is a triumph of egalitarian degradation. He considers the well-known habit of English juries to undervalue stolen goods as a sign that the whole people actively participated in the criminal justice process, whereas most historians primarily view this as a check on the unusual severity of the bloody code. Neither does the death penalty play a major role in Whitman's account of Colonial and Revolutionary America, except for the fact that, as in England, hanging was the standard mode. In fact, the death penalty is largely absent from his entire account until its abolition in various European countries after World War II. This leads me to a preliminary assessment of the long-term history of executions.

In the 1789 drawing of the guillotine, the only person near the convict looking him right in the eyes is a priest. For the artist, apparently, the confessor's presence was still self-evident. More generally, early modern capital punishment had at least four conspicuous elements: pain, publicity, infamy, and religion. The first two – denoted more precisely as punishment's being directed at the body's integrity and punishment's public, theatrical character, respectively – were most fundamental because they applied to the penal system as a whole. As I showed in several of my works, both elements declined in importance over the centuries. But they never totally disappeared. Pain's most notorious reappearance occurred during World War II, whereas the extermination in the gas chambers by contrast was highly concealed. For a recurrence of punishment's public character, we can rather point at recent calls, in America and Europe, for naming and shaming in the case of corporate offenses. Religion remained an important element in nineteenth-century solitary confinement and with or without it in women's prisons, in Catholic countries often run by nuns. Religion's role in punishment simply diminished with the overall decline of its influence in society. In modern democratic countries, to consult a clergyman of any persuasion is merely one of the services available to prisoners. Consequently, it does not appear that religion was one of the factors at work in

[36] Arasse 1989: 158. On the further history of the death penalty in France, including debates about its public character, see Grivet in this volume.

[37] Hay (Douglas), Property, authority and the criminal law. In: Hay (Douglas) et al., Albion's fatal tree. Crime and society in 18th-century England. New York (Pantheon Books) 1975: 17–63.

the long-term history of punishment. Its principal contribution consisted of the sacralization of executions, which led to the first slight increase in the status of convicts. In fact, that status is equally reflected in the other three elements that I identified. The extent to which they suffer pain, are considered infamous, or have to condone that others view their predicament affects their status as persons. But as I just argued, changes in capital punishment during the Revolutionary period can hardly be viewed as an extension of dignity. After this period, the status of convicts increasingly came to mean that of prisoners.

THE EMANCIPATION OF PRISONERS

Let me return to Whitman once more. His account from 1815 to 1933 revolves around imprisonment. Throughout the nineteenth century, both France and Germany knew separate régimes for privileged prisoners. In the German case, this was part of a formal system that comprised three types of imprisonment, "fortress confinement" being the most comfortable. Whereas France extended the privilege of comfortable treatment to political prisoners in particular, in Germany, persons of great moral worth, who included some political activists but also duelists, came to enjoy fortress confinement. The most notorious among these morally high-standing persons was Adolf Hitler after his beer hall putsch. This modest extension of privileged treatment to persons outside the aristocracy, as long as they were considered no real criminals, during the nineteenth century paved the way, still according to Whitman, for its generalization after World War II.

When it comes to the United States, Whitman considers forced labor and the prevalence of corporal punishment in nineteenth-century penitentiaries as prime symptoms of degradation. He attaches great significance to the fact that the Thirteenth Amendment, abolishing slavery, explicitly excluded convicts when properly tried. Not every scholar shares his interpretation that this clause made prisoners into slaves of a kind. Looking at the subject from a different angle, others view the new penitentiaries, erected from the 1820s onward, primarily as bastions of state power. There may be truth in this assertion, but state power is merely a static term. From a dynamic point of view, we are faced with recurrent changes in the degree of monopolization of force. As I argued some time ago, the extent and stability of state power in the northeastern United States in the early nineteenth century should be likened, even though the situation was not entirely similar, to that in Western Europe at the beginning of the seventeenth. Significantly, American policy makers usually preferred the Auburn system, which resembled the forced labor régime that had characterized European prisons already in the early modern period.[38] I will come

[38] For the European-American comparison of imprisonment, see Spierenburg (Pieter), From Amsterdam to Auburn. An explanation for the rise of the prison in 17th-century Holland and 19th-century America. In: Journal of Social History 20,3 (1987): 439–61. For an updated and more complete analysis of imprisonment in early modern Europe, the reader should consult Spierenburg (Pieter), The prison

back below to the question of the extent to which a monopoly of force was established in the United States. My playing down the view of the new penitentiaries as bastions of state power, on the other hand, does not mean that I support Whitman's thesis of increasing degradation. A major weakness of his book, for Europe no less than for the United States, concerns its prime focus on legislation and legal opinion. There is much less attention to changes in the actual prison conditions of the nonprivileged majority.

Prison conditions in the nineteenth and twentieth centuries are a central issue in the work of Herman Franke.[39] Although this is mainly confined to the Netherlands, his theory, based on Elias, is preferable to Whitman's. Let me begin with a few empirical examples. Although Franke states a couple of times that even the solitary confinement of the nineteenth century was somehow less atrocious than inmate life in previous periods, he still repeatedly emphasizes the great psychic suffering, often leading to suicide, involved in the cellular system. The real beginnings of the emancipation process, therefore, should be situated around 1900.[40]

On a European scale, Franke traces it back to the rise of professional criminology in the late nineteenth century. According to him, criminologists of various schools, even when they only measured skulls, were the first to show a scientific interest in individual prisoners. More specifically for the Netherlands, around 1900, several socialist leaders served a term in prison, an experience which shocked them. They turned the diffuse interest in convicts into an active movement, bent on ameliorating carceral conditions.[41] In the interbellum period, though, it was mainly the sensitivities outside that increased rather than the benefits on the inside. The Dutch were exceptional in long preferring the cellular system, which continued to be imposed on the majority of inmates until just after World War II. In other European countries, where research is still scarce for this period, the alleviation of prison conditions probably began earlier. When the Netherlands replaced solitary confinement with a régime of communal resocialization, privileges for inmates soon expanded. They were allowed to play sports, watch films or television, and make telephone calls. Some open and half-open prisons were established, and generally the possibilities of obtaining leave or interruption of a sentence increased. At the beginning of the 1970s, the first prisoner newspaper appeared. A few years later, inmates were allowed

experience. Disciplinary institutions and their inmates in early modern Europe. New Brunswick, NJ (Rutgers University Press) 1991.

39 I will refer here to Franke (Herman), The emancipation of prisoners. A socio-historical analysis of the Dutch prison experience. Edinburgh (Edinburgh University Press) 1995. This book is an abbreviated version of his Dutch dissertation of 1990. The suppressed sections mainly deal with parliamentary debates.

40 Compare the critical remarks in Spierenburg (Pieter), Four centuries of prison history: Punishment, suffering, the body and power. In: Norbert Finzsch & Robert Jütte (eds.), Institutions of confinement. Hospitals, asylums and prisons in Western Europe and North America, 1500–1950. Cambridge (Cambridge University Press) 1996: 17–35, see pp. 33–4.

41 Franke 1995: 203–7.

unsupervised visits by their partners for sexual purposes. This is only a selection from the many empirical examples of emancipation provided by Franke. During the 1980s, the pace of the emancipation process began to slacken, but most of the privileges acquired in the preceding decades survived.[42]

Intriguingly and despite Whitman's claim of increasing degradation, such a process of emancipation also took place in the United States. Its outline was already known to scholars, but the process is more amply documented in a recent book by Rebecca McLennan.[43] The bulk of her evidence is from New York, but she stresses that the Empire State served as a model for many other northern and western states. Again, the Old South went its own way. Chronologically, the American emancipation process did not lag behind Europe and it certainly predated the Dutch reform period. In the United States, changes in prison conditions were introduced just after the abolition of large-scale labor, with reform concentrated in the so-called Progressive age. One of its early markers was an interstate phenomenon, the convict newspaper *Star of Hope* whose first issue appeared in 1899. Among other things, the *Star* published letters from prisoners, signed with their number rather than with their name. In New York in the same year, humiliating practices such as the shaving of heads and the obligation to wear striped uniforms and to march in an excruciating fashion were abolished. Prison libraries were set up and inmates, most of them literate by then, were allowed to write letters. In the 1910s, Thomas Mott Osborne even introduced prisoner's councils in Auburn and Sing Sing, but these were discontinued later. More lasting was the introduction of films and sports. All these privileges first applied to white inmates only, but they were later extended to African Americans. Osborne's successors expanded the sports program and introduced occasional performances by singers and comedians.

Admittedly, cells often continued to be dirty and infested with vermin. Riots broke out repeatedly, as in the 1950s. Solitary confinement in dark cells still existed as a disciplinary punishment, and Alcatraz was opened as an institution devoid of privileges for the most hardcore federal convicts in 1934. These observations do not diminish the importance of the emancipation process. McLennan does not take her story much further than the 1920s, but Edgardo Rotman concludes that "... the concession of benefits and privileges during the Progressive Era had become accepted social practices that ultimately gave substance to the nascent prisoners' rights movement [in the 1960s]. Those concessions were largely the result of the policy of patterning the prison on the community."[44] This article's author, moreover, possesses material evidence for the continuation of the emancipation process until

[42] Franke 1995: 246–74.

[43] McLennan (Rebecca M.), The crisis of imprisonment. Protest, politics and the making of the American penal state, 1776–1941. Cambridge (Cambridge University Press) 2008.

[44] Rotman (Edgardo), The failure of reform: United States, 1865–1965. In: The Oxford history of the prison. Edited by Norval Morris and David J. Rothman. New York, Oxford (Oxford University Press) 1995: 169–97, see p. 192.

the end of the 1960s in the form of two CD's with Johnny Cash's concerts in Folsom and San Quentin, California, in 1968 and 1969. As is well-known, Cash was allowed to sing "San Quentin I hate every inch of you." The evidence for the process of emancipation of prisoners in the United States constitutes the clearest refutation of Whitman's thesis that degradation was the central element in this country's criminal justice history.

In order to explain the process of emancipation of prisoners, Franke draws on the work of Norbert Elias. Elias identifies several long-term developments in European societies that are broadly interrelated. These include civilization processes and the diminution of differences in power between social groups. To describe the interaction between two social groups with rather unequal power chances, Elias uses the conceptual pair of established versus outsiders. In that connection, the term 'emancipation' appears. The power relationship between the two groups may become (but does not necessarily always become) less unequal. This means that the outsiders emancipate. In order to fully understand the structure of such an emancipation process, we must be aware of Elias' concept of power. Like Foucault, Elias acknowledges that "power is everywhere."[45] It is a structural aspect of all human relationships. More clearly than Foucault, however, Elias maintains that power is always two-sided. There cannot be differences in power if only one group "possesses" it. In the relationship between baby and parents, for example, the latter are by far the more powerful party, but the baby also has a measure of power: When it cries, a parent will come and see. Power, moreover, can have various sources, among which is physical strength. In the baby's case, this is obviously not the source; it is the parents' wish to take care of their child in every possible way. When new or enlarged sources of power become available to an outsider group, it starts to emancipate.

Prisoners clearly constitute a bunch of outsiders. They are much less powerful than the various groups interacting with them, who include politicians, lawyers, bureaucrats, and guards. Nevertheless, according to the theory that power is always two-sided, prisoners have a measure of power. Consequently, we must identify their sources of power. Franke mentions two types of sources: sensitivity in the outside world against their suffering and obstruction by themselves. Prisoners can commit obstruction by failing to meet the expectations of the groups interacting with them, for example by not improving when improvement is the prison's official goal. They can do this even after their release by becoming recidivists, thereby showing that resocialization in prisons does not work. Obstruction, it seems to me, is a rather ambivalent source of power. Franke's argument assumes that policy makers' reaction to discovering that resocialization has failed is a further alleviation of prison conditions. At times, however, this discovery produces a call for greater harshness. This leaves sensitivity as the key element. When sensitivity in the outside world

[45] Elias' and Foucault's concepts of power are discussed more elaborately in Spierenburg (Pieter), Punishment, power and history: Foucault and Elias. In: Social Science History 28,4 (2004): 607–36.

against the suffering of inmates increases, this means that their source of power is enhanced. Consequently, they are able to negotiate an extension of their privileges. Conversely, when sensitivity in society at large diminishes, the life of inmates will tend to become harder. Is this what happened in the Western world since about 1980? To preserve the more or less chronological structure of this chapter, I must first return to the death penalty.

THE DEATH PENALTY: REINTRODUCTION, ABOLITION AND NEAR-ABOLITION

Few possibilities for emancipation are available to capital convicts, who have to die per definition. For them, the two principal forms of alleviation were the acceptance of the principle of making death as painless as possible and the change that spared them onlookers, except for a decreasing set of invited persons. The other major development with respect to capital punishment in the nineteenth and twentieth centuries was that ever fewer criminals met that fate. In France, for example, the annual number of executions per million inhabitants, documented since 1825, was slightly more than 2 then, but it quickly dropped to about 1. Averaged per five-year period, the number declined to about 0.2 in 1865–1870, after which it fluctuated between 0.1 and 0.4 until it peaked at nearly 0.5 after World War II. Note, however, that the French graph is interrupted during both world wars. The execution rate in France decreased to nearly zero in the 1970s.[46] In the United States, measured for North and South together, the decline set in somewhat later: per capita since the 1880s and in absolute numbers since 1935. Once again, the Northern states made the principal contribution to this decline.[47] The world wars had no significant effect on execution rates in the United States, but in Europe, this was clearly different. In Germany, the annual number of death sentences in 1942–1944 was about fifty times as high as the average in both the Weimar and the early Nazi years. There is no information on the number of executions in these war years, but for 1939, Evans lists 139 death sentences – and 219 executions![48] Obviously, he has included a number of judicial killings that were less than legal. The problem of which ones to count as legal and which as illegal is even greater for the occupied countries. There, World War II certainly brought an increase in execution rates, but as the interruptions in the French graph indicate, there is no consensus about the numbers.

46 Chesnais (Jean-Claude), Les morts violentes en France depuis 1826. Comparaisons internationales. Paris (Presses Universitaires de France) 1976: graph 9. Chesnais' graph is per 100,000 which I converted to per million for convenience's sake. On executions in modern France see also Grivet's contribution to this volume.

47 Banner 2002: 208. Most detailed and recent quantitative analysis in Allen (Howard W.) + Clubb (Jerome M.), Race, Class, and the Death Penalty. Capital Punishment in American History. With assistance from Vincent A. Lacey. Albany (State University of New York Press) 2008.

48 Evans 1996: 914–16 (table 1). The table goes back to 1860 but it presents no per capita figures and has gaps.

To more fully grasp both the secular decline of capital punishment and its return in relation to World War II, it is instructive to examine developments in the Netherlands, the second European country in abolition's chronology. In fact, the abolition in 1870 was neither total nor definitive. It was probably preceded by a decline in execution rates, but this is hard to determine with precision from the figures provided by Sibo van Ruller. In the whole country (Belgium, which was part of it until 1830, excluded), 442 death sentences were pronounced between 1814 and 1870, of which 75 were executed. Because the pardon rate progressively increased, the number of executions probably declined correspondingly.[49] Following the last public execution in Maastricht in 1860, all capital convicts were pardoned. Between 1814 and 1860, executions thus averaged 1.6 per year, which amounts to an average execution rate of about 0.5 per million. The legal change in 1870 caused the Netherlands to skip a phase with indoor executions, but the abolition of capital punishment applied only to civilian law. The death penalty remained part of military penal law, listing fifteen capital offenses and ordering execution by a firing squad without an audience. A separate clause, however, allowed capital punishment to be imposed only when the defendant's act had caused danger to the security of the state, and most lawyers agreed that this required a state of war.[50] Thus, even in the absence of research into court-martial archives, it is likely that the alleged deserter Chris Meijer, shot at the military compound in Doorn on May 12, 1940, was the first person legally executed in the Netherlands since 1860.[51]

Meijer's death sentence foreshadowed things to come. A lessened respect for life was not only present among Nazis and fascists but also among many of their opponents. This manifested itself in various ways, but for this work, I must confine myself to legal executions. As early as 1941, clandestine newspapers in the occupied Netherlands called for the execution of the leaders of the Dutch National Socialist Movement (NSB), and the following year, Queen Wilhelmina's radio message from London assured that no traitor would escape his or her deserved punishment. The exiled government made legal provisions for this in a series of decisions in 1943–1944, all called special or extraordinary. This designation referred in particular to the absence of a legislature that could authorize them (directly after the war most lawyers thought this procedure acceptable). The decisions included the creation of new punishable acts, for example by extending the range of the offense "assistance to the enemy." Nowadays, many lawyers consider this as a violation of the *nulla poena sine lege* principle. Most fatefully, the special decisions included the reintroduction of

49 Ruller (Sibo van), Genade voor recht. Gratieverlening aan ter dood veroordeelden in Nederland, 1806–1870. Amsterdam (Bataafsche Leeuw) 1987: 94–6 (count of death sentences based on number of pardon dossiers; since 1814, all death sentences were apparently followed by a pardon procedure) and 200 (tables 9b and 9c, indicating the increase in the percentage of pardons).

50 Bot (Erwin), De doodstraf onder de Bijzondere Rechtspleging. Master thesis, Erasmus University, Rotterdam 2005: 8–12, 20.

51 On Chris Meijer: http://www.dodenakkers.nl/oorlog/grafmonumenten/20-vuurpeloton.html (accessed May 26, 2010).

capital punishment into civilian criminal law, for the most serious wartime offenses. All this was decided without much debate. The cabinet and its advisers believed that it would be dangerous not to give in to some extent to the lust for revenge that was widespread in the country. The primary aim of capital punishment's reintroduction was to prevent lynchings and other forms of extralegal justice directly after liberation and to ensure immediate control for the returning authorities.[52]

These events make it clear that even when a country has reached a certain level of civilization, exceptional circumstances may lead to heightened feelings of revenge and an increase in judicial harshness. It can be argued that the Netherlands replicated, on a meso-level, the European experience of the sixteenth century. Back then, powerful rulers suppressed individual people's desire for private vengeance and raised the number of executions, thereby demonstrating their monopoly of force. In the Netherlands since 1940, the long-forgotten death penalty was reintroduced with the hope of satisfying feelings of revenge. In all, the Special Justice after the war (including a court-martial in the liberated region before the war's end) led to 159 death sentences and 42 executions, the last one in March 1952. Those put to death included a few Germans and one woman.[53] Until the end of 1947, the majority of the press and public opinion favored quick executions and the rejection of pardons. Since then, the call for revenge quickly disappeared, whereas the government usually preferred clemency. For decades, the death penalty was retained in military law, but the new constitution of 1983 included an article that proscribed it. Thus, 1983 is generally considered as the legal end of the death penalty in the Netherlands, although a few laws had to be adapted afterward to make them conform to the new constitution.

The major Western and Central European countries abolished the death penalty between 1949 (West Germany) and 1981 (France), whereas the United States witnessed an abortive abolition between *Furman v. Georgia* in 1972 and *Gregg v. Georgia* in 1976. In this volume, these episodes are analyzed in detail by Andrew Hammel and Marie Gottschalk, respectively. For my argument, it suffices to emphasize the paradox inherent in the comparison between the American and European experiences: a legal change under political pressure versus a political change in the absence of pressure.[54] In the United States, the death penalty is primarily a legal issue, with the Supreme Court deciding on the matter of its constitutionality, whereas in European countries, it is a political issue with the legislature deciding whether to retain or abolish it, usually at the initiative of the executive branch of government. Nevertheless, in several European parliaments, the abolition of the death penalty came about as a project of the political elite who was able to ignore majority opinion. By contrast, American officials, political and legal, are much more sensitive to public

52 Belinfante (A[ugust] D[avid]), In plaats van bijltjesdag. De geschiedenis van de Bijzondere Rechtspleging na de Tweede Wereldoorlog. Assen (Van Gorcum) 1978: 17–50; Bot 2005: 15–19, 22.

53 Most recent figures in Bosch 2008: 83–4.

54 Noted earlier in Banner 2002: 301.

opinion, which applies even to the nonelected justices of the Supreme Court. In Europe, it appears, the majority of the population ultimately accepted the values of their political leaders, which sealed the fate of the death penalty.

THE MODERN RETURN TO PUNITIVENESS

With the death penalty absent in Europe, the modern return to punitiveness revolves around imprisonment. At least two issues are important in this respect. One refers to the statistical question of incarceration rates and the general harshness of the criminal law as reflected in such rulings as 'three strikes and you're out'. The evidence regarding this issue is relatively easy to ascertain, even though there are methodological problems even here, such as which types of institutions qualify to have their inmates counted as prisoners. The other is the question to which extent the process of emancipation has been discontinued or even reversed. For an answer, we need data about prison conditions and inmates' rights from a number of countries, and this over several decades. Collection of these data requires an elaborate comparative investigation that cannot be performed within the framework of this historical essay. I restrict myself to referring to a few authors whose work touches on the question whether the United States is unique with respect to the new punitiveness or merely ahead of Europe. In terms of the graph presented at the beginning of this article, do we attach primary importance to the steepness of the curve or to the absolute numbers?

Authors with such divergent backgrounds as the sociologist Loïc Wacquant and the journalist Anne-Marie Cusac appear to support the position of uniqueness.[55] Wacquant speaks of the penal or neoliberal state that has totally replaced the welfare state. Notably, the abolition of the Aid to Families with Dependent Children (AFDC) program in the late 1990s constituted a landmark. The social profile of today's prisoners, Wacquant continues, is strikingly similar to that of (former) welfare recipients (this applies much less, however, to the gender profile). He furthermore stresses that penal administrators have given up every pretense of resocialization, prisons just being places for neutralizing and storing people. Although he maintains that the penal state has made intrusions into some European countries – and this under socialist governments – his analysis is perfectly attuned to the United States. For her part, Cusac opens with commenting on America's elevated incarceration rates, but she quickly leaves this subject for a historical and qualitative analysis. Her most original chapters deal with the increasing and often illegal use of devices such as restraint chairs and stun belts on prisoners, as well as tasers by the police, and

[55] Wacquant (Loïc), Crafting the neoliberal state. Workfare, prisonfare and social insecurity. Forthcoming; Cusac (Anne-Marie), Cruel and unusual. The culture of punishment in America. New Haven, London (Yale University Press) 2009.

she finds evidence of torture and sexual humiliation in American prisons akin to the practices at Abu Ghraib. Cusac further reports that the producers of several of the repressive devices export them but mainly to countries with dictatorial régimes, thereby underscoring the United States' uniqueness among Western nations.[56]

David Garland's *The Culture of Control* can be considered as a study maintaining that the United States is merely ahead of other nations with respect to a trend that is nearly universal in the Western world.[57] Garland identifies several factors that all imply a shift away from "penal welfarism." Although he takes his evidence from the United States and Britain, he considers the rise of the culture of control as characteristic for most of continental Europe too. Indeed, even his critics are able to come up with only a few counterexamples, and some of them not valid.[58] If we also take into consideration Wacquant's remarks that the penal state is on the rise in major European countries, it would seem that the argument that the United States is merely ahead of the others is persuasive. Amidst the modern trend toward punitiveness and control, the increase in incarceration rates stands out as the most tangible element. There are just a few partial counterexamples, such as the German Federal Republic during the 1980s, where the rates declined bringing the number of prisoners in 1990 back to the 1970 level.[59] In the Netherlands, on the other hand, the post-1970 rise was even more marked because it followed several decades of per capita decline. During a period of which the 1960s formed the nucleus, Dutch incarceration rates were among the lowest in the Western world. This was a period of great social optimism that Downes and van Swaaningen refer to as the Second Golden Age.[60] Does the return to punitiveness, then, imply the resurgence of pessimism?

Perhaps pessimism sounds too negative, since modern punitiveness also has a positive side to it. The idea that it has to do with an increasing compassion for crime victims plays a part in Garland's analysis and it is central to the work of Marie Gottschalk and Jonathan Simon.[61] It would be incorrect, therefore, to state that the

[56] See also my review, *Journal of Social History* 44, 1(2010) 290–292, where I argue that the situation before the sacralization of executions provides counterevidence to her thesis about the religious nature of punishment. Further, compare the essay by Colin Dayan in this volume showing the extensive use of solitary confinement in American prisons today.

[57] Garland (David), The culture of control. Crime and social order in contemporary society. Chicago (University of Chicago Press) 2001.

[58] As pointed out in Downes (David) + Swaaningen (René van), The Road to Dystopia? Changes in the Penal Climate of the Netherlands. In: Tonry (Michael) + Bijleveld (Catrien) (eds.), Crime and Justice in the Netherlands. Chicago (University of Chicago Press) 2007: 31–72, see p. 33.

[59] Salle (Grégory), La part d'ombre de l'état de droit. La question carcérale en France et en République fédérale d'Allemagne depuis 1968. Paris (editions EHESS) 2009: 135.

[60] Downes and van Swaaningen 2007: 36–9.

[61] Gottschalk (Marie), The prison and the gallows. The politics of mass incarceration in America. Cambridge (Cambridge University Press) 2006; Simon (Jonathan), Governing through crime. How the war on crime transformed American democracy and created a culture of fear. Oxford (Oxford University Press) 2007.

sensitivity in society at large, which in an earlier period was the motor behind the process of emancipation of prisoners, has vanished. Rather, a shift in the public's sensitivity has taken place from prisoners as its objects to crime victims as its objects, or more generally from perpetrators to victims. Around the 1960s, victims received scant attention, whereas perpetrators were often seen as themselves victims of unfavorable social circumstances. Viewed from one angle, this modern shift should be regarded as a decivilizing trend because, if it continues, its ultimate consequence would be to allow widespread physical retaliation in response to victims' anxieties. In any case, the evidence so far seems to indicate that the power of prisoners has somewhat diminished again. Viewed from another angle, the concern for victims involves more of a civilizing trend, because it is not simply a return to the age of feuding. Medieval concern for a victim was restricted to his or his family's right of private vengeance. Third parties did not particularly care. By contrast, the modern concern for victims involves sympathy for them from larger groups, often unrelated, within society. The movement against "senseless violence" that gained momentum during the 1990s stems from a rather diffuse anxiety about lethal incidents that should not happen.[62]

From the observation that modern punitiveness implies a shift away from the rehabilitative attitudes prevalent from the 1950s to the mid-1970s, it is a small step to an explanation in terms of a backlash at the 1960s. In this view, the modern culture of repression and control constitutes a reversal of the permissive and progressive culture that had its heyday in the 1960s. This is one of the conclusions emerging from Cusac's historical exposition. The argument is present even more forcefully, though still semi-implicitly, in the work of Wacquant. For one thing, he speaks of a remasculinization of the state in reaction to the women's movement. This new masculinity has powerful political managers posing as virile protectors against troublemakers. Second, Wacquant sees a reactivation of the stigma of blackness, in this case, of course, as a reaction to the civil rights movement. Once more nowadays, African Americans are viewed primarily as dangerous persons. The first factor in his argument, unlike the second, is universal rather than peculiarly American, but it is also the one that is flawed. The modern compassion with crime victims actually has its roots in the second feminist movement! This movement began with a focus on the issue of abortion, but toward the end of the 1970s, its concerns extended to sexual and domestic violence. For the first time, the more or less progressive attitudes of the sixties led to a preference for criminalization, presented as the only solution favorable to the victims.[63] This suggests that an explanation in terms of alternating

[62] Spierenburg (Pieter), A History of Murder. Personal Violence in Europe from the Middle Ages to the Present. Cambridge (Polity Press) 2008: 218–22.

[63] See esp. Gottschalk 2006: chapters 5 and 6. She argues that in the U.S., the anti-rape and battered women's movements became much more aligned with law-and-order politics than they did in Europe. Simon (2007: 108) also briefly comments on the link between feminism and the victims' movement

spirits of the age is too simple and that, again, we have to take the longer term into consideration. I will come back to this in the conclusion.

First, I should relate the preceding discussion to our principal subject, the death penalty. One way of doing this would be to state that attitudes toward capital punishment simply evolve with the flow. On neither of the two continents, for example, has the return to punitiveness extended to public tortures on a scaffold, which all but a few people consider as a phenomenon of the past that should remain so. Clearly visible from the early 1980s onward, the return to punitiveness proceeded within the framework of each continent's penal spectrum at that point in time. For the United States, this meant including the death penalty, which had just been declared constitutional again, whereas for Europe, this meant with the populace just having accepted the political elite's position that capital punishment was outside the moral value system. Consequently, in Europe, the subsequent increase in punitiveness referred to imprisonment alone and in the United States to both imprisonment and executions. The corollary of this argument would be that abolition of the death penalty in the United States is only possible after a drastic trend reversal.

But I am not content with such an easy answer, since after all, I believe that a broader historical-sociological theory is required. At this point, it is necessary to consider the work of Stephen Mennell who analyzes the American civilizing process, along the way comparing it with developments in Europe.[64] One of the principal differences he observes is that, unlike European countries, America never knew a single model-setting elite (as a reference group for what constitutes polite behavior and what, generally, are civilized values). Instead, there has been a succession of partially model-setting groups. Today, for example, a jet set of television and movie stars plus some popular singers that live in and around Los Angeles set the model for some people but not for everyone. As discussed earlier, in European countries, the model-setting elite – by that time, the political establishment – took the lead in abolishing the death penalty. Hence, Mennell partly attributes its retention in the United States to the absence of such an elite. In addition, he adduces my democracy-came-too-early thesis about the persistence of high homicide rates in the United States and extends this thesis to the death penalty.

The slogan that "democracy came too early" is a rhetorical statement, highlighting the different pace of historical developments on either side of the Atlantic. In Europe, it took centuries, marked by recurrent setbacks, before stable monopolies of force were established. At some point, resistance to the royal monopoly shifted from trying to destroy it to trying to co-possess it. In the latter case, the people were accustomed to being disarmed in day-to-day affairs; they accepted the monopoly as such but

in the United States, but he identifies the 1968 Safe Streets Act as the real root of the trend toward compassion with victims.

64 Mennell (Stephen), The American civilizing process. Cambridge (Polity) 2007.

wished to have a say in how it was used. On the American continent, on the other hand, democracy was introduced before the people had gotten accustomed to being disarmed. Consequently, an ethic of self-help and distrust in state agencies remain widespread among Americans. This does not mean that a monopoly of force did not emerge at all, which would fly in the face of the evidence. It means that there remain strong countertendencies to its full effectuation.[65] We may take the new penitentiaries of the nineteenth century, for example, as testifying to the existence of a monopoly of force, whereas the widespread and unrestrained possession of guns by private citizens until today testifies to the countertendencies.

In extending my democracy-came-too-early thesis from the subject of homicide to that of the death penalty, Mennell relies heavily on Zimring's association of capital punishment and popular justice, equally emphasizing that lynchings then and executions now concentrate in the South but adding that the weakness of the monopoly of force has always been greatest in the South. Moreover, Mennell interprets the ethic of self-help and the distrust in state agencies as a brake on civilizing developments, while considering abolition of the death penalty as reflecting civilizing developments. Thus, he concludes that "the political structures of American democracy have subtly constrained the workings of an underlying civilizing process that would not otherwise have been radically different from that seen in Europe."[66] I agree with his analysis to a large extent, but I wish to give the argument a different twist.

Returning to Europe, I observe that an important long-term historical development involves the gradual intensification of the demands made from below upon the representatives of the state at moderating the practical uses of their monopoly of force. The disappearance of the scaffold and the emancipation of prisoners form part of this moderation process, along with other changes not discussed here, such as increasing restrictions on police action. The crucial point is that the moderation in the uses of a monopoly of force is a function not only of civilizing processes but also of the diminution of power differences within society. This last factor ensures that we can view the sacralization of executions as a very early phase in the moderation process. Although it was not a particularly civilizing change, it did involve a slight raise in the status and hence the power of convicts. This long history of moderation characterized American society to a much lesser extent. Prisoners did emancipate there during a large part of the twentieth century, but capital convicts had fewer power chances. The relative weakness of the moderation process in American history can be connected to the democracy-came-too-early thesis. This connection results in the following paradox: As Americans are inclined to a lesser recognition of the existence of a monopoly of force, they have a lesser inclination to make demands for restraint on it.

[65] Discussed more fully in Spierenburg 2006.
[66] Mennell 2007: 151.

CONCLUSION

The principal analysts and theoreticians referred to in this chapter all contributed pieces of the puzzle, which I have tried, perhaps not to solve but to rearrange. In all societies and throughout history, the criminally condemned have in common that they feel the state's monopoly of force striking at their person in one way or another. Hence, every change in the treatment of the condemned is also a change in the way in which the monopoly of force is used. When successful demands are made on state agents for moderating the uses of their monopoly, the power of the condemned increases. This is a manifestation of the overall diminution of power differences that Norbert Elias views as one of the principal aspects of long-term change. In Europe, the sacralization of executions, involving a slight rise in the status and power of capital convicts, constitutes an early example of the moderation process. Subsequently, the ritual of religiously tainted executions was exported to Colonial America, which is one indication for this continent's more compressed long-term development. Crucial in this compressed development was the "too early" advent of democracy, which led Americans to remain particularly distrustful of a state monopoly of force and, paradoxically, inclined to make fewer demands for moderation in its uses. Nevertheless, some examples of moderation, in particular a phase of emancipation of prisoners, took place also in the United States.

In the last three decades or so, the power of the criminally condemned appears to have somewhat diminished again, but further research is needed to determine its extent with greater precision. For one thing, average prison terms have increased and the supermax régime has spread. The extent of ordinary inmates' privileges and rights, on the other hand, has certainly not been reduced to the nineteenth-century level. Moreover, these recent developments are coupled with a partially civilizing trend of increasing compassion with crime victims that balances between vindictiveness and solidarity. Taken together, these developments are, to a large extent, common to Europe and America. In European countries, however, where the determination of the political elites to reject the death penalty meets with no serious opposition, this punishment remains out of the picture. In the United States, next to prisoners being even worse off than their European counterparts, the popularity of the death penalty has markedly increased. Thus, the modern return to punitiveness is a trend common to most Western nations, but in the United States it is exacerbated due to the lesser inclination of its citizens to make demands of moderation on the use of the monopoly of force.

The principal conclusion of this thesis for Elias' theory runs like this: In the long run, civilizing processes and the decrease of power differentials between social groups go together and reinforce each other. In the short run, however, they sometimes proceed in opposite directions. The history of violence offers another example. In recent decades, respect for authority figures such as teachers or public transport officials has decreased, which led to an increase in aggression directed at them.

Recent developments in punishment and control are even more complex. They involve a less moderate use of the monopoly of force and a concomitant decrease in the power of the criminally condemned but also a civilizing trend toward compassion with crime victims. An analysis of these partially contradictory developments helps us in better understanding present-day society, but it cannot tell us how things will continue.

2

Did Anyone Die Here?

Legal Personalities, the Supermax, and the Politics of Abolition

Colin Dayan

My subject is solitary confinement and the ways in which it has been transmuted from an occasional tool of disciplinary convenience in our prisons – as punishment for infractions – into a widespread, normative, but concealed alternative death penalty in our judicial system.[1] Although issues of punishment and conditions of confinement in our prisons are two separate subjects, they come together and overlap in the ways we treat criminals.

Recent judicial activism – I think particularly of Justices Antonin Scalia and Clarence Thomas – has tried to remove conditions of confinement from Eighth Amendment scrutiny, making them part of the administrative prerogative, and hence to narrow the definition of punishment, thus emptying it of much of its actual, lived meaning. However, whether we regard prison as retributive or as rehabilitative, or as both, conditions of confinement do matter, not simply as an administrative issue or as an Eighth Amendment issue, but because, quantitatively and qualitatively, they have changed their character and in doing so changed the character of punishment – as well as the status of the condemned. Newer and ever larger categories of our population are swept up into the categories of the dehumanized and excluded.

Once, solitary confinement affected relatively few prisoners for relatively short periods of time. Today, most prisoners can expect to face solitary, for longer periods than before, and under conditions that make old-time solitary seem almost attractive. The costs are enormous. Supermaxes, also called "Security Housing Units," "Control Units," or "Special Management Units," typically cost two to three times more to build and operate than traditional maximum-security prisons.[2] The societal costs are far greater still: Of the approximately 2.3 million people in prison or jail in the United States – the highest documented incarceration rate in the world – how many

[1] This chapter draws in part on my forthcoming book, *The Law Is a White Dog*.

[2] For up-to-date information on supermax prisons, see "StopMax: Working to end solitary confinement," organized by the American Friends Service Committee: http://www.afsc.org/stopmax/.

may spend the rest of their lives without speaking to another human being – or returned to society damaged and disenfranchised, without redress?

Figures for supermax confinement are elusive, if not unreliable. The figures come from different dates and sources. According to Human Rights Watch, by 2002, more than 20,000 prisoners, or nearly 2 percent of the U.S. prison population, were being held in long-term solitary confinement.[3] "StopMax: Working to End Solitary Confinement" estimates that forty-four states have supermax facilities confining more than 30,000 people.[4] The most complete statistics I have found, however, from the "campaign to shut down control units," estimate that forty-three states confine over 100,000 prisoners.[5] The statistical problem is that conditions vary from state to state and in different institutions. From one year to the next, in some states, the percentage increase appears to be 1,000 percent – that is, a tenfold increase.[6] More importantly, such confinement is defined in various ways and goes under a range of names: not just supermax – which means institutions designed specifically for the permanent isolation of all their inhabitants – but also isolation, the hole, permanent lockdown, administrative segregation, or closed custody, special management, control or secure housing unit – which means segregated confinement within a larger institution, an isolation section that some call a "prison within a prison."[7]

Prisoners are confined for months or even years, with some spending more than twenty-five years in segregated – solitary – prison settings. And contrary to the perception that supermaxes house "the worst of the worst," it is often the most vulnerable – especially the mentally ill – not the most violent, who end up in indefinite isolation.[8] As I learned in my work in the Arizona supermaxes, placement there is often

3 "Out of Sight: Super-Maximum Security Confinement in the United States," Human Rights Watch, February 2000, http://www.hrw.org/legacy/reports/2000/supermax/Sprmx002.htm#P40_391 (accessed May 25, 2010).

4 In "The Prison Inside the Prison: Control Units, Supermax Prisons, and Devices of Torture: A Justice Visions Briefing Paper" (Philadelphia: American Friends Service Committee, 2003), Rachael Kamel and Bonnie Kerness describe the growth of the control unit prison: from half a dozen control units in 1985 to control units in forty-five states by 1997. See also Chase Riveland, "Supermax Prisons: Overview and General Consideration," U.S. Department of Justice, 1999, available at http://nicic.org/pubs/1999/014937.

5 MIM (Prisons), "Nationwide Survey of Control Units," http://abolishcontrolunits.org/research. The campaign to shut down control units is led by the Maoist Internationalist Ministry of Prisons.

6 For the confusion in defining the term "supermax" and in arriving at correct figures, see Alexandra Naday, Joshua D. Freilich, and Jeff Mellow, "The Elusive Data on Supermax Confinement," *The Prison Journal* 88 (2008): 69–93.

7 For the purpose of this chapter, I use the general though admittedly inexact terminology of "supermax" confinement to denote long-term isolation, whether in sensory-deprivation cells or supermax prisons.

8 Though both *Madrid v. Gomez*, 889 F. Supp. 1146 (N.D. Cal. 1995) and *Ruiz v. Johnson*, 37 F. Supp. 2d 855 (1999) judged long-term segregation facilities unconstitutional insofar as they held mentally ill inmates, neither decision confronted the psychic decompensation that threatened otherwise healthy individuals. In *Jones 'El v. Berge*, 164 F. Supp. 2d 1096 (W.D. Wis. 2001) and *Austin v. Wilkinson*, 189 F. Supp. 2d 719 (N.D. Ohio 2002), both courts granted a preliminary injunction prohibiting defendants from housing mentally ill prisoners in supermax confinement.

haphazard and arbitrary. It usually focuses on litigious inmates, those disliked by correctional officers, or alleged gang members.[9]

Next, as to quality: Once upon a time, solitary meant little more than a cell to oneself. Criminals were sent to solitary for defined – shorter or longer – periods of time, in the knowledge that they would get out, fairly soon, and return to the general prison population. Future infractions might send them back to solitary again, but again they would return from it. None of this is true today. The contemporary high-tech prison is a clean, well-lighted place. There is no decay or dirt. And there is no guaranteed exit.

This is not the "hole" popularized in movies like *Murder in the First* or *The Shawshank Redemption*. Under the sign of professionalism and advanced technology, idleness, sensory deprivation, and extreme isolation constitute the "treatment" in these units. And while they take trauma to its extreme, these places are rationalized as "general population units": the general population of those judged to be the inmates most likely to offend (defined as gang members or "security threat groups," the mentally ill, or "special needs groups," as well as protective custody inmates – ever-widening sections of the total prison population).

Most importantly, however, hidden in these details – and hidden there in part by the judicial activism I noted – lies a terrible change in our ways of punishing. The great struggle over the death penalty goes on. Given the way our country works, it may never end. But it is clear that there are some states that will not use it any longer, as there are other states that will continue to, and some that will go backward and forward over the issue. Just last week, a judge in Texas declared the death penalty unconstitutional, only to reverse himself a few days later and say that he needed to think about it a bit more.[10]

Probably we are, quietly, slowly, and fitfully, falling into line with other "civilized" countries and finding the company of China, as the other main proponent of judicial killing, distasteful. In its place, however – or, more precisely, alongside it – we have invented a new form of death penalty, one which needs no judicial decision, carries no decent shame, is not open to scrutiny, and already stands in danger of killing more people than the death penalty.[11] Long-term, open-ended, and often permanent,

9 Dayan, "Held in the Body of the State," *History, Memory, and the Law*, eds. Austin Sarat and Thomas R. Kearns (Ann Arbor: The University of Michigan Press, 1999), 183–249. For the most acute analysis of penology based on "status," see Scott N. Tachiki, "Indeterminate Sentences in Supermax Prisons Based upon Alleged Gang Affiliations: A Reexamination of Procedural Protection and a Proposal for Greater Procedural Requirements," *California Law Review* 83 (1995): 1117–48. See also Elizabeth Vasiliades, "Solitary Confinement and International Human Rights: Why the U.S. Prison System Fails Global Standards," *American University International Law Review* 21 (2005): 71–99.

10 See "Texas judge rescinds anti-death penalty ruling," http://www.google.com/hostednews/ap/article/ALeqM5hJjNzsQw2EiMdsxPajJMR64dM.

11 "In the Shadow of Death: Capital Punishment, Mass Incarceration, and Penal Policy in the United States," Marie Gottschalk's essay in this volume, demonstrates the entangling of the exceptional – the trajectory of capital punishment ("Death is different," as Brennan pronounced in *Furman v.*

supermax confinement kills – it kills physically and it kills the spirit. In the way it functions today, it is an efficient and largely hidden additional form of death penalty, not for murderers, but for ever-wider circles of malefactors (and, as we have seen to our shame, even some people whom we kidnap from foreign countries to bury in our prisons without any recourse such as trial or habeas corpus, but whom our legal idioms and traditions and social values alike proclaim to be innocent).

ICONS OF THE HUMAN

In *Baze v. Rees* (2008), the Supreme Court upheld Kentucky's method of execution by lethal injection. In a seven-to-two ruling, the Court rejected the claim that the effects of the three-drug protocol on the condemned qualified as cruel and unusual punishment under the Eighth Amendment. At issue in this case were the details of the injection's administration: the chemicals that are used, the training of the personnel, the adequacy of medical supervision, and the risk of error. The ritual correctness of state-sanctioned execution ostensibly assures humane, clean, and painless death. But the paralyzing drug pancuronium bromide leaves an improperly sedated inmate conscious but unable to move, breathe, or cry out. Although nineteen states prohibit the use of this chemical in the euthanasia of animals, the Roberts Court decided that it did not present "a significant risk of unnecessary suffering." What would an *insignificant* risk of unnecessary suffering look like?[12]

When considering the practice of lethal injection, we face the unsavory possibility that the dignified spectacle made visible to the observer in the viewing chamber shares nothing at all with the torture, mental and physical, going on behind the glass in the execution chamber. The rules of law and the leeway within them recognize certain forms of punishment as suitable for people of a certain "nature" or "character" – those labeled unfit, barbaric, subhuman, or the "worst of the worst." Once categorized as such, and stigmatized as criminals or threats, they can be restrained in their liberty, deprived of rights, and ultimately undone as persons. This legally binding incrimination, not always linked to specific actions and offenses, recycles human materials as the detritus of our new world order.[13]

Persons labeled as extraneous to civil society – whether slaves, criminals, or detainees – do not have *rights* as the term is normally used. Unseemly tensions

Georgia) – with widespread practices of mass incarceration and a new kind of death penalty, which she describes as "a death in slow motion for many prisoners."

12 *Baze v. Rees*, 128 S.Ct. 1520 (2008).

13 What I refer to as society's refuse, humans contained or quarantined in the local and the global call for "security," recalls Zygmunt Bauman's description of the poor and the stigmatized in *Wasted Lives: Modernity and its Outcasts* (Cambridge: Polity Press, 2004). What he describes as "the human waste disposal industry" is both essential to and the result of globalization. The prison, as Loic Wacquant and David Garland have also emphasized, is essential to this project of containment, the incapacitation of persons deemed noxious to society. See Loic Wacquant, "Deadly symbiosis: When ghetto and prison meet and merge," *Punishment & Society*, 3 (2001): 95–133, and David Garland, *The Culture of Control: Crime and Social Order in Contemporary Society* (Chicago: The University of Chicago Press, 2001).

characterize the rhetoric of humane treatment, and nowhere do the duplicitous claims of civilization become as obvious as in the recent uses of such terms as "dignity" or "decency" to justify the most extreme suffering. It is perhaps the cohabitation of calls for decency with the threat of barbarism that makes the lethal magic of state power less open to criticism.

The idea of a decent death puts us at the limits of reason, but there is something worse than physical execution by the state – its legal alternative: the haunt of the self made extinct, bereft of intimacy and affiliation, condemned to a permanently confined and solitary life. Situated beyond the terror of mortality, the person dies incessantly in new ways. In this chapter, I explore how increasingly refined technologies of death are sustained and promoted by the rhetorically powerful forms of law. I suggest that protracted and indefinite supermax confinement is a cruelty worse than death. Not an alternative to the death penalty, but instead its dark underside – redefining death as it expands criminality – the supermax is the background against which our fixation on the death penalty must be considered.[14]

If the United States has not abolished the death penalty in concert with its peers in the civilized world, it has gone far toward doing so, in two ways: first, by replacing it with life imprisonment; and second, by making that expression, again unlike other civilized countries, mean just that.[15] Solitary confinement has become the weapon of choice in the American punitive armory. It has drawn vast numbers of prisoners into its ever-growing maw. These include large numbers of people who are there not as perpetrators of serious crimes, but who find themselves enmeshed in "solitary" as part of what is mendaciously, if euphemistically, labeled "administrative segregation." People, in other words, who have committed no – relevant – crime find themselves placed apart from other prisoners, sometimes for what is claimed to be their own protection, sometimes for what is alleged to be the administrative convenience of prison officials, sometimes for baseless, unproven, and generally unprovable claims of gang membership.[16] The numbers are growing, and the profits from building and running such units are immense.

14 See Lorna Rhodes, *Total Confinement: Madness and Reason in the Maximum Security Prison* (Berkeley: University of California Press, 2004); Craig Haney, "Infamous Punishment: The Psychological Consequences of Isolation," *National Prison Project Journal* 8 (1993); Craig Haney and Mona Lynch, "Regulating Prisons of the Future: A Psychological Analysis of Super-Max and Solitary Confinement," *New York University Review of Law & Social Change*, xxiii (1997): 477–570; James Robertson, "Houses of the Dead: Warehouse Prisons, Paradigm Change, and the Supreme Court," *Houston Law Review* 34 (1997): 1003–63; Jamie Fellner and Joanne Mariner, *Cold Storage: Super-Maximum Security Confinement in Indiana* (New York: Human Rights Watch, 1997).

15 The United States is the only country that sentences juveniles to life in prison without parole. On November 9, 2009, the Supreme Court heard oral arguments in *Sullivan v. Florida* and *Graham v. Florida* in order to consider whether the Eighth Amendment has been violated in such cases.

16 For my account of the "no-exit" mechanisms of supermax confinement in Arizona's Special Management Unit 2, see Dayan, "Due Process and Lethal Confinement" in "Killing States: Lethal Decisions/Final Judgments," eds. Jennifer L. Culbert and Austin Sarat, *South Atlantic Quarterly* 107 (2008): 485–509, reprinted in *States of Violence: War, Capital Punishment, and Letting Die*, eds. Austin Sarat and Jennifer L. Culbert (New York: Cambridge University Press, 2009), 127–50. On the development

As if all this were not enough, and still more relevantly from our point of view, the length of detention in such units, for whatever reason incarceration has occurred, depends not on a sentence issued by a court, nor on any specific infraction by the inmate, but on the whim of the prison administration. Inmates can spend from a defined minimum of, on average, ninety days, through an average, in practice, of several years, to life – and without knowing either whether they will ever get out or how they might do so, and hence when. The regulations governing egress from solitary are cast in ways that actually make it impossible for constantly increasing numbers of inmates ever to leave.

Since Scalia's decision in *Wilson v. Seiter* (1991), as I have argued elsewhere, the possibility of claiming an Eighth Amendment violation for any "totality of conditions" – such as those found in the supermax – has been totally eroded.[17] These conditions – no longer legally recognizable – construct a new and capacious category of persons.

In the twenty-first century, the United States has created a specter of criminality. James Whitman's word "degradation," used to focus on the extremity of punishment here as opposed to Europe, not only describes the punitive, retributive bias of our prisons, but also explains our government's continued reservation to Article 16 of the United Nations Convention Against Torture and Other Cruel, Inhuman, or Degrading Treatment or Punishment (proposed by the United Nations in 1984 and ratified by the United States in 1994). Avoiding the definition of torture that includes the words "inhuman" or "degrading," the United States accepts the prohibition only insofar as the meaning of the phrase "cruel, inhuman or degrading treatment or punishment" is limited to the words in the Eighth Amendment.[18]

How did what used to be called "solitary confinement" become the penal philosophy behind entire prison facilities, built to detain "incorrigibles" for indefinite periods of time? In *Hutto v. Finney* (1978), after hearing about all kinds of barbaric physical abuses and hellish conditions of confinement, the Supreme Court upheld a lower court's order limiting the length of stay in the punitive-segregation unit of the Arkansas prison system to thirty days.[19] But as long as confinement in isolation is identified as an "administrative" precaution, not a "disciplinary" or "punitive"

of the supermax in Arizona, see Dayan, "Held in the Body of the State" and Mona Lynch, *Sunbelt Justice: Arizona and the Transformation of American Punishment* (Stanford: Stanford Law Books, 2009), 135–8, 168–9.

17 Colin Dayan, "Legal Slaves and Civil Bodies," *Materializing Democracy: Toward a Revitalized Cultural Poetics*, eds. Russ Castronovo and Dana D. Nelson (Durham and London: Duke University Press, 2002), 83–5; Dayan, "Legal Terrors," *Representations* 92 (2005): 60–2, 68.

18 James Q. Whitman, *Harsh Justice: Criminal Punishment and the Widening Divide Between America and Europe* (New York: Oxford University Press, 2003). See also Anne-Marie Cusac, *Cruel and Unusual: The Culture of Punishment in America* (New Haven and London: Yale University Press, 2009). For my discussion of the U.S. reservation to Article 16 and the significance of this reservation to the legal limits of torture, see Colin Dayan, *The Story of Cruel and Unusual* (Cambridge and London: MIT/Boston Review Press, 2007), 65–7; 79–82.

19 *Hutto v. Finney*, 437 U.S. 678 (1978).

exercise – in other words, not a punishment – there is no agreed-on time limit beyond which it can be judged cruel and unusual punishment.

In *Sandin v. Conner* (1995), Chief Justice William Rehnquist's decision redefined the constitutional limits of confinement and set the stage for legally designating the supermax prison as an administrative – not a disciplinary – necessity. Focusing on the nature of the hardship imposed, and not on the language of the state prison's regulations, as he had done in *Hewitt v. Helms* (1993), Rehnquist gutted the meaning of solitary confinement. The Supreme Court had previously stated in dictum that solitary confinement is a "major change in conditions of confinement" that should be governed by the same procedures as the deprivation of statutory good time (*Wolff v. McDonnell*, 1974), and lower federal courts had almost universally adopted this view.[20] In a five-to-four decision, the majority in *Sandin* rejected it and claimed that the inmate's disciplinary segregation in solitary confinement "did not present the type of atypical, significant deprivation in which a State might conceivably create a liberty interest."[21]

The Court reasoned that disciplinary confinement, "with insignificant exceptions," was similar in "duration and degree" to administrative segregation and protective custody: "disciplinary segregation, with insignificant exceptions, mirrored those conditions imposed upon inmates in administrative segregation and protective custody."[22] The distinction is thus legally erased between a normal, administrative order – applicable to all prisoners – and an exclusive situation, affecting only prisoners who have misbehaved.

So, when prison officials renamed punitive or disciplinary segregation as *administrative segregation*, they were in conversation with judges who had been only too willing to blur the distinction between administrative custody and punitive isolation.[23] A punitive transfer would require at least the minimum requirements of due process. But the legal effect of administrative transfer is that the prisoner cannot challenge a designation that is based most often on status alone.[24]

The courts demanded due-process procedures for disciplinary action, so the prisons segregated inmates just as harshly as before – with the loss of privileges and threat

[20] *Wolff v. McDonnell*, 418 U.S. at 572 n. 19.

[21] *Sandin v. Conner*, 515 U.S. 472 (1994), 486.

[22] *Sandin v. Connor*, 515 U.S. 472 (1994), 486.

[23] For a lengthy discussion of Rehnquist's maneuvering in *Sandin* and his logic that makes a fiction of protection, see Dayan, "Due Process and Lethal Confinement," 492–5. See also Dayan, "Held in the Body of the State," 210–12, for a discussion of the "institutional-risk score" that has nothing to do with the crime that put an inmate in prison, but is based on behavior after confinement. As William Bailey, the classifications specialist at the Department of Corrections in Phoenix, put it, "Classification is non-punitive in every single way. . . . We don't have any punitive measures anywhere in the classification system."

[24] In *Wilkinson v. Austin*, 544 U.S. 74 (2005), while the Court found that prisoners have a due process liberty interest in avoiding supermax placement, it upheld the written policy that includes annual review of such placement as comporting with due process. Most significantly, there is no substantive limitation on prison officials' ability to put prisoners in supermaxes in the first place.

of psychological harm – but called it by another name and thus escaped judicial censure. By a linguistic sleight of hand, prison officials made the illegal legal. Rules in Special Management Unit 2 in the Arizona State Prison Complex–Eyman, for example, claim that solitary confinement is not disciplinary, since inmates in "close" or "secure" quarantine are not being "punished." Instead, they are sequestered to promote order and security: an administrative judgment only.

How, to adopt the language of *Sandin*, do we define "the ordinary incidents of prison life"? What kind of rule can be used to ascertain whether a deprivation "imposes atypical and significant hardship on the inmate"? Or, to take up fully Rehnquist's rephrasing of the conditions necessary to give rise to due process protections: these "will generally be limited" to whatever "imposes atypical and significant hardship on the inmate in relation to the ordinary incidents of prison life."[25] What the Court accomplishes by putting "atypical and significant" in league with "ordinary" is to level the distinction, to make it difficult to prove when the due process clause should kick in – how atypical must something be in order to be extraordinary?

Conditions of confinement, not overtly as bad as the dank and filthy penitentiaries of old, are now accommodated to the neutralization of individuality. Punishment has been gradually reinvented as an alteration of mind. This change is as profound as it is legally illegible. It is as if with each court case, with each decision to make the prison more legal or to tailor its confines to constitutional expectations in the face of proliferating claims of cruel and unusual treatment, punishment becomes more refined and hidden, less vulgar and obvious.

WHERE DO YOU GET TO BE ALONE – FOREVER?

What do figures tell us about supermax confinement? As I have said, there is a lack of reliable data. Figures are hard to come by. Even when available, they are vitiated by a variety of problems.[26] According to one source, a total of 105,614 inmates in U.S. prisons are in Control Units – another name for supermax prisons or prisons within prisons.[27] They constitute 4.59 percent of the total prison population in state prisons. (Federal prisons are a separate matter).[28] This means that almost one prisoner of every twenty in state prisons in the United States is in a supermax.

The figures alone are awe-inspiring, even for those accustomed to the United States' tendency to be at the wrong end of scales on such matters. Their detail,

25 *Sandin*, 484.

26 See Alexandra Naday, Joshua D. Freilich, and Jeff Mellow, "The Elusive Data on Supermax Confinement," *The Prison Journal* 88 (2008): 69–93.

27 See "Nationwide Survey of Control Units," http://abolishcontrolunits.org/research (accessed March 14, 2010).

28 The contemporary supermaxes grew out of the twenty-three-hour lockdown policy at the federal prison in Marion, Illinois, which began in 1983 and continued as a means to silence dissent and punish the activism that gave rise to the prisoners' rights movement in the late 1960s and 1970s.

however, reveals some telling discrepancies. Of the fifty states, seven have no prisoners in such units – Hawaii, Idaho, Kentucky, Minnesota, North Dakota, South Dakota, and Utah. Two have fewer than 100 in supermaxes: New Mexico (48) and New Hampshire (60); and another five have similarly small numbers: Maine (100), Maryland (160), Rhode Island (166), West Virginia (184), and Indiana (262). These three categories of states, 14 in all, house a total of some 980 prisoners, or less than 1 percent of the national total, in such units. At the other end of the scale, four states – California, Ohio, Texas, and New York – with respectively 14,207, 13,013, 9,984 and 9,019, for a total of 46,223, account for almost half of the national total.[29]

Percentages too tell a curious tale: Those states that house no prisoners in such units are of course out of this particular loop. But others are not. Some states place only a tiny percentage of their prisoners in such units: Indiana (262) 1%; Maryland (160) 1%; New Mexico (48) 1%; and Alabama (483) places only 2% there; as do Connecticut (453) 2%; Georgia (1,345) 2%; Illinois (832) 2%; and New Hampshire (60) 2%.

Others stand out, not only for absolute numbers of prisoners in supermaxes, but for how large a percentage of their prisoners overall they place there: Alaska, with 500, places 10% of its prisoners in indefinite isolation; so does Washington (2,026) 10%. From here, the figures rise steadily: Missouri (3,286) 11% and Nebraska (468) 11%; Kansas (1,088) 12%; Montana (430) 12%; New York, as we saw, also 12%; then Nevada (2,155) 13%; Mississippi (3,140) 15%; North Carolina (6,756) 17%; and Colorado, with 4,374, places 18%; and this list is topped off finally, with a jump, by Ohio, whose 13,013 prisoners constitute fully 24%, virtually one prisoner in four, of its total.

These and similar sets of figures are worrying and suggest that the real explanation for these discrepancies may be far simpler – and more troubling too. Political colorings are insignificant: Democratic and Republican states seem to be fairly evenly scattered here. Regional spread is irrelevant. Density of population is not a factor. Entry into supermax prisons is a product on one hand of large numbers of arbitrary decisions by individuals on the ground, and possibly on the other of a variety of extrajudicial influences: the significance of prisons and of supermaxes to

[29] The large numbers of prisoners in supermax confinement in New York and California substantiate the argument that the political activism of prisoners during the 1970s was the catalyst for the contemporary use of solitary to isolate, degrade, and disable: For example, the riot at Soledad prison in California in 1970 and the killing of the black activist George Jackson at San Quentin in California, intensified the riot that had begun in part as a protest for better conditions and treatment at the Attica Correctional Facility in New York in 1971. I thank Marie Gottschalk for alerting me to the connection between the modern supermax and radical politics behind bars. In "Resisting Living Death at Marion Federal Penitentiary, 1972," *Radical History Review*, no. 96 (Fall 2006): 58–86, Alan Eladio Gómez focuses on the political awakening that led to "the prison authority's deployment of living death as a strategy to control radical inmates." See also Dylan Rodriguez's *Forced Passages: Imprisoned Radical Intellectuals and the U.S. Prison Regime* (Minneapolis: University of Minnesota Press, 2006) for his analysis of the site of incarceration itself as ground for a new understanding of resistance. Judged incorrigible and rendered anonymous, the imprisoned demand – through their activism – a redefinition of the very terms of personal and social identity.

a local economy, political strategies, and state traditions of severe confinement. A range that goes from 0% (Kentucky) or 1% (Indiana) to 24% (Ohio) leaves a worrying, not to say unpleasant taste.[30]

ATTENDING TO THE DEAD

Nearly two centuries ago, Bentham came to believe that solitude was "torture in effect": "When the external senses are restrained from action," in "a state of solitude, infantine superstitions, ghosts, and specters, recur to the imagination. This, of itself, forms a sufficient reason for not prolonging this species of punishment. . . . "[31] Nineteenth-century writers, including Dickens, Beaumont, and Tocqueville, used images of premature burial, the tomb and the shroud, to figure the severity of this death-in-life in the penitentiary. Since then, numerous critics of solitary confinement have focused on the harsh psychological effects of this practice, but we need to ask not only why this torturous confinement continues, but also how it has been legally justified and extended – normalized for an ever-larger group of prisoners. Moreover, the twenty-first-century export of indefinite detention to Guantánamo Bay – and its projected replacement by permanent or open-ended "preventive detention" here in the United States – alerts us to the strange staying power of this form of incapacitation.[32]

After years of analyzing the effects of supermax confinement on inmates' mental health, the Harvard psychiatrist Dr. Stuart Grassian defined the environment as "strikingly toxic." What he has called "a supermax syndrome" includes such symptoms as hallucinations, paranoia, and delusions. Inmates have difficulty remaining alert, thinking, concentrating, and remembering due to prolonged sensory deprivation.[33] During a *60 Minutes* episode on California's "Pelican Bay" broadcast on January 15, 1995, Grassian complained, "In some ways it feels to me ludicrous that we have these debates about capital punishment when what happens in Pelican Bay's Special Management Unit is a form of punishment that's far more egregious."[34]

30 Arizona, where I am most familiar with this practice of incarceration, puts 8 percent of its prisoners in supermaxes.

31 *The Works of Jeremy Bentham, published under the supervision of his executor, John Bowring* (Edinburgh, 1838–1843), vol. 1, 426. For Bentham on solitary confinement, see Janet Semple, *Bentham's Prison: A Study of the Panopticon Penitentiary* (Oxford: Clarendon Press, 1993), 129–33.

32 My forthcoming book, *The Law Is a White Dog*, tries to account for the capacious and constantly shifting legal forms of incapacitation in the United States. For a literary history of solitary and its gothic effects, see Caleb Smith, *The Prison and the American Imagination* (New Haven and London: Yale University Press, 2009).

33 Dr. Stuart Grassian, "Psychiatric Effects of Solitary Confinement," *Washington University Journal of Law and Policy* 22 (2006), 333, 354, and *Lee v. Coughlin*, 26 F. Supp. 2d 615, 637 (1998).

34 Grassian, *60 Minutes*, CBS, January 15, 1995. The interview with Mike Wallace followed and updated his first interview on Pelican Bay prison, "California's High Tech Maximum Security Prison Accused of Torture and Mental Abuse," *60 Minutes*, CBS, September 12, 1993. This report preceded and prompted *Madrid v. Gomez*, 889 F. Supp. 1146 (1995). Sally Mann Romano in "If the SHU Fits:

More than a decade later, on March 19, 2009, Governor Bill Richardson repealed the death penalty in New Mexico. He told the story behind the "most difficult decision" of his political life. After going to the state penitentiary where he saw the death chamber, he visited the maximum security unit that held those sentenced to life without any possibility of parole (LWOP).[35] "My conclusion was those cells are something that may be worse than death," he said. "I believe this is a just punishment." Even though his words recall the spiritually inclined prison reformers who invented the "separate system" or absolute isolation in early nineteenth-century Philadelphia, Richardson's sense of justice sounds more like vengeance without any hint of redemptive promise.[36]

Life and death are brought together under the umbrella of legal history. Whether legitimate punishment, necessary pain, or reasonable violence, these cultural expectations are produced, transmitted, and sustained in a legal idiom. We need to consider whether there is a distinction to be made between the legal personality granted the body strapped to the gurney, injected with chemicals, and made placid for the killing action and that of the person locked up in prolonged and indefinite solitary confinement. In other words, what is left of persons – living or dead – once the law has finished with them? In choosing to focus on the mind's entombment in supermax confinement, my polemic is not against judgment per se, and punishment too, but against the tendency in contemporary cases to reduce constitutional claims to the most basic terms: life and death, bodies emptied of minds, and hence deprived of the defining qualities of personhood. Such loss not only suggests the allegedly inferior status of offenders, but it also cultivates inferiority.

To date, the Supreme Court has not considered whether supermax confinement is itself unconstitutional. So the supermax in its evasion of constitutional claims

Cruel and Unusual Punishment at California's Pelican Bay State Prison," *Emory Law Journal* 45 (1996): 1112–13, outlines the clinical symptoms of sensory deprivation: "hyper-responsivity, perceptual distortions, hallucinations, massive free-floating anxiety, and difficulties with thinking, concentration, memory, and impulse control." This series of symptoms, called "Reduced Environmental Stimulation" syndrome, was codified in a series of studies on sensory deprivation conducted by Doctors Brownfield and Solomon in the 1950s, but had been identified in the nineteenth century. These studies were corroborated by the "Walpole Study" conducted by Stuart Grassian at the Massachusetts Correctional Institute at Walpole, which found that solitary confinement is "a major, clinically distinguishable psychiatric syndrome" that is "strikingly consistent among the inmates."

35 See Ashley Nellis and Ryan S. King, "No Exit: The Expanding Use of Life Sentences in America," July 1–3, 2009), The Sentencing Project: http://www.sentencingproject.org/doc/publications/publications/inc_noexitseptember2009.pdf.

36 "N.M. repeals death penalty," *Los Angeles Times*, March 19, 2009. Cost was also cited as a factor in the decision to repeal. See Ian Urbina, "Citing Cost, States Consider End to Death Penalty," *New York Times*, February 14, 2009. In some ways, the possible end to the death penalty makes it even more necessary to consider the connection between civil life and civil death (the latter being the condition of those imprisoned for life, warehoused in isolation units, as if buried alive). Jonathan Simon's "Capital Punishment as Homeowners Insurance" in this volume suggests how the support for "ultimate sanctions" – especially what he calls a "death sentence in disguise" – operates in tandem with, indeed, arises quite naturally from the rise in homeownership, the flight to the suburbs, and the pursuit of personal security in "gated communities."

has created the perfect crucible for transformation. Designed for basic necessities and nothing more, the structure itself dramatizes the minimal requirements of the courts. Awash in unnatural light, everything in the building – what can be seen and how, its location and design – promotes the control of deviance, the assurance of sameness. Its physical space marks the outer limits of social coercion, because it singles out those to be controlled.

The damage done by that control, no matter how great, cannot be redressed or even addressed legally as long as the mere necessities for life are met. If mere physical survival is what matters, if "basic human needs" or the "minimal civilized measure of life's necessities" remains the bottom line for humane – indeed constitutional – treatment, then these immaculate cages embody this new penology of deprivation. They are locales for perpetual incapacitation, where obligations to society, the duties of husband, father, or lover, and the traits of and criteria for personal identity are no longer recognized or validated.

LOCKDOWN

Working in the state prison systems in Arizona, I recognized the power of terminologies that kill, the violence of humane restraint and disciplinary segregation. In *The London Hanged*, Peter Linebaugh describes the "denaturing" of "men and women who fell foul of law" in eighteenth-century England. His "history of misappropriated things" provides a background to a new social order that depends on the putting away of those deemed unfit. He thereby captures something of the exploitation and dispossession in the United States that now lead to innovations in a civil society whose criminals become indistinguishable from the poor.

Dogs and blood. Obedience and belief. She could not be sure what the voices told her. She remembered asking to see a doctor. She could still smell the feces she had smeared on the walls. She started a fire in her cell. They took her to a smaller, darker cell. Locked down twenty-four hours a day in a 7′ by 12′ cell and shackled in cuff and chains, H.B. was allowed three fifteen-minute showers and three one-hour periods of exercise per week. Correctional officers said she made odd gestures, but she was left alone – no medication, no doctors. This was her punishment.[37]

How did a fifty-year-old African-American woman, diagnosed with chronic paranoid schizophrenia, end up in lockdown? Convicted of aggravated assault in 1981 and sentenced to ten years in prison, she was assigned to the Santa Maria Unit of the Arizona State Prison Complex, Perryville, a 312-bed maximum-security unit for women, in Goodyear, about two hours from Tucson. In 1991, Charles L. Arnold, attorney at Frazer, Ryan, Goldberg, Arnold & Gittler in Phoenix, acting as guardian on behalf of H.B., brought a case against Samuel Lewis, then director of the Arizona Department of Corrections (ADOC); Mary Vermeer, deputy warden of the Santa

[37] Name changed.

Maria Unit at the Perryville Prison; and David Fernandez, M.D., a psychiatrist employed by the ADOC. In the summer of 2008, I spoke to Arnold about the case. "Seriously mentally ill male inmates always had the chance to be treated at the Baker Unit on the grounds of the Arizona State Hospital on 24th Street and Van Buren in Phoenix," he explained. "But women had no options but lockdown."

Between May 12, 1989 and October 2, 1991, H.B. was in lockdown for 514 days – approximately 60 percent of her time in custody. Dr. Victor Pera, the psychiatrist employed by the ADOC to oversee mental health care, appeared before the Arizona Superior Court during H.B.'s commitment proceedings on October 18, 1991. Her attorneys hoped that she could be treated at the Arizona State Hospital, where medications could be forcibly administered if necessary:

Q. What have you noticed about H.B.'s behavior in your various interviews or examinations?

A. Well, she is hallucinating and delusional. My diagnosis is chronic schizophrenia. She is a very belligerent lady, who screams and hollers at you, does not listen to what you are saying, is very uncooperative and threatens.

Q. In what manner does she threaten?

A. She threatens that if you don't leave the room, she'll – verbally threatens, not physically. Set fire to her cell. Covered her walls with feces. Clammed up and became mute. We had to lock her down twenty-four hours a day. If she strikes out again, they will automatically put her in the hole, and they're liable to keep her there from six months to a year and a half. Which is incredible, and it will certainly – I mean, actually, it's pathetic that we have to treat people this way. You know, they tell us, she's in the Department of Corrections, she's been sentenced, she's got to carry out the sentence and whether she's sane or insane or whatever. We've got ladies that are locked down from six months to a year, to a year and a half.[38]

H.B. sat in the court during this testimony. Sitting next to her attorney, she demanded clarification: "Well, ask him how belligerent, how I was belligerent to him. That's a lie." Then, turning to the judge, she denied being delusional and begs to return to Perryville. "I'm tired around here just let me stay at prison and finish my time so I can go home." She continued:

> What I want to ask you is when I come out here they brought all my records with me in the van and my TV. That's all I had of my own. Well, can you tell me – can you – what I want to ask you, could you extend – I mean I said – I got about four more years to do. Drop that and let me go home. Okay, now he say I haven't had

[38] Court transcripts, Superior Court, Phoenix, Arizona (October 18, 1991), *Arnold v. Lewis* CIV 91–1808 (consolidated into *Casey v. Lewis*, 834 F. Supp. 1477, 1993). I thank Charles Arnold for his informative conversation with me, June 3, 2008.

all my physical. I had it, my physical by doctor, the lady doctor, white lady doctor. I'm tired around here just let me go home.

The two attorneys, H.B., the judge, the recorder and the psychiatrist had already been in the courtroom for two hours when H.B.'s lawyer began cross-examining Dr. Pera.

Q. Did you try to enroll her in any therapy groups?
A. No.
Q. Did you try to take her out of lockdown?
A. Oh, yes, sure. I talked to the warden, I talked to security, can we get her out of there, lockdown could damage even a perfectly normal person, maybe she would feel better. Their contention was no, we cannot take her out of there, because security cannot handle her.

Pera diagnosed her with "schizophrenia, exacerbation. A major mental disorder in which the individual is out of contact with reality. Hallucinating and delusional." Pera testified that H.B.'s situation, though extraordinary in itself, is nothing exceptional at the Santa Maria Unit. Seven or eight women, suffering from varying psychoses, are habitually locked down for extended periods of time. H.B.'s lawyer disagreed: "Now this – this situation is out of a prisoner-of-war camp situation or a concentration camp."

In September 1992, nearly a year later, her case came before Judge Carl A. Muecke of the U.S. District Court for the District of Arizona. Presiding over the weeklong hearing concerning H.B, he told the court that her treatment "has been worse than grossly inadequate or inhumane. It has been barbaric":

> Over this period of time, the defendants have punished plaintiff for her mental illness by throwing her in the hole for periods of time up to a year and leaving her there without any mental care in a highly psychotic state, terrified because of hallucinations, such as monsters, gorillas or the devil in her cell. In fact, one psychiatric expert states he wouldn't treat his dog the way defendants treated H.B.[39]

In *Arnold v. Lewis* (1992), Muecke concluded that the defendants had violated H.B.'s Eighth and Fourteenth Amendment rights by their deliberate indifference to her mental health needs. He issued a detailed injunction forbidding the defendants to place her in lockdown, isolation, seclusion, or restraints for any reason, especially as punishment for actions caused by her mental illness.

At the time of H.B.'s incarceration in the late 1980s, before supermaxes were the norm – and there are still none for women in Arizona[40] – ADOC had different methods of treating recalcitrant inmates, or the mentally ill unlucky enough to have

39 *Arnold v. Lewis*, 803 F. Supp. 246, 258 (1992).

40 To date, there are no separate supermax facilities for women in the United States, although there are isolation units within prisons.

been released into prison from state institutions. If they became violent or abusive, the "hole," the "self-abuser pod," and the "socialization chair" were the prescribed treatments. The isolation or temporary holding cells are triangular cells with a bench six inches deep. The bench runs the length of the hypotenuse of the cells. Once in there, inmates are "four pointed": held face down with their ankles secured by leg-irons and hands cuffed to wall or floor rings.

Though correctional officers are supposed to assess regularly inmate mental health, the logs are fragmentary, registering only intermittent observation. I was told by officers at the Arizona State Prison Complex–Florence, that clear boundaries were always maintained between staff and inmates. I learned that the "toughest problem for rookie officers" was being "conned" or taken in by "malingerers." I was shown a sign that had recently been placed in every unit:

STAFF/INMATE
MAINTAIN
PROFESSIONAL DISTANCE

"Not a slash," an associate deputy warden explained, but "understand it like a vertical bar, an absolute barrier between staff and inmates, humans and animals."

THE LAWFUL PRISON

In 1996, I first walked through special management units 1 and 2 (referred to as SMU 1 and 2) in the Arizona State Prison Complex–Eyman, just down the road from the Arizona State Prison Complex–Florence. Escorted by deputy wardens, I completed a series of interviews in an attempt to learn how the bounds of human endurance had been tested, the limits of cruel and unusual punishment extended, and human treatment redefined.

When it opened in October 1987, SMU 1, a 768-bed structure, was considered the model of efficiency and security. The unit is a cement building of unremitting monotony. Skylights in the hall provide only indirect access to natural light. Each windowless cell is eighty square feet and is equipped with a built-in bunk and a toilet-sink unit. The doors of the cells are heavy-gauge metal. The cement walls and ceilings in the halls are unpainted. The computer system monitors each inmate's movement and opens and closes cell doors. Human contact is reserved for what is known as "cell extraction." When an inmate refuses a transfer to another cell or fails to return his food tray, four or five guards in riot gear immobilize him. Tasers and gas guns are used as "nonlethal weapons." Sometimes attack dogs are "sicced" on stubborn inmates who refuse to "cuff up" or pass their trays through the food slots. A prisoner in SMU 1, with whom I corresponded for a year in 1999, described how dogs are used "as punishment or psychological torture." "The dogs do attack us," he wrote, they are "sicced on us by COs [correctional officers] for minute things that could be handled by talking, or spray, but now more and more inmates become victim to unreasonable dog attacks." Inmates are then removed from their cells with restraints that include at a minimum handcuffs or belly chains (chains fastened at the back with cuffs for the hands). A small place for exercise, called the "dog pen," with cement floors and walls twenty feet high, virtually another cell, provides the only access to fresh air.[41]

SMU 1 was surpassed by SMU 2. Completed in 1996, it was renamed Browning Unit on June 2, 2008, in honor of Army Staff Sergeant Charles R. Browning, previously a correctional officer in SMU 2, who died leading a convoy in Afghanistan. Also a 768-bed unit, it cost taxpayers $40 million. Given the cost of building supermaxes, an official in Arizona joked, "Why don't we just freeze-dry 'em?"[42] Situated on forty acres of desert, SMU 2 is surrounded by two rings of twenty-foot-high fence topped with razor wire, like a hazardous or nuclear waste storage facility. Held between the monotony of sand and concrete, the desert and the walls, I understood what the officers meant when they described the "no-frills' policy of the Arizona Department of Corrections.

On one of my first visits, a correctional officer explained, "We razed the desert, bulldozed it, tore up anything that looked green." The extruded-steel cell doors are punched through with holes, making them look "like irregular-shaped Swiss cheese," in the words of an ADOC architect. The stainless steel mirror, sink, and toilet are fastened with adhesives that cannot be chipped. Nothing inside the cells can be moved or removed. Inmates sleep on a poured concrete bed. The water supply to the toilet and sink can be shut off from a nearby control booth. Some officers find that turning off the water after just a few seconds in the morning is a good way to discipline inmates.

The cell doors have traps through which food trays can be passed, when, as one deputy warden put it, "they feed." Second-floor hallways have steel mesh floors so that the hallway below is visible. Skylights intensify the spectacle of light and immaculateness. Cell doors are reflected in the ultrashined floors, which the deputy warden praised as we walked through the halls during my first tour of SMU 2: "Looking good. Smooth as glass. From now on I'll have to wear sunglasses." Not only is the inmate isolated in his cell, but each cell is further isolated in a separate, steel-door-enclosed enclave of five or six similar cells. Officers and prisoners talk via intercom rather than face-to-face, giving new meaning to the policy of detention, incapacitation, and control.[43]

ALTERING THE MIND

In the new prison management practices, we confront a difficult metamorphosis. To incapacitate is to render incapable, to disable body and mind. Out of this death

41 Personal correspondence (name withheld), July 16, 1999.

42 Interview (name withheld), Arizona State Prison, Florence, August 25, 1995.

43 Interview with James McFadden, June 7, 1996.

and dispossession, a new status of being is promoted and legitimated for inmates. Supermaxes entail a substantial modification in the inmates' spatial and temporal framework of personal identity and memory. Since the body remains circumscribed in a passivity that has no analogy in normal daily life, the objects of understanding necessary to thinking can only be held onto in memory.

The residue of the past matters. But how long can the mind hold onto these fast-fading remains? In *An Essay on Human Understanding*, Locke described memory as a "tomb of dead ideas." He knew, however, that in time they erode into nothing. Once deprived of things to think about, of new impressions or sensations, what can one remember? Memory, preserving a continuous thought through time, is crucial to personal identity, as Locke defined it. If we take this definition as key to our reflection, then we see how this attention to mind and memory shaped the development of radical isolation in prisons. In *A Question of Torture*, Alfred McCoy explains how "sensory disorientation" and the "control over human consciousness for its own sake" became crucial after World War II to the CIA's secret efforts to develop new forms of torture: what he describes as "a hammer-blow to the fundamentals of personal identity."[44]

How does someone who is being forced out of his identity construct a narrative of such a transformation? If the mind is attacked without relief while the body is held in a cage, what can the law do about it? The relevant legal categories change upon imprisonment, when a person becomes human material no longer the subject of rights and duties. With refined, legally permitted methods of imposing helplessness and persistent deprivation, the prison becomes the site for unheralded metamorphoses.

In conditions of radical isolation, only the external shape remains, whereas personal identity – what makes you recognize yourself as yourself – is annihilated. You are then something other, watching over the death of what you once knew, the gradual decay of all that made you part of the world: "For, it being the same consciousness that makes a Man to be himself to himself," Locke wrote, "*personal identity* depends on that only."[45] Contemporary alterations of consciousness called "behavior modification," though still disingenuously cast as rehabilitation, are experiments in deprivation that cause what William James described as "the shrinkage of our personality, a partial conversion of ourselves to nothingness."

No longer to be able to think of oneself as thinking – or to recast this dilemma slightly, no longer to be thought about at all – is, as William James described it, to inhabit a status of the hypothetical: As *if* dead, these selves know something worse than natural death, the continual aftershocks of a death both legal and social: "If every person we met 'cut us as dead,' and acted as if we were non-existing things,

44 Alfred McCoy, *A Question of Torture: CIA Interrogation, From the Cold War to the War on Terror* (New York: Henry Holt and Company, 2006), 8.

45 John Locke, *An Essay Concerning Human Understanding*, ed. with an introduction by Peter H. Nidditch (Oxford: Clarendon Press, 1975): 2:27:10, 336.

a kind of rage and impotent despair would ere long well up in us, from which the cruelest bodily tortures would be a relief."[46]

THE MANY FORMS OF DEATH

Seven years before his death in 1704, John Locke published *The Reasonableness of Christianity, As Delivered in the Scriptures*. In this radical, subversive encounter with the history of law and belief, he made an analogy between the torment of hell and the torture of secular punishment: "Could any one be supposed, by a law that says, 'For felony thou shalt die,' not that he should lose his life; but be kept alive in perpetual, exquisite torments? And would any one think himself fairly dealt with, that was so used?" How, then, was such a condition of extremity as solitary confinement devised as a humane answer to state-sponsored execution? (At least, Governor Bill Richardson – like most prison officials – has no illusions about the humaneness of such confinement.) In the nineteenth century, reformers gave this fate worse than death a religious subtext. Indefinite containment demanded a submission of *mind* that has been seduced by the carnal and its temptations. This juridical incapacitation brought divine dispensation into the prisons of the United States.[47]

When the state decided to punish criminals psychically without executing them, a bold reimagining occurred. Hell came into this world. The criminal was circumscribed by the walls of a cell, condemned to solitude, locked in torment. This second death, psychic and in a sense unnatural – for now, let us call it "soul death" – is brought about without the death of the body. The inversion of spiritual and material replaces the law of heaven with the law of earth. In the fiction of civil death, broadly understood, the state reinvents what happens after literal death. In a secular world, the enthusiastic embrace of something vague like the *soul's salvation* allowed reformers to point to an abstraction, thus masking the concrete object of punishment: the *mind's unraveling*.

The physician and early abolitionist reformer, Benjamin Rush, understood permanent solitary confinement as a "humane" advance over public execution and the indiscriminate mingling of prisoners. But in "An Enquiry into the Consistency of the Punishment of Murder by Death, With Reason and Revelation" (1798), Rush revealed the questionable nature of his use of the word "humane." He argued that "the horrors of a guilty conscience proclaim the justice and necessity of death." And since God inflicted these "horrors of conscience" as "punishment," the most effective punishment would be to extend these torments through time, not curtail them by execution: "Why, then, should we shorten or destroy them by death, especially as we are taught to direct the most atrocious murderers to expect pardon in the future

[46] William James, *The Principles of Psychology*, vol. 1 [1890] (New York: Cosimo, Inc., 2007), 293–4.

[47] John Locke, *The Reasonableness of Christianity, As Delivered in the Scriptures* [1697] in *The Works of John Locke*, 10 vols. (London: Printed for Thomas Tegg; W. Sharpe and Son; etc., 1823), 7:6.

world? No, let us not counteract the government of God in the human breast: let the murderer live – but let it be to suffer the reproaches of a guilty conscience." He presumed that without any human contact, the prisoner might ultimately be reborn – but as what?[48]

If we bring together two nineteenth-century cases, we can better understand the manipulation of the two kinds of death in this country – physical and mental. Though ostensibly about different issues, they belong together. In 1890, the Supreme Court decided two cases that dealt with the limits of cruel and unusual punishment. The first, *In Re Medley*, applied the cruel and unusual punishment standard to solitary confinement in the case of a prisoner condemned to death; awaiting execution, he was condemned to isolation – an extra-added punishment. The second, *In Re Kemmler*, applied that standard to rites of execution.[49]

The Court in *In Re Kemmler* held that a current of electricity scientifically applied to the body of a convict is a more "humane" even if "unusual" method of execution than hanging, since its use must result "in instantaneous, and consequently in painless, death."[50] Electrocution was thus held to be a reasonable and humane means of inflicting capital punishment, not in itself cruel and unusual. The Supreme Court has never judged that solitary confinement itself is an unconstitutional punishment. But in *In Re Medley*, the Court described its effects:

> A considerable number of the prisoners fell, after even a short confinement, into a semi-fatuous condition, from which it was next to impossible to arouse them, and others became violently insane; others, still, committed suicide; while those who stood the ordeal better were not generally reformed, and in most cases did not recover sufficient mental activity to be of any subsequent service to the community.

The judges' opinion not only admitted the terror of isolation, but also considered how the removal to "a place where imprisonment always implies disgrace" branded the prisoner with a "peculiar mark of infamy."[51] The Court argued that the damage of solitary confinement resulted not from the immediacy of punishment but rather through extended suffering.

Now we have returned to the mental torture the *Medley* Court once found unacceptable. Beginning in Arizona in 1995, with a revolt by prisoners shackled on what was called the "death row chain gang," and then, more recently, in other states such as Texas, death row inmates – many of whom have committed no wrong while

[48] Benjamin Rush, *Essays: Literary, Moral, and Philosophical*, edited with an introductory essay by Michael Meranze [1806] (Schenectady, NY: Union College Press 1988), 86, 88. See Meranze's history of punishment in the late colonial and early republican periods: *Laboratories of Virtue: Punishment, Revolution, and Authority in Philadelphia, 1760–1835* (Chapel Hill: University of North Carolina Press, 1996).

[49] *In Re Medley*, 134 U.S. 160 (1890); *In Re Kemmler*, 136 U.S. 436 (1890).

[50] *In Re Kemmler*, 143–4.

[51] *In Re Medley*, 168–71.

in prison – are now institutionalized in supermaxes. They are condemned to this life-in-death – a double death penalty.[52]

UNREALITY AND LEGAL HISTORY

What counts as real in legal argument? To think legally is to be capable of detaching ways of thinking from what is being thought about. Perhaps this is what Judge Christian meant in *Ruffin v. Commonwealth* (1871), when he cautioned that the Bill of Rights, applied to a civilly dead convict, should be given "a reasonable and not a literal construction." To think in law means to reason in a special kind of way, and, as I seek to show, the application of legal rules creates a universe unto itself. The word-magic of legal fiction not only maintains and invigorates philosophies of personhood but engenders ambiguous effects on the politics of everyday life.

If intelligibility or a peculiar kind of logic – and not reality – is the aim, then we need to comprehend how the law has a history of such imagining made real. A resilient acceptance of unreality is a necessary part of legal history. At issue, for example, is not whether the condemned person's pain is real or not, but whether or not in the legal world an unspeakable situation is being described as uncontroversial.

It is not indifference to the category of personhood but rather an obsession with it that introduced another kind of person, anomalous and somehow extraneous to civil society. When prisoners come before the law, they are treated as if real only insofar as they have legal standing. Yet the constitutional status of prisoners has never been decided. So once in the courtroom, what seems obviously extraordinary becomes merely unusual. Once the doors are opened into the house of law, we find implausible metamorphoses that have the power to exploit and oppress. The intriguing thing is the thoroughly matter-of-fact way these horrors are dealt with legally.

Judicial reasoning has the power to give and to take away, to affirm personality and to deny it. A cure for all kinds of threats, reasonableness has always been a necessary presupposition for extending enslavement and disability. This legal rationality, however, is tied to figurative power, and its metaphors can become insistent and literal, operating, as Robert Cover famously wrote, "on a field of pain and death."[53] In our "secular" and "progressive" times, comprehensive forms of intimidation and punishment function as the backdrop to civil community. Nowhere

[52] Robert M. Ferrier in "'An Atypical and Significant Hardship': The Supermax Confinement of Death Row Prisoners Based Purely on Status – A Plea for Procedural Due Process," *Arizona Law Review* 46 (2004): 291–315, argues that placing death row inmates in supermax confinement, "solely on their status under sentence of death," arbitrarily exposes them to psychological harm and hence triggers a liberty interest: the protection of procedural due process guaranteed by the Due Process Clause of the Fourteenth Amendment.

[53] Robert Cover, "Violence and the Word," *Yale Law Journal* 95 (1985): 1601–29.

is oppressive state magic more accomplished than in cases of policing, imprisonment, and torture, where infernal treatment thrives under cover of necessity.

A MORE ARDENT LAW

The opposition between barbarism and civility – the key poles in eighteenth-century jurisprudence – retains its strategic force in today's legal terrain, even if the distinction is not as indisputable as we like to believe.[54] Those who put their faith in the cultivated evolution of legal principles may think it proper to make a sharp division between the Courts' so-called "hands-off" era (1776–1965) and the height of the "prisoners' rights" movement (1965–1986). It is reassuring to believe that, after ignoring the dank holes, vermin, and beatings, the courts responded to the harsh treatment of inmates in a triumph of enlightenment. But in Eighth Amendment cases in particular, it has become clear over time that though physically brutal treatment has been prohibited by the Supreme Court, psychological harm has been disregarded.[55]

Because the courts have defined horrific abuse out of recognition, inhuman treatment continues. Displays of cleanliness, as well as appeals to constitutional minima, basic needs, and humane treatment, allowed severe sensory deprivation and enforced isolation to evade Eighth Amendment claims. Through an often ingenious technical legalism, the court has paved the way for cruelty that passes for the necessary incidents of prison life. Extreme verbal qualifications make deprivation or injury matter only when "sufficiently serious," when involving "more than ordinary lack of due care," or inflicting "substantial pain."

Recent cases also permit punishments that do not necessarily leave scars or perceptible proof of injury. Instead, as Justice Blackmun warned in his concurrence in *Hudson v. McMillian* (1992), they place "various kinds of state-sponsored torture and abuse – of the kind ingeniously designed to cause pain but without a tell-tale 'significant injury' – entirely beyond the pale of the Constitution." We are permitted to fracture the mind in the way that we once broke bones.[56]

54 See *The Story of Cruel and Unusual* for my analysis of the history of Eighth Amendment jurisprudence from slavery to imprisonment to the meaning of "torture" in the Bush administration's War on Terror and the memos written to evade punishment for torture.

55 State prisoners could not claim the protection of the Eighth Amendment until *Louisiana ex rel. Francis v. Resweber*, 329 U.S. 459 (1947). The Court clarified that the Fourteenth Amendment prohibited "by its due process clause execution by a state in a cruel manner" (463). But whereas procedural due process asks whether there is a liberty or property interest that has been interfered with by the state – and, if so, whether the procedures attendant upon the deprivation were constitutionally sufficient – it is the Eighth Amendment that gauges the seriousness of the violation. Treatment *during* detention is not met by the question of due process, because there remains the issue of how extreme are harsh or inhuman conditions. The extent of the deprivation of the formulaic "basic human needs" (*Rhodes v. Chapman*, 452 U.S. 337, 347 [1981]) is not my concern; rather, I am interested in how such a narrow definition of *human* ignores the disintegration of personal identity that occurs during incarceration.

56 *Hudson v. McMillian*, 503 U.S. 1, 13–14 (1992). Linda Greenhouse in *Becoming Justice Blackmun: Harry Blackmun's Supreme Court Journey* (New York: Times Books: H. Holt and Co., 2005) ignores

Words like *decency* and *dignity* jockey for preeminence in these late-twentieth-century cases and alternate with less expansive phrases like "basic human needs" or "minimal civilized measure of life's necessities." The involvement of the law in prisoners' rights provided the terms by which apparent legitimacy masked conditions of incarceration. In miming the language of the law, these terms ensured that old abuses and arbitrary actions would continue. The formulaic call for *humane treatment* played easily into the hands of penal bureaucrats, only too ready to embrace such rhetorically powerful terms.

The notion of "evolving standards of decency" and the "dignity of man" in *Trop v. Dulles* (1958), for example, asserted a very sharp distinction, albeit later repudiated, between the civilized and inhumane treatment of prisoners. Chief Justice Earl Warren's opinion in *Trop* emphasized a flexible interpretation of the Eighth Amendment, recognizing mental suffering or anguish as crucial to the meaning of cruel and unusual punishment. He ruled that it was unconstitutional for the government to deprive Albert Trop of citizenship as penalty for desertion from the army. Though there had been "no physical mistreatment, no primitive torture," Warren emphasized that involuntary expatriation was far worse, for it meant "the total destruction of the individual's status in organized society." Had the government's position been upheld, Trop would have "lost the right to have rights." But during the years of the Rehnquist court (1986–2005) and since, most judges have ignored mental anguish as well as the enduring consequences of degradation.[57]

Perhaps nowhere is the pressure to reclaim and return to an earlier kind of law more evident than in supermax confinement. Since the judicial involvement in prisons in the 1960s, both federal district courts and the Supreme Court have extended and circumscribed the conditions deemed "humanly tolerable." To be turned into ghosts before and until actual death necessitated the redefinition of punishment. If one assumes that the criminal has no intrinsic worth, lacks those intangible qualities that constitute what we know to be human – increasingly the view of Clarence Thomas – then punishment must be retooled. A tormenting afterlife that makes no claims on the self is a limbo without end. No fear of violence, mutilation, or abuse, but the horrifying reality that there is nothing to fear. In this emptiness, terror is a welcome diversion, death – an unrealizable desire.

A PHANTOM PRECEDENT

It is worth considering what might have been. For all its apparent dependence on the past, the legitimating potential of the law sometimes relies on radical disregard.

Blackmun's concern with prisoners and with conditions that are "potentially devastating to the human spirit," as Blackmun writes in his concurrence in *Farmer v. Brennan*, 511 U.S. 825, 853 (1994), the year he left the Supreme Court. Increasingly outspoken in his later years on the Court, he spoke powerfully against *Wilson v. Seiter*, 501 U.S. 294 (1991), arguing that the Court's "unduly narrow definition of punishment blinds it to the reality of prison life" (*Farmer v. Brennan*, 855).

57 *Trop v. Dulles*, 356 U.S. 86, 101, 100, 101, 102, 101 (1958).

Useful precedent may be ignored. I turn to what I consider a decision that in fact was never given life by the Supreme Court. By focusing on its ghostly promise, its lost potential, we can begin to think about what has not yet been actualized, what has instead been forgotten in current juridical models of accountability.

In this spectral decision, *Laaman v. Helgemoe* (1977), Judge Hugh H. Bownes of the United States District Court for the District of New Hampshire held that confinement at New Hampshire State Prison constituted cruel and unusual punishment in violation of the Eighth Amendment. The far-reaching relief order articulated the broadest application ever of the Eighth Amendment to prison conditions. Following this decision, which focused on conditions of incarceration that made "degeneration probable and reform unlikely," the Supreme Court would soon make virtually irrelevant its own attentiveness to the effects of inhumane conditions of confinement. Instead of considering prisoners' intrinsic worth and enforceable rights, the Court adopted the strangely malleable *allowable suffering paradigm*, announced in Justice Rehnquist's opinion in *Bell v. Wolfish* (1979).[58]

Though much attention in *Laaman* was paid to the physical characteristics of the cell, such as inadequate lighting, poor ventilation, and lack of sanitation, this uninhabitability had its extension and analogue in the argument against debilitating methods of incarceration itself. Judge Bownes condemned "enforced idleness" as a "numbing violence against the spirit." Warning against the practice of placing inmates in "cages with nothing to do," Bownes emphasized the loss of self-worth "inherent in such a degrading experience":

> The experts confirmed the old saying that idleness is the handmaiden of the devil . . . Enforced idleness is a 'numbing violence against the spirit,' and causes good work habits to atrophy. It leads to degeneration because it severely undermines self-confidence, and the natural reactions to lowered self-esteem are either mental illness or antisocial behavior.[59]

Bownes perceived in the law what many of his contemporaries ignored: protective power. When does this protective power yield to rituals of vengeance, to practices that target the offender's self-respect? It is this damage that concerns me. American legal culture, especially Supreme Court jurisprudence, casts a cold eye on the mental suffering of prisoners.[60]

Legal interpretation requires that we recognize how new taxonomies of personhood are being created. For the Court, talk of private experience and subjective mental states has become irrelevant. We are far from the days of the Warren court (1953–1969), when attention to psychological anguish, dignity, and human worth

[58] *Laaman v. Helgemoe*, 437 F. Supp. 269, 325, 293, 325, 293 (1977). A year earlier, in the landmark case *Pugh v. Locke*, 406 F. Supp. 318, the judge described Alabama's prisons as "wholly unfit for human habitation" and considered the totality of unconstitutional conditions that made rehabilitation impossible and reform unlikely.

[59] *Laaman*, 293, 294, 318, 325.

[60] See James Q. Whitman, *Harsh Justice: Criminal Punishment and the Widening Divide Between American and Europe* (New York: Oxford University Press, 2003).

mattered. But imprisonment is, of course, a highly abnormal condition, and nowhere as much as in supermax units that isolate behavioral expectations from the realities of normal human experience. Thoughts and emotions are wrenched out of any meaningful context. Instead, extreme isolation, helplessness, and other mechanisms of incapacitation are incorporated into peculiarly vehement rites of degradation. So with the emphasis on "reasonableness" the courts endorse techniques that force inmates outside the precincts of thought and feeling but leave no marks on the body.

The conditions of indefinite solitary fulfill the assumptions of the state. Abandoned to depression and despair, branded as incapable or irresponsible, these inmates are to be fashioned anew: not reformed, but undone. In removing the social and emotional conditions necessary for agency, radical isolation creates the stigma of ineligibility. Craig Haney, who has spent years studying the psychological assault of supermax confinement, describes the "feeling of unreality," the blunting of perception, the threat of noxious transformation, the "extraordinary – I believe often needless and indefensible – risks to take with the human psyche and spirit": "The virtually complete loss of genuine forms of social contact and the absence of any routine and recurring opportunities to ground one's thoughts and feelings in a recognizable human context lead to an undermining of the sense of self and a disconnection of experience from meaning."[61] What seems arbitrary is instead behavioral readjustment, a project to annihilate individual identity through sensory deprivation.

WHAT'S IN A WORD?

Oliver Wendell Holmes warned, "We are not studying etymology, but law."[62] But the legal history of the word "wanton" is crucial to the case law concerning cruel and unusual punishment. Its use targets the power and privilege enjoyed by agents administering torturous treatment, whether prison correctional officers or interrogators of alleged "enemy combatants." In the spectacle of lust and shame recorded in the Abu Ghraib photos; the shackles, dogs, "restraint chairs," and permanent solitary confinement at Guantánamo Bay; and the treatment in supermax confinement in the United States, the drama of degradation turns on the relation between those who get to be wanton and others who count only as something of nonvalue: conceptually no longer *persons* who suffer cruelty or torture.[63]

[61] Craig Haney, "Mental Health Issues in Long-Term Solitary and 'Supermax' Confinement," *Crime and Delinquency* 49 (2003): 124–56.

[62] Oliver Wendell Holmes, *The Common Law* [1881] (New York: Dover Publications, Inc., 1991), 215.

[63] Throughout this analysis, I am in dialogue with Jeremy Waldron's "Inhuman and Degrading Treatment: A Non-Realist View," NYU Public Law Colloquium, April 23, 2008, which takes seriously my attention to terminology in *The Story of Cruel and Unusual* and acutely expands on it to include the meaning of the words "cruel, inhuman, or degrading" in the prohibitions of The Universal Declaration of Human Rights of 1948 and the International Covenant on Civil and Political Rights (ICCPR), 1976.

How could these treatments be legal? The answer lies in the extraordinary latitude that prison guards and officials enjoy, thanks to enabling Supreme Court decisions. Beginning in the 1980s with a series of cases challenging inadequacies in medical care, use of force, and conditions of confinement, the Court turned to a novel translation of *malice aforethought* for murderers into the *maliciously wanton* standard for prison officials. The full force of mental volition is transferred to the person of the prison official. The requirement that aggrieved prisoners show *deliberate* indifference by their keepers when claiming cruel and unusual punishment permits untoward rationalizations. This reasoning measures cruelty not by the pain and suffering inflicted but by the intent of the person who inflicts them. In the search for intent, the official who commits the act is vindicated, whereas the object of harm is ignored.

"Wanton" means you cannot be shamed; you cannot be humiliated. It applies only to the dominating, not to the subordinated. The latter are completely powerless before this word that curiously mixes caprice and wickedness: a profligate and maleficent magic. What does this term's applicability – to what kind of persons can it be applied – say about thought and feeling, cognition and affect? The language of wantonness in U.S. prison cases has fine-tuned the legal meaning of the Eighth Amendment prohibition on "cruel and unusual punishments." Qualitative distinctions, not simply dictionary definitions of "wanton," can illuminate the standards invoked by its use.

The history of punishment is also a history of language. The use of the word "wanton" in the current enterprise of degradation and punishment prompts us to consider how the ethical framework of judicial practice becomes darker, more doubtful, and more mysterious rather than more reasonable and more enlightened. More crucial perhaps than the decisions themselves is the language in which they are rendered. The compulsion to define grants a license for ambiguity. Quibbling over terms contributes to the pose of judicial caution, as it generates the hyper-legality that institutes judicial novelties the Eighth Amendment was designed to prohibit.[64]

In recent cases that judge challenges to conditions of confinement, it is striking that the trade-off between illegal and legal torment is also between those who administer discipline and those who lack it. But though the root meaning of wanton is lacking discipline, only officers who guard, order, train, and control – whose job is to impose control – are capable of wantonness. The insufferable becomes legal and torment

64 The focus on terminology and the opacity of law language are crucial to the history of the common law. In A *Concise History of the Common Law* [1929], 4th ed. (London: Butterworth & Co. [Publishers] Ltd., 1948), Theodore Plucknett memorably attests to the devious history of legal formulas in his discussion of "the very troublesome word 'malice': It is best regarded as a traditional form which only occasionally coincided with the natural meaning of the word" (419). If legal fictions fly in the face of fact, Plucknett argues that *legal forms* – better known as *terms of art* – have a life quite independent of what they ordinarily mean. Perhaps obvious, but what is most striking in his pages is how in early modern law, words were left to be vague and hoary, gaining force in their repetition and apparently profiting from their ambiguity.

legitimate through the manipulation of language. Judges like Antonin Scalia and Clarence Thomas, especially, obsessed as they are with the legal history of words, preempt the reality that those words label and describe. The more obsessive their task of definition, the more murky is the intelligibility of their arguments. From that opacity the law takes its power. Shifting the language of subjective blameworthiness to prison or governmental officials, legal decisions testify to the thorough calibration of the relationship between persons and things, between those capable of intent and the presumed unthinking recipients of punishment.[65]

In *Wilson v. Seiter* (1991) – still the crucial, precedent-setting case for my purposes – the plaintiff argued that if prisoners are deprived of "the minimal civilized measure of life's necessities," the Eighth Amendment is violated regardless of anyone's intent. But Justice Scalia, giving the intent requirement its fiercest play, raised the threshold of harm to the point where it ceased to be legally relevant. Writing for the five-member majority in the sharply divided decision – joined by Chief Justice Rehnquist, and Justices O'Connor, Kennedy, and Souter – Justice Scalia focused on the meaning and extent of *punishment.*

Scalia construes a legal idiom that makes the definition of punishment an excuse for depersonalization. If deprivations are not a specific part of a prisoner's sentence, they are not *really* punishment unless imposed by prison officials with a "guilty mind." No matter how much actual suffering is experienced by a prisoner, if the intent requirement is not met, then the effect on the prisoner is not a matter for judicial review. "The source of the intent requirement," Scalia reasons, "is not the predilections of this Court, but the Eighth Amendment itself, which bans only cruel and unusual *punishment.*" If it is not meted out by the sentencing judge, then "some mental element must be attributed to the inflicting officer before it can qualify."[66]

The Court thus requires not only an objective component ("was the deprivation sufficiently serious?"), but also a separate subjective component ("did the officials act with a sufficiently culpable state of mind?") in all Eighth Amendment challenges to prison practices and policies. In order to meet the second criterion, Scalia maintains that "the offending conduct must be *wanton*" – a term that even he admits is slippery in the context. Undeterred, he returns to *Whitley v. Albers* (1986) and the necessarily hasty response to a prison riot in which a prisoner – Albers – was shot by a guard.

65 Justice Thomas' concurrence in the *Baze v. Rees* (2008) judgment, joined by Scalia, exemplifies the return to a history of atrocity in order to reinvent the nature of suffering in the present. Thomas's focus on "historical practices" with old "tools" of intensifying death reads like a litany of horrors – disemboweling alive, burning at the stake, public dissection, to name just a few – and aims to prove the uncruel and unatrocious nature of lethal injection. What the pages and pages of examples do instead is to make us question the nature of "terror," reminding us of the inmate who suffers and not just the kind of punishments inflicted.

66 *Wilson v. Seiter*, 501 U.S. 294 (1991). In *The Story of Cruel and Unusual*, I analyze how the words themselves – from slavery and imprisonment to the torture memos of the Bush administration – in their combination of generality and emptiness ensured that old abuses continue, made legitimate by vague standards.

Even if "the conduct is harmful enough to satisfy the objective component of an Eighth Amendment claim, whether it can be characterized as 'wanton' depends upon the constraints facing the *official*."[67]

In appealing to a mentalist language of law, Scalia lingered on the word *wanton*. Once wantonness has become the test whereby prisoners may demand their constitutional rights, the objects of attention become state agents whose judgment can neither be predicted nor controlled. Prison officials are thus endowed with will, reason, and foresight. They might choose to be unreasonable. It is their concerns, thoughts, inclinations, fears, lapses, and strain that occupy the pages of this opinion, not the effects of their actions on the incarcerated. In an emergency situation, such as a prison riot that "poses significant risks to the safety of inmates and prison staff" and necessitates "excessive force" (*Whitley*), "wantonness consist[s] of acting 'maliciously and sadistically for the very purpose of causing harm,'" but in the context of inadequate medical care (*Estelle*), the standard for judging unconstitutionality does not depend on that "very high state of mind." Deliberate indifference will do. In *Wilson*, Scalia sees "no significant distinction between claims alleging inadequate medical care and those alleging inadequate 'conditions of confinement'" and applies the *Estelle* standard: "Since, we said, only the 'unnecessary and wanton infliction of pain' implicates the Eighth Amendment, a prisoner advancing such a claim must, at a minimum, allege 'deliberate indifference.'"[68]

In their discussion of ancient criminal law in 1898, Pollock and Maitland explained: "A mean must be found between these two extremes – absolute liability for all harm done, and liability for harm that is both done and intended." This attempt "to detect and appreciate the psychical element in guilt and innocence," they acknowledge, is doomed to failure.[69] The obsession with mentalist instead of behavioral explanations for crime has now resurfaced in the strangest of places. Obvious signs of violence disappear in quest of the unseen: What was the official, who also happens to be the malefactor, thinking? Was he "deliberately indifferent"? Did he have a "sufficiently culpable state of mind"? In this spectacle of deference to prison authorities, the Court seeks grounds and reasons after the fact. Evidence resides in the most obscure and unverifiable place: the private thoughts of prison officials.

If the objective severity of conditions is only judged unconstitutional when the subjective intent of those in control is present, Eighth Amendment violations are impossible to prove in practice. Justice Byron White, in a concurrence agreeing only

[67] The joint opinion in *Gregg v. Georgia*, 428 U. S. 153 (1976), which overturned *Furman v. Georgia*, 408 U.S. 238 (1972) and reinstated capital punishment, coined the phrase "unnecessary and wanton infliction of pain." *Whitley v. Alpers*, 475 U.S. 312, 320, 327. *Wilson*, 302 quoting *Whitley*, 320–321.

[68] *Whitley*, 312, 320, 327. *Wilson*, 302 (quoting *Whitley* 320–321). *Estelle v. Gamble*, 429 U.S. 97 (1976) 429. *Wilson*, 302, 303, 297 (quoting *Estelle*, 104, 106).

[69] Sir Frederick Pollock and Frederic William Maitland, *The History of English Law before the Time of Edward I* [1898] (Union, NJ: The Law Book Exchange, Ltd, 1996), 2: 475, 474.

in the judgment, joined by Justices Marshall, Blackmun, and Stevens, objected that previous decisions insisted that "the conditions are themselves *part of the punishment,* even though not specifically 'meted out' by a statute or judge." "Not only is the majority's intent requirement a departure from precedent," he concluded, but "it will likely prove impossible to apply in many cases. Inhumane prison conditions often are the result of cumulative actions and inactions by numerous officials inside and outside a prison, sometimes over a long period of time."[70]

What is the legal personality of the criminal, once caught between the decision decreed by the sentencing judge and the intent of the inflicting officer? As I have argued, if we follow the logic of *Wilson*, the full possession of the mental faculty (it gets to be wanton, malicious, obdurate, and willful) is transferred to the person of the official, whereas the mind of the prisoner, lost to the subtleties of legal interpretation, is eliminated. Literally stripped of the right to experience suffering, to know fear and anguish, the plaintiff becomes a nonreactive, defenseless object for whom harsh or even intolerable conditions – such as indefinite supermax isolation– are not legally an issue unless they leave a bruise.[71]

By the time Blackmun wrote his qualification to the decision in *Farmer v. Brennan* (1994), the year he resigned from the Court, he did not mince words about the dangers of Scalia's reasoning in *Wilson*, especially the narrow delimitation of punishment to the inmate's sentence by a judge. "The Court's analysis is fundamentally misguided; indeed it defies common sense. 'Punishment' does not necessarily imply a culpable state of mind on the part of an identifiable punisher." He argued that intentionality, requiring "an easily identifiable wrongdoer with poor intentions," guaranteed that "barbaric conditions," if not "a reign of terror," could continue, unmitigated and without redress.[72]

In concentrating on the culpable mind of the punisher – and the attribution of responsibility that comes with it – this judicial reasoning, by making inmate claims ineligible, does not so much objectify as depersonalize the prisoner: the animate object given up to the state.[73] The insistence on mental elements in determining criminality is not new, given that the purview of early English law was confined to intentional wrongs. Yet the stakes of legality become disquieting when justices

70 On the definition and theory of *mens rea*, with an analysis of its meaning from early to modern law, see F. B. Sayre, "*Mens Rea,*" *Harvard Law Review* 45 (1932): 974–1026. *Wilson*, 297, 298, 306.

71 See Dayan, "Legal Slaves and Civil Bodies," *Materializing Democracy*, 83–5 and "Legal Terrors," *Representations*, 60–2.

72 *Farmer v. Brennan*, 854, 857, 855, 853.The legal nonrecognition of mental or emotional injury due to prolonged detention in maximum security units is demonstrated in *Madrid v. Gomez*, 889 F. Supp. 1146 (1995), a case heard by Chief Judge Thelton Henderson in the United States District Court for the Northern District of California. Though Henderson admits that confinement in the Special Housing Unit "may well hover on the edge of what is humanly tolerable for those with normal resilience," he held that such conditions remain within the limits of permissible pain for inmates not in the "specific population subgroups identified in this opinion" (1280). See Dayan, "Legal Slaves and Civil Bodies."

73 Richard A. Posner, *The Problems of Jurisprudence* (Cambridge, MA: Harvard University Press, 1990), 168.

translate wrongdoing in criminal cases into wanton intention in civil law. Once states of mind characterized as "indifferent," "unreasonable," or "malicious" are ascribed to those who harm without liability to punishment, something vicious is done to the object of harm, now reduced to a mere body controlled by administrative power. Subjectivity, though it takes its definition from criminal law, is the privilege of those in control: not only the prison officials, but the judges whose linguistic maneuvering has lethal effects on those whose lives depend on their words.

SUPERMAX CONFINEMENT, GLOBAL EXPORT

To return to my earlier question: Is there a distinction to be made between the legal reasoning that condemns persons to physical death and that which incarcerates persons in conditions that deprive them of everything associated with consciousness, with human life: its affiliations and care? Perhaps it is not surprising that more attention is paid to the abolition of the death penalty than to consideration of the death-in-life of supermax confinement. For just as the courts concentrate on the physical needs of prisoners – "basic human needs" and nothing more – the public continues to focus on physical, not psychic, death. There is a reason for this. Prisoners are considered unfit, disabled in mind – nothing more than brute matter – so here legal reasoning and popular prejudice coincide.

The Prisoner's Litigation Reform Act (PLRA), signed into law by Bill Clinton on April 26, 1996, dramatically curtailed prisoner litigation into the next century. Designed to limit what was said to be a massive increase in "frivolous" inmate litigation, the PLRA permits preliminary injunctive relief related to prison conditions, but it erects substantial hurdles that must be negotiated before such relief can be given. To get an injunction, a plaintiff must prove that every plaintiff or member of the proposed class has suffered actual physical injury, thus prohibiting damages for mental injury. The prisoner must prove that the request for relief is narrowly focused, extends no further than necessary to correct the injury, and is the least intrusive means necessary to correct or prevent the harm.

What remains once civil has been replaced with penal life? The objects of oppressive state magic are also racially marked, making life imprisonment count in a blatantly phenomenal and therefore pervasively spectral manner. Though alive, they are incessantly dying in new ways. Situated beyond the terror of mortality, these persons work powerfully on the minds of the as-yet included.

Again, let us ask: Who are the prisoners put in supermaxes? Most generally, they are murderers, nonmurderers, suspected or certain terrorists, the insane or the sane, the assaultive and nonassaultive. All suffer the same fate. They are all supposed threats to "security," however prison management chooses to define it. But the majority of prisoners held in supermax confinement are labeled "security threat groups." These alleged gang members usually have no disciplinary infractions; they are locked down allegedly for the safety of the rest of the prison population. The incarceration of "dangerous terrorism suspects" on our soil without due (or indeed, any) process of law also trades on the promise of security. The new global logic of punishment promises democracy while requiring no judge and jury. It also ensures the broader establishment of super-maximum security units.[74]

On May 21, 2009, President Obama introduced, as if a novel idea, the protracted incarceration of alleged terrorists. In spite of admirable intentions, his proposed "legitimate legal framework" – what he also described as "an appropriate legal regime" for preventive detention – is both unprecedented within the law and unconstitutional. It is not unprecedented in actuality.[75] It remains indistinct from the worst, though least-discussed, excess of Guantánamo: the use of indefinite isolation as psychological torture. Sensory deprivation is the form of discipline preferred by prison management. Now it is offered as the solution to the Guantánamo disgrace. The "rendering" of prisoners as packaged goods during delivery to be later sealed off and warehoused thus presaged their future.

By legitimizing incapacitation without proven crimes or violations of law – and without trial – President Obama regularizes the anomalous and rationalizes solitary torture. He reimagines *preventive detention* offshore as *prolonged detention* on the mainland. Not as degraded or mendacious a euphemism perhaps as "enhanced interrogation techniques" for torture, but a euphemism for supermax isolation nevertheless. In the wily magic of changing terminologies, "prolonged detention" replaces both "indefinite detention" and "administrative segregation" – the latter already an evasive, legally convenient renaming of "solitary confinement."

What the United Nations Convention Against Torture, as well as human rights groups such as Human Rights Watch, Amnesty International, and others have long singled out as torturous solitary-confinement practices in the United States, and what Guantánamo detainees have revealed to be the most horrific part of their detention – its systematic psychic cannibalism – President Obama presents as what every reasonable American should admit as worthy of our heritage: "the power of our most fundamental values." He asks us to bear in mind: "Nobody has ever escaped from one of our federal supermax prisons, which hold hundreds of convicted terrorists." His proposal, he says, resulted from approaching "difficult questions with

[74] Sheryl Gay Stolberg, "Obama Would Move Some Terror Detainees to U.S," *New York Times*, May 22, 2009, at A1. See also William Glaberson, "President's Detention Plan Poses Fundamental Test: Absence of Trials Challenges a Principle," *New York Times*, May 23, 2009, at A1. For labeling and incapacitation according to status, see Dayan, "Due Process and Lethal Confinement," *South Atlantic Quarterly* 107 (2008): 485–507, reprinted in *States of Violence: War, Capital Punishment, and Letting Die*, eds. Austin Sarat & Jennifer L. Culbert (Cambridge and New York: Cambridge University Press, 2009).

[75] Thirty-three international terrorists, some with ties to al-Qaeda, already are detained in the federal supermax prison in Florence, Colorado. See "Supermax Prisons in U.S. Already Hold Terrorists," *The Washington Post*, May 22, 2009, http://www.washingtonpost.com/wpdyn/content/article/2009/05/21/AR2009052102009_pf.

honesty and care and a dose of common sense." When did common sense become so difficult, honesty so terrifying?[76]

The incapacitated, the as yet improperly apprehended legal person is sufficiently unreal to make claims on our habits of thought. If more-or-less tangible objects can be either "property" or "persons" in the eyes of the law, what we consider subjects of legal rights and duties can also be stripped of these attributes. We are obliged to consider the creation of a species of depersonalized persons. Deprived of rights to due process, bodily integrity, or life, these creatures remain persons in law. The reasoning necessary to this terrain of the undead sanctions the irrational: the reasonable extension of unspeakable treatment into an unknowable future.

When law is called on to ascertain a "rational" basis for sustaining the dominion of the dead and the ghostly, much depends on assumptions that most of us claim to find intolerable. But recent events continue to prove how much we can tolerate, how easy it is for fear, dogma, and terror to allow us to demonize others, to deny them a common humanity, the protection of our laws, to do unspeakable things to them. In a morally disenchanted world, daily cruelty and casual violence accompany the call for order, the need for security.

[76] The White House, Office of the Press Secretary, "Remarks By the President on National Security," May 21, 2009. My recognition of the institutionalized witchcraft of the state and the psychic cannibalism it practices is indebted to Misty L. Bastian, "'Bloodhounds Who Have No Friends': Witchcraft and Locality in the Nigerian Popular Press," *Modernity and Its Malcontents: Ritual and Power in Postcolonial Africa*, ed. by Jean Comaroff and John Comaroff (Chicago & London: The University of Chicago Press, 1993), 133–4. Bastian describes the witch's contempt for, while retaining uncanny intimacy with, her victims: "She becomes a psychic cannibal, worse than a murderer, because she treats other human beings as though they were meat and her prey."

3

Capital Punishment as Homeowner's Insurance

The Rise of the Homeowner Citizen and the Fate of Ultimate Sanctions in Both Europe and the United States

Jonathan Simon

INTRODUCTION: ULTIMATE SANCTIONS, CAPITAL CRIMES

The fate of capital punishment is often considered one of the decisive differences between Europe and the United States. In the analysis that follows, I argue that in important respects, the approach of both toward capital crimes are converging. This convergence may or may not arrive soon on the issue of execution of death sentences, but there is convergence on the increasing demand on both continents for "ultimate sanctions," which I define as incapacitative imprisonment that ends either in an execution or a natural death in prison. My subject, however, is not LWOP, or specific sentencing laws at all, but instead a kind of citizenship, growing on both continents (at least before the financial crisis), which can be expected to coalesce as public support for ultimate sanctions against murderers (and perhaps some other categories of especially feared crimes like terrorism and child sexual abduction). The strength of this citizenship and public represents an important political constituency to sustain capital punishment where it exists, and to restore it should current restraints on executions weaken.

In previous work, I have argued that punitiveness in the United States has been a political project aimed at shoring up the legitimacy and efficacy of state power in a conjuncture where both fear of violent crime and mistrust of government have

The author gratefully acknowledges research help from Jack Bouboushian, Berkeley Law Class of 2010, Joe McGrath, PhD, candidate in Law, Cork University, visiting student, UC Berkeley, and Marie Guerin, visiting student, UC Berkeley, law student at Université Bordeaux IV Montesquieu. The chapter also benefitted greatly from the comments of the other participants in this volume, especially Juergen Martschukat and Austin Sarat. Naturally all errors of fact and speculation belong to the author.

been persistent (if not continuous).[1] In more recent work,[2] I have been exploring the spatial and phenomenological dimensions of this project, specifically the distinctive context of the privately owned housing estate and a liberalizing (or even bubble-like) residential real estate market. It is this latter mouthful that I propose to discuss through the metaphor of homeowner's insurance. Building on the work of sociologists, geographers, and historians, I argue that the political sensitivity or salience of crime fear is, all other things being equal, higher where subjects begin to interact with the political in and through their ownership and interest in their home.

As I will develop further in this chapter, this means more than just widespread homeownership. For various cultural and historical reasons, some European nations (for example, Ireland, Italy, Norway) and some U.S. states (for example, Minnesota, Michigan, and Iowa) have had a very high portion of homeownership compared to others, but without having a strong sense of political identity based on that property relationship. Whereas a high proportion of homeownership (among voters, if not the populace as a whole) is clearly a precondition for the "homeowner citizen" to become an important political public, the mere fact of homeownership does not seem to have a particularly strong impact on political identity (although some economists have long argued that it has powerful economic consequences). Rather, I suggest, two other conditions seem necessary to give rise to the homeowner citizen as political force: (1) the marketing of homes as a source of personal security (as epitomized by the much-lambasted "gated communities" in the United States, but much more generally in U.S. suburbs and gentrified city neighborhoods); and (2) the rapid inflation of home prices over a sustained period (ten years or more) effectively transforming the home from shelter and/or lifestyle into a primary form of economic security.

From the mid-1990s through the late 2000s these three conditions (a growing portion of homeowners, marketing security in homes, and a rapid inflation of housing prices) prevailed in varying degrees almost everywhere in both Europe and the United States, but with large degrees of difference. In a few of the nations in the Council of Europe and in a few states of the United States most caught up in what has now been called the housing bubble, all three conditions grew at a high rate. David Garland has written of "high crime societies" where a "culture of control" becomes the common sense among both citizens and political leaders, a common sense that includes a heavy salience of crime insecurity and support for harsh

[1] Jonathan Simon, *Governing through Crime: How the War on Crime Transformed American Democracy and Created a Culture of Fear* (Oxford University Press, 2007); James D. Unnever and Francis T. Cullen, "The Social Sources of Americans' Punitiveness: A Test of Three Competing Models," *Criminology*, 48 (2010): 99.

[2] Jonathan Simon, "Consuming Obsessions: Housing, Homicide, and Mass Incarceration since 1950," University of Chicago Legal Forum, 2010: 165–204.

incapacitative sentences.[3] In what we might think of as high "homeowning/high crime fear societies," support for ultimate sanctions does not necessarily reflect a positive demand for retributive justice, a displaced form of racial or ethnic animus, or even a commitment to the actual execution of capital criminals. Instead, it reflects a sense of vulnerability, anchored in the home, to crimes that put at risk the security in the home.

Homeowner citizens do not assume that this will prevent every tragedy, nor can they be easily reassured by statistics that many long-serving prisoners no longer pose a risk to them. Instead, ultimate sanctions, irreversible exclusion through execution, or permanent imprisonment operate as kind of a hedge against the risk that governments will fail to prioritize the needs of citizen-homeowner-victims over the needs of prison administrations or the demands of human rights. It is in this sense that we might think of it metaphorically as a form of "homeowner's insurance." Although ultimate sanctions cannot compensate for losses the way insurance literally does, we might think of it as providing a layer (however thin) of coverage against the distinctive threat that violent crime poses to home values.

This goes beyond the incapacitation of specific criminals subjected to ultimate sanctions, because one effect of the very availability of an ultimate sanction is to establish an anchor point against the possibility that governments will use their discretion to release all manner of prisoners earlier than scheduled. Thus Californians continue to support a death penalty that over 35 years has only produced 13 executions (with almost 700 prisoners accumulated on death row) because during the same period, the politics behind the death penalty much more successfully produced a revolution in sentencing which saw noncapital murder sentences move from under 10 years (in 1970) to 25 or 30 years for those relatively few murderers who make it through the parole process at all.[4]

In what follows, I will briefly flesh out my spatial phenomenology of homeownership and crime fear and the "homeowner citizen" as it has operated in the United States to support ultimate sanctions. As a step toward a more adequate comparative analysis of these trends, I will present some information on general trends in European housing and punishment patterns and brief case studies of Ireland and the Netherlands. The implications of this analysis for the future of abolition are necessarily contingent. To the extent that the bursting of the housing bubble in both the United States and Western Europe in 2008, along with structural pressures toward more flexible and greener residential patterns, leads to a reduction in the scale and economic importance of homeownership, publics in both regions may become less attracted to ultimate sanctions and less likely to respond to the emergence of alarming crime examples with demands for them. However, to the extent

3 David Garland, *The Culture of Control: Crime and Social Order in Contemporary Society* (University of Chicago Press, 2001).

4 This co-rise of mass imprisonment and capital punishment after 1975 is one of the many lessons I take from Marie Gottschalk's *The Prison and the Gallows: The Politics of Mass Incarceration in America* (Cambridge University Press, 2006)

that the long-term trend remains one in which larger portions of the Western middle class will identify primarily with their home rather than their job as an anchor of economic security, support for ultimate sanctions can only grow, underscoring the importance of either national or European Community law setting powerful antipopulist limits to such sanctions.

ULTIMATE SANCTIONS

The death penalty has been abolished in Western Europe for more than twenty years but "capital punishment" lives on. Although no member state of the Council of Europe may execute a prisoner for any crime, even murder, many of them face increasing political pressure to keep perpetrators of highly publicized murders incapacitated in prisons for the rest of their natural life. Crimes like the Jamie Bulger killing in Merseyside, England, in 1993, or the murder of crime reporter Veronica Guerin near Dublin, Ireland, in 1998, have led to demands for severe punishment.[5]

The nature of these de jure and de facto "natural life" terms (or "death in prison" sentences) is very much up for debate in the courts of the European Community.[6] The best guess at the moment seems to be that an irreducible life sentence, at least if handed down to a relatively young person with decades to transform themselves, would run afoul of the best reading of contemporary European Community law.[7] Long sentences, however, which could theoretically result in release prior to death but under which many prisoners might well expect to die inside, seem likely to survive judicial challenge even under the European Convention on Human Rights.

Surprisingly, the situation is not that different in the United States. Outside of a handful of mostly southern states, capital punishment seems to be a virtually symbolic punishment with no more than an execution every few years.[8] Even in a bastion of execution, like Texas, executions have fallen off considerably.[9] But as executions dwindle in both the United States and more decisively in Europe, political demand for ultimate sanctions – long prison sentences that differentiate the most feared categories of offenders like terrorists, serial killers, and sexual predators – is growing. Often this can mean an irreversible life sentence in which an offender is sentenced to die in prison.

5 Ian O'Donnell, "Imprisonment and Penal Policy in Ireland," *The Howard Journal*, 43 (2004): 253.

6 Dirk Van Zyl Smit, "Outlawing Irreducible Life Sentences – Europe on the Brink?" (unpublished paper 2010).

7 Van Zyl Smit, "Outlawing Irreducible Life Sentences – Europe on the Brink?"

8 David Johnson and Franklin Zimring, *The Next Frontier: National Development, Political Change, and the Death Penalty in Asia* (Oxford University Press, 2009), 23 (defining countries in Asia with less than 1 execution per 25 million population as having a "symbolic" death penalty).

9 John Schwartz, "Death Sentences Dropped, but Executions Rose in 2009," *The New York Times*, December 17, 2009, http://www.nytimes.com/2009/12/18/us/18death.html?_r=1&scp=9&sq=executions&st=cse.

My home state of California is a good example of a state where capital punishment is largely symbolic yet retains a significant position both politically and legally, and under which an unprecedented number of prisoners face the likelihood of dying in prison. In California, more than 2,500 prisoners have been sentenced to "life without parole" since 1990. Tens of thousands more are facing life sentences that allow for parole after a fixed minimum, but only on the recommendation of a politically appointed parole board and the ultimate confirmation by the governor.[10]

Support for ultimate sanctions (including capital punishment where it is available, but if not, the longest possible prison sentences with the least possibility of early release and the easiest capacity of law enforcers to reincarcerate), independent of other sources of support such as racial threat, rising homicide rates, or will be highest in those nations in Europe and those states in the United States that have experienced the sharpest increases in the economic and demographic significance of home ownership over the past decade or two.

Of course, support for and use of ultimate sanctions by any particular country is going to be determined by multiple factors, including the degree to which ultimate sanction policies come up for public discussion at all, the existence of party competition over this terrain, and the "availability" of alarming examples of crimes that might warrant ultimate sanctions (capital crimes in effect). But the emergence of the homeowner citizen tilts the risk sensibilities of publics to make them much more sensitive to crime information and much more poised to seek remedies that guarantee the permanent removal from society of those viewed as a dire threat to personal security.

These claims need to be tested by work that is empirical and comparative. What follows does not promise to be adequate to either objective, but to develop more completely the theoretical account of the homeowner citizen and ultimate sanctions and to draw some examples that can help specify possible dynamics for empirical testings.

THE HOUSE OF FEAR

We do not normally think of homeownership as making people more punitive (although official propaganda constantly refers to homeowners as more responsible citizens).[11] Most economic theories of punitiveness emphasize the interests of

[10] Which results in fewer than fifty life-sentence prisoners being paroled in an average year, up from fewer than ten a year in the 1990s. See, John Irwin, *Lifers: Seeking Redemption in Prison* (Routledge, 2009). The European Court of Human Rights has held that life and other long-sentenced prisoners under its jurisdiction must have their release considered by a court or court-like body insulated from the political process, presumably to avoid just such a nightmare as California now has. See *Weeks v. United Kingdom*, 2 March 1987, see Dirk Van Zyl Smit and Sonja Snacken, *Principles of European Prison Law and Policy: Penology and Human Rights* (Oxford University Press, 2009), 332.

[11] Criminology would remind us that many features associated with homeownership, including income, age, marital status, parental status, and exposure to crime risk, are more likely to be the real causes

producers rather than consumers.[12] Still the relationship between homeownership and harsh crime policies fits the actual timing of U.S. trends in punishment more than familiar arguments about racial backlash and neoliberal disciplining of the work force.

In his path-breaking study of postwar Detroit, Thomas Sugrue argues that the city's high level of homeownership made its middle-class residents acutely sensitive to both fear of crime and racial block busting due to their exposure to declines in home values, leading to much quicker and more complete flight to the suburbs than in cities that remained oriented toward rental units for their middle classes (like Chicago).[13] Mike Davis traces the parallel construction of the gated suburbs and fortified downtowns of California and its massive prison system;[14] a point explored in more literary terms by essayist Joan Didion in her memoir of California.[15]

Although this crime-fear-based real estate risk is often associated with the "white flight" years of the 1960s and 1970s, it has become a far more generalized phenomenon nowadays, no longer associated primarily with large midwestern cities undergoing deindustrialization and racial turnover; indeed, it is now reflected in the very form and distribution of new housing construction all over the country (at least until the financial crisis halted new construction in 2008).

Renters, naturally, are not indifferent to crime fear, but although they may fear personal harm at the hands of criminals, crime in general is not a fundamental threat to their security so long as they enjoy sufficient resources to move to a different area should the local crime profile become genuinely alarming to them.[16] Renters do not have the potentially large financial risk tied to a specific property that owners do. Although renters may be overall less wealthy than owners, this wealth is almost certainly not as sensitive to crime fear as homeowners'. For renters, the most important

of any punitiveness detected in homeowners. I would agree and take these effects to be a given in asserting that the political identity and ultimately public action (in the form of ballot initiatives and conventional elections among others) of homeowners will support more punitive crime policies.

12 For example, Christian Parenti, *Lockdown America: Police and Prisons in the Age of Crisis* (Verso, 2000); But see Barry Vaughn, "The Punitive Consequences of Consumer Culture," *Punishment & Society*, 4 (2002): 195, and Ian Loader, "Ice Cream and Incarceration: On Appetites for Security and Punishment," *Punishment & Society* 11 (2009): 241.

13 Thomas Sugrue, *Detroit and the Origins of the Urban Crisis: Race and Inequality in Postwar Detroit* (Princeton University Press, 1996).

14 Mike Davis, *City of Quartz: Excavating the Future in LA* (Verso, 1989); Mike Davis, *Ecology of Fear: Los Angeles and the Imagination of Disaster* (University of California Press, 1998).

15 Joan Didion, *Where I Was From* (Knopf, 2003).

16 I realize that I am ignoring the fact that some renters in certain locations may become very committed or invested in their rental property, either through strong personal association with the location or because of legal rights, like rent control, that may create a quasi-property right in the rental. However, overall from the perspective of economists, renters are inherently more mobile than owners. Indeed, an interesting body of economic work now attempts to estimate the effect of high homeownership on unemployment rates to see if that lack of mobility results in longer or deeper unemployment. See, A.J. Oswald, "A Conjecture on the Explanation for High Unemployment in the Industrialized Nations: Part I," University of Warwick Working Paper, No. 475 (1996).

factor in their long-term economic security is likely to be their job security and their employability. Jobs may move from some neighborhoods due to crime, but they are generally displaced elsewhere nearby; crime by itself does not shrink an economy.[17] Thus the most important economic security concerns of renters are generally quite insulated from crime of any kind (especially violent crime; property crime may be a different kind of threat).

Renters, if they intend to remain renters, might be expected to look to the state primarily for what it can contribute to the stability and health of the labor market (although they may, of course, be drawn by noneconomic values to other issues like the environment, civil rights, or crime, for that matter). If crime does become alarming, renters may support greater state measures to prevent it, but they are unlikely to rate these over issues of labor market security, entitlement access, educational opportunities, and so on.

Because of the extraordinarily nondiversified risk involved in a typical consumer home loan (with 10 or even 20 percent of the home price put up by the owner – a portion that increases as the mortgage is paid down), homeowners have a different relationship to crime. Since crime is almost always associated with place, neighborhoods and the values of the homes in them have long been sensitive to concerns about crime. Whereas the renter can wait out rumors of worsening crime to see if the neighborhood seems alarming to them, the homeowner must consider what potential buyers think of the neighborhood and try to stay ahead of any threat of a significant downgrading of the neighborhood's desirability. The renter may choose to prioritize local knowledge over the often more alarmist tone of media reports on crime, whereas the homeowner has to consider even alarmist reports as potentially significant because of their ability to diminish the value of the home.[18]

The American experience suggests that this relationship between homeownership and fear of crime has fed on itself.[19] If homeowners are more sensitive to crime threats to the neighborhood's property values, they are likely to assign significant value to

[17] Indeed, one of the treats of my childhood in Chicago's Hyde Park neighborhood was driving out to the suburbs to visit some of my parents' favorite restaurants that had followed many of their customers to the southern suburbs.

[18] Indeed, one of the most bizarre aspects of the relentless marketing of homeownership as a good economic move in the United States is the fact that it violates the most axiomatic rule of investing, namely diversification. In borrowing many times their annual income to purchase a home, Americans are tying their wealth to about the least diversifiable asset in the world – a distinct and unique piece of real property whose value depends almost entirely on the reputation of the local environment.

[19] I describe this logic more fully in Jonathan Simon, "Do These Prisons Make Me Look Fat? Moderating America's Consumption of Punishment," *Theoretical Criminology*, 14 (2010): 1. The gated community is perhaps the most notorious example of how housing estates have morphed to perform security in their very appearance (albeit perhaps merely the appearance of security), but there are clearly other ways of signaling security including private police, alarm systems linked to private security firms, fencing around the home, and the like. The gated community has thus far been rejected in England, but this does not mean the niche for a successful way to signal the crime security of housing units has not or is not emerging there. See Benjamin Goold, Ian Loader, and Angelica Thumala, "Consuming Security: Tools for a Sociology of Security Consumption," *Theoretical Criminology*, 14 (2010): 3.

housing opportunities that are resistant to crime threats. But the more homes have come to be marketed precisely on their security, the greater the pressure exerted by this logic. Gated communities are the logical outcome of this marketing strategy, and even without gates, most suburban housing relies on isolation and separation to signal security from crime. But isolation and separation also operate to reinforce the sense of vulnerability. To the extent that these strategies fail to keep criminals away, they may make it less likely for neighbors or police to perceive the danger and intervene.[20]

The U.S. experience also suggests that this kind of homeownership crime sensitivity can be politically productive. Like renters, most homeowners in the United States remain very dependent on job security for their overall economic security (indeed loss of a job can lead directly to loss of the home to foreclosure). Thus homeowners remain interested in the work government can do to provide job security and overall economic growth, but their nondiverse home value risk gives them a distinctive interest in crime politics.

The trends in high housing price growth U.S. states like California, Florida, and Arizona (until the bubble burst, of course) suggests that where inflating home prices over a sustained period of time creates a sense that economic opportunity is tied to the value of the home, the political salience of crime reaches its apex. In this kind of setting, the homeowner comes to identify their basic economic security not with their *job* but with their *home*. Crime has little impact on jobs, but it has a very powerful effect (at least in the U.S. context) on home prices. It is for this reason that some of the states that have had historically high rates of homeownership – Minnesota, for example – have never developed a high level of populist punitiveness. Whereas California may have a lower overall level of homeownership (because of the very high prices and the high portion of relatively poor immigrants), its high home prices mean it has a significant number of homeowner citizens who have come to view their home as their primary claim on middle-class legitimacy, a trend exacerbated by the disappearance of the high-end defense manufacturing jobs that had once provided access to that status.[21]

If homeownership and the economics of house prices have created a potential public of citizens whose view of the political is positioned in site-specific risks of the home, it may matter a great deal how large the scale of this public is and how rapidly home prices are inflating. The spread of mass private homeownership in the United States since the 1930s has meant a great expansion in the portion of the middle class that fit this profile of a homeowner citizen. Prior to the 1940s, people who did not inherit real property were unlikely to ever own it unless they inherited wealth, or had earned a lot and were able to invest in a house in their older years. With the

[20] This logic is evident in a whole subgenre of American thriller films that involve violent criminals menacing citizens in their rural or ex-urban home, for example, *The Desperate Hours* (1955), *In Cold Blood* (1967), *Straw Dogs* (1971).

[21] Didion, *Where I Was From*.

New Deal and the spread of the thirty-year fixed-rate mortgage, families with steady jobs could purchase a home at the beginning of their family and child-rearing lives.

Sociologists and historians have pointed to the rise in reported violent crime and homicide, in particular in the United States during the 1960s and early 1970s, as contributing to the political climate in favor of punitiveness that had become dominant by the 1980s.[22] But it was not crime by itself (even crimes as eye-catching as homicides) that generated a citizenry that recognized itself in the figure of the potential crime victim. Something else was mediating between the two, setting the context in which violent crime and homicide posed a politically salient threat, and in which ultimate sanctions would figure prominently. Consider that the United States experienced a strikingly similar increase in homicides in the 1920s and early 1930s without unleashing a sustained war on crime or producing a culture of control.[23] What changed? In the 1920s, American homeownership was growing, but the great majority of Americans continued to rent their domicile. The 1950 census marked the crossover point where a majority of homes were owner-occupied, a figure that reached nearly 70 percent by 1970. Thus between the crime waves of the 1920s and the 1960s, America, especially its fast-growing metropolitan areas, became a nation of homeowners.

The America that began to absorb the alarming images of violent crime, riots, and assassinations in 1968 was increasingly doing so from (or aspiring to) a piece of real estate with some margin of safety from danger (a concept fast becoming dubbed as "the American dream"). It was in this context of what we might call homeowner citizenship – that many began to recognize themselves in the appeal to crime victims that politicians were beginning to make in the 1970s and 1980s.[24]

This marked in America a watershed in the way citizens thought about security and the operation of the national government. The New Deal had taught a generation or two of Americans to look to the national government as at least a partial source of economic security against the vagaries of age and the markets through both entitlement programs and deft management of the fiscal and monetary policies. But the relatively full employment policies of the Johnson and Nixon administrations yielded less and less in appreciation from voters.

22 Most powerfully in Garland's *The Culture of Control.*

23 Of course, the 1920s was the prequel to the great real estate run-up of the late twentieth century, and some of the same places would experience the recent real estate bubble, for example, Miami, Los Angeles, and Oakland. Intriguingly it was also an era in which a politics of crime suppression gained some considerable traction.

24 As Katherine Beckett showed in her important study, *Making Crime Pay: Law and Order in Contemporary American Politics* (Oxford University Press, 1997), public opinion surveys show that identification of crime as a major national priority followed rather than preceded discursive mobilization concerning crime among politicians. However, it is not surprising that *before* the war on crime, few Americans were ready to view crime as primary focus for the federal government to address. Nor does it show that a growing alarm about crime was not already gathering salience in the lives of Americans, even if it remained prepolitical in form.

By the late 1970s and early 1980s, many Americans saw their economic future in the value of their private home, not their job. The first to feel this way were retirees in California's hottest real estate markets. It was these "crabgrass warriors,"[25] who had worked in California's well-paid blue-collar defense industries, who found themselves in retirement with homes suddenly worth many times what they paid for them and the possible danger of being forced out between the rising tide of market-based property taxes and their fixed (if generous) pensions. The short-term result was Proposition 13, a ballot initiative that amended California's constitution to cap property tax increases at 2 percent plus the rate of inflation (allowing market-rate resets only when the property is sold), altering forever the fiscal landscape of the state and undermining the high-quality public schools that property taxes had once supported.

Taxes were quickly joined to crime (sometimes conjoined with busing or other desegregation initiatives that undermined the neighborhood school connected to a particular home location) as major threats to the "homeowner citizen's" ability to stay in their home and benefit from its economic value. In addition to low taxes, mass imprisonment has been the most consistent policy preference of these citizens.

After stalling in the very high interest rates of the late 1970s and early 1980s, the U.S. housing market (both prices and the home-owning population) began to grow again in the 1980s. After the recession of the early 1990s, growth turned into what now appears to have been a bubble, with astronomical growth in home prices in some parts of the country (California, Florida, Nevada among others) and considerable expansion of the population in the market. This meant expanding homeownership to economically far more precarious families, a policy pursued aggressively by both the Clinton and Bush administrations. In the name of creating better and more secure neighborhoods, this owning-society vision was pushed into the cities that had remained the strongest redoubt of renters (there was no large pool of wealthy renters waiting to be convinced) through loan mechanisms that now appear to have been highly problematic.

This period, roughly 1994–2007, saw the growth of imprisoned population reach all-time highs in the midst of the greatest decline in crime in U.S. history. It was also the period in which the growth in mass imprisonment began to come mostly from the lengthening of prison sentences, especially for violent crimes (or at least people deemed violent), rather than from the flood of drug arrests and the more aggressive approach toward imprisoning marginal offenders.[26] Whereas the tougher approach included long determinate sentences, and policies like "truth in sentencing" designed to eliminate sentence reduction measures, an important and

[25] See Kenneth Jackson, *Crabgrass Frontier: The Suburbanization of America* (Oxford University Press, 1987); Lisa McGirr, *Suburban Warriors: Origins of the New Right* (Princeton University Press, 2001).

[26] Zimring divides the great American imprisonment boom into three periods. The third, beginning in the 1990s, is primarily driven in his view by lengthening prison sentences. See Franklin Zimring, "Imprisonment Rates and the New Politics of Criminal Punishment," *Punishment & Society*, 3 (2001): 161.

growing segment of this deep punishment base to mass incarceration involved life sentences, mostly for murder. Support for executions and capital punishment seemed to peak and decline in that same period (in 1994, for example, New York finally adopted capital punishment, only to abandon it by the end of the decade), but the nationwide political trend toward the other ultimate sanction, imprisonment without substantial hope of release, has consolidated and expanded.

It is this period, roughly 1994 through 2007, and those places, California, Florida, and Arizona, among others, that epitomize the idea of capital punishment as a kind of "homeowner's insurance." In all three places we can detect traces of older penal cultures that supported capital punishment, especially the lynching culture of violent racial subordination that has been linked to the modern propensity to execute.[27] All three are states that fought hard to retain capital punishment, but compared to states like Texas, Oklahoma, or Virginia, these are states where execution seems less central to public support than the weight of the death penalty on a political and legal structure that keeps murderers locked up practically forever and overall sentences long.[28] It is in these states, and with this kind of public commitment to ultimate sanctions (even without actual executions), where the homeowner citizen seems to hold the key to punitiveness in general and capital punishment in particular. For abolitionists, these citizens may seem especially promising targets for strategies that focus on permanent imprisonment as an incapacitative alternative to actual death sentences. Such a solution, however, will also depend on the willingness of those citizens to trust government not to yield to pressure from prisoners, prison administrators, and eventually courts to allow parole.

It might do to leave this analysis here. It is possible careful quantitative analysis using multiple regression techniques could probe the salience of this homeowner citizen on actual variations in overall punitiveness (measured by imprisonment rates), as well as on public support for capital punishment between American states with different concentrations of homeowner citizens. Instead I want to pivot to consider how this homeowner citizen might figure in the emergence of Europe's well documented, if less celebrated, punitive turn. Imprisonment rates are growing virtually across Europe. In many countries, this reflects a growing role for long prison sentences (formally considered an American disease) and especially life sentences for murderers. In seeking to account for this punitive turn and variations therein, European scholars have given prominent attention to the influence of political economy and in particular the split within Europe between more market-oriented nations like the United Kingdom and Ireland and more social-democratic-oriented nations like Sweden and Norway, with various nations in between, including Germany, France,

[27] Franklin Zimring, *The Contradictions of American Capital Punishment* (Oxford University Press, 2003).

[28] Jonathan Simon, "Why Do You Think They Call It CAPITAL Punishment: Reading the Killing State," *Law & Society Review*, 36 (2002): 783.

Belgium, and the Netherlands. More market-oriented nations, more "neoliberal" societies, are thought to be more punitive.[29]

"Neoliberalism," however, is an umbrella term for a wide range of developments including deregulation of previously regulated economies, lowering and flattening of progressive tax systems, shrinkage of social provisions, and the movement of access from a rights-based to a more market-based system, the growth of financial capital at the expense of other sectors, as well as the loss of influence by unions over the political system (in contrast to a growth in corporate influence). The growth of homeownership is no doubt a part of this larger constellation of changes in the governance of post-industrial societies.[30]

The role of the homeowner citizen in the rising political salience of crime fear throughout Europe may contribute to the analysis of the punitive turn and to understanding sources of long-term support for capital punishment. Support for tough-on-crime policies, especially capital punishment, has often been treated, including by this author, as the pursuit of largely symbolic, noneconomic values. But the homeowner citizen is not so much rejecting economic values as a goal for political engagement as recognizing a new economic interest in the state's penal capacity, in the added insurance value it adds to the home prices that constitute their central economic interest. This also explains the apparent paradox of the neoliberal state that promises to shrink but instead expands its penal sector.

PUNITIVENESS AND WESTERN EUROPEAN HOUSING MARKETS, 1994–2007

Perhaps because the U.S. incarceration rate rose so dramatically and became qualitatively separated from European penal practices it is only recently that a substantial literature has accumulated documenting that virtually every nation in Western Europe[31] experienced increases in incarceration during the 1990s. In some nations, for example the Netherlands, this has been building since the

[29] Loic Wacquant, *Punishing the Poor: The Neoliberal Governance of Insecurity* (Polity, 2009); Michael Cavadino and James Dignan, *Penal Systems: A Comparative Approach* (Sage Publications, 2006).

[30] The rise of mass private homeownership certainly predates neoliberalism in the United States (where it began actually as a New Deal project), but the securitization of residential real estate marketing and the shift toward a bubble like inflation of housing prices have paralleled the path of neoliberalism in Europe (with England moving toward more ownership in the 1980s, and countries like Ireland, the Netherlands, and Spain in the 1990s and 2000s).

[31] Although I will not be consistent in referencing "Western" Europe throughout this part of the chapter, I should emphasize that the further discussion is based entirely on nations that belonged to the "West" during the Cold War and, for the most part, have been prosperous democracies since World War II (Spain became a democracy in the late 1970s, and Ireland remained a very poor country by European standards until the 1990s). Penal patterns in the "Eastern" sector of Europe are only beginning to receive sustained attention by criminologists in the United States and Western Europe. Although the basic dynamic between homeownership and political identity that I suggest here can be expected to operate in the East, the politics of penal policy in these countries appears to remain quite different.

TABLE 3.1. *Housing markets and punitiveness (as measured in growth of imprisonment)*

Countries rank in each category	Home prices (1985–2002) rank of 10[32]	Home ownership growth 1970s to 2000 rank of 7[33]	Home ownership rank of 7 in 2000[34]	Imprisonment rate growth 1977–2004[35] rank of 10
Spain	1	4	1	3
Belgium	2	NA	NA	7
Ireland	3	7	3	2
Netherlands	4	1	6	1
UK	5	3	4	4
France	6	NA	NA	8
Italy	7	NA	NA	5
Sweden	8	5	5	6
Norway	9	2	2	9
Germany	10	6	7	10

early 1980s.[36] In others, like the United Kingdom, a decided upward pattern only emerged in the mid-1990s.[37] That this growth has occurred mostly in the absence of sustained crime increases suggests that important changes in penal politics and policy are going on. The distributions highlighted in Table 3.1 are consistent with the possibility that homeowner citizens are beginning to make their political identity felt in the democracies of Western Europe.

Any effort to think comparatively about the politics of punitiveness must begin by acknowledging the multiple institutional and cultural factors that have been identified as potentially "active" in unleashing punitiveness (or to use Michael Tonry's useful metaphor, there are multiple "risk factors" for the politics of mass imprisonment).[38] One of the most noted factors is the degree (or lack thereof) of insulation between penal decisions and politically sensitive agents (especially elected officials). Where decisions about punishment, especially in the kinds of

32 Kostas Tsatsaronis and Haibin Zhu, "What Drives Housing Price Dynamics: Cross-Country Evidence," *BIS: Quarterly Review* (March 2004).

33 Andrew J. Oswald, "A Conjecture on the Explanation for High Unemployment in the Industrialized Nations: Part I."

34 Oswald, "A Conjecture on the Explanation for High Unemployment in the Industrialized Nations: Part I."

35 Michael Tonry and Catrien Bijleveld, "Crime, Criminal Justice, and Criminology in the Netherlands," *Crime and Justice*, 36 (2007): 1, 15; Ian O'Donnell, "Imprisonment and Penal Policy in Ireland," (Ireland); Sonia Snacken, "Penal Policy and Practice in Belgium," *Crime and Justice*, 36 (2007): 127, 128.

36 David Downes, "Visions of Penal Control in the Netherlands," *Crime and Justice*, 36 (2007): 93–126.

37 Timothy Newburn, "'Tough on Crime': Penal Policy in England and Wales," *Crime and Justice*, 36 (2007): 425–70.

38 Michael Tonry, "Determinants of Penal Policies," *Crime and Justice*, 36 (2007): 1.

well-publicized crimes that make up the potential pool for capital punishment (or alternative ultimate sanctions) are made by elected judges, or where elected officials can pass directly on the release of a violent offender from prison, populist punitiveness is likely to drive growth in imprisonment rates.[39] Another is the degree of overall party competition as opposed to consensus and coalition building within the overall political culture of a particular nation. In the U.S., politicians learned to challenge each other on their fidelity to crime victims (usually measured in their readiness to inflict harsh punishment), but they had long operated in a political culture of head-to-head competition as opposed to consensus building among a permanent class of party officials; had crime not come along, other opportunities to enforce such competition would have.

Among European nations, there are major differences in the institutional factors that shape punitiveness, as well as social factors like poverty, crime rates, and immigration. The present study does not purport to untangle the cross-cutting effects of these variables on both imprisonment and on housing markets. The data in Table 3.1 should only be taken as an illustration of the possible covariance of (change in) both punitiveness and housing markets, with the objective of providing a provisional sense of where in Europe we might expect to see the formation of the kind of homeowner citizenship described earlier, and to find signs of a punitive politics of ultimate sanctions.

Imprisonment rates are a very limited measure of the punitiveness of a country,[40] but it is a measure heavily relied on by comparative scholars in the field. There seem to be three patterns, between 1985 and 2002, worth noting. The top five countries in the growth of housing prices in the Western European countries analyzed here, and the top five countries in the growth of imprisonment rates, during the somewhat longer time period 1977–2004, are the same with one exception on each side. Italy comes in fifth in growth in imprisonment while experiencing only modest growth in its housing prices, and Belgium kept prison rates relatively level for the Western European norm but experienced the second-highest growth rate in housing prices among them. The remaining countries in the top five, however, show a relatively close fit.

Spain experienced the highest growth in home prices and the second-highest growth in incarceration. Ireland experienced the third-highest increase in home prices and third-highest increase in incarceration. The United Kingdom had the fifth-highest increase in home prices and the fourth-highest increase in incarceration (perhaps because incarceration and home prices began to grow earlier there than in the rest of Europe so there was less of a pop in the late 1990s). The Netherlands was fourth in home prices and far ahead in first place for the growth of incarceration. It is noteworthy that these nations include both strong neoliberal nations

39 Joachim Savelsberg, "Knowledge, Domination, and Criminal Punishment," *American Journal of Sociology*, 99 (1994): 911.

40 See generally Natasha Frost, "The Mismeasure of Punishment," *Punishment & Society*, 10 (2008): 277.

(Ireland and the United Kingdom) and others less unambiguously market oriented (Spain and the Netherlands). They include countries with a high degree of party competition (United Kingdom, Spain) and countries that have a strong tradition of consensus governance (Ireland and the Netherlands). Perhaps most importantly, they include countries with a long history of having high imprisonment rates by European standards (United Kingdom and Spain), as well as those with a history of penal moderation (the Netherlands and Ireland). We would expect all of these factors to influence the degree to which American-style tough-on-crime politics and penal policies would take hold in European countries.

These four countries enjoyed the strongest housing markets between the mid-1980s and the recent financial crisis. If, as I argued earlier, the presence of homeowner citizens makes a state or nation easier to mobilize around crime-fear politics, these are the countries in Western Europe where we might expect to find a growing responsiveness of government to crime fear generally and to long prison sentences in particular. My hypothesis is that in all of these countries, you have a growing segment of the middle classes whose fundamental sense of economic and social security is (or was, during the period) oriented toward the value of their homes, and that this anchoring is driving them away from the politics of government security for income[41] and toward government policies that are perceived as guaranteeing the value of homes, including support for low taxes (at least on property) and high incarceration policies.

The data on housing markets in Table 3.1 provide only a very imprecise measure of how homeowner citizens may be distributed throughout Western Europe. The left-most column ranks nations in terms of the inflation of housing prices from the 1980s until the period before the recent financial crisis (which has disordered housing markets). These are not necessarily the countries with the highest proportion of homeowners (the rank for 2000 appears in the third column from the left). Some, like Ireland and Spain, have historically been countries of high homeownership but low prices, which, beginning in the early 1990s, both experienced extraordinary increases in the prices of houses (along with robust labor markets and a general rise in affluence). In the Netherlands, historically a country of low homeownership, a strong trend toward ownership began in the 1970s and continued across the decades, along with a strong price inflation beginning in the 1990s. The United Kingdom, which was historically near the middle of the European norms for homeownership, saw a significant surge in ownership beginning in the Thatcher years of the early 1980s and also a major run-up in prices since the 1990s.

While the data in Table 3.1 are too incomplete and too imprecise to test any relationship between homeownership and punitiveness, the different rankings suggest that the rise in home prices has been more closely associated with growing

[41] Of course, many of these same countries (particularly Ireland) were experiencing very tight employment markets, so these voters did not necessarily believe they were choosing between home and job security.

punitiveness than simply the growth in the overall level of homeownership. The two may often work together because the growing pool of people who expect that they should try to buy a home have helped push the prices up. Those countries that already had a lot of homeowners, which then experienced a tremendous surge in the value and wealth associated with the price of those homes (Ireland, Spain), might be the most disposed to homeowner-driven populist punitiveness.

At the bottom of the rankings, there is a similar degree of fit between those countries where both home prices and incarceration rates remained relatively stable during the period. Sweden was eighth of ten Western European countries in home price inflation and sixth in incarceration growth. Norway came in ninth in home prices and ninth in incarceration growth. Germany was dead last in both categories. In political economy terms, Norway and Sweden are emblematic of the social-democratic governance pattern associated with the Nordic countries with high taxes, significant regulation of the economy, and relative social stability. Germany, Europe's last major export manufacturer, combines a strong social state with more conservative cultural and social values. All three are often contrasted with the United Kingdom and other neoliberal countries as nations that are unlikely to respond to populist pressures with punitive sanctions for criminals. Table 3.1 also suggests that whatever their institutional readiness for crime politics, compared at least to other nations in this survey of Western European countries, Germany, Norway, and Sweden are not likely to have high concentrations of homeowner citizens. Although all of these countries saw an expansion of their homeownership in the 1990s, and a rise in incarceration rates, none experienced the kind of rapid inflation of prices most likely to set off the changes in interest and expectation associated with the homeowner citizen. In these countries, I am hypothesizing, citizens overall remain highly committed to their jobs as their primary platform of economic and social security and feel little pull toward policies that back their home investment with deterrence and incapacitation against crime and penal leniency.

In the middle are three countries that have a considerable degree of separation between housing and incarceration. Belgium, as we have noted, had the second-highest house price inflation in Western Europe but belongs in the bottom tier of the league table of incarceration growth. In fact, Belgium experienced an overall decline in convicted criminals sentenced to prison in the 1990s, but sent more arrestees to pretrial incarceration, and significantly increased sentence length for some crimes has resulted in a modest (by overall European standards) increase in incarceration.[42]

This modest growth actually disguises a major inflammation of civil society around violent crime, and a responsive wave of populist punitive sentiment checked by a political culture of consensus politics and insulation of criminal justice from political officials. After many decades of relative penal stability, Belgium's incarceration rate began to go up in the 1990s. Belgian civil society has been mobilized by a growing concern with violent crime and failures of law enforcement since the early

[42] Sonja Snacken, "Penal Policy and Practice in Belgium," *Crime and Justice*, 36 (2007): 127–216.

1980s. This culminated in 1996 with the Dutroux scandal, a series of rape-murders perpetrated by a Belgian prisoner on parole, which mobilized huge marches and initiated Europe's most significant victim's rights movement. The rape-murder a year later of a young female immigrant helped take the crime issue away from the anti-immigrant far-right party and allowed the mainstream parties to reclaim the issue for themselves. The resulting compromise was a bifurcation in which the government sought to reduce overall use of prison for criminal offenses while increasing preventive detention of arrestees and lengthening prison sentences for violent crimes and sexual offenses. Whereas the structure of Belgian political institutions remains a powerful check on the growth of incarceration, the mobilization of Belgian civil society around crime is well underway. Thus even though Belgium may remain in the bottom half of Western European imprisonment growth, its high home price inflation suggests that homeowner citizens are emerging in Belgium and responding to the politics of crime fear.

Italy and France both are arguably examples of countries that seem to combine growing populist punitiveness with limited growth in incarceration. Italy, which was seventh among the ten Western European countries analyzed in home prices and fifth in incarceration, has experienced a sustained period of top-down rhetoric on crime from the mercurial populist Sylvio Berlusconi who has served as prime minister several times in the time period and who has often focused his zeal on illegal immigrants and other law breakers. Italy seems an example of a nation without a strong homeowner citizen base but where growing intolerance of immigration and intense political competition had built up incarceration.

France, which had the fifth-highest home price inflation and was second from the bottom in growth of incarceration, has combined considerable use of tough-on-crime rhetoric by its political leaders, with minimal actual growth of imprisonment. The French political class, apparently across the political spectrum, remains rather dubious about the benefits of incarceration.[43] As a result, tough talk, and even tough new legislation, has been checked by refusal of successive governments to construct sufficient new prison space for a substantial increase in penal scale. Yet the existence and growth of both tough-on-crime rhetoric and popular concern about crime, perhaps fueled by the emergence of homeowner citizens, make France a potential recruit to the high-punishment, "ownership" societies of Europe.

ULTIMATE SANCTIONS IN EUROPE

The array of national statistics analyzed in Table 3.1 can only provide the crudest indicators of where growing concentrations of homeowner citizens may be creating the political conditions for a general rise in punitiveness, but what, if anything, can it

[43] Sebastian Roche, "Criminal Justice Policy in France: Illusions of Severity," *Crime and Justice*, 36 (2007): 471.

really tell us about the fate of capital punishment and ultimate sanctions in Europe? As Sebastian Roche notes, the elements of a "harsh penal policy" can include many distinct features, including the death penalty (with or without the actual executions, as in the United States), mandatory minimum sentences, increases in prison population, and tough-on-crime rhetoric among them.[44] The historical structure and conjunctural dynamics of a particular nation will have a lot to do with how a successful politics of harsh punishment translates into specific materializations of policy or rhetoric. In the United States, we tend to see all four elements in many states, although some lack the death penalty, and many lack actual executions, whereas others have abundant prison growth. In Western Europe, France is a good example of a country where populist punitiveness has translated into tough-sounding talk and legislation but little actual growth of imprisonment, and even consolidation of opposition to capital punishment.[45] The Netherlands is a good example of where growing populist punitiveness has translated into substantial growth in imprisonment because of strong and consistent political leadership support for building prisons and toughening prison sentences for some categories of offenders.[46]

At present, capital punishment has been abolished throughout Western Europe (and indeed all of the states of the EC, which includes most other European sovereign states) and appears to have permanently lost the majority cultural acceptance it once had even during the abolition process. The point at which national abolition occurred varies greatly, from 1964–1969 (moratorium into abolition) in England and Wales to 1990 for Ireland (although it had not carried out an execution since 1964). In most countries, the new penalty for ordinary murders was set at life, although some, like Spain, set the ultimate sentence at a term of years.[47] In virtually all of these countries, however, it was expected that in the normal course, life prisoners would be released when they no longer posed a significant danger, with some setting minimum terms within the murder statute and others creating administrative laws dictating parole procedures.

In France, a whole life term, for example, can be applied to a murderer who kills and rapes a child under fifteen years of age. In Ireland, the deliberate murder of a *Garda*[48] officer or a prison officer can result in a forty-year capital murder term. In most cases (Switzerland being an interesting exception), this truly ultimate sanction is narrowly limited by substantive elements of the crime. In some cases, Ireland being one, the ultimate sanction is a residue of negotiations attending the final abolition

44 Roche, "Criminal Justice Policy in France," 475.

45 Roche, "Criminal Justice Policy in France," 475.

46 Downes, "Visions of Penal Control in the Netherlands."

47 Spain along with Croatia, Slovenia, Portugal, and Norway are the European countries that replaced capital punishment with something less than life. Se, Appelton and Grover, Op. Cit., 603. The original intent may well have been to produce a clear barrier to whole-life sentences, but compared to European norms of life meaning ten years or less, Spanish sentences may become highly punitive.

48 Garda Síochána na hÉireann, literally, "guardians of the peace of Ireland," the Gaelic term for national police force of the Republic of Ireland.

of the death penalty (*Garda* demanded special protections to support the general abolition of capital punishment). In other cases, however – France, for example – the ultimate sanction is new and is a product of populist anger over well-publicized crimes contemporaneous with the adoption of the law.

It is possible that this consensus against capital punishment has now become such a strong anchor of European identity[49] that this turn to abolition is permanent, regardless of the growth of a punitively oriented homeownership class. One should note that the actual process of national abolition in most of the Western European countries took place during the decades (1960s, 1970s, and early 1980s) before any kind of substantial populist politics of crime fear had developed in Europe (as it already had in the United States). Where such a politics is already underway, perhaps fueled by the growth of homeowner citizenship, I would argue that it will be much harder for elite decisions to abolish to receive popular acceptance (the states of the former Soviet bloc are the obvious testing ground for this).[50] Moreover, should European human rights constraints break apart and a renewed national politics of capital punishment reemerge in the midst of the robust politics of crime fear operating in virtually every European nation today, homeowner citizens would likely emerge as a vanguard base for a movement to restore capital punishment.

Two points are worth making about the commitment of homeowner citizens to capital punishment and to lesser but still harsh ultimate sanctions (like permanent imprisonment). First, homeowner citizens do not recognize themselves in many of the critiques of capital punishment that have fueled its rejection in Europe. Because they view capital punishment primarily as a tool of protecting the rights of homeowners against the social and economic risk posed by violent criminals, homeowner citizens rightly reject the charge that they are racists or that this policy is necessarily a ritual designed to constitute a racialized community (as it may remain for some states in the American South). Indeed, as Sonya Snacken suggests for the case of Belgium, sometimes the politics of crime victims and homicide can build bridges across ethnic and immigration divides and allow the dominant political parties to seize the law-and-order mantle away from the far-right, anti-immigrant parties that often innovate in the introduction of such discourse to European politics.[51]

Second, because homeowner citizens are generally in favor of reduced taxes and a more limited state (they are neoliberal in that sense), they do not recognize themselves in the charge that capital punishment builds up the power of the state. They are more likely to view capital punishment as a service to private citizens provided by the state in its classic and limited penal form.[52] Indeed, to a certain

49 Katherine Heard, "Performances of Abolition? Transatlantic Discourse on Capital Punishment and the Execution of Saddam Hussein," this volume.

50 Agata Fijalkowski, "European Policy on the Death Penalty," this volume.

51 Snacken, "Penal Policy and Politics in Belgium."

52 As Frank Zimring argues, Americans tend to see capital punishment as a benefit for private citizens. While Zimring emphasizes the private interest in vengeance, the homeowner-citizen concept helps

extent, capital punishment (at least in the idealized form citizens may imagine it) can appear less bureaucratic and less prone to institutional insulation from populist demands than prisons.

Even if capital punishment has now become a culturally unacceptable option for at least Western Europe, there is reason to believe that the growth of homeowner citizenship in European countries, combined with the extent of political competition on crime politics, will likely lead to growing pressure for the other form of ultimate sanction, namely permanent imprisonment without intention to release or reintegrate. Although it is difficult to generalize, the work of Dirk Van Zyl Smit suggests a trend toward increasing the minimum terms that can be set by judges or mandated by statute for certain killers deemed more of a threat. Moreover, throughout many of the countries we have discussed, both those with substantial imprisonment growth and those without, there has been a growing populist concern with violent crime and sex offenses (the two kinds of crime with the most direct impact on house prices).

Since the late 1980s, for example, the United Kingdom has moved toward allowing judges flexibility in setting a minimum prison sentence that a life prisoner must serve before the possibility of release, including the theoretical possibility of a "whole life" sentence.[53] The Netherlands has never specified a minimum sentence for life and has yet to release any life prisoner sentenced since the 1980s when life sentences began to go up substantially. Ireland, which paroled lifers in as early as seven years in the 1980s and early 1990s, shifted in the late 1990s to a possible twelve- to fourteen-year minimum for murder.[54]

The conditions likely to produce homeowner citizenship as a political identity are spreading throughout Western Europe, because home prices have been inflating well beyond the general rate of inflation (until the financial crisis) in virtually every Western European country (with the possible exception of Germany). The main measure of punitiveness considered in Table 3.1 – growth in imprisonment – probably understates the influence of the distinctive concerns of homeowner citizens. Many of the countries in the lower half of imprisonment growth, including France and Belgium, as well as some high-growth countries like the Netherlands, have chosen to target increased prison sentences against violent and sex offenders – precisely the categories most feared by homeowner citizens – while balancing the effect on the actual population imprisoned by reducing sanctions against drug and property crimes.

In the last sections of this chapter, I want to discuss two examples from Table 3.1 of high homeownership countries that have substantially increased punitiveness as measured by imprisonment to try and identify some of the dynamics that may

us see how even incapacitative security (which we generally think of as a public good) can also be viewed as a private service. Franklin Zimring, *The Contradictions of American Capital Punishment* (Oxford University Press, 2003).

53 Newburn, "'Tough on Crime': Penal Policy in England and Wales."

54 Ian O'Donnell, "Imprisonment and Penal Policy in Ireland," *The Howard Journal*, 43 (2004): 253.

drive support for restoration of capital punishment or harsh ultimate sanctions in Europe.

IRELAND: HOMEOWNER-BASED FEAR IN A LOW-CRIME SOCIETY

In their impressive and comprehensive account of Irish penality from the birth of the Republic to the middle of this decade, Shane Kilcommins[55] and his colleagues describe a country that, at least since World War II, maintained a small prison population and mostly thought of itself as a low-crime society. As late as 1983, and despite an alarming rise in the homicide rate in the late 1970s, a contemporary observer noted that the Irish were, even relative to Europe as a whole, "not obsessed with crime."

Ireland's relatively stable and low prison population turned up sharply beginning in the middle of the 1990s. This happened despite a falling crime rate throughout the period and fewer committals to prisons. Kilcommins and his colleagues attribute this to an increase in the number of longer-sentenced prisoners causing the daily population to rise despite fewer crimes and committals. They see in this period the beginnings of the kind of "culture of control" that Garland described in the United Kingdom and the United States, but still on a much lower level.

The Irish approach to ultimate sanctions is similar to that of many other Western European countries. Death sentences were handed down rarely after the middle of the twentieth century and even more rarely carried out. There were only eighty murder convictions between the end of World War II and 1962, of which only eighteen were sentenced to death and only three hanged.[56] The law of homicide was reformed by the Criminal Justice Act 1964 that abolished the death penalty for piracy, some military crimes, and most murders. Capital punishment remained available for treason, certain military offenses, murder in the course of terrorism, and the deliberate murder of a known officer of the *Garda* or prison service.

In 1990, Ireland moved toward the European norm of compete abolition by eliminating the death penalty. Although no major political party supported retention, some leaders did support the arguments of the *Garda* that police and prison officers required an extra measure of deterrence. Thus the crime of capital murder was created that requires a mandatory forty-year prison sentence (although it can be reduced up to ten years for good behavior). Only four people have received the forty-year sentence for capital murder since 1990.

There is evidence here, albeit sketchy, of the emergence of the punitive "homeowners citizens" that I hypothesize (or at least fear on the part of the political elites to the emergence of such mentalities). First, consider the homeowner side of the

[55] Shane Kilcommins, Ian O'Donnell, Eoin O'Sullivan, and Barry Vaughan, *Crime, Punishment and the Search for Order in Ireland* (Institute of Public Administration, 2004).

[56] Kilcommins et al., "Punishment and the Search for Order in Ireland," 55.

equation. Although Ireland always had higher rates of homeownership than Europe as a whole (and therefore had much less room for homeownership expansion in the 1990s and the 2000s than most Western European nations), most properties were worth very little, and the real estate market was anything but dynamic.[57] Beginning in the mid-1990s, however, real estate was at the forefront of the general explosion of economic growth. Unemployment dipped to historic lows as foreign corporations built factories in the Republic, but citizens seemed genuinely dizzied by the remarkable inflation of their home values that rose faster during this period than in either California or New York.[58] To many Irish families, their long-paid-for house had become the pathway to securing retirement or launching offspring into responsible lives, or both. To the young, getting in on the ground floor of the real estate market was competing with career ladders in planning their future. As in California, this led to a speculative dimension that pushed the real estate market into a bubble-like formation.

By the end of the 1990s, after more than a decade of unceasing and sometimes spectacular increases in home prices, we might expect homeowner citizens to begin revising their expectations on the state from a concern with keeping employment full to a concern with protecting citizens in their private ownership and enjoyment of their property. Irish business journalist David McWilliams describes just this kind of housing-based transformation going on in Ireland: "The property boom – the soaring prices of houses, the associated lending, building, commuting and working – has not just changed the economy, it has changed us – the Irish people – profoundly."[59] Moreover, McWilliams's descriptions of the new form of Irish homeownership, primarily the U.S.-style suburban sprawl (that McWilliams calls "the BabyBelt"), has come along with a political identity emphasizing both withdrawal from collective solidarity and a profound sense of fear and anxiety that suggests a society primed for a boom in crime fear:

> In last year's by election, less than thirty percent of the BabyBelt voted. As far as they are concerned, the government can't do anything for them except leave them alone . . . Then a tragedy occurs and they clamber for politicians to do something. But . . . what are the politicians expected to do, protect the "speed bump" moms from themselves in large SUVs?[60]

57 Ireland's remarkable economic boom and the role of homeownership and housing prices in that boom (as well as a prescient warning of a crash) are dissected in David McWilliams, *The Pope's Children: The Irish Economic Triumph and the Rise of Ireland's New Elite* (John Wiley & Sons, 2006).

58 Gregory Connor, Thomas Flavin, and Brian O'Kelly, "The US and Irish Credit Crises: Their Distinctive Differences and Common Features," Irish Economy Note No. 10, March 2010.

59 McWilliams, *The Pope's Children*, 68.

60 Ibid., at 71. McWilliams is describing a burst of activism that developed in the suburbs after a child was run over by a driver in a large SUV, and which took the form of demands for speed bumps. Even though this was not framed as a crime problem per se, it is exactly the kind of fear-based mobilization I would expect from homeowner citizens.

As in California and in a number of other Western European countries, it is not crime in general but homicide in particular that seems to have been key to building a political consensus to toughen sanctions (especially ultimate ones). The key year seems to have been 1996, when several disturbing rural murders (always a frightening prospect for the suburban homeowner) were capped off by two highly publicized Dublin murders, those of *Garda* Detective Jerry McCabe and crime reporter Veronica Guerin.[61] As Kilcommins and colleagues explain:

> These killings were defining moments in the debate about law and order in Ireland. They were the catalyst for a hardening in political attitudes. Crime control became a national priority and it was as if a state of national emergency had been declared. The Dail was recalled for a special debate, and, during the general election campaign which took place in 1997, public concern seemed to be at an all-time high, as reflected in the sudden prioritization of law and order issues in the opinion polls.[62]

Although Kilcommins and colleagues can find little evidence that the public priority of crime was sustained, there seems to be plenty of evidence that the official approach to murder changed. After the abolition of capital punishment for ordinary murder in 1964, the mandatory sentence for murder was life, but the *Irish Times* reported in 1990 that juries rarely brought in murder verdicts, returning only two murder convictions out of fourteen sought in two terms of court during the late 1980s.[63] Even when life sentences were handed down in Ireland, the real time served was generally less than eight years between 1976 and 1980, but jumped to thirteen years between 1996 and 2001.[64] The major political agent of this transformation was Justice Minister Michael MacDowell:[65]

> In August 2003 the Minister for Justice, Equality and Law Reform stated that henceforth no lifer would have his or her sentence reviewed before ten years had elapsed. This was on the basis that "it might have filtered out into the criminal underworld that that taking of a life might only result in seven years . . . I'm trying to get across to them that that will soon be a dangerous delusion. He added that he

61 Guerin's case received enormous publicity both in Ireland and abroad, with Hollywood contributing a major movie with her name in 2003. Although Guerin displayed extreme or even foolhardy courage in pursuing direct contact with Irish drug criminals and criticizing them openly in her reporting, the death of the young wife and mother who was twice attacked in her home before the final, fatal attack could well have been seen by the public as evidence that decent people were not safe in their homes.

62 Ibid. 137.

63 Paul Carney, "Juries now rarely bring in murder verdicts," *The Irish Times*, June 2, 1990.

64 Kilcommins et al., Op. Cit. 248; O'Donnell, "Imprisonment and Penal Policy in Ireland," 261.

65 Grandson of an Irish revolutionary Eoin MacNeill and the founding member of the Progressive Democrats; served as Attorney General and then Minister of Justice for Ireland from 1999 to 2007, just as the real estate boom and crime panic played out. McDowell openly criticized Irish judges for granting bail too easily and for failing to implement mandatory sentences. This kind of attack on judges has been a signal pattern for elected politicians facing a public increasingly made up of homeowner citizens who feel mistrustful of insulated political elites.

> wanted it to be twelve years before any life sentence prisoner was even granted day release. In order to "restore public confidence" a life sentence was going to be "a very severe sentence."[66]

Although these terms remain short compared to California murder sentences, they are clearly contributing to mounting Irish prison populations, and even though the surge of populist punitiveness in the wake of 1996 seemed to disappear quickly in Irish public opinion surveys, the pattern suggests that political elites are now highly sensitive to the possibility of appearing insufficiently concerned about keeping the public safe from violent criminals who appear to menace them in their homes. This was strongly suggested by considerable public and then political support for a homeowner named Nally initially charged with murder or manslaughter after fatally shooting in the back a trespasser near his rural home. Nally was initially convicted of manslaughter after a court refused to let him put on a full self defense theory before the jury; after an appellate court ordered a retrial permitting the full defense, Nally was acquitted. The Nally case has led the Irish law to be formally changed to allow that a homeowner may use deadly force when they reasonably believe it to be necessary to defend family or home. The law, popularly known as "Nally's Law" is, in effect, a form of ultimate sanction, and one directly connected to the citizen as homeowner.[67]

THE NETHERLANDS: RISING FEAR IN A CORPORATIST STATE

The Netherlands is the country with the most dramatic turnaround in penal severity in Western Europe.[68] Once celebrated by criminologists as the central example of tolerance as a penal virtue, the Netherlands had the lowest incarceration rates of any moderate- to large-sized country in Western Europe between 1970 and 1990.[69] The Netherlands' low level of incarceration reflected not just a reluctance to criminalize marginal forms of deviance (like drug use or sex work) but a basic leniency in the punishment of even very serious crimes. For example, of sixty-three people convicted of homicide in the Netherlands in 1970, only fourteen received three or more years in prison (with a strong presumption of early release through parole).[70] By 2002, it had become, next to the United Kingdom, the heaviest incarcerator in Western

66 Indeed, O'Donnell quotes McDowell and the chairman of the parole boards as publically taking the position "that even in the absence of aggravating factors, a term of at least 12 to 14 years would be served before release on licence was considered."

67 See, Olga Craig, "Right to defend yourself: Ireland has changed law, so why can't Britain?" Telegraph .co.uk, http://www.telegraph.co.uk/news/uknews/law-and-order/6844727/Right-to-defend-yourself-Ireland-has-changed-law-so-why-cant-Britain.html (last visited September 10, 2010).

68 The classic statement is David Downes, *Contrast in Tolerance: Post War Penal Policy in the Netherlands and England and Wales* (Oxford University Press, 1993).

69 Cavadino and Dignan, *Penal Systems*, 113.

70 Robert Heiner, "The Growth of Incarceration in The Netherlands," *Federal Sentencing Reporter*, 17 (2005): 227.

Europe. In the intervening three decades, the Netherlands' rate of incarceration growth rivaled that of the United States.[71] What changed?

Recent scholarship on Dutch punitiveness points to a number of factors that sociologists would expect to contribute to such a surge. Foremost among them is immigration, from former Dutch colonies as well as Eastern Europe. The unprecedented level of immigration has led most visibly to the formation of right-wing nationalist politics. It may well also have contributed to popular anxiety about crime as well as the efforts of government officials to stay on top of such anxieties with administrative decisions to extend greater imprisonment. Second, the Netherlands experienced a real growth in homicides, with a tripling of the homicide rate between the 1960s and the 1990s (more or less the same period during which many U.S. states experienced high levels of homicide).[72] Beginning in the 1990s, this began to reflect itself in public opinion and politics as fear of crime.[73] As Sebastien Roche has argued, it is hard to imagine a real takeoff in crime-fear politics without heightened homicide rates.[74]

On the institutional level, the Netherlands shares with many low-incarceration countries a considerable degree of administrative control over punishment (which might be thought to insulate penality from political pressures) as well as a consensus-oriented political structure that has played down partisan competition (until recently). In the Dutch case, however, elites have clearly chosen to stay ahead of populist punitiveness in the public by using their administrative power to expand punishment. Indeed, much of the Dutch incarceration expansion was carried out without major new pieces of crime legislation,[75] although it appears such legislation is now coming online.[76] Procedural reforms in the early 1980s gave Dutch prosecutors greater power under the existing principle of "expediency" to resolve cases with fines or probation up to crimes that could require six years in prison without judicial supervision. By the middle of the 1990s, it was clear that whatever the intentions behind the reforms (which may have aimed at continuing Dutch low-incarceration policies), the result was the growing use of unconditional prison sentences through the courts that now found this a growing portion of their business.[77] This seems to have only accelerated a shift toward increasing prison populations beginning as early as 1975, and ratified further by prison construction in the 1990s.[78]

71 Michael Tonry and Catrien Bijleveld, "Crime, Criminal Justice, and Criminology in the Netherlands," *Crime and Justice*, 36 (2007): 1, 3.

72 Tonry and Bijleveld, "Crime, Criminal Justice, and Criminology in the Netherlands," 20.

73 Downes, "Visions of Penal Control in the Netherlands," 105.

74 Roche, "Criminal Justice Policy in France: Illusions of Severity," 532.

75 Tonry and Bijleveld, "Crime, Criminal Justice, and Criminology in the Netherlands," 11.

76 Downes, "Visions of Penal Control in the Netherlands," 119 (discussing new Three-Strikes law).

77 Josine Junger Tas, "Recent Trends in Sentencing Policies in the Netherlands," *European Journal on Criminal Policy and Research*, 6 (1998): 484.

78 Junger Tas, "Recent Trends in Sentencing Policies in the Netherlands," 485 (reversing a trend toward declining incarceration that began in 1837).

As with France and Belgium, Dutch decision makers seem to have sought to target enhanced penal sanctions to specific crimes rather than supporting a general expansion of imprisonment. Dutch prosecutorial discretion and the availability of longer sentences for violent and sex offenses have clearly been part of the rise of prison populations through at least the late 1990s.[79] There is also evidence from the mid-1990s of "a heightened sensitivity and social awareness both of violence and of sex offences, such as rape, sexual abuse, incest and assault on homosexuals," and that "what worries [Dutch] people more than anything else is the increase in violence."[80]

Michael Cavadino and James Dignan point to the neoliberal turn of Dutch policy as moving it from what they call the corporatist/welfarist camp toward the punitive neoliberalisms of the United States and the United Kingdom, although they are somewhat puzzled by the fact that the Dutch welfare state remained (at least as of 2006) relatively strong.[81] Is it possible that it is not neoliberalism in general (the Dutch welfare state remains comparatively generous) but rather the rapid rise in Dutch home prices and the creation of a defensive homeowner citizenry that is making itself felt? Even though the Dutch may have retained a welfare state, the inflation of home prices has created the kind of new wealth among formerly work-centered citizens that we might well expect to lead to an increasingly populist punitiveness.

A crucial intervening factor would be alarming crimes that help center the ordinary citizen, in or near their homes, as at risk in crime. Against the background of three decades of rising homicide rates and increased immigration, the past decade has seen a number of highly publicized killings that have highlighted the potential intersection of these trends, especially the political killings of a populist political candidate, Pym Fortuyn, and of Dutch documentarian Theo Van Gogh, which have helped consolidate an elite-based culture of control in the Netherlands.

There is evidence of this kind of homeowner citizenry behind the populism of Fortuyn's meteoric political rise. According to Peter van der Veer, much of Fortuyn's financial backing was linked to the housing boom and what van der Veer specifically calls "the populist emotions that are intimately tied to real estate prices."[82]

> His friends brought Fortuyn's ashes to his holiday villa in Italy, and the Dutch were regaled with endless gossip about the men and women financially backing Fortuyn's party. These were mostly rich real-estate developers with a somewhat

[79] Junger Tas mentions sex offenses and robberies as well as violent crimes generally as crimes where relatively stable commitment patterns were producing more pressure for prison cells through longer sentences, but says nothing specific about murder in general or use of the whole-life sentence. However, crimes against life are mentioned as one of the five crimes most responsible for the growth of detention in the 1980s and early 1990s. Junger Tas, "Recent Trends in Sentencing Policies in the Netherlands," 484, 495.

[80] Junger Tas, "Recent Trends in Sentencing Policies in the Netherlands," 492–4.

[81] Junger Tas, "Recent Trends in Sentencing Policies in the Netherlands."

[82] Peter van der Veer, "Pym Fortuyn, Theo Van Gogh, and the Politics of Tolerance in the Netherlands," *Public Culture*, 18 (2006): 1–14.

> shady reputation and a total lack of political savvy. It is perhaps relevant that they had greatly benefited from the real-estate boom of the 1990s (when house prices rose 300 percent), and in this sense were close to populist emotions that are intimately related to real-estate prices.

Likewise, as early as the 1980s, the Netherlands saw crime become a bigger concern for civil society as the rights of crime victims, and the incidents of violent crime, became a recurrent theme of the Dutch media.[83]

Cavadino and Dignan point to the Netherlands as an example of a highly centralized penal state (a tendency that favors stability over all else) whose corporatist masters have chosen to take it in the direction of penal "managerialism" and greater preventive segregation (especially of those marked as violent).[84] Distinguished Dutch sociologist Josine Junger Tas ends her 1998 review of Dutch Sanctions with the prediction that "all the indicators suggest that a more repressive and retributive system has now been firmly rooted in Dutch society and it will remain so for some considerable time."[85]

All of this is consistent with the deliberate use by Dutch governments of ultimate sanctions as a tool of reassurance and penal risk management against at least a modest number of violent deviants. Life sentences remain relatively unusual in the Netherlands, but their numbers are growing, and unlike other European life sentences, it is not clear whether the Dutch ever intend to release life prisoners.

CONCLUSION

Whereas capital punishment may be dead for good in Europe and dying in the United States, its passage does not mean the end of "ultimate sanctions" – that is, exclusionary sanctions designed to effectuate a long-term and possibly permanent separation of violent criminal deviants from the community. In this essay, I have argued that support for ultimate sanctions may depend in part on the growth of a class of late modern citizenry that views its social and economic security as rooted less in their jobs, or their social rights, than in their privately owned home (and the real estate market for that home) – the "homeowner citizen." It is clear that the conditions for this kind of citizenship proliferated in the United States after 1950 and throughout Europe after 1980. Even though concentrations of such homeowner citizens vary considerably across Europe (and across various U.S. states), there is growth across the board.

The growth of residential real estate markets in Western Europe has accompanied a growth in punitiveness and arguably in the demand for ultimate sanctions, offering

83 Junger Tas, "Recent Trends in Sentencing Policies in the Netherlands," 495.

84 Cavadino and Dignan, *Penal Systems*, 123; See also Junger Tas, "Recent Trends in Sentencing Policies in the Netherlands," who describes the Dutch welfare state as becoming substantially less generous.

85 Junger Tas, "Recent Trends in Sentencing Policies in the Netherlands," 504.

limited evidence of my claim. The connective force may be a body of "homeowner citizens" who see their interests in state power primarily in its law enforcement function (rather than the welfare or regulatory fuction) and especially in its ultimate sanctions. This latter point is particularly salient to the concerns of this volume and chapter. It is possible that the crime fears of European publics can be largely addressed through more aggressive policing and more efficient and reliable courts (which have historically been lacking in many European states). But homeowner citizens are distinctly less likely to find solace in either better police or more reliable court bureaucrats. They want guarantees that those criminals whose crimes are most salient to property-based fear and loss of value – that is, violent crime and sex crimes – once identified, will be permanently removed from society. Given the effective removal of capital punishment as an option from European penality, I would suspect that this homeowner-based demand for incapacitative sanctions will take the form of pressure for irreversible life sentences. Since these are likely to be unacceptable to Human Rights courts, the future is likely to bring greater political conflict and thus politicization around these issues.

The dramatic collapse of the real estate prices in North America and Western Europe and the accompanying Great Recession as financial institutions have failed or been bailed out as a result of lending in that market have clearly put a moratorium (at least) on further expansion of the homeowner citizenry (as well as cast some portion back into nonownership). Independent factors, especially the energy crises and concern about global climate change, may put longer-term restraints on the growth of homeownership, especially the security-oriented suburban estate that has become the global gold standard for the most desirable housing. If younger families find that moral and economic incentives lead them to rent apartments near their work rather than buying homes in distant suburbs, we may well be seeing the high watermark of the homeowner citizenry and its populist punitiveness.

If, however, the present economic crisis turns out to be a mere pause in the shift from industrial to real estate capitalism in Western Europe, we can expect continuing pressure for a restoration of ultimate sanctions (even if not the death penalty) by Western European publics who find themselves, however reluctantly, pushed into a homeowner citizenship and the decidedly second-best politics of penal segregation. In that case, everything depends on the willingness of the European Court of Human Rights to back up its hints that a real and substantial chance at release is a fundamental right for life-sentenced prisoners in Europe.

PART II

On the Meaning of Death and Pain in Europe and the United States: Viewing, Witnessing, Understanding

4

The Witnessing of Judgment

Between Error, Mercy, and Vindictiveness

Evi Girling

The global production, exchange, and consumption of images of punishment have created a new landscape for penal sensibilities that our preoccupation with local and national legal orders needs to embrace as a cultural as well as a comparative project.[1] This landscape posits new challenges for the scope of comparative reflection on the death penalty. It is a volatile landscape where the narcissism of small differences and legal cultures seems to prevail, and where it is no longer – if it ever was – possible to understand local penal sensibilities toward the death penalty without a comparative perspective.[2] The fates of the death penalty are to borrow Robertson's apt but rather ungainly term 'glocal'[3] – imagined globally and acted locally. This chapter explores one key aspect of this glocalization of the cultural lives of capital punishment – the global witnessing and local meanings of the act of judgment of death.

This chapter explores the cultural lives of act(s) of judgment in liberal democracies at a time of global witnessing. My interest follows on from earlier work that examined the Benetton death penalty advertising campaign[4] and European campaigns to end the death penalty as instances of these global exchanges. This chapter's focus on judgment draws inspiration from Culbert's discussion of the problem of

[1] Penal sensibilities and their attendant penal cultures have, in the main, been apprehended as 'local' in nature and mostly circumscribed by nation states. The intricate repertoire of images and narratives of punishment for worldwide audiences invites us to reconsider the 'local' character of such ensembles and the challenge they pose for the salience of locality in penal politics and culture.

[2] See Evi Girling, "'Looking Death in the Face': The Benetton Death Penalty Campaign," *Punishment & Society* 6(3) (2004): 271, and Evi Girling, "European Identity, Penal Sensibilities and Communities of Sentiment" in *Perspectives on Punishment: The Contours of Control*, Sarah Armstrong (ed.) (Oxford: Oxford University Press, 2006).

[3] Roland Robertson, "Glocalization: Time-Space and Homogeneity-Heterogeneity," in *Global Modernities*, M. Featherstone, S. Lash, R. Robertson (eds.), (London: Sage, 1995).

[4] See Girling, "'Looking Death in the Face'," 271, and Girling, "European Identity, Penal Sensibilities and Communities of Sentiment."

judgment in capital punishment.[5] Her contribution explores the problem of judgment in the Supreme Court's language in the process of limiting and defending the practice. Here I wish to reflect on the processes and impact of a 'witnessing of judgment' in what Appadurai has descripted as mediascapes – new scapes in a world of flows enabled by an exponential rise in electronic advances and capabilities for the dissemination of information.[6] Translocal cultures and communities of sentiment[7] challenge the distinctiveness and relative inertia and stability of nation-state arrangments within which our comparative endeavor (or, one could say, chimera) of understanding the fates of the death penalty is usually situated. The flows of people, discourses, and images that have become cliché both in popular culture and the sociological imagination posit challenges for the traditional fixed landscapes[8] on which our exploration of the death penalty and the divination of its fates has long concentrated.[9] These flows stand in varied and unpredictable relationships to local institutional practices and cultures, resulting in what Appadurai has called disjunctures, where the local manifestation of 'problems' can only be apprehended in contexts that are translocal.[10] The creation of 'communities of sentiment' transcends local political, cultural, and juridical orders. In this chapter, I explore the implications of these communities of sentiment – people who imagine and feel things together as 'communities of judgment'. Judgment on distant shores, with its attendant local moral and legal comfort procedures, invites and is made morally vulnerable to a translocal witnessing. The global spectacle of moral and legal comfort procedures in states that kill invites further consideration in this chapter.

Witnessing the act of punishment is inherently a comparative project, inviting contemplation between the general and the particular (the punishment of death and the death-worthiness of the person facing it), the seen and the unseen (what do we see, what is possible/appropriate to see when witnessing the punishment of death), the ideal and the real, the then and now. It is precisely this comparative contemplation that renders witnessing potentially subversive in a way that allows for what

5 Jennifer Culbert, *Dead Certainty: The Death Penalty and the Problem of Judgment* (Palo Alto: Stanford University Press, 2008).

6 Arjun Appadurai, *Modernity at Large: Cultural Dimensions of Globalization* (Minneapolis: University of Minnesota Press, 1996).

7 Arjun Appadurai, "Disjuncture and Difference in the Global Cultural Economy," *Theory, Culture, and Society* 7(2–3) (1990): 295 (short version). See also Benedict Anderson, *Imagined Communities: Reflections on the Origin and Spread of Nationalism* (London: Verso, 1991 [1983]).

8 Appadurai, *Modernity at Large*, 33–6.

9 Appadurai describes the world of flows in terms of a set of 'scapes': ethnoscapes (the movement of groups of people), mediascapes (electronic capabilities for disseminating information), technoscapes (the distribution of technology), financescapes (the transnational exchanges of economy and finance), and ideoscapes (the interaction of ideologies). See Appadurai, *Modernity at Large*.

10 Arjun Appadurai, "Disjuncture and Difference in the Global Cultural Economy" in *Media and Cultural Studies: Keywords*, Meenakshi Durham and Douglas M. Kellner (eds.), (Oxford: Blackwell Publishing, 2006).

Sarat has called 'new narrative possibilities' about the death penalty.[11] Nowhere is this global witnessing more evident than in transatlantic political, legal, and cultural exchanges regarding the practice of capital punishment. New media contexts and communities of sentiment/judgment have challenged established 'manners of viewing'[12] of capital punishment through an intimate proximity to the scene of punishment *and* judgment, with important implications for the future of penal sensibilities and, importantly for this volume, their attendant narratives/scripts for reforming action. 'Manners of viewing' of the death penalty have always embraced the theoretical and epistemological position of the spectator; from the curious and raucous crowds at the scenes of executions and lynchings described by Foucault and Gattrell, to the carefully choreographed and controlled (un)witnessing of 'non-event' executions in the United States in the twenty-first century.[13] More recently, the furtive and intimate viewing of executions (judicial and extrajudicial) on YouTube and other video-sharing websites, of 'extraordinary' executions such as that of Saddam Hussein[14] or routine executions of other states with more public protocols and practices of execution such as Iran and China, have brought the juridically local and particular into the everyday lives of global audiences.

There are two important anticipated consequences of these new media contexts. Firstly, they transform the very nature of witnessing through 'intimate proximity' to punishment and judgment, thus potentially transforming and challenging the cultural work of judgment and moral/legal certainty. Secondly, this intimate proximity recasts the scope and audience of local moral comfort and legal certainty procedures, especially at a time when new abolitionist strategies are gaining ground.[15] What are the prospects and consequences of this new cosmopolitan epistemological vantage point[16] for the 'witnessing of judgment' in capital punishment? This epistemological vantage point reveals and ponders the local fractured narratives of 'reasonable doubt' within the United States and its atavistic search for the potent and elusive moral, legal, and factual certainty. Narratives of error and the failure of mercy animate abolitionist witnessing in the United States as well as, somewhat less predictably, play a key role in the cultural lives of the death penalty after abolition in Europe. This

11 Austin Sarat (ed.), *When the State Kills: Capital Punishment and the American Condition* (Princeton: Princeton University Press, 2001), 250.

12 Wendy Lesser, *Pictures at an Execution: An Inquiry into the Subject of Murder* (Cambridge, MA: Harvard University Press, 1993).

13 See Mona Lynch, "The disposal of inmate #85271: Notes on a routine execution," *Studies in Law, Politics, and Society*, 20 (2000): 3–34, and Timothy Kaufman-Osborn, *From Noose to Needle: Capital Punishment and the Late Liberal State* (Ann Arbor: University of Michigan Press, 2002).

14 See Katherine Heard, Chapter 5 in this volume.

15 See discussions by Timothy Kaufman-Osborn, "A Critique of Contemporary Death Penalty Abolitionism," *Punishment & Society* 8 (2006): 365–83; Austin Sarat, "Conclusion: Toward New Abolitionism" in *When the State Kills*; and Austin Sarat, "Innocence, Error and the New Abolitionism: A Commentary," *Criminology & Public Policy* 4 (2006): 45–54.

16 See also Daniel Levy and Natan Sznaider, "Memory Unbound: The Holocaust and the Formation of Cosmopolitan Memory," *European Journal of Social Theory* 5 (2002): 87–106.

preoccupation with the aesthetics of justice, error, and mercy stand in somewhat uneasy juxtaposition with the the old abolitionism of the Council of Europe and European Union discourse on the death penalty, discussed by Fijalkowski and Yorke in this volume. As I have indicated elsewhere, the 'European' war against the death penalty may appear to have been won, but the cultural lives of the death penalty in Europe are only just beginning.[17]

THE WITNESSING OF JUDGMENT: PROXEMICS AND PENAL EXCESS

More than any other criminal sanction, the death penalty demands witnessing. Witnessing implies a state of consciousness beyond 'seeing' as a spectator and encompassing the idea of 'seeing through'.[18] The spectator in the case of the death penalty is haunted by the very impossibility of seeing and knowing. This haunting usually focuses on witnessing and knowing the moment of death, that final act in the state's judicial disposal of life.[19] Yet witnessing extends beyond seeing and knowing the final act of capital punishment and encompasses the witnessing of judgment. It is not only the performance of death that is being witnessed but also the performance of the act of judgment. As Culbert eloquently describes, the act of judgment displays an unknowability – a lacunae at the very heart of the process[20] that is reminiscent of the lacunae at the heart of knowing death in capital punishment. As I shall discuss further in this chapter, it is precisely at this void where aesthetics of moral certainty and admonitions of reasonable doubt and the 'decision not to decide'[21] stand for the judgment itself.

'Witnessing the death penalty' has remained a powerful metaphor to live by and imagine the judicial taking of life. Abolitionist campaigns have often used narratives of witnessing the legal process that leads to execution. European campaigns against the death penalty invite close and intimate witnessing of the day-to-day practices of capital punishment, arguing not only for the abolition of the death penalty in principle but also directing intervening in individual cases. Intimate witnessing in this process involves the continuous dialectic between the general and the particular. The reporting of capital punishment cases in the United States makes familiar reading in the European press, partly due to the political process and international politics of European abolitionism[22] and partly due to the cultural lives of the death penalty in Europe.[23] The case-by-case reporting elaborates on narratives

[17] See Girling, "European Identity. . . . "

[18] David Garland, "The Cultural Uses of Capital Punishment," *Punishment Society* 4 (2002): 459–87. See also Girling, "Looking Death in the Face."

[19] See Sarat, "To See or Not To See: On Televising Executions," in *When the State Kills*; Kaufman-Osborn, *From Noose to Needle*; and Girling, "Looking Death in the Face."

[20] Culbert, *Dead Certainty*.

[21] Ibid.

[22] Ian Manners and Ray Whitman, "The 'Difference Engine': Constructing and Representing the International Identity of the European Union," *Journal of European Public Policy* 10 (2003): 380–404.

[23] See Girling, "European Identity. . . . "

of mercy and error that animate the collective imagination of these communities of sentiment and judgment. Inasmuch as the death penalty enters European media discourse, it tends to do so through the spectacle of error and mercy. Regardless of the morality or the legality of the punishment itself, the act of judgment finds itself on the dock along with the punishment itself. European political identity has been understood to have embraced an old abolitionist strategy based on appeals to human rights and civilized sensibilities toward punishment (see Fijalkowski, Yorke, and Hammel in this volume).

Execution rituals are 'transgressive political rituals' that always hold the potential for multiple readings.[24] Acts of judgment are similarly transgressive, with the potential for multiple readings and witnessing that can provide moments of political and cultural epiphany. The judgment of death, similarly to the execution itself, opens up narrative possibilities for challenging the pretences of the liberal state.[25] As Garland describes in a different context, 'civilized sensibilities' in punishment depend on a series of prior social conditions that position and link the punisher to the punished: an effective state, secure disinterestedness on the part of key actors and groups, and a degree of solidarity that links punishers to punished.[26] These are what one could broadly describe as the *proxemics* of the act of judgment, which contribute to the ambient moral certainty and legitimacy of the judgment demanded by the spectator. In this context, I am using the term proxemics loosely to evoke not the physical distances between people as they interact, but moral spacing, the moral proximity and distance[27] in the act of judgment and its witnessing. They could be described as essential for the witness's and bystander's moral comfort and moral certainty.

THE DANCE OF NAKED VINDICTIVENESS: OF MIRRORS AND NIGHTMARES

Let us briefly explore an example of the impact of the proxemics of judgment and its global witnessing in Saddam Hussein's execution. Saddam Hussein's execution is often associated with the circulation of both official and furtive video recordings of his execution through a 'cameraphone witness':

> If you could film a nightmare it might look like what appeared on Google video last night... The sooty video showed the complete execution of Saddam Hussein. In the way of nightmare it was both startling and inevitable. Also in the way of a nightmare it was murky with gaps in the action and sudden moments of horrifying clarity.[28]

24 David Garland, "Penal Excess and Surplus Meaning: Public Torture Lynchings in Twentieth-Century America," *Law & Society Review* 39 (2005): 793–834.
25 See also Kaufman-Osborn, *From Noose to Needle*.
26 Garland, "Penal Excess . . . ," 830.
27 Zygmunt Bauman, *Postmodern Ethics* (Oxford: Blackwell, 1993).
28 "The Cameraphone Witness," *New York Times*, December 31, 2006.

Saddam Hussein was sentenced to death on November 5, 2006 by an Iraqi High Tribunal[29] and was hanged on Saturday, December 30, 2006. Whereas European Union countries welcomed the fact that Saddam was to be held responsible for his crimes, there was either silence on or condemnation of his death sentence and subsequent execution. The reaction from Europe predictably adopted the official discourse of old abolitionism. Politicians from EU countries expressed general approval of Saddam's conviction but they also tended to express their general opposition to and disapproval of a sentence of death.[30] The official EU statement was that 'establishing the truth and ensuring accountability for the crimes committed during the past regime will assist in furthering national reconciliation and dialogue in Iraq in the future. The EU opposes capital punishment in all cases and under all circumstances and it should not be carried out in this case either.'[31]

What kind of witnessing did Saddam's execution make possible?[32] 'Seeing' is not the same as witnessing. Witnessing involves something more than seeing – it is "seeing through." In that sense, did the broadcasting of images from Saddam Hussein's execution enable any form of witnessing of capital punishment in the United States and Europe? In some ways, it could be argued that Saddam Hussein's execution deployed atavistic technologies and symbols of state execution. Lethal injection (Kaufman-Osborn, in this volume) is now the preferred method of execution, but the gallows along with the electric chair remain potent cultural symbols of punishment by death.

The debate about how much of Saddam's execution should be broadcasted started in anticipation in the week preceding his execution. In the United States, among the main networks there was broad agreement that there should be some 'visual documentation' of Saddam Hussein's fate.[33] On Saturday, December 30, 2006,

29 For a discussion of the probity and procedure of Saddam Hussein's trial (i.e., whether it should have been subject to international justice or Iraqi justice), see Kevin Heller, "A Poisoned Chalice: The Substantive and Procedural Defects of the Iraqi High Tribunal," *Case Western Reserve Journal of International Law* 39 (2007). Available at SSRN: http://ssrn.com/abstract=939909.

30 "In Quotes: Reaction to Saddam sentence," *BBC News*, December 27, 2006. Available at: http://newsvote.bbc.co.uk/mpapps/pagetools/print/news.bbc.co.uk/1/hi/world/middle_east/6211761.stm.

31 "EU Presidency Statement on the Verdict of Saddam Hussein," http://www.europeanlawmonitor.org/News/Latest-EU-News/The-verdict-of-Saddam-Hussein.html.

32 In the United States, the constitutional debate about recording and broadcasting executions continues in view of the Supreme Court's reticence to allow cameras into the execution chamber. Sarat, "To See or Not to See," advocates shredding the veil and paradox of 'private' public executions in the United States by allowing the televising of executions. In this way, he claims, the American public will be required to take full responsibility for the acts that are carried out in their name.

33 "TV Executives Debate whether to Show Execution," *New York Times*, December 29, 2006. The article reports that NBC news was contemplating broadcasting "a wide shot of Saddam hanging." The producers discussed balancing the need of doing it with a "measure of taste" without "stand[ing] in the way of history" (ibid). Similar concerns were also expressed by ABC that cited "Taste and propriety are the two key guidelines" (ibid). In the United Kingdom, the main TV channels agonized over transmitting footage from the execution in their morning news programs.

Saddam Hussein was executed. As was widely predicted, the Iraqi government filmed and released an official video of the execution. The official video showed Saddam Hussein being led to the gallows but stopped short of showing the actual moment of execution. It was from this stock of images that the original broadcasting of the execution drew. The official video is a silent record of a solemn occasion. The enduring images and sounds of Saddam Hussein's execution reached a worldwide audience from a different source: the furtive filming through a mobile phone camera smuggled into the execution chamber – the 'cameraphone witness'.[34] This footage is in stark contrast to the stilted silent footage of the official release. It included audio in Arabic and lasted for just over two and a half minutes. Unlike the official video, it included images of Saddam Hussein's body swaying from the noose immediately after the execution. The violence of the moment of the taking of life remains offstage, hidden away from the restricted view of the mobile phone user. The moment of death happens off-camera and below the scaffold.

The footage is described as 'blocky, shadowy,' shot by a 'nervous witness.'[35] This is a furtive look – the witness nervously attempting to cover up his endeavor and in the process frequently appearing to turn the gaze of the camera away from the gallows. The conditions of filming mean that the source of lighting for the clandestine video is provided by the the official recording of the execution. The memoralization of the execution is ever present through a number of flashes that seek to memorialize the execution. The genre of the banal stands in sharp juxtaposition to the purported solemnity of the execution. It has been noted that the constraints of the medium give the televised view its degraded/furtive quality[36] What the unofficial video brings to our senses are the sounds of an execution. The silence of the official video gives an aura of solemnity that the 'furtive' video shatters – the sounds of the clandestine video reveal angry exchanges and taunts.

One can conjecture that had Saddam been hanged in a stadium, the execution may have been so alien as to preclude a 'witnessing' of executions in the United States or Europe. It would have been too exotic to enable meaningful witnessing of the event. One of the most potent features of this execution is that it used 'Western' tropes and props of justice and execution rituals just enough to hold a mirror of recognition to European and American audiences. It was the similarity to the historical 'Western' executions that enabled the witnessing, the seeing through. Saddam's execution has come to be marked as a botched one, enabling a witnessing that seems to be almost impossible for the carefully choreographed nonevent executions of the late liberal state. A botched execution is more usually described as one in which pain is revealed during the taking of life. Yet this was a story of a botched process and botched staging. This was a botched execution in which narratives of a perceived ineffectiveness of

34 "The Cameraphone Witness," *New York Times*, December 31, 2006.

35 See note 27 in this chapter.

36 Ibid.

the new Iraqi state and the sectarian nature of Iraqi politics took center stage. It was, however, the tipping point of a spectacle of revenge and sectarianism at the time of his execution and during his trial that marked the execution as botched.

The new mediascapes have been testing what has remained for the most part a theoretical debate on the impact of televising executions. More images from the whole execution process have been emerging from China, Iran, and North Korea in recent years – these images are easily accessible on the Internet but rarely enter public debate or attain the visibility achieved by Saddam Hussein's execution. One of the key arguments used by those supporting the broadcasting of executions is that televised executions would educate the public about capital punishment and its political and physical effects, opening new narrative possibilities in our conversations about the death penalty. Let us now explore the extent to which the intimate witnessing of Saddam Hussein's execution nurtured such narrative possibilities.

Despite repeated statements that the execution process was in line with Iraqi law in terms of the time elapsed between sentencing and execution and the conduct of the appeal process, there was still criticism in mainstream press, discussion groups, and the blogosphere of the 'unseemly' haste to execute Saddam – what many perceived to be indicative of the partiality and cursory nature of the process. Commentaries on Saddam Hussein's execution were generally prefaced by statements explaining that Saddam's actual guilt was not in question – what was in question was 'due process', which was politically paramount. The implication was that the staging of 'due process' had failed in this instance. The original and ongoing (see note 14) debate of whether Saddam ought to have been tried by the International Criminal Court or an Iraqi tribunal fueled a continuous comparison of the two different judicial settings and their staging of justice.[37] The courtroom drama of Saddam's trial was widely reported.[38] The trial, sentencing, and appeal process set in motion a reporting frame of incompetence, sectarianism, and farce. In that sense, the botched execution started before Saddam Hussein ever climbed the gallows. The lack of staging, the lack of control over the manner of viewing of this execution revealed for the media commentators a fumbling state, a state unable to control the execution. Reports focused on the 'disorderly' nature of execution and the tattered image of a government in control that was left behind. President Bush said 'felt like they fumbled the – particularly the Saddam Hussein – execution.'[39] Charles Krauthammer of the *Washington Post*, among many others, described the execution as a 'rushed, unholy mess'.[40] The haste between sentence and execution appeared to be particularly

37 Heller, "A Poisoned Chalice."

38 "Courtroom Chaos Halts Saddam Trial: Testifies For First Time, Encourages Iraqis To Resist Americans," CBS News, March 15, 2006. Available at http://www.cbsnews.com/stories/2006/03/15/iraq/main1404526.shtml.

39 "Bush: Saddam Hanging Botched," *USA Today*, January 17, 2007.

40 Charles Krauthammer, "The Hanging: Beyond Travesty," *Washington Post*, January 5, 2007.

vexing for U.S. commentators.[41] The trials and executions in Nuremberg were held up as an example of what a good processing of Saddam's death may have looked like, a successful holding at bay of the press, a single military photographer, destroyed negatives, cremated bodies quietly dumped.[42]

Those supporting the death penalty have often opposed the televising of executions,[43] fearing that any televised execution could not fail but make the inmate appear as the victim and therefore demanding undeserving pity. After all, at the particular moment of death, the life of a defenseless human being is taken. Saddam was suddenly placed as the victim of taunts, the victim of not being able to finish his prayers before he was dropped to his death.

Similar to the lynchings described by Garland (2005), Saddam's execution was marked by penal excess of vengeance and vindication, and a performance of restoration of the honor of the victims of his regime. This 'naked vindictiveness' was one of the features of the execution that twenty-first-century observers found most distasteful. In the aesthetics of the late liberal execution process, there is no place for displays of revenge.[44] What did twenty-first-century observers take to be the elements of revenge? Interestingly, the cues were not visual but auditory. It was the voices that appear to taunt Saddam with the name of one of his enemies whose son he had had killed.

'The world saw Saddam falling through the trap door, executed not in the name of a new and democratic Iraq, but in the name of Sadr, whose death squads have learned much from Saddam.'[45] The motive of revenge was read in the timing of the execution to coincide with a holiday for the Sunni population (from where Saddam had most of his supporters).

The overdetermination of vengeance in Saddam's execution directed our gaze toward the perpetrators of that death, the very people that the private 'disposal' process of execution effaces from the scene of punishment.[46] There was little danger that our gaze would have stayed firmly on the condemned. In fact, it is the perpetrators, their performance and their motives, that take center stage. Even the 'cameraphone witness' with the furtive, amateur, shaky footage cannot efface his presence as a partisan witness. The genre of home – or cameraphone – video keeps its maker behind the scene and out of sight but ever present.

The themes of sectarianism and partisanship were central in articulating what was perceived to be the 'penal excess' of Saddam's death. In some ways, the issue of pain, which has been seen as central in the management and staging of death by

41 "Iraq Probes Hussein Execution," CNN, January 2, 2007. Available at http://edition.cnn.com/2007/WORLD/meast/01/02/saddam.execution/index.html.

42 Norman J. W. Goda, "What Saddam's Botched Execution Means," History News Network, January 8, 2006. Available at http://hnn.us/articles/33747.html.

43 Philip Wiese, "Popcorn and Primetime vs. Protocol: An Examination of the Televised Execution Issue," *Ohio N.U. L. Rev.* 23 (1996): 257.

44 See Lynch, "The disposal of inmate #85271" and Kaufman-Osborn, *From Noose to Needle*.

45 Krauthammer, "The Hanging."

46 See footnote 44.

the late liberal state into a 'virtual non-event,'[47] is evaded even in the cameraphone video. The terror and pain of death does not receive much attention. Somehow the emotion to be effaced is not pain and terror but the 'unseemly', unashamedly vindictive staging of emotion on which the death takes place.

WITNESSING JUDGMENT: THE STAGING OF ERROR AND MERCY

Witnessing of the death penalty can also occur in the spectacle of the banal. This spectacle involves witnessing the exits and turns of some capital cases as they go through a legal and procedural labyrinth. The final possible spectacle in each of those cases is either the granting or withholding of mercy.

European campaigns against the death penalty concern themselves with the condemned at the final stages of their journey. As I have pointed out elsewhere, the condemned but not yet executed pose particular challenges and awkward juxtapositions in the narratives of the state.[48] They are, in Austin Sarat's words, 'suspended in a place between life and death: living, breathing, but with a rapidly closing horizon of possibility. Because everyone knows that their pleas for clemency most likely will be denied, they become rhetorical and political stand-ins for various of law's failures and symbols of martyred innocence, victims of legal incompetence, or of racial discrimination.'[49] He argues that these pardon tales are predominant cultural genres of communicating error in clemency petitions and involve narratives of 'You got the wrong man,' 'It ain't fair,' 'If you'd led my life you'd understand,' 'Accept my contrition, grant me mercy, spare my life,' and of 'the death penalty as a tool of racism.' The same conventions and narratives permeate the reporting of capital cases in the European press – each presenting a cautionary tale for the perils of judgment, of apprehending the wrong man,[50] of legal error, of mitigation, of the limits of mercy, and of racism.

The witnessing of judgment is important to different extents for both new and traditional abolitionism.[51] Traditional abolitionist arguments invoke the sanctity of life and continually point to the moral horror of a 'state that kills.' In the United States, traditional abolitionism elaborates on the inherent cruelty of punishment

47 See Kaufman-Osborn, *From Noose to Needle*.

48 Girling, "Looking Death in the Face."

49 Austin Sarat, "Memorialising Miscarriages of Justice: Clemency Petitions and the Killing State," in *When Law Fails: Making Sense of Miscarriages of Justice*, Charles Ogletree and Austin Sarat (eds.) (New York: New York University Press, 2009).

50 In European campaigns, the use of the term is much more open than 'the wrong man' focus of the innocence movement in the United States, reflecting some of the more subtle narratives of innocence and miscarriages of justice discussed by Carol Steiker and Jordan Steiker, "Seduction of Innocence: The Attraction and Limitations of the Focus on Innocence in Capital Punishment," *Journal of Criminal Law & Criminology* 95 (2005): 587.

51 The witnessing of judgment has a long history in the United States, especially in the so-called extrajudicial, lynch-mob executions. In those events, the quasi-judicial process was opened up to the spectator through the public apprehension and trial of the accused (see Garland, "Penal Excess . . . ").

by death that makes it incompatible with the Eighth Amendment's prohibition of cruel and unusual punishment. 'New abolitionism' began gaining prominence after what some considered to be its apotheosis in *Furman*, and by the late 1990s, this new discourse had successfully shifted the terms of the death penalty debate in the United States from questioning the morality and legitimacy of execution to the one in which minimizing the risk of error and safeguarding due process has become politically and juridically paramount. The choice (and shift) from traditional to new abolitionism has been presented as a pragmatic strategy aiming to dislocate some of the foreclosures of earlier debates. With new abolitionist arguments, one could be against the death penalty and not pass judgment on the moral positions of others – disrupting the impasse in what has been termed the U.S. culture wars, in which the death penalty debate had been situated so far.

Human rights organizations, such as Amnesty International, and other regional specifically anti-death penalty movements such as Together against the Death Penalty, World Coalition against the Death Penalty, Reprieve, and Hands off Cain have conceived their role vis-à-vis the death penalty as bearing witness to the practices of states that kill by providing information about the extent of the use of the sanction and problems in the practice, with the aim of turning bystanders into actors and putting pressure on states to act to limit or abolish the practice. The rise of new abolitionism in the United States, with its scrutiny of the processes of the machinery of death, has also brought a witnessing as 'seeing through' the process and the moment of judgment. Through the work of such organizations and the concerted effort of the EU and the Council of Europe, narratives of the wrongness of the death penalty and error and arbitrariness are deeply entwined in the regional message within the EU, but also for American audiences and policy makers.

The drama and spectacle of exoneration and error is central in sustaining abolitionist discourse and the work of European abolitionism. Inasmuch as European abolitionism can be said to be important to a European identity,[52] 'error' of 'fallibility' is also central. The emphasis on error and arbitrariness has become one of the recurrent motifs for reporting death penalty stories both in the United States and Europe and animates both new and old abolitionism. In this context, the witnessing of judgment in U.S. capital punishment occurs on the one hand at a national level embedded in new abolitionist strategies that seek to expose the problems and perils of American capital punishment, and on the other hand at an international level, where the spectacle of judgment is witnessed by an ostensibly abolitionist continent. The predicament of disjuncture is therefore at the heart of witnessing the ultimate punishment – the witnessing of judgment, both within the United States and in Europe, that 'throws into question and strips self evidence from [. . .] their own juridical experience.'[53]

52 Girling "European Identity. . . . "

53 Ewald (1986), cited in Adam Sitze, "Capital Punishment as a Problem for the Philosophy of Law," *CR: The New Centennial Review* 9.2 (2009): 221–70.

PROXEMICS OF JUDGMENT: THE HAUNTING OF ERROR

Contemplating the possibility of error and the moral and political consequences of 'wrong' execution and miscarriages of justice has produced what can be described as the 'haunting of error' for the act of judgment in capital punishment. The specter of error and the problem of mercy haunts both current U.S. retentionism and European abolitionism. Both narratives speak to the perils of judgment in capital punishment.

The problem of innocence and of the overproduction of death by the U.S. practice of capital punishment has put the issue of the standard of proof and its attendant moral comfort procedures in the limelight and at the heart of debates about the reform/retention or abolition of the death penalty. The search for a higher threshold of certainty beyond reasonable doubt has permeated both academic and popular debates. When the former governor of Illinois, George Ryan, introduced the moratorium on executions in Illinois that was to send shivers down the legal spines of executing states at the turn of the millennium, he said that the death penalty system was 'fraught with error and has come so close to the ultimate nightmare . . . Until I can be sure with *moral certainty* that no innocent man or woman is facing a lethal injection, no one will meet that fate.'[54] Governors of other states, such as Mitt Romney (Massachusetts) and Frank Keating (former Governor of Oklahoma), deliberated on raising the standard of proof in capital cases from 'proof beyond a reasonable doubt' to a 'moral certainty standard.'

The term 'beyond reasonable doubt' does not find comfort and sits uneasily in Supreme Court discourse and courtroom talk. It is forever begging and denied definition – an almost mystical concept in a world of clearly articulated legal talk. The term was reintroduced in the 1970s, but all tiers of courts have been reluctant to use a language that would provide a clear-cut definition for jurors. 'Moral certainty' rejoined the term 'reasonable doubt' in the 1990s,[55] when, after a series of cases, the Supreme Court decided to allow the term but again refused to define it. Yet despite its ambiguous and precarious legal position, 'moral certainty' has become part of the repertoire of appropriate responses to the overproduction of death and the problem of innocence in the American capital punishment system.

'Moral certainty' and 'reasonable doubt' have long been part and parcel of moral comfort procedures designed to alleviate the moral anxieties and moral peril of those who are averse and have most to lose from engaging in acts of judgment.[56] Even though the use of the term 'reasonable doubt' is often thought to be intended for the

[54] Mick Dumke, "Ryan Joins Death Penalty Fight, Seeks 'Moral Certainty'," The Chicago Reporter, January 2001. Available at http://www.chicagoreporter.com/index.php/c/Inside_Stories/d/2000_in_Review:_Ryna_Joins_Dealth_Penalty_Fight,_Seeks_'Moral_Certainty'.

[55] *Cage v. Louisiana*, 498 U.S. 39 (1990).

[56] James Q. Whitman, *The Origins of Reasonable Doubt: Theological Roots of the Criminal Trial* (New Haven: Yale Law Library Series in Legal History and Reference, 2008), 6.

protection of the innocent accused, James Q. Whitman shows that reasonable doubt was introduced in the late seventeenth and eighteenth centuries as a moral comfort procedure, a process of conscience by which jurors could make the decision for blood to be shed. According to Whitman reasonable doubt was 'designed to protect the souls of the jurors against damnation and was never intended to be used as a standard of proof.'[57] Eternal damnation would befall a juror who convicted an innocent defendant. So in fact the guilty verdict had risks for both the accused and the juror. The 'reasonable doubt' standard provided a way in which the jurors could safely convict 'as long as doubts about the guilt were not reasonable.'[58] Whitman attributes the confusion of the law over 'reasonable doubt' in the 'vestigial ambiguity' of the moral and evidential work of the doctrine of reasonable doubt. Whitman provides a useful discussion of the jurisprudential distinction between proof procedures and what he describes as *moral comfort procedures*: 'Proof procedures, as the name suggests, aim to achieve proof in cases of uncertainty. Moral comfort procedures, by contrast, aim to relieve the moral anxieties of persons who fear engaging in acts of judgment – persons such as early modern criminal jurors.'[59] I argue further in the chapter that in the age of uncertainty, the distinction between proof procedures and moral comfort procedures is more fragile than Whitman first suggests. Whitman, however, goes on to acknowledge the complexities of the relationship:

> The pursuit of the truth can always serve as a means of easing the sense of moral responsibility: If we can claim that our decision was dictated by "the truth," we can disclaim our personal responsibility for making it. We can say something like what the medieval church lawyers said about their highly rule-bound procedures: that *the law* made the decision. We can declare ourselves to be simple servants of the truth, rather than judges with undiluted moral responsibility.[60]

The American death penalty system operates through legal and administrative procedures that efface personal moral responsibility for decision makers and criminal justice actors throughout the process, but the discourse of moral responsibility in the face of error continues to haunt capital punishment.[61]

There are certain features of judgment in capital punishment that encourage, facilitate, and prolong the haunting of error and moral responsibility. Judgment in capital punishment may be well contained in discrete juridical moments/events (of the finding of guilt, of the death sentence, of the decision not to grant clemency, etc.). In the cultural lives of capital punishment, however, judgment is an unfinished, contested, and ongoing project that starts with the first report of the crime, and the

[57] Whitman, *The Origins of Reasonable Doubt*, 3.
[58] Ibid.
[59] Whitman, *The Origins of Reasonable Doubt*, 6.
[60] Whitman, *The Origins of Reasonable Doubt*, 20.
[61] See Kaufman-Osborn, *From Noose to Needle*, chapter 2 and Sarat, *When the State Kills*, chapters 4 and 5.

certainty of death only becomes unequivocal in the last few hours before execution. This places a different and more onerous set of demands on the moral comfort procedures of jurors, judges, and 'witnesses'. The endless iterative spectacle of judgment is not amenable to the moral comfort procedures of premodern jurors; moral responsibility cannot be effaced or evaded.

The jury of the modern capital trial has no illusions that it sits in 'final judgment', but can better be described as engaging in a decision not to decide,[62] first by relying on the 'gold standard' of DNA both during the trial and, equally importantly, as a fail-safe 'scientific comfort procedure' by which their decision, if erroneous, will remain reviewable should new DNA evidence come to light. It is illuminating that all proposals for a higher standard of proof in capital cases and for achieving a higher degree of certainty (including moral certainty) involve placing DNA evidence at the heart of 'proof procedures'. The reliance on DNA evidence seems to delimit moral risk in decision making. Secondly, the jury's decision not to decide relies on the perception of the role of clemency as the ultimate fail-safe of the American capital punishment system.[63]

James Q. Whitman argues that the current jury system does not engender 'meaningful moral qualms'.[64] Yet his account glosses over the second of the two stages of capital trials – the sentencing stage, which is arguably the most morally perilous stage. This is the most liminal stage of the trial process, in which the condemned stands between life and death. The pursuit of truth can evade moral responsibility, as we will see in further discussion, yet the sentencing stage of the trial ultimately has to determine whether the particular person (the person, not the truth of the events) before them is 'death-worthy' – deserves to die. This act of judgment in capital cases in the United States is reserved for 'death qualified' jurors – jurors who believe that the death penalty should and can be imposed. This could be arguably the only narrative of moral certainty in capital jury trials. In the face of jurors managing ambiguous instructions and contradictory evidence, the only certainty is that 'someone', 'somewhere', who has committed a certain offense, deserves to die. In the context of this contingent and complex evidence and jury instructions,[65] where the declaration of guilt becomes a 'symbolic act' in the expectation that every aspect of their decision both with regards to facts but also the death-worthiness is to be scrutinized and reviewed through procedural safeguards ensuring appeals, scientific evidence that may come to light after the trial, and finally through the exercise of a final judgment through executive clemency, the moral certainty of punishment by death never quite crosses the divide between the general and the particular.

62 Culbert, *Dead Certainty*.

63 Ibid.

64 Whitman, *The Origins of Reasonable Doubt*.

65 See Mona Lynch, "Stereotypes, Prejudice, and Death in Life-and-Death Decision Making" in *From Lynch Mobs to the Killing States*, Charles Ogletree and Austin Sarat, eds. (New York: New York University Press, 2006) for an account of the ambiguous contexts in which jury decision making takes place.

The maze of appeals, science, and executive clemency in modern capital cases means that juries are charged with the responsibility of making a declaration of 'death-worthiness', not deciding death. Arguably the spectator, witness, and bystander have a similar role in the act of judgment. The spectator and bystander, however, are not 'death qualified', thus opening up narratives of moral responsibility that can challenge state killing and sustain the conditionality of that first declaration of death-worthiness. The routine witnessing of judgment sets a train of events that appear to confirm the conditionality and reversibility of judgment.

Robert Weisberg argues that the margins of error are situated within a "boundary dispute" between law and justice.[66] Judgment in capital punishment, with its moralized rhetoric, creates particular challenges for this boundary dispute for the system, its lay actors, and its lay observers. Weisberg's discussion shows that there is a third party in this boundary dispute, which stands in an equally liminal relationship to both justice and law, and this is the new category of unassailable 'amoral' fact in the form of DNA evidence that 'categorically' exonerates the wrongly or about to be convicted. Between legal certainty and moral certainty lies the spectrum of scientific 'unassailable certainty.'[67]

The 'haunting of error' described earlier is qualitatively different from the concerns with moral certainty/reasonable doubt of premodern jurors. The haunting of error in premodern capital trials was on the conscience of the jury and their soul. In the practice of capital trials in the United States in the twentieth and twenty-first centuries, there are temporal and system spectra in the haunting of error. The first relates to the moment of judgment – an extended moment that, beyond its juridical life, begins with the reporting of a case/crime and ends with the executive clemency/mercy or execution. Through this journey, there is an 'unfinished', contingent, and inherently unknowable element to the work of judgment, which creates and sustains a lacunae of moral responsibility. The haunting of error thus becomes not one of moral responsibility, but an actuarial concern. Error here is not a moral problem that can be attached to individual decision makers – it is a system-haunting problem. Judgment itself cannot be erroneous until it is final. The judgment could have been reversed at any stage of the sentencing process (and subsequently at the appeals stage) by 'scientific evidence'. Finality of judgment comes in the face of executive clemency that in itself is not framed as a judgment but as a decision to allow the original judgment of the 'death-worthiness' of a particular defendant to stick.[68] The critical moment of judgment is not the decision to deprive of life, but a decision not to grant mercy. This is the point at which responsibility for the imminent execution can be at its most visible and its most corporeal, and also the point at which responsibility and the proxemics of judgment can be witnessed.

66 Robert Weisberg "Margins of Error" in *When the Law Fails*, 71.

67 Ibid.

68 See Culbert, *Dead Certainty*, chapter 6.

MORAL COMFORT IN AN AGE OF UNCERTAINTY

'Miscarriages of justice' are key events in the witnessing of judgment. It has been argued that miscarriages-of-justice narratives are narratives about the failure of law rather than the failure of judgment.[69] However, as I have discussed earlier, moral responsibility cannot be unequivocally abrogated, and moral comfort procedures have global as well as local audiences. Ogletree and Sarat point out that when the law fails, 'it is not the initial failure but the story that is told of the nation's response.'[70] It is to these stories that I turn to now.

Zygmunt Bauman argues that morality involves (individual) responsibility toward the other, which is evidenced by empathy and commitment.[71] Unconditionality is essential to his idea of responsibility – responsibility in Bauman's view is not a contract; it cannot be abrogated, alleviated, or in this case, be completely subsumed under moral comfort procedures. The decision not to decide in capital cases exposes the fault lines in the aesthetics of moral responsibility and the fragility of moral comfort procedures, and draws attention to the final act of judgment (the granting/denial of clemency) from which there are no easy exit rules of moral responsibility, and where the moral and the political stand in uneasy juxtaposition. Modernity has blunted moral sensibilities, and in modernity, humankind has exchanged 'moral struggle for the seductive sureness of ethical codes' thus 'becom(ing) morally indifferent.'[72] The jurors, in ceding their moral responsibility to the state, are engaging in the defining moral trade-off of modernity – 'accepting regulation in place of moral choice.'[73] Yet moral responsibility and the language of morality and ethical decision making still haunts the practice of capital punishment[74]: Thurschwell notes that the law of capital punishment cannot escape the struck-by-the-vocabulary of moral judgment and moral responsibility. There is, he argues, a 'truly awesome responsibility of decreeing death for a fellow human,'[75] and no amount of regulation, or decision not to decide, and faith in science as the final arbiter can satisfy the aesthetics of responsibility from the witnessing of judgment. In the spectacle of fragmented and challenged moral comfort procedures and the unspeakability of reasonable doubt, we are faced with modernity's challenge – the 'excruciating difficulty of being moral.'[76]

The differences and unresolved tensions between traditional and new abolitionist responses to the possibility of error can be conceptualized along the distinction

[69] See Ogletree and Sarat, *When Law Fails*.

[70] Ibid., 7.

[71] Bauman, *Postmodern Ethics*.

[72] Carole Smith, "The Sequestration of Experience: Rights Talk and Moral Thinking in 'Late Modernity'," *Sociology* 36 (2002): 43–66, 44.

[73] Ibid.

[74] Adam Thurschwell, "Ethical Exception: Capital Punishment and the Figure of Sovereignty," *South Atlantic Quarterly* 107 (2008): 571.

[75] Ibid.

[76] Bauman, *Postmodern Ethics*.

between risk and uncertainty.[77] The peril of judgment for new abolitionism is the risk entailed in the regulation of capital punishment. The logic of the risk society is paramount here, acknowledging and regulating the operational imperfections of complex systems and assessing their threat to state legitimacy. Miscarriages of justice are in this respect system risks that can be calculated and weighed against other risks[78] and most importantly accepted for what they are without moral consequences on individual judges/juries. Ewick points out that the term 'miscarriage of justice' 'connotes a failing of monumental scale . . . an event – a decision, a verdict, an act – that is exceptional, a singular betrayal of the established ideals and practices of law'.[79] In European reporting, miscarriages of justice are unexceptional, routine, but at the same time emblematic of why capital punishment cannot be reinstated.[80] Uncertainty of outcome does not lend itself to actuarial concerns.

For old abolitionism, these are not regulation dilemmas but moral perils. One of the central narratives of European abolitionism is the lesson that 'Europe' has learned from World War II – of the impossibility of moral certainty in the exercise of state power when the unimaginable becomes real. This is the narrative that permeates the abolitionist identity of Europe – lessons from her past, frequently recounted, that do not so much speak of risk and its regulation as of the inherent uncertainty in the regulation of unfettered power exposed by World War II. The intimate witnessing of judgment helps to shore up support and to ensure through narratives of moral (un)certainty and the fragility of moral comfort procedures that the real from across the Atlantic and across the globe becomes unimaginable. The problem of judgment lies at the heart of capital punishment; the decision not to decide may provide actuarial comfort but does not satiate the aesthetics and proxemics of moral certainty for the ever more intimate and ever relentless witnessing of judgment. A relentless witnessing that, paraphrasing one of the commentaries on Saddam Hussein's execution:

> In the way of nightmare it [is] both startling and inevitable. Also in the way of a nightmare it [is] murky with gaps in the action and sudden moments of horrifying clarity.[81]

77 Pat O'Malley, *Risk, Uncertainty and Government* (London: Glasshouse Press, 2004).

78 Discussing the risk of error as a system risk situates it within an economy of risks that states routinely manage. For an intriguing recent exchange, see the exchange between Steiker (2005) and Sustein and Vermuille (2005) about the life-for-life trade-off of capital punishment, assuming both executions of innocent defendants and a deterrent effect: the trade-off of the risk of executing innocent defendants or the risk of more deaths of innocent victims.

79 Patricia Ewick "The Scale of Injustice," in *When the Law Fails*, 303.

80 One of the first acts of the Criminal Cases Review Commission in the United Kingdom was to review a number of cases involving capital cases (executed in the 1950s and 1960s) and reverse their convictions. This work was seen as a symbolic declaration of the importance of miscarriages of justice to capital cases.

81 "The Cameraphone Witness," *New York Times*, December 31, 2006.

5

Unframing the Death Penalty

Transatlantic Discourse on the Possibility of Abolition and the Execution of Saddam Hussein

Kathryn A. Heard

INTRODUCTION: AN EXECUTION WORTH A THOUSAND WORDS

In the early morning hours of December 30, 2006, Saddam Hussein was executed by hanging in the depths of an Iraqi military bunker. Unbeknown to the officials orchestrating the execution, witnesses smuggled video and camera phones into the makeshift death chamber. Within several hours of Hussein's last breath, images of his execution flooded popular media channels; the resulting photographs and videos ranged in scope from documenting the precise moment at which the noose was placed around Hussein's neck (see Figure 5.1) to a full digital account of his execution.[1] Reactions to his execution were swift and unequivocal. American President George W. Bush hailed the news of Hussein's death as an "important milestone on Iraq's course to becoming a democracy that can govern, sustain, and defend itself."[2] Across the Atlantic, European officials on both a supranational and local level roundly condemned the execution. European Commissioner for Development and Humanitarian Aid Louis Michel declared: "One cannot fight barbarism with means that are equally barbaric. The death penalty is not compatible with democracy."[3] Even British officials, representing an administration that had been a staunch ally of the United States during the invasion and subsequent liberation of Iraq, criticized the use of capital punishment. British Foreign Secretary Margaret Beckett, in a statement released by Downing Street, stressed that her

[1] Saddam Hussein's execution can be viewed in total at: http://www.youtube.com/watch?v=AfJrZSRj-fE. Please understand that this video contains graphic footage, and YouTube advises viewer discretion.

[2] White House Press Conference (December 30, 2006). As quoted in: Tariq Ali, "Lynched by the Mob," *The Guardian (UK)*, December 30, 2006. This article can be found at: http://www.guardian.co.uk/commentisfree/2006/dec/30/post852 (accessed January 6, 2007).

[3] "Hanging of Saddam 'Barbaric' – Top EU Official," *AlertNet: Alerting Humanitarians to Emergencies (Reuters)*, December 30, 2006. It can be found electronically at: http://www.alertnet.org/thenews/newsdesk/L30630950.htm (accessed January 6, 2007).

FIGURE 5.1. The execution of Saddam Hussein, December 30, 2006.[4]

government "did not support the use of the death penalty in Iraq or anywhere else."[5]

These statements are compelling for several reasons. At once both declarative and imperative, they capture a set of assumptions and anxieties about the contemporary application of and campaign against the death penalty. The competing qualifications of capital punishment as barbaric and as essential for democracy offered by Commissioner Michel and President Bush, respectively, are of particular interest: They signal a growing ideological divergence between the European Union and the United States on what can rightly be construed as justice. In the discerning eyes of European officials, the use of capital punishment in Iraq – although condoned by the newly installed post-Hussein government – represents a troubling and pervasive American influence that threatens the global advancement of civilization. Indeed, Michel's words imply that the complete and total abolition of capital punishment is necessary to achieve fully the democratic ideals associated with European norms of civilization: liberty, equality, and the unassailable right to life. The appeal to such rhetoric, however, cannot be confined solely to the European Union and its representatives. President Bush invokes the same liberal principles, albeit to a much

[4] The image of Hussein's execution is available at: http://www.guardian.co.uk/news/blog/2006/dec/30/inpicturesrea (accessed January 6, 2007).

[5] "Hanging of Saddam 'Barbaric' – Top EU Official."

different end. Not only does he regard the execution of Hussein as a necessary component for the successful completion of the American overseas mission, but he also determines that it serves as a catalyst for Iraq's political transformation and progression toward eventual self-governance. When these statements are taken together, it is possible to see that the furor surrounding Saddam Hussein's execution is twofold: It is both a response to the death of a dictator renowned for his proclivity toward genocide and a site in which discourse over the continued legitimacy of capital punishment as a method of democratic governance is reproduced, demarcated, and reinforced. The latter aspect informs this chapter.

Narrowly construed, the purpose of this chapter is to use the rhetoric generated by the execution of Saddam Hussein as a point of departure to examine if, and how, the language of democracy and civilization provides an effective means of establishing a transatlantic consensus on the viability of abolition.[6] It questions: How do Commissioner Michel and President Bush's statements reveal broader cultural attitudes regarding the persistence of the death penalty and, more specifically, its efficacy as a form of punishment? Furthermore, how does the European belief in abolition as a particularly "European" trait influence the possibility of America's own eventual achievement of the eradication of the death penalty? And finally, if the ideals of democracy and civilization do fail – as I contend they indeed will – to provide an adequate forum for discourse on the possibilities of abolition, what recourse remains for those committed to anti-death penalty policies?

In exploring these questions, this chapter is loosely divided into three parts. The first part examines in more depth the responses to the photographs offered by each government. Drawing from the notion of framing advanced by Judith Butler, I argue that both the European Union (as the figurehead of the European nations in the American-led Coalition of the Willing) and the United States read the photograph in Figure 5.1 as a threat to the established meaning and narrative of the war. This reading of the image, I insist, was necessitated primarily because of the unprecedented and unexpected nature of what it depicted; to mitigate the image's perceived threat, engagement by both Commissioner Michel and President Bush with the troubling aspects of the photograph would be needed. The second part of this chapter expands on this argument by linking the concept of framing to that of performativity. It traces both Europe and America's contentious relationship with the death penalty, deploying performativity as a means by which to develop a more nuanced understanding of what the rhetoric of abolition and retention have come to constitute for each. The third and concluding section of this chapter contends that

[6] Austin Sarat and Christian Boulanger, "Putting Culture into the Picture" in *The Cultural Lives of Capital Punishment: Comparative Perspectives*, eds. Austin Sarat and Christian Boulanger (Stanford: Stanford University Press, 2005), 34. Following the argument made by Sarat and Boulanger, I understand "abolition," "abolitionist," and "abolitionism" to mean the complete eradication of capital punishment. In contrast, "retention," "retentionist," and "retentionism" refers to ideas which "support the legal institution of capital punishment and countries where it is still practiced."

contemporary transatlantic discourse on capital punishment, and its heavy reliance on terms associated with democracy, barbarism, and civilization, can be understood as one means by which Europe and the United States attempt to understand themselves and their relationship with capital punishment. It argues that what is important about the execution of Saddam Hussein and the ensuing reactions is not whether the execution was indeed barbaric, nor whether it represented a substantial step toward or away from the development of a free-standing Iraqi democracy. Rather, what is important are the multiple ways in which hierarchical language was deployed as a means to structure and order the actions of individual nations, a practice that drastically endangers the project of global abolition through the misunderstanding and misconception of mutually employed terms. I argue that one way forward from such a discursive bind is to refocus on the image with which we began and the very elements that prompted such a political kerfuffle; indeed, by isolating the portions of the image that represented a threat to the stability of contemporary capital punishment dialogue, it might – just might – be possible to move away from the inadequacy of its current vocabulary and toward a new, unframed vision of abolition.

TECHNOLOGIES OF WAR: PHOTOGRAPHY, EMBEDDING, AND THE DISRUPTIVE POSSIBILITIES OF NEW MEDIA

To understand precisely why Commissioner Michel and President Bush's words have significant implications for the study of abolition, it is first necessary to clarify the underlying concepts and ideas central to this chapter. To this end, I suggest we turn our attention to two fundamental precepts: first, to the power of photographs to contain and constrain meaning; and second, to how responses to an image deemed "deviant" can be considered an attempt to realign and reorient its contents to fit more concretely within a given socio-political context. Indeed, it is possible to ask: What qualities inherent to the photograph were judged to be so intrinsically troublesome that pronouncements of barbarism, civilization, and democracy were considered not only useful, but necessary for its interpretation? The answers to this question are complex; however, by examining in further detail the politics of photographs, frames, and the war, it will be easier to see just how a clandestine photograph captured in the heart of the Middle East has everything to do with the possibility of abolition.

Simply stated, the photograph capturing Hussein's execution – to paraphrase Timothy Kaufman-Osborn's reading of the photographs documenting the torture of Iraqi prisoners of war at Abu Ghraib[7] – does not speak for itself. Photographs, argues Susan Sontag, exist within a complex field of historical, social, and ideological meanings, such that the images are not merely representative (but also not wholly interpretative) of the actions and persons they contain.[8] Images like the one

[7] Timothy Kaufman-Osborn, "Gender Trouble at Abu Ghraib?" *Gender & Politics* 1 (2005), 599.

[8] Susan Sontag, *Regarding the Pain of Others* (New York: Farrar, Straus, and Giroux, 2003), 26.

reproduced in Figure 5.1 provide their viewers with a visual frame that brings them closer to the "human cost of war, famine, and destruction in places that may be distant both geographically and culturally."[9] In doing so, photographs convey affect; that is to say, they require that the viewers engage in acts of translation such that they acquire meaning within their own cultural or political consciousness. But what entails an act of translation? For Sontag, it can be as straightforward as the caption accompanying a photograph in a newspaper or a more intricate written exegesis in a periodical; what remains the same in each instance, though, is the presence of human narratives to make sense of a discrete and atomic image.[10] Under this interpretation, photographs alone do not have the power to incite political transformation because they are considered naturally momentary, but once situated within a specific cultural and political context through an affective narrative, they acquire the potential to evoke a moral or ethical response and lay the "tracks for how important conflicts are judged and remembered."[11]

Sontag's insistence that photographic images alone have no meaningful capacity to motivate their viewers to political action due to their noninterpretative nature and reliance on human narratives does not adequately account for the sheer scale of the political furor following Hussein's execution. This is not to say that the image of his execution does not require interpretation and translation (as it very well does, as will be seen from further discussion), but rather to suggest that the image *itself* is not nearly as innocuous as Sontag would make it seem. In her most recent work, *Frames of War*, Judith Butler takes up Sontag's notion that photographic images provide visual frames that bring the viewer close to distant – and potentially troubling – subject matter. However, unlike Sontag's belief that such images only take on meaning when interpreted within the viewer's own cultural and political setting, Butler determines that photographs themselves actively participate in the viewer's understanding of the subject matter by virtue of delimiting what is knowable, what is true, and what can be seen. She writes:

> We do not have to be supplied with a caption or a narrative in order to understand that a political background is being explicitly formulated and renewed through and by the frame, that the frame only functions not only as a boundary to the image, but as structuring the image itself. If the image in turn structures how we register reality, then it is bound up with the interpretative scene in which we operate. The question for war photography thus concerns not only what it shows, but how it shows what it shows.[12]

On this reading, photographs produced under the conditions of war are by no means benign. The photographer, the state, the subject, and even the angle of the camera

9 Judith Butler, *Frames of War: When Is Life Grievable?* (New York: Verso, 2009), 68.

10 Sontag, *Regarding the Pain of Others*, 83.

11 Susan Sontag, "Regarding the Torture of Others: Notes on What Has Been Done – and Why – to Prisoners, by Americans," *The New York Times Sunday Magazine* (May 23, 2004), 25.

12 Butler, *Frames of War*, 71.

itself subtly shape and manipulate the viewer's field of vision. For Butler, what is included is as important as what is excluded, just as the photographer's political sympathies are as important as her employer's. The frame, once the photograph reaches the public eye, is no longer visible and, accordingly, imparts the appearance of neutral observation to the viewer; this perceived appearance obliquely structures the viewer's perceptions of and reactions to the image's subject. As a result, the photographic image is not simply waiting for the interpretative assistance provided by narratives á la Sontag, but rather engages in interpretation even *before* being exposed to film, etched on a digital memory card, or viewed by a member of the public.

The heavy hand frames have in our interpretation of certain events is well illustrated by the role of the media in the second Iraq war – the setting of this chapter's inquiry. Throughout the invasion and later occupation of Iraq, the Bush administration tightly controlled the release of any media even tenuously war-related. Embedding, a Department of Defense-sponsored program that enabled journalists to report from the frontlines of battle due to their strategic placement within military convoys, defined precise ground rules as to what was considered acceptable, and thus distributable, news. An embedded journalist "traveled only on certain transports, looked at certain scenes, and related home images and narratives of only certain kinds of actions."[13] The Embedment Manual issued by the Department of Defense exemplifies this perspective perfectly, as members of the media corps in Iraq were to be briefed "in advance about what information is sensitive and what the parameters are for covering this type of [classified] information."[14] Furthermore, if a journalist encountered potentially sensitive information while in the field and wished to include it in her report, "the commander [might have] offered access to it if the reporter agreed to a security review of their [sic] coverage or asked [the reporter] to remove that information."[15] The regulation of what could be reported extended so far as to mandate that the bodies of the injured and dead soldiers (including the shrouded American coffins returning home from abroad) were not to be photographed for fear of undermining popular support for the war. Ultimately, embedded reporting provided the Department of Defense with the means of controlling the greater narrative scope of the second Iraq war; indeed, it was able to deploy the power of the state to promote a particular photographic interpretation by purposefully crafting the appearance of objectivity and reality in the work released by embedded reporters.[16] Iraq was, for the viewing publics of the United States and

[13] Butler, *Frames of War*, 64.

[14] "Embedment Manual" in *Embedded: The Media at War in Iraq*, Bill Katovsky and Timothy Carlson (Guilford, CT: The Lyons Press, 2003), 401–417. The full text of the manual can also be found at: http://www.concernedjournalists.org/ground-rules-embedded-reporters-iraq (accessed February 20, 2010).

[15] Katovsky and Carlson, "Embedment Manual," 407.

[16] Here, it is important to note that embedded reporters traveling with American military convoys were *not* always from the United States because it broadens the scope and impact of the frames discussed above. When embedment first began, the media corps was indeed comprised mostly of selected and respected newspaper and television reporters from the United States. Many – if not most – other

the European Union, intended to be a carefully controlled and highly sanitized mission.

Put bluntly, the image of Hussein's execution followed neither the prescription for wartime reporting nor the general rules elucidated earlier by Butler for the control of photographic affect. Taken not by members of the embedded media corps, but rather by a seemingly chaotic group of Iraqi witnesses wielding camera phones, the image transgressed and disregarded the frames considered by the Department of Defense to be necessary for the maintenance of the war's meaning writ large. Audiences in both America and the European Union saw almost immediately the implications of the invasion of Iraq: The introduction (or, perhaps, continuation) of American practices like capital punishment,[17] rowdy crowds clamoring for the "spectacle" of execution that has rarely been seen in Western countries since the nineteenth century, and the very real cost the war had on sentient bodies. Stated differently, in place of the previous images of camouflaged patrols bloodlessly securing the entrances to key cities and outposts, viewers instead found pictures and videos depicting the noose around Hussein's neck and the long arms of unknown Iraqis reaching out to adjust it. Furthermore, the accompanying cellular phone video footage[18] revealed that the moments before Hussein's execution were quite hostile; the guards charged with keeping order in the death chamber instead disrupted it, shouting Shiite militia slogans to the Sunni Saddam.[19] When witnessed this way,

nations did not provide embedment "services" for their reporters. Furthermore, these "other nations" were primarily European in character because the nations of Europe represented the second-largest majority of coalition troops after the United States. These journalists (termed "unilaterals" by the United States) were welcome to travel to Iraq independently, but they had to provide for their own security detail and transportation once in the country. Traveling without the aid of sanctioned military convoys yielded wartime images that did not have to be approved by the Department of Defense, but as the invasion escalated and nonmilitary movement across Iraq became increasingly risky, more and more unilaterals traded journalistic freedom for the relative safety offered by the embedment corps; ultimately, this meant that nations like Britain and Germany – close allies of the United States following the events of September 11, 2001 – gained a meaningful way of controlling their own narrative and continued support of the Iraq war. Consequently, the vast majority of the images emerging from Iraq during the invasion and occupation stages were the result of embedding and subject to censure, regardless of the reporter's initial country of origin or official affiliation with the American Department of Defense.

17 In Saddam Hussein's Iraq, executions were deployed as a means by which to suppress political dissent. Indeed, at least 114 crimes carried the sentences of the death penalty. After the invasion of Iraq, however, U.S. administrator L. Paul Bremer discontinued the practice, stating that "the former regime used certain provisions of the penal code as a means of oppression, in violation of internationally acknowledged human rights." In May 2005, capital punishment was reinstated under American supervision for a smaller set of crimes – and, as was widely believed, to prepare for the execution of Hussein. For more, see: Jonathan Finer and Naseer Nouri, "Capital Punishment Returns to Iraq: Public Welcomes Practice Suspended After U.S. Invasion," *The Washington Post*, May 26, 2005. This article can be found electronically at: http://www.washingtonpost.com/wp-dyn/content/article/2005/05/25/AR2005052501970.html (accessed September 11, 2010).

18 See *supra* footnote 2.

19 Sabrina Tavernise, "For Sunnis, Dictator's Degrading End Signals Ominous Dawn for the New Iraq," *The New York Times*, January 1, 2007. This article can be found electronically at: http://www.nytimes

the image of Hussein's execution appears to conform not to the controlled frames of peacekeeping and occupation put forth by the embedded reporters traveling with Western military forces, but rather to historical photographs documenting vigilante lynchings in the Jim Crow-era American South – lynchings whose modern connotations of lawlessness and untempered violence[20] are very nearly the precise opposite of the narrative desired.

In this instance, the photograph documenting Hussein's execution acts as an *unframed image*[21] – that is, an image that makes vulnerable the continued and unchallenged operation of the dominant frame. With the weakening of the dominant frame, discrete individuals now had unrestricted visual access to the manifest consequences of the war's larger political aims, as well as to the more specific penal tactics deployed in the realization of such goals. As such, the post-execution conditions were set, depending upon the cultural and political contexts in which the image was received, for "astonishment, outrage, revulsion, admiration, and discovery."[22] The varying affects that an unframed image may elicit from its viewers, argues Butler, both call into question a "taken-for-granted reality" *and* expose the "orchestrating designs of the authority that sought to control the [original] frame."[23] Thus, if we take seriously the notions of framed and unframed images, we see that the United States and the European contingent of the Coalition of the Willing are placed in a tricky rhetorical situation: To prevent the larger narrative of the Iraqi enterprise from collapse, they must bring the unframed image back into proper affective alignment, but to do so, each government must first engage with the image's subject – Hussein's imminent expiration on the gallows – in such a way as to render it sensible, and thus a legitimate or illegitimate consequence of the war's objectives, to its respective audiences. In short, for both the United States and the European Union, an ex post facto, culturally specific frame was needed.

It is at this point, with the invocation of an ex post facto frame to contain and control an unframed image, that a pause for further elaboration is needed. This chapter's appeal to the notion of an unframed image may unwittingly imply that the image of Hussein's execution lacked any serious affective potential prior to the attempts made by Western governments to lend it interpretative stability, and that, once stabilized, the image is evacuated of its transformative force and the narrative continuity of the

.com/2007/01/01/world/middleeast/01sunnis.html?pagewanted=1&ei=5088&en=9a4812fde9db44e5&ex=1325307600&partner=rssnyt&emc=rss (accessed May 29, 2010).

20 Amy Wood, *Lynching and Spectacle: Witnessing Racial Violence in American, 1890–1940* (Chapel Hill: University of North Carolina Press, 2009), 2.

21 For the remainder of this chapter, I will use the term "unframed" to refer to any image that does not conform to or represent a dominant mode of interpretation. In this instance, the image of Saddam Hussein's execution is "unframed" because it does not adhere to the policies mandated by the Department of Defense's Embedment Manual and, writ largely, the intended war narratives of the United States and its allies.

22 Butler, *Frames of War*, 11.

23 Butler, *Frames of War*, 12.

Iraq war soldiers on unscathed. This vein of argumentation, however, runs the risk of throwing out the baby with the bathwater by failing to account for the uniquely disruptive nature of the photograph itself; indeed, I want to suggest that what is so theoretically enticing about the statements made by President Bush and Commissioner Michel are the ways in which they seek to make uncontestable an image that is meaningfully and perpetually contested – and what is elided or valorized in their respective processes. As established earlier, an unframed image is an image that breaks from and challenges existing and dominant narratives. What is, however, particularly compelling about the unframed image of Hussein's death is that it does not mandate or elicit a particular response from its viewers because it occupies "no single time and no specific space."[24] Put in more concrete terms, the use of an officially unsanctioned recording medium (cellular phone technology) to capture Hussein's execution and the viral channels (social networking sites like Facebook and YouTube) through which it was subsequently distributed guaranteed that the image was "shown again and again, transposed from context to context."[25] Its sheer mobility ensured not only that it would be successively framed and reframed through private and non-state-mediated encounters with the photograph, but that this subaltern witnessing would also, perhaps negatively, condition the possibility of a single public interpretation like that encouraged by wartime embedding. As such, what I term an ex post facto frame is then the scramble made by American and European governments to impose interpretative boundaries on an image that is, at its core, narratively dislocated.

The importance of this dislocation for the study of abolition cannot be underestimated. Indeed, Hussein's execution temporarily hijacked the staid and cohesive flow of transatlantic war reporting and left in its wake the imprint of a hastily constructed gallows and interpretative dissonance. It is here, in the penumbra created by the combined and related influences of dissonance and dislocation, that we can at long last begin to see how the unframed image's depiction of the death penalty – and the ensuing responses offered to it – reveals much about the prospects for its eventual eradication.[26] It is now possible to ask: How do the opposing attempts to settle the meaning of the unframed image by American and European authorities demonstrate particular political or cultural convictions relating to the legitimacy of the death penalty as a means of dispensing justice? Furthermore, how are we to understand the discrepancy between their statements, with President Bush appealing to capital punishment's supposedly democratizing effect and Commissioner Michel decrying its presence as evidence of society's barbarism, if both ultimately remain committed to the war's broader political aims? Finally, and most critically,

[24] Butler, *Frames of War*, 78.
[25] Butler, *Frames of War*, 78.
[26] To paraphrase the original title of this project.

what precisely do these statements, borne from a geographically distant and unexpectedly high profile event, *do* for us as transatlantic abolitionists? To take the initial step toward answering these questions, let us (albeit temporarily) leave behind photographs and turn our attention to the prescriptive power of words. In doing so, we come to the principle objective of this chapter: To understand how the responses offered to the dislocated image of Hussein's execution are the products of particular discursive histories – histories that are seemingly rooted in the supposition that the transatlantic experiences of capital punishment have been, and will continue to be, meaningfully divergent.

THE REFRAMING POWER OF PERFORMATIVE SPEECH AND THE CONVENTIONS OF CAPITAL PUNISHMENT

Performance Theory

Certain configurations of words, argues J.L. Austin, possess the performative power to "accomplish a deed through the very act of their enunciation." They may at differing times, for example, inflict bodliy injury, render a marriage binding or dissolved, or instigate war. In this sense, words – when ordered correctly and situated in the appropriate context – harbor a productive capacity; that is, they differentiate, variegate, consolidate, and, ultimately, totalize specific social, cultural, and political norms in the pursuit of some end.[27] To locate how words acquire such a constitutive character, Austin directs our theoretical attention toward "total speech situations"[28]; examining the confluence of locutionary, perlocutionary, and illocutionary acts in speech, he argues, will illuminate how words garner the discursive power to impart a new social reality purely through their articulation. Understanding the ways in which these modes of speech operate and overlap provides the tools with which it will be possible to dissect the statements offered by Commissioner Michel and President Bush following Hussein's execution and the dissemination of the unframed image; this dissection, it is hoped, will demonstrate precisely how these statements appealed to culturally specific renderings of capital punishment as a means to reframe the image's fraught meaning and, through this, regain narrative control over the broader military mission in Iraq.

By way of following Austin's prescription to investigate total speech situations, let us turn to a specific example through which the nuanced differences and similarities motivating locutionary, perlocutionary, and illocutionary acts can be articulated. In

[27] The use of Foucaultian terminology here was inspired by this excellent work: Tomoko Masuzawa, *The Invention of World Religion: Or, How European Universalism was Preserved in the Language of Pluralism* (Chicago: The University of Chicago Press, 2005), 20.

[28] J.L. Austin, *How to Do Things with Words* (Cambridge, MA: Harvard University Press, 1975), 52, 148; see also Judith Butler, *Excitable Speech: A Politics of the Performative* (New York: Routledge, 1997), 3.

From Noose to Needle,[29] an excellent and compelling work on the complicated role of capital punishment in the late liberal state, Timothy Kaufman-Osborn does just this by modifying one of Austin's own examples:

> Consider this hypothetical incident of extrastate violence: Two thugs, one menacing and the other somewhat less so, stand on either side of a man who has failed to make good on his gambling debts. The first turns to the second and says, "Shoot him." The second, after some hesitation, raises a pistol and kills the hapless debtor. Shortly after having read Austin's posthumous text, I observe this event. In my capacity as witness, I describe what I saw to the police: "The first man said to the second, 'Shoot him,' meaning by 'shoot' to fire the gun and by 'him' to refer to the deceased."[30]

When Kaufman-Osborn relates to the police both the action (the shot fired) and the person to whom the action was directed (the ill-fated debtor), he captures a locutionary act; that is, in his role as a knowledgeable bystander, he uses his statement to illustrate the relationship of the menacing thug's words ("shoot" and "him") and their meanings to one another. Yet Kaufman-Osborn, as a seasoned political theorist, recognizes that much more is at work (and punitively at stake) in this situation and amends his hypothetical statement to the police:

> But my philosophical sensibilities primed, I soon realize that this does not exhaust what transpired via this utterance; and so I explain to the police that the second man wavered, and hence that he must have been *persuaded* by the words of the first to commit this deed.[31]

In contrast to his initial locutionary-laden version of the shooting, Kaufman-Osborn amends his account of the shooting to incorporate the consequences of the words deployed by the thug. This revision reveals an important correlation present in the imaginary tableau that had previously gone unnoticed: The man in possession of the gun only shoots the unfortunate debtor *because of* the persuasive efforts made by the first man in his desire to induce the hoped-for action. Put differently, Kaufman-Osborn's statement to the police portrays the kill shot administered to the debtor as a *consequence* of the words articulated by the more menacing thug. In shifting the focus from the relationship between certain descriptive words to the consequences brought about through their utterance, Kaufman-Osborn transforms his statement to account for the presence of a perlocutionary act instead of the more one-dimensional locutionary act. But, once again, Kaufman-Osborn remains unsatisfied with his portrayal of the event:

> And yet, as I explain to the now exasperated officers, there is still more to this utterance, for I have yet to capture the sense in which it was itself an action.

[29] Kaufman-Osborn's interpretation of dignity in this volume, although not explicitly engaging with performativity as in his earlier works, will become important in later sections of this chapter.

[30] Kaufman-Osborn, *From Noose to Needle*, 25.

[31] Kaufman-Osborn, *From Noose to Needle*, 25; emphasis in original.

> Specifically, when the first man said, "Shoot him," he *ordered* the second to do so. Although this utterance may indeed have set in motion the train of actions that led to the debtor's death, it was a deed in its own right.[32]

This final rendering of the death of the debtor privileges an illocutionary act; it is a deed that is performed simply in virtue of articulation. Whereas the previous statements to the police provided an account of the shooting that depicted the relationship between the actors and the eventual consequences of their words, Kaufman-Osborn's last iteration captures the certain sense of immediacy present in the shooting. Indeed, an utterance is an illocutionary one if it is, in and of itself, enough to accomplish an end and make manifest its import *at the instant of its articulation.*[33] When this provision is then imposed on Kaufman-Osborn's Austinian example, the force of the words metaphorically replaces the force of the bullet in effecting the debtor's death – the moment the thug says, "Shoot him," the debtor's lifeless body falls to the street.

What might we learn by extracting this theory of language from the thugs-and-debtors situation and applying it to the American and European governments' encounters with an unsanctioned and viral image of Hussein's execution? In other words, how can we understand Commissioner Michel and President Bush's statements to be functioning as performative utterances? To make the initial foray into answering these questions, we must preliminarily leave aside any differences in their appeals to civilization, barbarism, and democracy present in their respective statements, and instead direct our focus to the actions these statements sought to induce: the ascription of a culturally and politically uniform narrative onto the unframed image as a means through which to render its disruptive potential moot; in doing so, it is possible to ascertain just how such assertions presume an illocutionary, and thus productive, force.

The primary way in which Commissioner Michel and President Bush seek to circumvent any lingering or permanent dissonance in narrative affect is simply through their engagement with the photograph. It is assumed that in doing so those who have yet to encounter the photograph – and, presumably, even those who already have come into cognitive contact with it – would instantaneously acquire a mental ex post facto frame through which to appropriately perceive and interpret its subject. Less obviously, but perhaps more importantly, such engagements with the photograph also signal Commissioner Michel and President Bush's intent that their utterances will still the viral dissemination of the photograph by assigning to it an official affect; through this ascription, the image's potential to shock and awe – to borrow from tactical wartime terminology – is neutralized and it consequently ceases to be an object of global interest. Even through this initial exegesis, the statements issued by Commissioner Michel and President Bush move away from

[32] Kaufman-Osborn, *From Noose to Needle*, 25; emphasis in original.

[33] For more on this, please see Butler, *Excitable Speech*, 2–17.

both the purely descriptive function of locutionary speech and the consequentialism of perlocutionary speech and shift, even if just infinitesimally, toward the possession of an illocutionary force.

This categorization of Commissioner Michel and President Bush's desire to reframe the image along performative lines is, however, still incomplete because it does not yet provide an accounting for the inclusion by each actor of substantially different organizational norms. At first blush, their respective references to barbarism, civilization, and democracy easily recall Kaufman-Osborn's earlier treatment of locutionary and perlocutionary acts in the thugs-and-debtors example: Such statements seek to describe the meaning of one term (the norm) to another (the death penalty) in a manner that privileges their consequences. For example, when Commissioner Michel declares, "One cannot fight barbarism with means that are equally barbaric. The death penalty is not compatible with democracy,"[34] he determines that because the supposedly unjust practice of the death penalty was deployed as a form of justice in Iraq, the larger civilizing mission of the Iraq war has been improperly compromised. A similar rhetorical framework, albeit one that is inverse in its meaning, can be applied to the statement made by President Bush. This reading of their statements, however, oversimplifies both the complexities of meaning that are contained in the deployment of such terms and how such meanings may actually *compel* their ultimate illocutionary, and thus potentially reframing, power.

By way of understanding how the meaningfully complex terms utilized by Commissioner Michel and President Bush possess a constitutive character, let us turn briefly, if somewhat incongruously, to the example of marriage. When I take a marriage vow and say, "I do," I offer a description of the action in which I am participating, an action that may be deemed either true or false depending upon the context in which it is uttered. An "I do" offered to a random individual that I happen to encounter on my walk to my neighborhood's coffee shop in the morning does not a marriage vow make; yet if I say the same words to this individual in the company of an authority vested by the state of California (such as a justice of the peace or an appropriately accredited religious official) to perform marriage ceremonies, the "I do" then executes the action it names: a marriage vow.[35] If we were to examine both of these potential marriage situations through the lens of locutionary speech acts, any meaningful distinctions motivating their separation would be lost; indeed, we can imagine an instance in which a bystander outside of the coffee shop and a decidedly unenthused attendant at my wedding offer the same interpretation of the events they had just witnessed: "She said 'I do,' which is a marriage vow, to another person, meaning an individual other than herself." If, however, the disaffected attendant

[34] See Kaufman-Osborn, *From Noose to Needle*, 25. Here, Kaufman-Osborn compels theorists of both the death penalty and performativity to ask in what sense death sentences may be considered illocutionary. For the purposes of this chapter, however, I alter Kaufman-Osborn's question slightly.

[35] This example is deployed by Austin in "Performative Utterances" as well as in Kaufman-Osborn's *From Noose to Needle*.

were to give a perlocutionary account of my utterance, she would note that, directly following my proclamation of "I do," I formally entered into the state of marriage with another person because I was prompted to do so by the officiate; whereas this description negates the possibility of the "I do" offered to the random individual on my walk to the coffee shop as an invocation of a marriage vow, it does not yet fully articulate how the words themselves induce a legally binding state of matrimony. If we understand my utterance of "I do" at the courthouse as an illocutionary act, not only do we see that it ushers in a new and palpable reality (that of the marital state) at the moment at which it was articulated, but that it had the legitimate power to do so because it presumed – in a way that locutionary and perlocutionary speech acts are unable to – that the individual to whom I uttered the vow was both a willing participant in the ceremony and recognized by the state of California as a person capable of entering into such a commitment.

Hence, marriage vows, when approached from a perspective that takes into consideration their total speech situation, derive their performative force from their illocutionary appeal to what Austin terms conventions.[36] The efficacy of speech acts, he writes, depends on "an accepted conventional procedure having certain conventional effect, that procedure to include the uttering of certain words by certain persons in certain circumstances."[37] In the marriage example, then, the performative utterance of "I do" has the force to bring into being a state of matrimony because it recalled not only the accepted social practice of marriage as an act between two willing and appropriate people, but because it also had to be witnessed, and ultimately sanctioned, by a representative of the state in order to be accepted as valid. To assume otherwise, as I did when I muttered, "I do," to the stranger on the streets of Berkeley and expected to be married from that moment forward is, for Austin, distinctly infelicitous.[38]

If the logic of conventions is applied to Commissioner Michel and President Bush's statements, their competing qualifications of the image as either "barbarous" or "democratic" emerge as attempts to locate an appropriate context for it such that their assertions automatically induce productive witnessing – or, illocutionary reframing – within their respective audiences. For traditional theorists of performative speech acts (like Austin), however, this application is not a happy one. In the case of the marriage vow detailed earlier, the conventions that endowed it with its performative force were not articulated within the actual utterance;

[36] Although I use the term conventions, Austin has, at different times, also used the terms "ritual" or "ceremony." Both Butler in *Excitable Speech* (at page 3) and Kaufman-Osborn in *From Noose to Needle* (at page 26) note these differences; for the purpose of this chapter, however, I will adhere to the term "conventions" because I believe it more accurately captures the confluence of historically grounded forces that legitimate an illocutionary act's force.

[37] Austin, *How to Do Things with Words*, 14.

[38] Jürgen Martschukat, "Nineteenth-Century Executions as Performances of Law, Death, and Civilization," in *The Cultural Lives of Capital Punishment*, eds. Austin Sarat and Christian Boulanger (Stanford: Stanford University Press, 2005), 51; see also Kaufman-Osborn, *From Noose to Needle*, 26.

instead, it distinguished itself from a perlocutionary act precisely because of its reliance on the presence of the correct social context and political circumstances to aid in the creation of a new reality, a reliance that allowed it to relinquish its ties to descriptive necessity. However, if the context in which the utterance is performed is *relocated to the setting of the iteration itself*, as our earlier determination to investigate the complexities of meaning present in Commissioner Michel and President Bush's statements urges us to do, then any clear distinction between the perlocutionary and illocutionary elements of speech collapses. This is not to suggest that perlocutionary and illocutionary acts should be considered as one and the same within Commissioner Michel and President Bush's utterances, but rather that they exhibit an interdependency that, when properly understood, has significant ramifications for the study of transatlantic capital punishment practices.

To see more concretely how this interdependency between perlocutionary and illocutionary acts is established, as well as how it simultaneously effects the reframing of Hussein's execution and cultivates a space in which to advocate for abolition, a substantive return to the works of Judith Butler is required. In *Bodies that Matter* and *Excitable Speech*, Butler charges that Austin's determination that an utterance's productive authority can only emerge in the context of commonly accepted conventions is insufficient. To follow Austin's prescription, she insists, is to misunderstand and misrepresent the coercive nature of modern power. She writes that performativity "must be understood not as a singular or deliberate 'act,' but rather as the reiterative and citational practice by which discourse produces the effects that it names."[39] On this understanding, conventions *qua* Butler render an utterance apprehensible to its audience and subjects by operating within and recalling "networks of meaning, modes of behavior, and institutions."[40] Their efficacy, as Jürgen Martschukat clarifies Butler, depends on their ability to connect to multiple points of reference that "allow for the performative act to make sense and unfold a specific meaning at a certain moment in history."[41] Butler's (and Martschukat's) reading of Austin does not discount the productive force of a performative utterance – it is instead to say that its power is *reflexive*, that is, it draws from and then subsequently suppresses previously existent webs of practices in order to constitute itself and its meaning afresh.

This means, on the one hand, that Commissioner Michel and President Bush's utterances exist within a never-ending series of utterances and, on the other hand, that they make sense only when taking into account the ensembles of practices, meanings, and values that gave rise to them. When the meaning of the war was rendered narratively and politically rudderless in the face of the unframed image

39 Judith Butler, *Bodies that Matter* (New York: Routledge, 1993), 2.
40 Martschukat, "Nineteenth-Century Executions as Performances of Law, Death, and Civilization," 50.
41 Martschukat, "Nineteenth-Century Executions as Performances of Law, Death, and Civilization," 50.

of Hussein's execution, their statements sought to recapture and recreate rhetorical stability through a "citation" to other recurring performative speech acts.[42] In this sense, their references to the "barbaric" and "democratic" natures of capital punishment recall nothing more than "historically specific compressions of meaning, brought about by the repetitive citation of utterances, attitudes, and behaviors within a culture."[43] Thus, when Commissioner Michel and President Bush assign ostensibly normative and perlocutionary descriptions to the act of capital punishment in the unframed image, they are, in fact, seeking to remedy the image's dissonance and dislocation by appealing to words and meanings that are already in possession of an illocutionary impulse. On this account, the productive distance between perlocutionary and illocutionary acts shrinks, and Hussein's execution emerges reframed.

Thus far, this section has sought to advance a portrayal of Commissioner Michel and President Bush's statements that locates their performative power in the interdependency between their respective descriptions of the act the unframed image captures and the productive force contained within their articulation of such descriptions. If, however, these statements are to be evaluated for any transatlantic abolitionist potential, the norms to which they appeal – and how they themselves are meaningfully constituted – must be understood in greater detail. It is now possible to ask: What is particular to the European and American experiences with capital punishment such that Commissioner Michel and President Bush may appeal to their normative differences in pursuit of a performative utterance – and have such utterances successfully render a volatile image popularly sensible? The answer to this question is both expansive and complex, but by narrowing our focus to the curious histories of transatlantic capital punishment practices following the conclusion of World War II, it will be easier to see just how the terms used by Commissioner Michel and President Bush are, as Butler argues, subjective compressions of historical meaning that can be deployed to expansive performative effect.[44]

Performing Cultural Capital Punishment

In September 1977, a Tunisian immigrant convicted of the torture and murder of a female acquaintance had the dubious honor of being the last person executed in Western Europe in the twentieth century.[45] Hamida Djandoubi's death by French guillotine generated no particular accolades or condemnations; indeed, for what would later be hailed as a major turning point in the history of Western civilization, the execution was remarkably uneventful. In the year of its final execution, Europe

42 Martschukat, "Nineteenth-Century Executions as Performances of Law, Death, and Civilization," 50.

43 Martschukat, "Nineteenth-Century Executions as Performances of Law, Death, and Civilization," 51.

44 For an altogether different account of how discourses of civilization and barbarism operate transatlantically, please see Andrew Hammel in this volume.

45 Franklin E. Zimring, *The Contradictions of American Capital Punishment* (New York: Oxford University Press, 2003), 16.

did not differ drastically from the political climates found elsewhere in the world. Most noticeably, Europe and the United States were exceptionally similar in their approaches to and amount of executions. As Franklin Zimring observes, "In 1977, only one person was executed in the United States: Gary Gilmore became the first offender put to death in a decade. But that same year, France beheaded two homicide offenders."[46]

Given what we know about Commissioner Michel's statement following Saddam Hussein's execution, the general silence that greeted Hamida Djandoubi's death – at least to our anachronistically situated ears – seems decidedly underwhelming and odd. Yet Zimring locates a specific reason for the lack of fanfare following Europe's final civilian execution: During times of political unrest and social instability, any popular debates over the merits of retaining or abolishing state-sanctioned executions noticeably recede.[47] Accordingly, in the late 1970s, during a period in which Europe was still reeling from the economic and cultural fallout of World War II, political elites held closed-door policy meetings with the intent to eradicate the death penalty through "leadership from the front." This intent was radically at odds with the prevailing popular mood; indeed, at the time in which political support for the death penalty began declining, the general European public was still in favor of its retention: When the death penalty was formally abolished in Germany, for example, over 74 percent of the populace supported its use for crimes relating to murder.[48] Although public approval of the death penalty would remain high in European countries for the next several decades, political elites firmly held to the belief that the practice of the death penalty was inherently incompatible with the direction and mood of the new, post-Holocaust Europe. Unyielding leadership from the front appeared the only way in which to ensure Europe remained on the path to achieve its civilizational *telos*[49]; in other words, the first steps in eradicating the death penalty were understood to be significant leaps away from the barbarism epitomized by the Holocaust.

In light of the lack of European discourse concerning capital punishment's gradual but steady elimination, it is all the more surprising to witness the sharp shift in policy objectives and the growth of international, European-led abolitionist movements. From the closed-door meetings of Europe's political elite has sprung an almost *de rigueur* belief in the necessity for capital punishment's worldwide eradication. But, again, nothing of this attitude was witnessed at the execution of Hamida Djandoubi. How are we to reconcile the disconnect between these two capital punishment realities? Furthermore, what lends the latter reality its lasting normative power? These questions can be resolved through a quick glance at the historical rise and

46 Zimring, *Contradictions of American Capital Punishment*, 16.

47 Zimring, *Contradictions of American Capital Punishment*, 26.

48 Zimring, *Contradictions of American Capital Punishment*, 23.

49 For more on this, please see: James Tully, "The Kantian Idea of Europe: Critical and Cosmopolitan Perspectives" in *The Idea of Europe*, ed. Anthony Pagden (New York: Cambridge University Press, 2002).

political influence of the European Union and the Council of Europe. By the mid-1980s, every Western European nation had formally abolished the death penalty. At approximately the same time, human rights activists were lobbying to strengthen the European Convention on Human Rights' (ECHR) commitment to the "right to life." Almost through coincidence of circumstance, Protocol No. 6 to the ECHR emerged as a means to ensure that no European citizen would ever come under the penalty of death again.[50] In 1983, the ECHR was opened for signature and ratified with astonishing speed. Within months of its ratification, the human rights framework was "extended to provide for mandatory abolition of death penalties for all of the European nations involved in the Council of Europe."[51] Abolition had become, in other words, naturalized under international and transnational law – in order for aspiring and would-be Council of Europe countries to apply for and gain access to the wealth of the politically consolidated European nations, they would need to demonstrate a commitment to the right to life by removing the death penalty from their punitive practices.

Thus, we can see that the right to life vocabulary has become an integral aspect to the framework of Europe's governing bodies. What makes Protocol No. 6's lasting influence important for this chapter's purpose is the realization that the rhetoric surrounding human rights has increasingly become equated with the normative qualities associated with civilization. Zimring argues: "Once a group of nations agrees that the standards governing the death penalty policy of individual states should be international, this creates the mandate to judge other countries on the death penalty, whether or not those other states agree with the standard imposed."[52] To paraphrase Zimring, the total and unequivocal abolition of capital punishment becomes the standard against which all other nations' judicial practices are assessed. But, as demonstrated earlier, the civilized standard takes on a new and coercive aspect: It is codified under supranational, international, and transnational European law. On this account, human rights, the death penalty, and the rejection of barbarism emerge as conflated notions under the institutional framework provided by the EU and the Council of Europe.

In the same year that Hamida Djandoubi became the last person to be executed in Western Europe, Gary Gilmore became the first person to be executed in more than a decade in the United States. Incongruously, in the eleven years prior to his death, public support for the death penalty had reached an all-time low; indeed, a Gallup poll reported that opponents of the death penalty outnumbered its proponents, 47 percent to 42 percent.[53] During this time of unprecedented abolitionism, citizens began pressuring their state legislatures to pass formal legislation that would explicitly

[50] Zimring, *Contradictions of American Capital Punishment*, 29.
[51] Zimring, *Contradictions of American Capital Punishment*, 29.
[52] Zimring, *Contradictions of American Capital Punishment*, 39.
[53] James R. Acker, "The Death Penalty: An American History" *Contemporary Justice Review* 6 (2003), 171; see also: Stuart Banner, *The Death Penalty: An American History* (Cambridge, MA: Harvard University Press, 2002).

outlaw the punishment of death for any crime. As James Acker notes, by the end of the 1960s, fourteen states had largely complied with their citizens' demands.[54] By all accounts, it appeared that the United States in the mid-twentieth century was moving closer – albeit at a glacial speed – to the complete and total eradication of the death penalty, buoyed in large part by a wave of public support.

This push for the permanent elimination of capital punishment as a tool for dispensing justice culminated in the landmark 1972 Supreme Court decision in *Furman v. Georgia*.[55] The justices, in a lengthy five-to-four decision, determined that the practice of capital punishment *as it stood in the cases before them* violated the Eighth Amendment's cruel and unusual punishment clause. Indeed, one of the more vocal justices on the bench for *Furman*, Justice William Brennan, declared that capital punishment is "unusual in its pain, its finality, and in its enormity. [. . .] Death is truly an awesome punishment. The calculated killing of the human being by the State involves, by its very nature, a denial of the executed person's humanity."[56] Echoing this sentiment, Justice Potter Stewart wrote:

> The penalty of death differs from all other forms of criminal punishment, not in degree, but in kind. It is unique in its total irrevocability. It is unique in its rejection of rehabilitation of the convict as a basic purpose of criminal justice. And it is unique, finally, in its absolute renunciation of all that is embodied in our concept of humanity.[57]

Taken together, these two statements appear reminiscent of the "right to life" vocabulary that emerged in the European Union's own turn toward abolition. But instead of being a marker of civilization and the rejection of barbarism, the "right to life" terminology seen in *Furman* takes on a decidedly populist bent. Not only did the cases considered in *Furman* come before the Supreme Court as a result of legal action claims spearheaded by civilian organizations such as the National Association for the Advancement of Colored People (NAACP), but throughout the written opinions in this case, the justices rely heavily on the perceived public opinion on the legitimacy of the death penalty by analyzing state legislation and jury behavior.[58] The justices' reliance on public opinion demonstrates how the rule of the majority – raw democracy – was a crucial factor in America's early experiment with abolition. As Justice Brennan concluded, "The objective indicator of society's view of an

[54] Acker notes that these states were all located outside the American south: Alaska, Hawaii, Iowa, Maine, Michigan, Minnesota, New Mexico, New York, North Dakota, Oregon, Rhode Island, Vermont, West Virginia, Wisconsin. In "The Death Penalty: An American History," 6.

[55] *Furman v. Georgia*, 408 U.S. 238 (1972).

[56] *Furman v. Georgia*, 408 U.S. 238 (1972).

[57] *Furman v. Georgia*, 408 U.S. 238 (1972).

[58] For more on this argument, please see: Austin Sarat and Neil Vidmar, "Public Opinion, the Death Penalty, and the Eighth Amendment: Testing the Marshall Hypothesis" *Wisconsin Law Review* 171 (1976).

unusually severe punishment is what society does it with it."[59] Thus, to extend the logic of Justice Brennan, if a democratic society deems capital punishment to be cruel and unusual through its incompatibility with its social standards, then its continued practice is no longer constitutional.

The popular support evinced for the abolition of the death penalty in 1972 makes Gary Gilmore's death by Utah firing squad a mere five years later particularly jarring. What produced such a dramatic shift in public and judicial opinions? The answer, for David Garland, is surprising. He argues that the period of abolition in American history was artificially supported by sustained periods of growth in the domestic economy; following World War II, crime rates decreased, standards of living increased, and consumers felt relatively safe in their homes and lifestyles. Accordingly, public support for criminal rehabilitation waxed at the same time as support for capital punishment waned.[60] With the advent of the 1970s and 1980s, however, the United States entered a period of persistent economic hardship as the nation entered a recession, unemployment rates skyrocketed, prices on basic goods were artificially inflated, and crime rates increased dramatically. Furthermore, shifting gender and familial roles shook the foundations of society, contributing to an anxiety-laced social sphere in which the appeal of conservative values grew greater every day. Garland writes, "The new social and cultural arrangements made late-modern society a more crime-prone society, at least until such new crime-control practices could be put into place to counter these tendencies."[61] Thus, when the Supreme Court reconsidered the constitutionality of capital punishment in 1976's *Gregg v. Georgia*,[62] the Justices determined that the principles of crime deterrence and victim retribution provided sufficient and rational cause for the reinstatement of state-sanctioned executions. Consequently, the reinstatement and retention of the American death penalty became intimately tied to the needs and desires of the nation's constituents.

The preceding paragraphs sought to make explicit how the competing terms of barbarism, civilization, and democracy became associated with culturally and historically specific understandings of the death penalty. At crucial points in both the United States and the European Union's evolving relationship with capital punishment, legal decisions were made that became conflated with *normative* choices. The development of Protocol No. 6 alongside the European Union's political predecessor of the Council of Europe imbued its institutions and practices with the valuation of the "right to life" doctrine – a doctrine that emerged from historically specific experiences with barbarism. Correspondingly in the American case, the Supreme Court's reliance on public opinion is evident in its thorough evaluation of state legislative documents, jury practices, and more, a practice that infuses the

59 *Furman v. Georgia*, 408 U.S. 238 (1972).

60 David Garland. *The Culture of Control* (Chicago: University of Chicago Press, 2001), 88.

61 Garland, *The Culture of Control*, 91–92.

62 *Gregg v. Georgia*, 428 U.S. 153 (1976).

retention of capital punishment with a seemingly democratic nature. Thus, with the conflation of legal choices and normative values, the practice of capital punishment materializes as a repository of cultural beliefs and can function as a "touchstone" for their later performative enactment by Commissioner Michel and President Bush.

CONCLUSION: TOWARD AN UNFRAMED VIEW OF THE DEATH PENALTY AND THE POSSIBILITIES OF ABOLITION

Following the release of the torture photographs taken at Abu Ghraib, Henry Giroux wrote:

> Meaning does not rest with the images alone, but with the ways in which the images are aligned and shaped by larger institutional and cultural discourses and how they call into play the condemnation of torture (or its celebration), how it came about, and what it means to prevent it from happening again.[63]

Allowing for the appropriate substitution of capital punishment for torture and an Iraqi military bunker for Abu Ghraib, Giroux's argument prompts us to realize that the American and European struggle to impose interpretative boundaries onto an unframed and dislocated image does not simply derive from a blind – although politically pressing – need to recover their narrative authority on matters relating to the regulation of the Iraq war. Instead, we see that the manner in which Commissioner Michel and President Bush seek to reclaim this authority from the hands of sub-state actors and individual witnesses is intrinsically tied to their respective society's cultural, political, and legal norms relating to the status of capital punishment. In calling upon terms like "civilization," "barbarism," and "democracy," Commissioner Michel and President Bush drive a wedge between the transatlantic experiences of capital punishment, effectively differentiating one punitive culture from the other; this differentiation allows both Commissioner Michel and President Bush to totalize their cultural capital and performatively "forget" that their historical narratives of the death penalty share significant overlap in its popular support (which still remains high in both the European Union and the United States), status as abolitionist (the United States, however short-lived, preceded some states in the contemporary European Union in the formal abolishment of civilian executions), and its derivation in Western liberal traditions. In each instance, the performative forgetting of the similar aspects of the other state's relationship to capital punishment by declaring it either barbaric or democratic only serves to both prematurely stagnate any dialogue on the eventual possibility of global abolition and negate the opportunity to develop tangible transatlantic policies that could unite the European

[63] Henry Giroux, "What Might Education Mean After Abu Ghraib: Revisiting Adorno's Politics of Education," *Comparative Studies of South Asia, Africa, and the Middle East* 24 (2004), 9.

Union and the United States with respect to the legitimacy of capital punishment as a penal practice.[64]

Thus, by way of concluding, I want to take up Giroux's final clause and transform it into a politically salient question: How do the ways in which both Commissioner Michel and President Bush engage with the image tell us something about the possibility of abolition? In other words, how may we, as abolitionists, use this event to illuminate the potential for preventing such punitive displays of state power "from happening again"?

One compelling answer to these questions recalls the interdependency of perlocutionary and illocutionary acts. When we utilized Butler to determine that the historically constituted description of an action possesses the necessary force to compel a specific understanding of an image, could we not also utilize her again to bring about the converse? That is to say, could not these performatively constituted

[64] This vast transatlantic divide on discursive matters of capital punishment retention and abolition is well illustrated by the uproar surrounding Texas' four-hundredth execution. On the eve of Johnny Ray Connor's execution, the European Union issued a special declaration denouncing capital punishment and its role in the American judicial system. The Portuguese then-president of the twenty-seven-nation governing body issued this statement on August 21, 2007:

> The European Union strongly urges Governor Rick Perry to exercise all power vested in his office to halt all upcoming executions and to consider the introduction of a moratorium in the state of Texas. [. . .] There is no evidence to suggest that the use of the death penalty serves as a deterrent against violent crime and the irreversibility of the punishment means that miscarriages of justice, which are inevitable in all legal systems, cannot be redressed.

This statement displays all the earmarks typical of present-day dialogue between the United States and the European Union regarding the application of capital punishment. What is particularly intriguing about this specific instance of dialogue, however, is the response offered by Texas. Robert Black, the spokesman for the governor of Texas, responded to the European Union:

> Two hundred and thirty years ago, our forefathers fought a war to throw off the yoke of a European monarch and gain the freedom of self-determination. Texans long ago decided the death penalty is a just and appropriate punishment for the most horrible crimes committed against our citizens. While we respect our friends in Europe . . . Texans are doing just fine governing Texas.

In the U.S. capital punishment system, the situation of Texas is unique. Following 1976's *Gregg v. Georgia* and the Supreme Court's subsequent reintroduction of capital punishment after its experimentation with abolition failed, the United States executed 1,090 death-row prisoners. Of these, Texas carried out approximately a third. When Robert Black's response to the European Union is viewed in conjunction with Texas' history as the most prolific instigator of juridical executions in the United States, the image of the United States he creates is one of radical democracy. In choosing to employ words such as "forefathers" and "yoke of a European monarch" and "death penalty" within the same sentence, Black evokes a mental image of capital punishment in America: of frontier justice, citizens gathering to deliberate on the harms done to them as a whole, and an American judge sentencing hardened criminals to death just as easily as his forefathers had thrown off the rule of European colonialism. This parallel that Black drew between the current American (Texan) legal system and the vision of democracy as tied to the death penalty haunts contemporary European conceptions of and relations to capital punishment, prompting statements like the one issued by the European Union immediately above and, more generally, Commissioner Michel's statement in the wake of Saddam Hussein's execution.

meanings of capital punishment practices be susceptible to being stood on their head simply through the invocation of yet another performative utterance or action? Butler, it seems, would agree with this potentiality:

> By understanding false or wrong invocations as *reiterations*, we see how the form of social institutions undergoes change and alteration and how an invocation that has no prior legitimacy can have the effect of challenging existing forms of legitimacy, breaking open the possibility of future forms. When Rosa Parks sat in the front of the bus, she had no prior right to do so guaranteed by any of the segregationist conventions in the South. And yet, in laying claim to the right for which she had no *prior* authorization, she endowed a certain authority on the act, and began the insurrectionary process of overthrowing those established codes of legitimacy.[65]

In applying Butler's admonitions to the work contained in this chapter, it is possible to see that one way in which to challenge (and subsequently move past) the domination of the "barbaric" versus "democratic" rhetoric pervasive in contemporary capital punishment discourse is for lay persons to forcefully assume performative authority. This means that, in the face of Commissioner Michel and President Bush's attempts to reframe Hussein's execution, subaltern witnesses to the photo must openly push back against their invocations of particular perlocutionary terms.

But if we do so, what performative or affective avenues are open to us? Put differently, what can be more effective in producing abolition than appeals to barbarism, democracy, and civilization? In assessing this subset of questions, a return to the image with which we started is necessary. Indeed, when both Commissioner Michel and President Bush performatively engage with Hussein's execution, they occlude one prominent component of the image: Saddam Hussein himself. Instead of responding to the depiction of the imminent death of a very real and tangible person, both governmental authorities choose to speak in broad terms about the historical meaning and political consequences infusing the practice of capital punishment. In order to claim performative authority á la Rosa Parks, abolitionists must engage defiantly and openly with contemporary portrayals of capital punishment and the occlusion of human life as a means by which to render palpable the undignified technologies of death that our current discourse supports.[66]

Along this vein, it is fitting to close with a return to Susan Sontag who, at the outset of this chapter, provided the initial impetus toward the discursive dissection of Hussein's execution and the performative utterances that followed in its wake. In *On Photography*, Sontag writes: "Photographs state the innocence, the vulnerability of lives heading toward their own destruction, and this link between photography and

65 Butler, *Excitable Speech*, 147; emphasis in original.

66 My determination that we must engage with the presence of a *person* in the unframed image of Hussein's execution coheres to a certain degree with Timothy Kaufman-Osborn's appeal in this volume to the dignity of an individual in assessing the methods and modes of execution.

death haunts all photographs of people."[67] As Butler points out, Sontag's evocative lament bears a striking resemblance to Roland Barthes who, in *Camera Lucida*, argued that all photographic images capture a future potentiality for the continuation or destruction of life. He writes of how a particular photograph he encountered "bespeaks of Lewis Payne in jail waiting to be hanged":

> He *is going to die*. I read at the same time: *This will be* and *this has been*. I observe with horror an anterior future of which death is at stake (*dant le mort est l'enjeau*). By giving me the absolute past of the pose (aorist), the photograph tells me death in the future.[68]

Photographs of imminent executions, on these combined readings, have the power to make manifest to the viewer the inevitability of human death. Although Barthes ultimately concludes that this affective quality of photographs is not limited solely to images of the juridically condemned, his treatment of Lewis Payne's death nonetheless reveals much about how modern death penalty abolitionists can engage with images that capture imminent expiration to advance performative interpretations of their subjects that can break free from the dominant modes of transatlantic discourse. By focusing on the "absolute pastness of life"[69] captured in the celluloid representation of Hussein's execution, abolitionist rhetoric itself can emerge as an unframed – and discursively and radically dissonant – alternative to state-based articulations of barbarism, civilization, and democracy that only serve to maintain the transatlantic status quo.

[67] Sontag, *On Photography*, 70.

[68] As cited in Butler, *Frames of War*, 97; emphasis in original. Original quotation can be found in: Roland Barthes, *Camera Lucida: Reflections on Photography*, trans. Richard Howard (New York: Hill and Wang), 85.

[69] Butler, *Frames of War*, 97.

6

Executions and the Debate over Abolition in France and the United States

Simon Grivet

INTRODUCTION

In the summer of 1976, France experienced one of its most severe droughts ever. The drought hit the farmers hard and preoccupied Valery Giscard d'Estaing's government.[1] A strong heat wave also afflicted the country for most of the summer. Later in July, the slump of the franc, which lost 8 percent of its value against the dollar, brought more worries to government officials. Along with Britain and Italy, the country was facing the monetary consequences of the economic crisis: Inflation and unemployment were other symptoms of this dire situation.[2] In the middle of the traditional summer vacations, plagued by the late-July heat, many in France enthusiastically followed Guy Drut's victorious race at the Olympic Games in Montreal, Canada.[3] In brief, the public had many topics of concern during that summer other than the fate of Christian Ranucci, a twenty-two-year-old man held under sentence of death at the Baumettes' prison in Marseilles for the murder of a young girl. His execution on the morning of July 28 came as a surprise.[4]

While campaigning in 1974, President Giscard d'Estaing expressed a "deep aversion" to the guillotine. Ranucci's defenders believed he was innocent, whereas others thought his youth warranted clemency. If Ranucci's crime had incited outrage and desire for stiff punishment, the newspapers after his execution were mostly critical of the death penalty. In fact, Ranucci's execution reignited the death penalty debate in

[1] Cf. "Worst Drought since 1921 Threatens All Sectors of the French Economy," *New York Times*, June 22, 1976.

[2] Cf. Clyde H. Farnsworth, "Decline in Franc Arouses Concern," *New York Times*, July 21, 1976.

[3] Frank Litzky, "Drut Takes High Hurdles Gold," *New York Times*, July 29, 1976.

[4] See Reuters, "In First Execution since 1973, France Guillotines Slayer," *New York Times*, July 29, 1979.

I would like to thank Jürgen Martschukat and Austin Sarat for inviting me to participate in this remarkable project. This work was greatly improved by remarks made by all the participants, especially those of Kathryn Heard and Jürgen Martschukat. Jonathan Simon's benevolence was also very helpful.

France.[5] True, there were two more executions in 1977. But the abolitionist cause, strongly supported by Robert Badinter, grew in popularity. After the Socialist victory in May 1981, Badinter became justice secretary and obtained the abolition of the death penalty.

On the path to the abolition in France, execution and its echo in the social and political realms played an important role. The aim of the following pages is to examine and compare the consequences of executions on the death penalty debate in France and the United States. Ideas of exemplarity and dissuasion have formed the core of the pro-death penalty discourses, but they directly contradicted both American and French practices that constantly and systematically hid executions from the public. The process of concealing executions began in the 1830s in New England, and it was finally adopted in France in 1939 after the publication of pictures taken during Weidmann's execution in Versailles. If the example was so vital, why take so many precautions to hide it? Numerous abolitionists like Albert Camus pointed out this glaring contradiction. Others, like philosopher Michel Foucault, believed that the hiding process was another sign that the punitive process itself was evolving from the terrible and ingenious tortures that aimed at the body of the condemned to the contemporary urge for *discipline* aimed at the prisoner's soul. According to this perspective, decency and the evolution of public sensibility are core elements in this history.

In this context, comparing discourses, films, or articles about executions in France and the United States offers surprising results. In France, the law after 1939 forbade *any* report on executions. The press, and later radio and television, could only repeat the official declaration that was as brief and abstract as the final judgment delivered by the court. Anyone violating these stringent regulations was liable to pay a very large fine. Circumstances of executions, attitudes of the condemned – prostration, cries, dignity or prayer – attitudes of magistrates and lawyers, official witnesses, and so forth – all of this was hidden and could only be known by private confessions or through a special account like the executioner's memoirs.[6] No one could oppose capital punishment in France as a consequence of learning concrete details about the guillotine in action because this information was largely kept secret. The American situation was quite different, because the press successfully defended its right to access and report on executions. Lawyers used the First Amendment and the rights of the press to guarantee reporters' access to death chambers. Although a prohibition on pictures remained firmly in place, articles clearly depicted executions and the participants' feelings.

France followed an abolitionist path and did away with the guillotine in 1981. This decision took place while reports on executions were forbidden by law. Abolition

5 Cf. Reuters, "Guillotine Debate Raging in France," *New York Times*, December 26, 1976.

6 See, for example, Jean Ker, *Le carnet noir du bourreau, les mémoires d'André Obrecht qui exécuta 322 condamnés* (Paris: Editions Gérard de Villiers, 1989).

in the United States has failed so far in the majority of states despite a wealth of articles and debates on the concrete aspects of execution. Shall we then conclude that execution – the true face of capital punishment – plays no role in the abolition debate? How are executions framed by public opinion? Why does it sometimes appear acceptable and other times completely scandalous to execute someone?

Sensibility and its evolution in both countries certainly account for some of the answer. Violence in both societies presented different images. Violence, homicide, and criminality have different meanings in each country, but it is striking to see how capital punishment reveals parallel evolutions. In both countries, there were fewer and fewer executions in the 1950s and 1960s compared to the first part of the twentieth century. Paths only diverged in the recent period after the Supreme Court decision *Gregg v. Georgia* in 1976, which reinstated the death penalty.[7] The links, influences, and back-and-forth between the two countries make the death penalty difference all the more vexing and difficult to explain. A classic attempt relies on political science: The French abolition would rest on an elitist political process that does not directly consult the people, because French public opinion favored the guillotine by a margin of two-to-one, whereas most members of Parliament (MPs) were abolitionists. There is truth in this explanation. The lack of direct consultation certainly insulated Parliament and helped MPs to vote on some unpopular piece of legislation at the time, such as abortion and abolition of the death penalty. Others would argue that the European context displayed such a strong and consistent pattern of abolition that it was only a matter of time before France would follow the same path. Moreover, France had a strong abolitionist tradition going back to 1791 with Gaultier de St Fargeau, and Victor Hugo and Jean Jaures would later carry the torch as well.

This work will argue, however, that the evolving meaning of execution could well be a determining factor. The 1939 ban on public execution and its contemporary gag order profoundly affected capital punishment in France. It became indeed some sort of secret ceremony to which even the victims' relatives were not allowed. On the other hand, in the United States, executions came more and more to resemble ceremonies held almost entirely for the victims' relatives. Very few people argued in the 1990s that the death penalty seriously discouraged criminality. Executions seem to have two meanings in contemporary America: They express the horror and shock of the community regarding very disturbing and horrible murders; and they show compassion for the victims' relatives by killing the guilty. Abolitionists see this as vengeance, others as respect due to the relatives' grief. Thus a systematic opposition to the death penalty by the victim's relatives would be a key factor in bringing abolition in the United States. Abolitionists have understood this and consequently put a great deal of energy toward this key constituency.

7 *Gregg v. Georgia*, 428 U.S. 153 (1976).

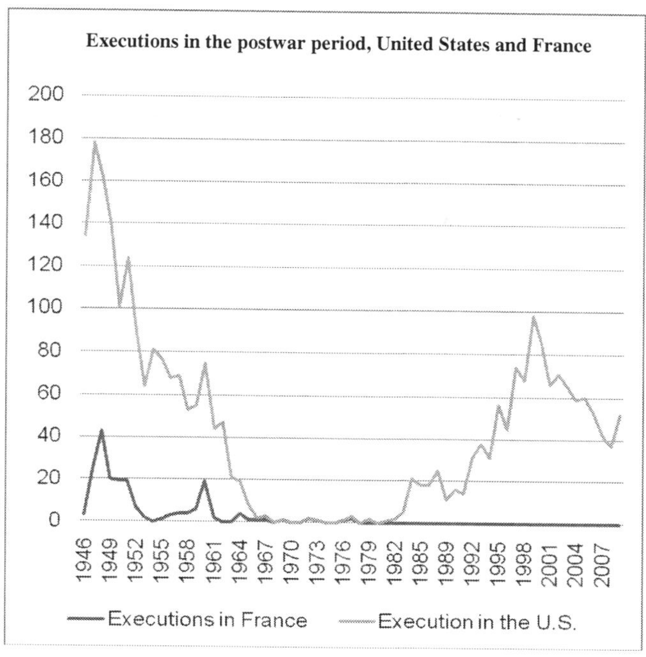

FIGURE 6.1. Executions in the postwar period, United States and France.

Trends in Executions, Strength of the Debate

The postwar period was strikingly different in the two countries.[8] The United States celebrated a victory that brought with it the status of a superpower, hegemony, and wealth, whereas France went through a long period of reconstruction that was not only material but also political and moral. After the liberation of its territory during the summer of 1944, French society went through an agitated period characterized by some rough justice against "collaborators" (those who abetted the German occupiers), social tensions when the Communist Party emerged as the number-one political force in the country, and criminality stemming from wartime destruction, displaced people, prisoners, and so forth. In the last years of the 1940s, French jurors displayed a draconian severity, with hundreds of murderers being sent to the guillotine. But remarkably, this bloody period did not last long, and in the 1950s, executions became sparse. The phenomenon was not only the result of a greater clemency on the part of Fourth Republic presidents Vincent Auriol (1946–1953) and

[8] Sources for graph data: for the USA *Death Penalty Information Center* (DPIC), available at http://www.deathpenalty.org; for France, I have relied on the work of writer and crime historian Sylvain Larue who maintained an impressive website and database dedicated to the guillotine (http://site.voila.fr/guillotine/, last visited May 24, 2010).

René Coty (1953–1958), but it also resulted from an evolution in attitude among jurors themselves.

This trend mirrored the American situation until the 1960s, when the suit brought by the National Association for the Advancement of Colored People – Legal Defense Fund (NAACP-LDF) in the federal courts brought about a de facto moratorium on executions. In America, the execution peak happened in the mid-1930s, during the Great Depression, a very troubled period indeed. There is ample evidence, both local and general, to draw a strong parallel between the dire social situations endured by many and the increasing levels of criminality. Intending to carry out a simple robbery, desperate people often went into shops with loaded weapons and, when met with unexpected resistance, often shot and killed their victims. It constituted a capital crime and was treated as such by the justice system.[9] The war years were less bloody, although there were violent events inside the country. But after the victory, with the economy enjoying a remarkable period of growth, homicides became less common and executions began to drop. This continued to be the case until the crisis of the late 1960s resulted in social upheavals and riots in ghettos from Watts to Cleveland and Detroit. Then criminality and its primary indicator – the homicide rate – increased again. This context brought electoral success to law and order politicians, who were favorable to capital punishment.[10]

Executions decreased in numbers, but it would be difficult to argue that support for capital punishment was eroding significantly. No massive protests against executions were recorded, and capital punishment as a specific issue was not debated very strongly on either side of the Atlantic. France and the United States had known frantic and feverish debates on this issue – the 1830s and 1840s in America, the Fallières presidency in France around 1908 – and the contrast with the postwar years was strong. In America, criminal justice was still left mainly to the states. Federal courts only intervened when injustice, bigotry, and racism had reached an embarrassing level, as in the Scottsboro Boys case in 1932 in Alabama.[11] The Federalist doctrine of the time severely restrained the courts' capacity to intervene. This led to some tragic decisions, like *Francis v. Resweber.*[12] Willie Francis, an African American, had been convicted of murder in Louisiana and sentenced to execution in the electric chair in September 1945. On the day of his execution, the portable electric chair used by the State of Louisiana malfunctioned – it was badly

9 See, for example, the case of Edward Anderson, hanged at San Quentin, February 15, 1935, for the murder of a movie theatre cashier during a robbery. Sheila O'Hare, Irene Berry, and Jesse Silva, *Legal Executions in California, A Comprehensive Registry, 1851–2005* (Jefferson, NC and London: McFarland & Company, Inc., 2006) 361.

10 See David Garland, *The Culture of Control: Crime and Social Order in Contemporary Society* (Chicago: University of Chicago Press, 2001).

11 Cf. *Powell v. Alabama*, 287 U.S. 45 (1932). See James E. Goodman, *Stories of Scottsboro* (New York: Vintage, 1995).

12 *Louisiana ex rel. Francis v. Resweber*, 329 U.S. 459 (1947). See Arthur Selwyn Miller and Jeffrey H. Bowman, *Death by Installments: The Ordeal of Willie Francis* (New York: Greenwood Press, 1988).

maintained, and the executioner was suspected of being intoxicated – and Francis, although hurt badly, did not die. A divided Supreme Court authorized a second attempt at executing Francis. Five justices rejected the double-jeopardy argument because it did not apply to the states at the time. More striking, however, was the fact that they did not see that sitting Francis on the electric chair a second time would constitute "cruel and unusual punishment," because "there is no purpose to inflict unnecessary pain nor any unnecessary pain involved in the proposed execution."[13] Confronted with this regrettable "accident," "this Court must abstain from interference with State action," wrote F. Frankfurter in his concurring opinion, "no matter how strong one's personal feeling of revulsion against a State's insistence on its pound of flesh."[14] Justice Burton, writing for the minority, condemned this "death by installments" that ran counter to the legal electrocution "only approved in a form that eliminates suffering."[15] Francis was executed in 1947; no protests were heard.

More generally in the United States, public opinion did not question the painless aspect of the "modern" methods of execution: electrocution and the gas chamber. The Supreme Court validated the former at the end of the nineteenth century, and lower courts in Nevada and California authorized the gas chamber in the 1920s.[16] It was generally held that these methods killed almost instantly, caused unconsciousness in seconds, and were humane ways of ending criminal lives. The usual observers, being reporters or prison officials, became accustomed to the situation. For example, in California, doctors monitored executions in the gas chamber and filled a "lethal gas record" that indicated the progression from the apparition of cyanide vapors to the death of the condemned – that is, when the heart stopped. These records clearly showed troubling signs of consciousness – movements, inhalation, grimaces – but doctors tended to ignore them and filled the record with the last words and attitudes of the condemned.[17]

In France, the guillotine was the topic of numerous debates about pain and execution. Although the machine was thought to give a perfect death because Dr. Guillotin famously proclaimed that his invention killed painlessly ("you feel almost nothing, just a cold feeling in the neck"), important questions and criticism remained until the early twentieth century. Doctors, scientists, and scholars had

13 *Idem* at 464.

14 At 470–471.

15 At 474.

16 See *In Re Kemmler*, 136 U.S. 436 (1890). Also on the gas chamber, see *People v. Daugherty*, 40 Cal. 2d 876 (1953).

17 See, for example, "Lethal Gas Chamber Execution Record" in "Richard J. JENSEN, #A-28419," California Department of Corrections Records, San Quentin Execution Files, California State Archives, Sacramento (hereafter CDCR, SQEF, CSA), F3918: 328, ("*Very stoical and resigned. Reviews his case rationally but with marked hatred against Judge Scott. One of his last statements was that his biggest regret is that Judge Scott will not be sitting on his lap in the chamber. He shakes hands with thanks for his care and treatment*").

to explain why decapitated heads sometimes exhibited expressions or movements. They tried to determine when exactly consciousness really ended. In 1796, German anatomist Thomas Sömmering (1755–1830) published a paper in *Le Moniteur* in which he argued that the self – the personality – was still alive in the separated head, thus provoking intense pain. Sömmering's thesis received refutations from French doctors like Pierre-Jean-George Cabanis (1757–1808), who thought that any movement seen on the head could be attributed to "natural irritability" and was not the results of pain and conscience.[18] In his *Reflexions*, published in 1957, Camus repeated some dreadful stories about decapitated heads exhibiting signs of life such as eyelid movements and the like, but he did not argue anymore that consciousness somehow remained after the fall of the blade – a sign that the controversy had lost most of its strength.[19]

In the United States, when citizens disapproved of an execution, they very rarely demonstrated. Picketing often did take place when the case involved some left-wing politics (e.g., the Mooney case, the Wesley Robert Wells case in San Francisco in the 1950s) or some well-known prisoner (Chessman). Generally, citizens wrote to their governor and pleaded with him to obtain clemency.[20] The abolitionist movement remained limited in the postwar years, although state associations frequently brought the issue before their respective legislatures. It drove investigative efforts and detailed reports, but when the actual vote came to the floor, abolitionists usually lost even when pursuing a limited objective like a five-year moratorium.[21] Capital punishment became more and more a symbolic feature of the justice system in America. At the same time, markedly progressive policies were implemented: To the apparatus of probation and parole, the "penal welfarism" of the 1950s and 1960s added group treatment, psychoanalysis, and a remarkable leniency that allowed certain murderers to be set free after as little as seven or eight years behind bars.[22] Support for the death penalty was slowly eroding in the United States, but executions did not play a major role in the process.

In France, executions were discreetly organized at dawn, behind prison walls. The public ignored the gory details: the crying of the condemned, his possible resistance and so forth. French public opinion did react strongly to executions, but their reactions were directed at those taking place in United States. In the complicated

18 On this debate, see Ludmilla Jordanova, "Medical Mediations: Mind, Body and the Guillotine," *History Workshop* 28 (1989): 39–52. Also recently in French, Grégoire Chamayou, "La querelle des têtes tranchées: Les médecins, la guillotine et l'anatomie de la conscience au lendemain de la terreur," *Revue d'histoire des sciences* 61, no. 2 (2008): 333–365.

19 Cf. Arthur Koestler and Albert Camus, *Réflexions sur la peine capitale* (Paris: Gallimard, Folio, 1957, 2002).

20 See, for example, Theodore Hamm, *Rebel and a Cause: Caryl Chessman and the Politics of the Death Penalty in Postwar California, 1948–1974* (Berkeley: University of California Press, 2001).

21 Cf. Subcommittee of the Judiciary Committee on Capital Punishment, "Report Pertaining to the Problems of the Death Penalty and Its Administration in California," in *Assembly Interim Committee Reports*, ed. California State Printing Office (Sacramento: Assembly of the State of California, 1955–1957).

22 See Garland, *The Culture of Control.*

and often contradictory relationship between the two countries, justice and competing conceptions of fairness played an important role. Two executions in the postwar years raised vigorous protestations in France: the Rosenbergs in 1953 and Caryl Chessman in 1960.

The Rosenbergs' execution in June 1953 can be analyzed as an episode of the Cold War: Presumed atomic spies were executed – a traditional punishment for traitors – and the enemy effectively exploited the affair for ideological ends. Clearly, the Communist Party was instrumental in building the spectacular protest movement in France and in rallying scores of intellectuals and artists to its cause. But the *Comité pour la Défense des Rosenbergs* also counted such non-communist persona as half a dozen Catholic bishops, Gaullists, and Socialist militants. The Christian bimonthly *La Quinzaine*, for example, relayed numerous Catholic protestations against "the possibility of electrocuting two innocent people." After the execution, the same publication denounced the U.S. actions as an immoral and dangerous act that would only worsen the international tension between the United States and the USSR.[23] What made all those people protest was not capital punishment, however, although the electric chair certainly seemed cruel to most French people. The main cause for protests was a feeling of unfairness, injustice, and incomprehension toward the American justice system that had allowed the defendant's own brother to testify for the prosecution.

In 1960, French public opinion expressed the same outrage when California authorities finally executed Caryl Chessman after a twelve-year incarceration. Once again, the Chessman case provided a classic example of complete incomprehension on the part of the French. To most of the French people interviewed in the press, what made Chessman's death unbearable was its timing: That he should be put to death twelve years after the crime was simply inconceivable. *Le Monde* correspondent in Washington, Jean Knecht, wrote, "When one has witnessed American enthusiasm for certain causes, one is but dumbfounded by the weakness of their reactions to some inhuman aspects of a trial, whose length, 12 years, is already a challenge to justice."[24] By contrast, to most seasoned and legally qualified American observers, the Chessman case mostly demonstrated that even a death-row inmate could have his claims litigated all the way to the U.S. Supreme Court.

The Meaning of Execution

A Common Evolution Toward 'Decency', Namely Hidden Executions

On the eve of World War II, both France and the United States had ceased public executions. In earnest, the process of bringing the gallows behind prison walls was already a century old in the United States. Louis Masur demonstrated how

[23] See (in French), Yvon Tranvouez, "Guerre Froide et progressisme chrétien. '*La Quinzaine*' (1950–1953)," *Vingtième Siècle. Revue d'histoire*, no. 13 (1987): 83–94.

[24] Jean Knecht, "Chessman doit être exécuté lundi," *Le Monde*, May 2, 1960.

Northeastern states like New York, Pennsylvania, or Massachusetts took the gallows out of the public eye in response to abolitionist pressure and shifting cultural and social views of pain, decency, and public order.[25] Nonetheless, public executions survived in some states, mostly in the South, and the last public execution took place in 1936 in Kentucky, when Rainy Bethea, an African American, was hanged for the rape and murder of a seventy-year-old woman. Public executions paralleled tolerance for the public display of violence and cruelty. The South had a number of lynchings from the end of the nineteenth century to the 1930s.[26] The phenomenon, although in sharp decline in the twentieth century, might explain why public executions were tolerated longer in the Southern states.[27]

In France, the Enlightenment period and the Revolution were watersheds not only for the judicial system but for punishments as well. In the *Ancien Régime*, Michel Foucault and many other historians underlined the strength of *l'éclat des supplices*, or the shining tortures, a specific regime of public punishment consisting in elaborate rituals of cruel beating and burning accomplished after a procession around the city.[28] The exact meaning of these ceremonies remains a matter of debates. Bée argued that it reveals the existence of a "sentencing myth." By executing criminals with such exquisite attention to details, the executioner accomplished a form of sacrifice that saves society from monstrous crimes. For Bée, the shining of torture had a religious foundation. For Pascal Bastien, who examined how two Paris bourgeois wrote about executions in their respective diaries, its origin was political. The main questions, according to Bastien, were what message an execution transmitted to the people and how they reacted to it? Finally, Michel Foucault's well-known perspective, centered on the "punishing power," linked the shining of torture to the very nature of monarchy: Executions were bloody, cruel, and horrible because every crime was a personal offense to the king. All agreed, however, that public executions were a representation, a form of bloody theatre, greatly appreciated by enthusiastic crowds.

Enthusiasm and joy displayed by the public at executions disheartened and shocked Enlightenment thinkers. Bastien did not find unruly behavior near the scaffold in Paris. Most of the time, the public joyfully participated and followed

[25] Louis P. Masur, *Rites of Execution: Capital Punishment and the Transformation of American Culture, 1776–1865* (New York: Oxford University Press, 1989).

[26] See, for example, the statistical analysis contained in Stewart Emory Tolnay and E. M. Beck, *A Festival of Violence: An Analysis of Southern Lynchings, 1882–1930* (Urbana: University of Illinois Press, 1995).

[27] See, for example, James W. Clarke, "Without Fear or Shame: Lynching, Capital Punishment and the Subculture of Violence in the American South," *British Journal of Political Science* 28, no. 2 (1998): 269–289; Stuart Banner, "Traces of Slavery: Race and the Death Penalty in Historical Perpective," in Charles J. Ogletree and Austin Sarat, eds., *From Lynch Mobs to the Killing State, Race and the Death Penalty in America* (New York and London: New York University Press, 2006) 96–116.

[28] Cf. Michel Foucault, *Surveiller et punir* (Paris: Gallimard, 1975). And Pascal Bastien, "Fête populaire ou cérémonial d'Etat? Le rituel de l'exécution publique selon deux bourgeois de Paris (1718–1789)," *French Historical Studies* 24, no. 3 (2001): 501–526. And Michel Bée, "Le spectacle de l'exécution dans la France d'Ancien Régime," *Annales. Economies, Sociétés, Civilisations* 38, no. 4 (1983): 843–862.

rituals that wore recognizable marks and symbols to illustrate specific crimes. This complicated theater of law appeared a waste and a disgrace to the new enlightened elite of the Revolution. The new Republic overwhelmingly reduced the range of punishment and embraced imprisonment. This rationalization did not erase public rituals all of a sudden. Galley slaves and convicts still carried a heavy load of rituals, superstitions, and popular beliefs. Executions, however, underwent a radical transformation with the adoption of the guillotine. Under the *Ancien Régime*, criminals were killed using a specific method according to their status (e.g., only aristocrats were beheaded whereas ordinary criminals were tortured and strangled). The Revolution applied the same swift mechanical beheading to everyone.

Executions with the guillotine entailed a whole new set of rituals.[29] A key aspect was its swiftness: It took only a few seconds to seize the condemned, lay him down on the bench, have his head positioned, and let the blade fall. The struggle between the executioner and the condemned, punctuated by cheers and comments of the crowd, disappeared. During the nineteenth century, France went through no less than five different political regimes, yet the guillotine remained. Public executions came under heavy criticism as the century witnessed half a dozen popular revolutions and urban riots. The guillotine lost its scaffold and was simply mounted on the street behind rows of soldiers and policemen. In Paris, executions left the famous *Place de Grève* by the City Hall and moved to more distant locations like the Roquette near la Bastille. The time was also changed to dawn to discourage as many spectators as possible.

In 1885, senators voted for Agenor Bardoux's bill to have executions held privately. This vote followed an unusual survey of some fifty of the most important French magistrates. E. Taïeb analyzed this remarkable survey and showed that most judges supported hidden executions because the guillotine in public ended up being a problem for public order and a challenge to what they considered "good mores."[30] If solemnity and dignity could not be achieved, public executions appeared counterproductive. Some magistrates went on record to say that those 'problems' were only discernable in Paris and not in the *Province*. But no magistrate believed executions ought to be completely private, without any sort of publicity. On the contrary, according to Taïeb, some judges believed that executions ought to be organized for other prisoners to observe. Others elaborated specific witness lists. Most importantly, judges usually agreed that an execution conducted behind prison walls but witnessed by a number of selected journalists could be adequate. This model, close to the American practice, was flatly rejected by the Assembly, where conservatives

29 On that topic, see Daniel Arasse, *La Guillotine et l'imaginaire de la Terreur* (Paris: Flammarion, 1987). Available in English, *The Guillotine and the Terror* (London and New York: Allen Lane/Penguin Press, 1989).

30 Cf. Emmanuel Taïeb, "Le débat sur la publicité des exécutions capitales, usages et enjeux du questionnaire de 1885," *Genèses*, no. 54 (2004): 130–147.

received the support of abolitionists who felt that executions should be public or not carried out at all. This remained unchanged until 1939.

A Secretive Judicial Operation

In 1939, Eugen Weidmann, a German conman and murderer, was sentenced to death and executed before the gates of the Versailles prison. Weidmann's case had attracted public opinion: After a long investigation resembling a film noir, he had been convicted of no less than five murders. His execution, originally set for 4 A.M., was delayed by thirty minutes. The new executioner, Henri Desfourneaux, who had only recently replaced the seasoned Anatole Deibler after his untimely death, hesitated, waited, and finally proceeded to carry out the execution at 4:30 A.M.[31] By that time, the sun had begun to rise, and photographers who had packed into surrounding balconies took many shots of Weidmann being brought to the deadly machine and meeting his fate.

The scene of hundreds of spectators watching the event like another entertainment shocked many observers. A journalist for *Paris-Soir* wrote the following day that, "Around the place Louis Barthou, the activity is extraordinary. A disgusting crowd is squeezed into the cafes, this unruly crowd is devouring sandwiches (. . .) there are jostling, clamors, whistling."[32] But it was nothing compared to the outrage after the weekly *Paris Match* published a couple of pictures clearly depicting the whole execution. Prime Minister Daladier used the new power granted to him to face the tense international situation: He signed a decree-law that set executions behind prison walls, with only a handful of official witnesses and no journalists. What Bardoux's bill could not achieve in 1885, Daladier was able to do thanks to the special powers granted him in 1939. Some observers applauded: An editorialist in *Paris-Soir* even wrote that, "In America, at the Sing-Sing prison: one room, a bench for the six witnesses, the electric chair and that's all."[33] Nonetheless, the decree really appeared to be a gag order because the press was forbidden to publish any detail on the execution itself. The sole authorized material would be the dull and evasive official declaration of execution.

The year 1939 forms a key point in French capital punishment history. From that year on, executions took place secretly, and only a few officials would know the exact date once the President had rejected clemency. In the middle of the night, as the executioner and his team set up the guillotine, the prison warden, various officials (judges, D.A., etc.), and the condemned's lawyers would silently walk to the condemned's cell and wake him up. He would be told that his application for clemency had been rejected and that he was to be executed shortly. The condemned was allowed confession and mass with the prison priest, a last letter, cigarette, and

[31] Gérard A. Jaeger, *Anatole Deibler, L'homme Qui Trancha 400 Têtes* (Paris: Editions du Félin, 2001).

[32] Cf. "Devant la prison de Versailles, Weidmann a expié ce matin à 4h32," *Paris-Soir*, June 18, 1939.

[33] Cf. Pierre Wolff, "La Guillotine en privé, bravo!" *Paris-Soir*, June 27, 1939.

rum. Once the condemned was given to the executioner's team, everything went fast: seized and laid on the bench, the blade would fall almost immediately.

The French ritual never changed after that. The confidentiality of the execution date underlined its secretive aspect. Once the president had rejected the condemned's clemency application, only his lawyers and a couple of magistrates shared the news of the upcoming execution, which generally followed the next day. Condemned men themselves were not told exactly *when* the sentence would be carried out. Journalists were kept out of the prison and had to do with very little information. Authorities never granted victims' relatives any privilege to witness the execution. To quote Albert Camus' famous 1957 *Reflections on the Guillotine*: "Society does not believe his own words. (. . .) If one wants the penalty to be exemplary (. . .) the machine should be put on a scaffold, place de la Concorde, at 2 P.M. before a crowd and also broadcast live on TV for those who could not be there. We must do that or stop talking of exemplarity."[34]

In the United States, the transfer behind prison walls never led to such secretive setups for several reasons. For one, the press enjoyed constant and reliable access to executions. In Minnesota, authorities at the end of the nineteenth century tried to enforce a gag order, but it proved ineffective. At the beginning of the twentieth century, reporters were allowed again to witness executions, and their articles were run on front page. A botched execution, narrated in details in the newspapers, brought abolition to that state.[35] The main limitation courts imposed on press reporting of executions was that of pictures: No camera was ever allowed to film an execution for television. Secondly, with that sort of access, authorities were eager to convey the idea that they were using the best available technology to execute condemned persons. Once the electric chair or the gas chamber replaced traditional hanging, the wish to display the remarkable technology was undeniable. Finally, this relative openness had another more paradoxical explanation. After 1945, a strong rehabilitative ideal dominated various departments of corrections around America. It was particularly the case in California, where Clinton Duffy, an avowed abolitionist, was San Quentin's warden and responsible for the executions. Most senior employees in the California Department of Corrections, headed by Richard McGee, considered capital punishment an archaic and useless tool to fight criminality. They believed their expertise and "treatment" method could "cure" most criminals. For the handful of desperate cases, psychiatric care seemed preferable to the gas chamber.[36] These liberal positions explain why San Quentin public tours always included a view of the gas chamber and why most curious *male* citizens willing to witness an execution had

[34] Albert Camus, *Reflections on the Guillotine, an Essay on Capital Punishment* (Michigan City, IN: Fridtjof-Karla Publications, 1960).

[35] Cf. John D. Bessler, "The 'Midnight Assassination Law' and Minnesota's Anti-Death Penalty Movement, 1849–1911," *William Mitchell Law Review* 22, no. 2 (1996): 577–659.

[36] Cf. Clinton T. Duffy, 88 *Men and 2 Women*, 1st ed. (Garden City, NY: Doubleday, 1962).

their wish granted. McGee, Duffy, and others believed an informed citizenry, after open debates, could not help but conclude that capital punishment was outdated.

A Special Program for Victims' Relatives?

The most important evolution in American rituals is related to the role devoted to the crime victims' relatives. Their presence at executions went through several stages that are not easily explained. At least in California, victims' relatives were unofficially welcomed until 1950. However, few of them actually witnessed executions. Before World War II, being a crime victims' relative was something shameful. Those who came to see the murderer of their loved ones pay the price for his crime did not enjoy specific privileges, although their presence was usually noted by the press. Then in 1950, California authorities sharply changed this unofficial policy by strictly following the Penal Code, which did not mention victims' relatives among the authorized witnesses. After that, crime victims' relatives were not allowed to witness executions anymore.

In California and elsewhere in the United States, when executions were again carried out after the ten-year hiatus between 1967 and 1977, it seemed like a different world. While lawyers and federal courts discussed the death penalty's constitutionality, the victims' movement gained a strong recognition and obtained remarkable reforms that gave victims and their families specific privileges in the judicial system – from the early contacts with the police or D.A. to trial, sentencing, parole hearings, and so forth. On the topic of capital punishment, crime victims' associations followed the lead of law-and-order politicians and demanded that death sentences be indeed carried out.[37] In California, Georges Deukmejian, Attorney General and later governor, embodied this tendency. His career was built on an uncompromising support for capital punishment and, more globally, law-and-order politics. In 1986, together with crime victims' families associations and other conservative groups, he led the fight to oust California Supreme Court Justice Rose Bird and two other liberal justices who had invalidated most death sentences before them.

Victims and their relatives became the number-one reason most politicians declared support for capital punishment. According to this logic, crime victims' relatives had to be accommodated to witness executions. Usually they expressed the hope that the spectacle would bring them "closure" and peace of mind. When the federal government executed native terrorist Timothy McVeigh, video feeds had to be organized because there were many witnesses to accommodate.[38] Executions in contemporary America have almost become a privatized ceremony for the victims' relatives. Most Penal Codes in the United States now guarantee a right for victims' relatives to witness executions. In California, the new execution chamber built at

37 Daniel Weintraub, "Father Fights System He Feels Aids Guilty," *Los Angeles Times*, March 2, 1985, A1.

38 See Jim Yardley, "Execution on TV Brings Little Solace," *New York Times*, June 12, 2001, A26.

San Quentin has a viewing area for victims' relatives separated from the official witnesses, the press, and the condemned's family.[39]

The Role of Executions in the Debate Over Abolition

In America, a Recent and Powerful Theme

Executions today occupy a major part of the capital punishment debate in America. This is a relatively recent phenomenon. During the 1960s, when the lawyers of the NAACP-LDF challenged the constitutionality of the death penalty before federal courts, discrimination and possible inequality in the treatment of various capital defendants formed the core of the matter. In the late 1990s, as the litigation strategy had stopped bringing new success for the abolitionist camp, innocence became a new, powerful, and fertile ground to fight the death penalty. With the spectacular consequences of DNA analysis in a few well-publicized cases, a fundamental axis of the abolitionist discourse regained a lot of weight: A judicial system that kills risks committing definitive errors.[40] This theme remains strong and vivacious today and it certainly has the capacity to convince even hardcore death penalty partisans to reconsider their position. Execution itself does not constitute a major point in the contemporary debate. Botched executions had played a role in the past. For example, Minnesota abolished capital punishment in 1917 after a vigorous press campaign had denounced a botched hanging. But, as recalled earlier, Louisiana's condemned Willie Francis was indeed electrocuted twice after the first attempt failed.

In recent years, sensibility evolved on the question of pain and suffering. In other areas of life, like medicine, pain has become unbearable. Norms and mores in the United States and in the Western world toward the treatment of animals also changed. Society would not accept barbaric or inconsiderate treatment of animals even in circumstances when they have to be killed. These evolutions show through the adoption of new execution methods. Ronald Reagan famously compared execution and getting rid of an agonizing horse on a ranch: While it used to be done with a rifle, science brought euthanasia by lethal injection. Lethal injection is the contemporary face of American capital punishment because it seems clean and completely painless. Other methods fell in discredit after vigorous litigations or scandals. The gas chamber was declared unconstitutional in 1994 by Judge Marilyn Patel after a long suit initiated by the ACLU.[41] The ACLU unearthed and brought together not only archives describing executions at San Quentin between 1938 and 1967, but also records pertaining to the latest executions in 1992–1993. These documents proved

39 See online at http://www.cdcr.ca.gov.

40 Cf. Jim Dwyer, Peter Neufeld, and Barry Scheck, *Actual Innocence: Five Days to Execution and Other Dispatches from the Wrongly Convicted*, 1st ed. (New York: Doubleday, 2000).

41 *Fierro v. Gomez*, 865 F. Supp. 1387 (1994). On pain and execution, Austin Sarat, *Pain, Death, and the Law: Law, Meaning, and Violence* (Ann Arbor: University of Michigan Press, 2001).

that a condemned in the gas chamber does not fall unconscious before ten to sixty seconds and that during that time, he suffers a great deal. The electric chair was eliminated after several botched executions in Alabama, Georgia, and Florida.

Lethal injection seemed so perfect that some victims' relatives witnessing an execution thought that the murderer "had it too good."[42] With the use of the curare derivative bromide pancuronium, which paralyzes the condemned, no sign of pain can be easily detected. In the wake of the much publicized McVeigh execution by injection in 2001, several doctors and medical experts like the Columbia anesthesiologist Mark Heath began to suspect that the execution protocol was not as perfect as it seemed. It marked the beginning of a series of state and federal lawsuits that profoundly changed the clean and sober image of lethal injection. The public learned about mistakes in dosing sodium thiopental, which rendered anesthesia ineffective when the condemned received his dose of curare. Inadequate or poor training of execution team members in California and elsewhere helped explain the numerous botched executions since the implementation of lethal injection in Texas almost three decades ago.[43]

With its complicated 2008 decision in *Baze v. Rees*, the U.S. Supreme Court finally intervened in the debate over lethal injection and more generally elaborated its vision and interpretation of the Eighth Amendment's key clause regarding "no cruel or unusual punishment."[44] A narrow majority agreed that there were not enough elements to forbid the use of the three-drug cocktail in the lethal injection procedure. This landmark decision may foreclose other suits in the years to come, but the simple intervention of the Supreme Court more than a century after its electric chair decision demonstrates how uneasy the judicial system is with carrying out executions. Never before had the question of pain inflicted on the condemned been so central in the debate about the death penalty. Chief Justice Roberts acknowledged that "some risk of pain is inherent in any method of execution" and added that "the Constitution does not demand the avoidance of all risk of pain in carrying out executions," but the Eighth Amendment clause does prohibit situations in which there is a "substantial risk of serious harm."

Even though lawyers representing R. Baze have failed to convince a majority of the Supreme Court that the three-drug protocol used in lethal injection put the condemned at "substantial risk," it does reveal how closely executions are now scrutinized by the courts. It has become extremely complicated for the State to kill. Some commentators predicted that the situation might be an insoluble predicament:

42 See, for example, Ken Ellingwood, "Freeway Killer's Final Moments Strangely Calm; Execution: One victim's relative feels cheated; other are relieved," *Los Angeles Times*, February 24, 1996.

43 Among a growing and massive bibliography, see Deborah W. Denno, "The Lethal Injection Quandary: How Medicine Has Dismantled the Death Penalty," *Fordham Law Review* 76, no. 1 (2007): 49–128. On California, cf. Howard Mintz, "California judge declares lethal injections unconstitutional," *McClatchy – Tribune News Service* (2006).

44 *Baze v. Rees*, 553 U.S. 07-5439 (2008).

Executing by lethal injection requires a good level of medical technique that doctors, for obvious ethical reasons, do not want to provide. The strong demands of the law and the trend toward constantly reducing pain in executions explain why it is a topic so central today in the American debate on capital punishment.

In France, a Struggle to Define the Guillotine's Meaning

Nothing comparable ever existed in France. Once the guillotine was adopted in 1792, it remained the sole legitimate method of execution in France until abolition in 1981. During some very troubled periods, like the months following the Liberation (1944), the firing squad was used as a substitute. The guillotine became a remarkably ambiguous object in French contemporary culture: an instrument of emancipation and liberty when it chopped the head of Louis XVI in 1793; a symbol of oppression and tyranny during the Reign of Terror. Later, *la veuve* (the "widow") acquired dark fame that was supposed to discourage wrongdoers from committing crimes. But on the other hand, it came to embody capital punishment in itself. When Victor Hugo defended his son Charles, who had written an article describing a gory execution during which the condemned had rebelled, he replaced capital punishment with "the guillotine," a female noun in French. Slowly, as he described the changes in rituals, the machine became a real character, a monstrous feminine character: "I thought that the guillotine (. . .) had begun to adjudicate itself, that *she* felt *she* was an outcast, and that *she* got used to it (. . .) I felt *she* began to hide *her*self." Later, as his son was prosecuted for "outrage" and "lack of respect for the law," he said to the jurors, "And the day after the bloodiest and gloomiest times, she wants to be admired! She demands respect or she declared herself abused, she sues and wants damages. . . . "[45] This episode, which illustrates the important meaning a simple mechanical device can take, may explain why the guillotine was never replaced in France.

It could also be that the guillotine was both reliable and fast. There were no reasons to modify the execution method after World War II. Scores of condemned died on the guillotine between 1946 and 1953. Abolitionism appeared weak and limited. A couple of great trial lawyers like Albert Naud or Henri Torrès, some religious dignitaries, and some leaders on the Left and in the Christian democracy movement composed this movement that ritually presented the same abolitionist bill at the National Assembly. But at the time, the bill did not receive enough support among other MPs to even trigger a debate in the full chamber.

Abolitionists rejected the traditional view that executions had any exemplary value. They stressed the risk of error and the fact that murderers finally executed were usually not the "worst of the worst." But the tastes of the time and contemporary sensibilities were not compatible with an all-out attack on execution and the

[45] Cf. Victor Hugo, *Oeuvres Complètes*, 15 vols., vol. 10, "Politique" (Paris: Bouquins, Robert Laffont, 1985) 309–316.

guillotine. A form of decency and modesty brought abolitionists to avoid denouncing executions themselves. A good example can be found in the most celebrated abolitionist movie of the 1950s, *Nous sommes tous des assassins* (*We Are All Murderers* [1952]) by André Cayatte. Cayatte, a former trial lawyer and a Communist sympathizer, chose to attack capital punishment for its unjust and barbaric aspects. However, he refused to represent the guillotine in action. His main character, René Le Guen, comes from the skid row around Paris. He is an alcoholic who learned to kill during the German Occupation, when he became an agent of the Resistance. When peace returns, Le Guen cannot control his murderous fury and shoots three people in a public bath as police come to arrest him. His trial is quickly seen as the movie centers on Le Guen's captivity in *La Santé*'s death row.

Cayatte exhibits two different strategies for his abolitionist credo. Firstly, more or less strong discourses held by certain key characters in the movie: one by a chaplain who opposes capital punishment because of the universal value of human life; another by a psychiatrist who pleads for scientific response to criminal folly, among other things. Secondly, Cayatte denounces the horror of execution, essentially by dramatizing both the condemned's tragic and uncertain wait – because he does not know when he will be executed – and the rituals directly leading to the execution – the officials slowly walking to the condemned's cell to wake him up in the middle of the night, guards running to him and seizing him, and so on. One of the best shots of this often too didactic movie happens when Cayatte films the crowd of officials slowly moving toward the condemned's cell only preceded by guards, walking without shoes to be silent. Fear and disgust surely rise in any spectator together with the feeling that we are all, as a society, somehow responsible for this legalized murder.

Cayatte's approach attempts to play on the spectator's moral sensibilities. Like the press of his time, he does not depict the execution itself when executioners seize the condemned, lay him on the bench, bring down the "glasses" and let the blade fall. In contrast to journalists, no law forbade him from doing so. It is a filmmaker's choice to avoid this potentially difficult scene that could have brought him accusations of exposing spectators to a blood-stained and horrific scene.

In America, Robert Wise, who filmed *I Want to Live!*, a passionate plea to prove Barbara Graham's innocence, six years after Cayatte's work, made radically different choices. He had been at an execution personally, meeting the condemned the night before the execution and, on a Friday morning, witnessing the gassing of James Reese.[46] The last third of the movie is dedicated to the recreation of Graham's execution. The spectator follows every detail of the gas chamber preparation. He then shares Graham's terrible wait, including a last-minute stay as she is about to enter the chamber. Her death itself is presented with realistic features. Although Wise replaced invisible cyanic gas vapors with a somewhat benign-looking white smoke, all the gestures and attitudes adopted by Susan Hayward are faithful to most gas chamber

46 Cf. James Reese's file "James REESE, #A22284A," CDCR, SQEF, CSA F3918:297.

records kept in the archives. However, Hayward's act betrays the prejudice of the time by not depicting the suffering of the condemned. She almost immediately falls unconscious and shows only limited gestures. Spectators neither see her drooling nor showing evident signs of stress or pain. In a word, Wise filmed a very acceptable and decent execution that would not have shocked spectators. American movies like *I Want To Live!* reflected a more open and transparent attitude toward execution, but their influence on the debate may not have been stronger than that of their French counterparts.

In France, the quasi-absence of executions during most of the 1960s, and ambiguous declarations on the guillotine by President Pompidou, and later Giscard d'Estaing, were important in preparing for the victorious debate of 1976–1981.[47] Public opinion certainly supported the death penalty when Buffet and Bontemps, two prisoners whose failed mutiny resulted in the assassination of a guard and a nurse at the Clairvaux prison, were executed in 1972.[48] Badinter's account, *L'Execution*, published shortly thereafter, is one of solitude and incomprehension. Crowds cried for revenge and death outside of the tribunal in Troyes during the trial. The execution itself, organized at dawn on November 29, 1972, did not raise unusual controversy. Badinter's book did not sell well.[49]

When Giscard d'Estaing was elected president in 1974, the political climate was beginning to shift. Giscard had narrowly won against Mitterrand, and the President intended to win over some voters from the left with liberal reforms, including the legalization of abortion, suffrage at age eighteen, and the like. On the "difficult" topic of the death penalty, the President expressed "abhorrence" for executions but wished that a thorough analysis be organized. In the case of Christian Ranucci, a twenty-one-year-old man from Southern France sentenced to death for stabbing a young girl after her abduction in Marseilles, abolitionists reasonably hoped for clemency. Not that Ranucci's crime did not warrant the guillotine according to the times' standards, but serious doubts remained about the young man's guilt.[50] Days before the young girl's abduction, a man wearing a red pullover was seen twice in the area talking to children, and near the girl's body, police found a similar red pullover. Ranucci never wore red and, after initially confessing to the murder, stringently denied being the culprit. Ranucci's execution in Marseilles at the end of July 1976 was the first of Giscard's mandate and was generally reproved by the press. Even on public television, at that time still controlled by the State, news anchor Roger Gicquel was allowed a candid abolitionist speech.[51]

47 See for example this piece published in the *Los Angeles Times* in 1971: Don Cook, "Guillotine: Will Blade Fall Once Again in France?" *Los Angeles Times*, October 14, 1971, A1.

48 Cf. Reuters, "Two Guillotine Executions Stir Debate, Grim Memories in France," *Los Angeles Times*, December 8, 1972, H2.

49 Robert Badinter, *L'exécution* (Paris: Grasset, 1973).

50 For a vigorous counter-investigation, see Gilles Perrault, *Le Pull-over Rouge* (Paris: Ramsay, 1978).

51 Watch online at http://www.ina.fr/economie-et-societe/justice-et-faits-divers/video/CAA7601747401/la-guillotine.fr.html (last visited March 29, 2010).

After Ranucci's execution, only two other condemned died on the guillotine in June and September 1977. The debate grew in intensity, especially when Robert Badinter convinced jurors in Troyes to spare Patrick Henry's life. Henry had abducted a young boy, demanded a ransom from his parents, and finally strangled his victim. Although no doubt existed regarding Henry's guilt, Badinter decided to plead mostly against capital punishment itself. In his book *L'abolition*, he explains, "I excluded resorting to the description of the horrors of execution. Jansenist by temperament, I refused any rhetorical exploitation of the guillotine." However, the concrete aspects of an execution need to be explained to the jurors, and Badinter kept looking for the right words: "I looked for the most striking image in the sparest form to express what the execution was all about. To guillotine someone, it's nothing else than to take a man, and cut him, as he is alive, in two pieces. It's as simple and unbearable as that."[52] This striking and simple formula – "take a man and cut him in two pieces" – proves Badinter's gift of eloquence.

As a lawyer, however, he knew he also had to place jurors in front of their responsibility as a sentencing authority whose words would probably be the final verdict, since President Giscard d'Estaing did not seem a man to grant a child killer clemency. This was why he closed his plea for Patrick Henry with an evocation of the future when, according to Badinter, capital punishment would be abolished and jurors would have to live with the fateful decision of having sentenced Henry to death. The jury – nine citizens of Troyes and three magistrates – deliberated for only an hour and a half. They found Henry guilty as charged of the abduction and murder of young Philippe Bertrand, a capital crime. But to the last question: "Are there any attenuating circumstances?" a majority of jurors answered yes, thus saving Henry's head and sending him instead to prison for life.

The Troyes' surprising verdict did not mean the end of capital punishment in France, with two other condemned being guillotined in June and September 1977. But it clearly demonstrated that even in the least favorable settings, the cause of abolition could win. It also gave Badinter legitimacy and moral authority, which made him the perfect choice for Mitterrand as a Justice Secretary. Mitterrand openly declared his abolitionist stance during a televised interview a few weeks before the vote in 1981. After Mitterrand's election in May, Badinter presented his abolitionist bill in September. The Left voted yes, as did sixteen MPs from the Right, including Jacques Chirac. There would be no more executions in France.

A few months later, Texas executed its first condemned by lethal injection. The new, "clean" and discrete method became the norm throughout the United States. A flurry of executions followed, reaching a peak of ninety-eight a year in 1999. The trend is admittedly declining, but still, fifty-two condemned were executed in 2009 and twenty-one in 2010.[53]

52 Cf. Robert Badinter, *L'abolition* (Paris: Fayard, 2000).

53 Source: http://deathpenaltyinfo.org/executions (last visited May 24, 2010).

CONCLUSION

How important were executions in all these processes? In France, Badinter, in both his pleadings and actions, powerfully expressed something that the lack of executions in the 1960s and 1970s had also suggested: Not only were executions with the guillotine unbearable, but as a shameful display of cruelty, they belonged to the past. Abolitionists tried to express and convey the horrors of the deadly machine. A strong tradition can be identified, from Victor Hugo to Albert Camus in literature and from André Cayatte to Claude Lelouch or Jose Giovanni in film. All those productions brought to readers and spectators the anguished wait of execution day, the fear and disgust that participants tried to hide since the law prohibited the press from openly describing executions, and the legal apparatus that certainly hid a number of episodes that may have accelerated the process of abolition. On the other hand, however, most citizens knew what the guillotine was all about. What needed to be dismounted were ideas of exemplarity and usefulness against criminality or to the victims' relatives. In that context, Ranucci's contested execution and Henry's trial in Troyes between July 1976 and January 1977 were important points in the debate in France.

In the United States, the public had more information about executions. The press was, in most states, authorized to cover executions. For thirty years, federal courts have developed a robust jurisprudence that now ensures the press' right to cover all of the execution from beginning to end.[54] Lawsuits pertaining to execution methods and especially to lethal injection have crippled capital punishment and forced authorities to reveal embarrassing details.[55] Since the recent Supreme Court decision in *Baze v. Rees*, lethal injection has received a fragile authorization to exist. Litigations about execution methods, articles about botched executions, and the like reveal that capital punishment in today's America does not enjoy the same tranquil popularity it did only fifteen years ago. Does that mean abolition is a reasonable, short-term perspective? Some signs could indicate just the opposite.[56] But debate and qualms about executions, together with other themes – wrongful convictions, cost of capital punishment, and so on – certainly indicate a favorable climate for abolitionists.

[54] See Kurt Streeter, "Serene Inmate Never Wavered as His Execution Drew Near," *Los Angeles Times*, March 28, 2001, A3. Also G.M.M., "The Executioner's Song: Is There a Right to Listen?" *Virginia Law Review* 69, no. 2 (1983): 373–403.

[55] See about California, Howard Mintz, "Untrained Executioners: Documents Reveal Little Preparation for Lethal Injections," *McClatchy – Tribune Business News* (2006).

[56] An execution with the electric chair in 2010, without much reaction; see Josh White, "Murderer and rapist Powell dies in Virginia electric chair," *The Washington Post*, March, 19, 2010, A01.

PART III

Abolitionist Discourses, Abolitionist Strategies, Abolitionist Dilemmas: Transatlantic Perspectives

7

Civilized Rebels

Death-Penalty Abolition in Europe as Cause, Mark of Distinction, and Political Strategy

Andrew Hammel

"Since Beccaria, Sonnenfels and other worthy and popular authors have declared war on the death penalty and torture, everyone now wants to be an 'enlightened thinker,' and a horde of writers has formed itself behind them."

– Christian Gottlob Gmelin (1785)[1]

INTRODUCTION

On July 28, 1978, the French National Assembly passed Loi 78–888. The law changed several articles of the French Code of Penal Procedure governing the selection of juries in the *cour d'assise* (the tribunal that tries the most serious felonies). Before the law was passed, members of each jury were selected from a list assembled by local commissions. This method had been criticized as elitist, because the commissions tended to favor "respectable" citizens. The new law specified that jury lists would henceforth be composed by random, public selection of names from the voting rolls.

The new law alarmed Robert Badinter, the French lawyer and anti-death penalty activist whose tireless advocacy against capital punishment had earned him the nickname *Monsieur Abolition*. In his 2000 memoir of the abolition struggle, Badinter described his reservations about the law. A lifelong Socialist, Badinter denied a desire to return to nineteenth-century juries of *notables*, who were disposed to defend "order and property at any price."[2] However, he observed that under the previous law,

[1] Eberhard Schmidt, "Goethe und das Problem der Todesstrafe." Schweizerische Zeitschrift für Strafrecht 63 (1948): 444–64.

[2] Robert Badinter, Abolition: One Man's Battle Against the Death Penalty, trans. Jeremy Mercer (Boston, Northeastern University Press, 2008), 159.

Where a published English translation of a source exists, I will use that translation. All other translations of foreign-language sources are my own. I would like to thank Dieter Reicher of the University of Graz and Tim Newburn of the London School of Economics for permission to cite forthcoming works, and my fellow participants at the conference "Is the Death Penalty Dying?" held at Amherst College in April 2010, for their excellent comments and suggestions.

jurors were "discreetly chosen" in a way that favored "professionals, civil servants, and managers." In these circles, Badinter argued, there is a "more advanced level of education and culture than in the average population," and therefore, "there tends to be a higher percentage of abolitionists and, more generally, supporters of a moderate approach to criminal penalties." Badinter acknowledged that the reform made juries more democratic, but feared that participation of the "average population" in the sentencing process would lead to more death penalties. Indeed, French juries did hand down a slightly larger number of death sentences after the reform. However, none of those sentences was carried out before the French parliament's 1981 vote to abolish the death penalty.

Badinter's tactical objection to more "democratic" juries reflects two key aspects of movements to abolish capital punishment in Europe. First, these movements were conceived and led by elites, often from within the legal profession. Second, one of the most persistent obstacles to abolition was pro-death penalty sentiment among the population. European abolitionists quickly concluded that the "average population" would never accept abolition, at least in the short term. Accordingly, elites designed rhetorical and political strategies for abolition that bypassed public opinion. This chapter addresses the role of elites in developing the campaign to abolish capital punishment in three western European nations: Germany, France, and the United Kingdom. In the first part of the chapter, I will briefly define relevant terms. The second part presents a historical overview of the gestation and development of the idea of abolition. It slowly developed from the pet project of a few Enlightenment-era criminal-law reformers to the settled consensus position of the educated elite – and recently, to the majority position in many Western European countries. In the third part, I consider questions raised by the historical overview. Amid all the Enlightenment ferment over human rights and rational government, how did this one issue – capital punishment – acquire such a prominent profile? In the diverse linguistic and cultural landscape of Europe, how did a surprisingly strong consensus develop on the issue of capital punishment while other issues continued to generate division?

I argue that the anti-capital punishment consensus depended on several broader social shifts. Changing sensibilities and attitudes toward punishment played a role. Throughout the nineteenth century, elites in Western Europe and the United States developed new ways of thinking about the death penalty, moving the suffering of the offender and the brutality of the spectacle closer to the center of their concerns. These changing sensibilities have been described by David Garland and Pieter Spierenburg, among others. However, what I want to stress is the outward-facing, signaling aspect of this issue – what publicly endorsing abolition says about a speaker's social standing and aspirations. Abolition's status as a mark of distinction had as much to do with transitory social configurations and political constellations as with principle. Opposition to capital punishment emerged as a mark of distinction by which elites could signal their distance from the masses and their adherence to a "progressive" system of values. This characteristic of abolition made it a favored cause among the liberal professions and the progressive members of the bourgeoisie. Denouncing capital punishment set one apart from advocates of absolutism and articulated a critique of the self-righteous brutality of judicial reactionaries. Yet, unlike some radical causes, it entailed neither a fundamental transformation of society nor a challenge to powerful economic interests. These characteristics, I argue, remained relevant well into the twentieth century and were instrumental in abolition's eventual victory on the European continent.

DEFINITIONS AND ASSUMPTIONS

I will use "abolition" to refer to a law or high court decision that institutes a nationwide ban on capital punishment for crimes within the normal jurisdiction of nonmilitary courts. Under this definition, a nation could be counted as having "abolished" capital punishment even while retaining a few scattered death penalty laws for treason or sabotage, for example. The "elite" will be divided into two broad categories: public intellectuals and the policy/bureaucratic elite. Zygmunt Bauman's loose definition of public intellectuals is helpful: "a motley collection of novelists, poets, artists, journalists, scientists and other public figures who felt it their moral responsibility, and their collective right, to interfere with the political process through influencing the minds of the nation and moulding the actions of its political leaders."[3] The policy/bureaucratic elite may include professors, high-ranking civil servants, and members of the liberal professions. Although well-educated, they are generally not as prominent as public intellectuals and rarely seek the spotlight. This group roughly corresponds to the intelligentsia, recently defined as those who are "concerned with practical knowledge to apply within their organisational roles in society, whereas intellectuals are associated with theoretical, universalist concerns from positions more alienated from immediate social reality."[4]

The concept of social distinction that I use in this chapter should emerge from the context and the specific examples I provide. Nevertheless, it would be remiss not to refer to Pierre Bourdieu's analysis of the way individuals use aesthetic and political judgments as tools of social "distinction" to establish their claims to a particular position within the hierarchy of social class present in all societies.[5] Drawing on Bourdieu, I maintain that every political commitment an individual broadcasts to the outside world is a product not only of that person's interior convictions,

[3] Zygmunt Bauman, Legislators and Interpreters: On Modernity, Post-Modernity, and Intellectuals (Cambridge: Polity Press, 1987), 1.

[4] Giles Scott-Smith, The Politics of Apolitical Culture: The Congress for Cultural Freedom, the CIA and Post-War American Hegemony (New York and London: Routledge, 2002), 15 (citing Ahmad Sadri, Max Weber's Sociology of Intellectuals (Oxford: Oxford University Press, 1992), 69–70, 73.

[5] See generally Pierre Bourdieu, Distinction: A Social Critique of the Judgment of Taste, 11th ed., trans. Richard Nice (Cambridge, MA: Harvard University Press, 1981).

but – precisely *because* the individual chooses to broadcast it to the outside world – also makes a statement about that person's self-image and social aspirations.

Finally, it will be useful to introduce the work of German sociologist Norbert Elias, whose theory of the "civilizing process" will inform the analysis of changing punishment norms presented in this chapter. In his classic *The Civilizing Process*[6] (first published in 1939) and later works, Elias showed that the social practices we associate with "civilization" – such as codes of dress and courtliness; table manners and the proper use of utensils; respect for the dignity and autonomy of others; a decrease in general interpersonal violence in society; and the tendency to remove bodily functions, illness, and death behind a curtain of privacy – originated among the social elites in the fourteenth and fifteenth centuries in Europe, then gradually spread throughout society, as those lower in the social hierarchy copied the "refined" manners of their social betters. Elias's review of the historical record also suggested a gradual decline in the level of interpersonal violence in Western societies since the medieval era, driven by the increasing interdependence and complexity of modern societies, as well as the formation of strong, centralized governments.[7] In addition to growing social interdependence, the civilizing process also involves the gradual spread of patterns of increased discretion, courtesy, and respect for life from social elites to groups lower in the social hierarchy. As will be shown further in this chapter, Elias' theory has been adopted (with some modifications) to explain long-term changes in patterns of violence and punishment beginning in the early modern era.

With these preliminary definitions out of the way, I now turn to a brief historical overview of the role capital punishment has played in European intellectual discourse.

HISTORICAL DEVELOPMENT OF THE ABOLITION IDEAL

The Enlightenment: Rationalism Trumps Revenge

The modern European death penalty abolition movement was launched by Cesare Beccaria, a minor Italian nobleman, when he was twenty-six. His book, *On Crimes and Punishments*, grew out of discussions within a group of young, philosophically minded Italian noblemen.[8] First published in 1764, *On Crimes and Punishments* is a brief Enlightenment manifesto for reform of the entire criminal law. Beccaria accepted the principle that wrongdoers must be punished, but, drawing on social

6 Norbert Elias, The Civilizing Process: Sociogenetic and Psychogenetic Investigations (Oxford: Wiley-Blackwell, 2000).

7 For an excellent application of Elias' thought to the evolution of violence in modernizing societies, see Jonathan Fletcher, Violence and Civilization: An Introduction to the Work of Norbert Elias (Cambridge: Polity Press, 1997).

8 Aaron Thomas, "Preface," in Cesare Beccaria: On Crimes and Punishments and Other Writings, Aaron Thomas, ed. (Toronto: University of Toronto Press, 2008), xvii.

contract theory, argued that punishment should inflict only that level of suffering necessary to prevent the crime at issue. Beccaria's famous treatise remained, according to one historian, "the most influential tract on penal policy well into the second half of the nineteenth century."[9]

In a chapter entitled "On the Death Penalty,"[10] Beccaria concedes that executions may be necessary during times of unrest, but when the "calm rule of law" prevails, their only purpose can be to deter criminals. Yet experience has shown that executions do not deter men from committing crimes. Further, executions harm public morals: "the death penalty becomes a spectacle and for some an object of compassion mixed with indignation." It is not the intensity of punishment that deters, Beccaria argues, but rather its length. Setting criminals to hard labor for life creates an example that will impress citizens for years to come. It also discourages those who, out of "fanaticism or vanity," might welcome martyrdom at the hands of the state. The death penalty is nothing but an "example of cruelty," all the more absurd in that it is a killing committed in the name of laws that "execrate and punish homicide." Most human societies have indeed practiced capital punishment, Beccaria admits, but "this objection amounts to nothing in the face of the truth – against which there is no legal remedy – that the history of mankind gives us the impression of a vast sea of errors, in which a few confused truths float about with large and distant gaps between them." The philosopher's plea for abolition will at first be drowned out by the "cries of so many people who are guided by blind habit," but it is Beccaria's sincere wish that "benevolent monarchs" should take his arguments to heart.

The reaction to *On Crimes and Punishments* was "swift and widespread."[11] A French translation appeared in 1765, and Voltaire, in the guise of a "provincial lawyer," published a favorable commentary on it. Voltaire echoed Beccaria's argument on the usefulness of hard labor as punishment, and observed that many murderers who had been transported transformed themselves into respectable citizens by virtue of being forced to work.[12] If executions are nevertheless deemed necessary, Voltaire argued, they should be exceptionally rare. Voltaire's commentary ensured the book a wide audience, given that he was, at the time, one of the western world's most famous men. In 1830, Goethe recalled: "You . . . have no idea of the influence Voltaire and his great contemporaries had in my youth, and how they governed the whole civilized world."[13] Translations into English followed, and by the 1780s, most catalogs of books for sale in America included an edition of Beccaria's essay, and

9 Richard J. Evans, Rituals of Retribution: Capital Punishment in Germany 1600–1987 (Oxford: Oxford University Press, 1996), 127.

10 Cesare Beccaria, On Crimes and Punishments in "On Crimes and Punishments and Other Writings," 1–86.

11 Thomas, "Preface. On Crimes and Punishments . . . ," xxiii.

12 Voltaire, Commentary on the Book On Crimes and Punishments by a Provincial Lawyer, in "On Crimes and Punishments and Other Writings," 113–152.

13 Johann Wolfgang von Goethe, Faust: A Tragedy (An Authoritative Translation, Interpretive Notes, Contexts, Modern Criticism) (New York: W. W. Norton & Co, 1976), 542.

newspapers serialized the book for their readers.[14] Just twenty years after the publication of Beccaria's book, German criminal law scholar Christian Gottlieb Gmelin, quoted in the epigraph to this chapter, could remark that "everyone" wanted to join Beccaria and other writers in "declaring war" on the death penalty and torture.

Beccaria's critique of capital punishment, although by far the most famous, was not the only one brought forth by the Enlightenment. In his legislative commentary *Grundsätze der Polizey* (roughly, "Principles of Policy"), published in several volumes in the early 1770s, Austrian jurist and professor Joseph von Sonnenfels advocated strict restrictions on capital punishment.[15] The state, he argued, may exact capital punishment only when other means to defend order are insufficient. As soon as the offender is in custody, this potential rationale no longer applies, since the danger he poses is neutralized. Generally, therefore, the death penalty should only be imposed in emergencies such as insurrections or plague quarantines. In any case, death may only be inflicted when other penalties would not be sufficient to deter potential wrongdoers. Like Beccaria, Sonnenfels pointed to the nondeterrability of criminals motivated by fanaticism or revenge. Nevertheless, Sonnenfels stopped short of repudiating the death penalty entirely. As one historian put it, Sonnenfels, to keep the ear of the absolutist rulers he served, was "eager to prove that he was not motivated by free-thinking, radical-humanitarian motives, but rather by concern for the welfare of the state." However, where he could, Sonnenfels advocated more humane policies by "smuggling them through the back door of utilitarianism."[16] Jeremy Bentham also argued against capital punishment at the beginning and end of his long career, although his arguments were somewhat diffuse and had relatively little impact.[17]

The Condemned as Subject: New Themes in the Nineteenth Century

In the nineteenth century, new tones began to enter into the abolitionist discourse of public intellectuals. Whereas the late eighteenth century had seen them abstracting from individual cases to construct principled critiques of capital punishment, the Romantic era saw a new focus on the suffering of the individual. Victor Hugo's seminal *The Last Day of a Condemned Man*[18] takes the form of a first-person journal written by an educated gentleman who is condemned to death by a Paris court.

14 Louis P. Masur, Rites of Execution: Capital Punishment and the Transformation of American Culture, 1776–1865 (New York and Oxford: Oxford University Press, 1989), 53.

15 Joseph von Sonnenfels, Grundsätze der Polizey (Munich: C.H. Beck, 2003, condensed reprint), §§ 377–87.

16 Robert A. Kann, Kanzel und Katheder: Studien zur Österreichischen Geistesgeschichte vom Spätbarock zur Frühromantik (Vienna: Herder, 1960), 187–8.

17 Hugo Adam Bedau, "Bentham's Utilitarian Critique of the Death Penalty," The Journal of Criminal Law, 74 (1985), 1033–65.

18 Victor Hugo, The Last Day of a Condemned Man, trans. P. Hesketh Fleetwood (London: Smith, Elder & Co., 1840).

The unnamed narrator does not dispute his guilt of the crime, the details of which are never mentioned. The focus is exclusively on the stations of the man's fate, from verdict to temporary custody in the Bicêtre prison awaiting the outcome of his pleas for clemency, to his final transfer to the place of execution. In jail, the man is horrified by the sudden loss of status conferred by his education and social rank – the sight of filthy, uneducated fellow prisoners pointing to him and calling him "comrade" induces a mental breakdown. As he comes closer to execution, however, it is the thought of his extinction that drives him to new heights of anguish. Hugo plays the full register of melodramatic techniques to highlight the man's suffering. Shortly before his scheduled execution, for instance, his young daughter is brought to see him, but she fails to recognize him in his wretched condition. An official visits with news of the decision on his last application for clemency (we are not told the outcome), and the prisoner falls to his knees, groveling and begging for his life.

The critical reception of *The Last Day*, which was initially published anonymously, shows its power. Jules Janin called the book "atrocious" and "three hundred pages of agony," complaining that "success can never justify, nor talent excuse – no, nothing can pardon an author who shows such obstinacy in dissecting the soul of a man and disturbing the peace of a nation." An anonymous reviewer praised the novelist's evident horror of capital punishment but took issue with the "cold solemnity" of the prose. Charles Nodier expressed respect for the author's "dark and energetic" talent but declared he would never read the novel again, nor even "think of it during the day, for fear of descending again into its dark night."[19] In 1832, Hugo brought out a new edition of *The Last Day* in which he acknowledged his authorship. He appended a long afterword in the form of a direct attack on the death penalty.[20] In this essayistic tour de force, Hugo invokes almost all the tropes of the modern European critique of capital punishment: Capital punishment does not deter crime, belongs to a bygone era of brutality, debases those who witness it, inflicts needless terror on the condemned, and flouts Christian principles. Justifying his decision to make the narrator of *The Last Day* anonymous and to leave his crime unspecified, Hugo called it "a great point of Human Right" that capital punishment be abolished for "all persons, innocent or guilty, before all courts, juries or judges." In 1848, as a delegate to the National Assembly of the short-lived Second Republic, Hugo echoed this language by calling for the "pure, simple, definitive" abolition of capital punishment in a famous speech.

Hugo was not a lawyer, and distrusted legal discourse. One perceptive study noted: "Hugo, the authentic man of letters, revolts against their double abuse by those who confound justice with the letter of the law. Behind legalistic eloquence lies the ugly

[19] Paul-Francis Smets, Le Combat Pour L'Abolition de la Peine de Mort: Hugo, Koestler, Camus et d'Autres (Louvain-Le-Neuve: Académie Royale de Belgique, 2003), 12–15.

[20] Victor Hugo, "The Last Day of a Condemned Man," 157–92.

reality of man's inhumanity to man."[21] Robert Badinter, the French lawyer/politician who later presided over abolition, described Hugo's accomplishment thus:

> Before him, Beccaria [and others] denounced the death penalty as useless. But they appealed more to reason than to emotion. Victor Hugo aimed at the heart. He was the first to place the condemned man at the center of the debate. He brought to life the agony of waiting that precedes the agony of execution. The writer employs these descriptions to trump the philosophers and jurists. One cannot topple the scaffold with arguments but with words which give birth to images and emotions. Hugo, the novelist and poet, puts the reader in the place of the condemned man.[22]

The horrified reactions of Parisian critics to *The Last Day* testify to Hugo's success. Even in the essay opposing capital punishment, Hugo combined rational arguments with unsparing descriptions of state killing's grisly reality. Hugo cites one execution in which the guillotine failed to sever the female prisoner's head, and the executioners had to "finish the job" by pulling violently at her body.

With his emphasis on the individual, subjective experience of the condemned, Hugo exemplifies the late-eighteenth-century shift in subjectivity described by Charles Taylor. Before the late eighteenth century, Taylor argues, "the background that explained what people recognized as important to themselves was to a great extent determined by their place in society, and whatever roles or activities attached to this position." Under the influence of Enlightenment thinkers such as Rousseau and Herder, a new form of inwardness gradually develops, in which people come to think of themselves having inner depths. The "new idea" that the late eighteenth century brought with it, argues Taylor, is that there is "a certain way of being human that is my way," and that one should realize that way of life as authentically as possible.[23] Hugo uses this innovation to build a universalistic case against the death penalty: The fact that it subjects a unique individual with human dignity to stretches of intense fear and anguish, before finally ending his existence, is *alone* sufficient to condemn it.

This critique of capital punishment, couched in the language of subjective human experience and universal human rights, conferred several strategic advantages on abolitionists. First, unlike arguments derived from Beccarian or Benthamite rationality, the execution-as-needless-suffering argument bypasses the formalities of legal and political debate and thus cannot be refuted in those terms. For the same reason, the argument grounds a claim for "pure, simple and definitive" abolition regardless of the nature of the crime, evidence of guilt, or social context. The argument also

21 Kathryn M. Grossman, The Early Novels of Victor Hugo: Towards a Poetics of Harmony (Geneva: Libraire Droz S.A., 1986), 123.

22 Badinter, in Marie-Laure Prévost, Victor Hugo: l'homme océan (Bibiothèque Nationale de France, Paris: Le Seuil, 2002), 58.

23 Charles Taylor, Multiculturalism: Examining the Politics of Recognition (Princeton, NJ: Princeton University Press, 1994), 30, 31.

provides a justification for ignoring the will of the majority. If executions are intrinsically evil, opposition to capital punishment is a moral imperative that cannot be made dependent on the vagaries of public opinion.

Hugo's reframing of the issue of state killing as a moral absolute incommensurable with ordinary calculations of public welfare continues to deeply influence abolitionist discourse. As Franklin Zimring recently observed:

> [The international abolitionist's] appeal to execution-free penal codes as a basic constitutional requirement for a civilized state performs a number of rhetorical functions for the international abolitionist. Seeking out the high ground of limits on government power renders all the traditional death penalty disputes about what terrible crimes and criminals deserve, about deterrence, about risks of error and fairness in administration, literally beside the point. As soon as the human rights/limited government premise is accepted, the policy conclusion is automatic. There are no contingencies, no balancing of costs and benefits, and no reasons to consult public sentiments about crime.[24]

The subjectivist turn in abolitionist discourse also added another aspect of social distinction to the abolitionist position. The Enlightenment critique showcased the educated man's ability to distance himself from the "primitive" and "backward" revenge instincts that drove the unlettered masses. This aspect of social distinction continues to play a vital part in abolitionist discourse. The introduction of the execution-as-needless-suffering trope now ensures that opposition to capital punishment *also* highlights one's refined sensibilities and capacities for empathy. The opponent of capital punishment distances himself from an impulse associated with the unlettered mob (blood revenge), while simultaneously affiliating himself with an sentiment associated with the the Romantic idea of refined sensibility (empathy with social outcasts).

The nineteenth century also saw a similar development of sensibilities among British elites. We see a transition from the utilitarian arguments of Bentham or the abolitionist lawmaker Samuel Romilly toward a more personal, subjective frame. William Makepeace Thackeray's 1840 essay "Going to See a Man Hanged"[25] is an example. Thackeray, then a struggling twenty-nine-year-old writer, conceived of the idea of witnessing the execution of François Benjamin Courvoisier, a French valet who had killed his employer. After a brief, heavily publicized trial (based on his confession), Courvoisier was sentenced to death and executed on July 6, 1840.

"Going to See a Man Hanged" begins in a nearly jaunty tone: Thackeray and his companion X (a politician who, Thackeray notes, had voted for the abolition of capital punishment) had spent most of the night socializing with renowned London

[24] Franklin E. Zimring, The Contradictions of American Capital Punishment (Oxford: Oxford University Press, 2003), 45–6.

[25] William Makepeace Thackeray, The Letters and Private Papers of William Makepeace Thackeray (Cambridge, MA: Harvard University Press, 1946), 451–5.

wit "Dash," who "kept the company merry all night with appropriate jokes about the coming event." On the morning of the execution, Thackeray and X arrive early at Snow Hill near Newgate Prison. Even at that early hour, thousands of commoners had gathered outside the walls of the prison to see the hanging. Merrymaking occupied the "extraordinarily gentle and good-humoured" crowd: Vendors sold food, men clambered up trees and drainpipes to get a better view, and wags entertained bystanders with political harangues and bawdy jokes.

As the awful event approached, however, Thackeray's apprehension grew. The sight of the gallows itself shocked him, and he was unable to witness Courvoisier's actual execution: "I could look no more, but shut my eyes as the last dreadful act was going on which sent this wretched guilty soul into the presence of God." Thackeray's pre-execution ambivalence disappeared: "The sight has left on my mind an extraordinary feeling of terror and shame. It seems to me that I have been abetting an act of frightful wickedness and violence, performed by a set of men against their fellows; and I pray God that it may soon be out of the power of any man in England to witness such a hideous and degrading sight." The ironic moralist of *Vanity Fair* is nowhere to be seen in the heartfelt conclusion of Thackeray's essay: "I feel myself ashamed and degraded at the brutal curiosity which took me to that brutal sight; and I pray to Almighty God to cause this disgraceful sin to pass from among us, and to cleanse our land of blood." Like Hugo, Thackeray highlights the prisoner's psychological suffering. Drawing from accounts published after the execution, Thackeray reconstructs Courvoisier's last days: "As the day of the convict's death draws nigh," Thackeray observes with pathos, "it is painful to see how he fastens upon everybody who approaches him, how pitifully he clings to them and loves them."

Historian V.A.C. Gatrell notes that Thackeray's text crosses a "great divide" in that "pity for a common murderer and disgust at those who took his life had never been so nakedly expressed in print before."[26] To be sure, earlier generations of British writers had expressed squeamishness at executions, but only in those cases in which the convict's social background was roughly comparable to the writer's. Generally, Gatrell observes, not a word was wasted on convicts from London's teeming slums. Thackeray's essay shows the educated British elite developing a critique of capital punishment based on disgust at its brutality and on compassion for the condemned, regardless of social class.

Changing Sensibilities in Theoretical Perspective

Norbert Elias's theoretical framework of the civilizing process, discussed briefly in the first part of this chapter, has proven fruitful to historical criminologists. Several

26 V.A.C. Gatrell, The Hanging Tree: Execution and the English People, 1770–1868 (Oxford: Oxford University Press, 1996), 296.

recent studies have found that the murder rate in Western Europe and England, for instance, decreased by something like 90 percent between the fourteenth century and the present, despite the advent of much deadlier weapons.[27] After assessing other potential causes, these studies conclude that the drop in interpersonal violence was largely a product of evolving social sensibilities. The decline in violence, which had gained momentum in the early modern era, gathered further strength in the nineteenth century, which also saw the spread of mass literacy and urbanization in many continental European countries.[28]

David Garland has argued that Elias's model also helps explain the decreasing harshness of punishment: "[I]t seems perfectly clear that Elias' analysis of the development and characteristics of modern sensibilities has a profound importance for the study of punishment, which, as I have argued, is a sphere of social life deeply affected by conceptions of what is and is not 'civilized.'"[29] Civilization fosters the ability to empathize with people of different social backgrounds. This empathy leads to internalized restraints on urges to do violence to others. This growing capacity for empathy and aversion to violence, in turn, reduces the level of condemnation and sheer hatred felt for criminals, and fosters a legal and moral order that accords even dangerous criminals basic respect and a chance at rehabilitation. Garland, drawing on work done by Pieter Spierenburg,[30] traces the development of elite sensibilities:

> This developing sensitivity [to public executions], growing from a mild ambivalence in the seventeenth century to the self-declared humanitarianism and sentimentalism of the eighteenth and nineteenth, was first and foremost a characteristic of elites. "Conscience formation" and the refinement of manners were features of "polite society," of the upper and middle classes who came to pride themselves on their delicacy and to despise those beneath them for their lack of culture and civilization. It was considered a mark of their uncivilized character that the lower-class crowds "continued to be attracted to the event until the end" long after the rulers had withdrawn from such scenes, having ceased to take pleasure in the brutal execution of justice.[31]

In the first half of the nineteenth century, the rhetorical shift among elite abolitionists was driven by a two-step dynamic that corresponds closely with Elias's framework.

27 Ted Robert Gurr, "Historical Trends in Violent Crime: A Critical Review of the Evidence," Crime and Justice 3 (1981): 295–353; Manuel Eisner, "Modernization, Self-Control, and Lethal Violence: The Long-Term Dynamics of European Homicide Rates in Theoretical Perspective," British Journal of Criminology 41 (2001): 618–38.

28 A. R. Gillis, "Literacy and the Civilization of Violence in 19th-Century France," Sociological Forum 9 (1994), 394.

29 David Garland, Punishment and Modern Society: A Study in Social Theory (Chicago, IL: University of Chicago Press, 1990), 216.

30 Pieter Spierenburg, The Spectacle of Suffering: Executions and the Evolution of Repression (Cambridge: Cambridge University Press, 1984).

31 Garland, "Punishment and Modern Society," 227.

Condemned criminals began to be viewed as autonomous subjects whose suffering was worthy of concern in its own right. In a related process, elites began to see executions as inherently cruel and distasteful. Gatrell, in his study of capital punishment in Great Britain, broadly endorses the Eliasian framework, but notes that the humane sentiments displayed by elites were rarely unalloyed:

> [H]umane feelings prevail when their costs in terms of security or comfort are bearable; when they can be productively acted upon; and when they bring emotional and status returns to the "humane". Culturally dominant groups most deplore brutality when the state's authority or their own is strong enough to obviate the need for its outward display.[32]

Gatrell's formulation neatly balances the *interior* process of refinement of sensibilities against the implications – in terms of social distinction and political context – of its *exterior* manifestation.

In contrast to the European movement against capital punishment, the American movement was often explicitly religious, reflecting a liberal Protestant theology that stressed reform and the offer of salvation to all who accepted Jesus Christ. Opposition to capital punishment was also often seen as a natural accompaniment to opposition to slavery and efforts to improve treatment of animals, which also became objects of progressive activism in the first half of the nineteenth century. As in Europe, emotional identification with the condemned offender and distrust of the crowd were driving factors in abolition. As historian Stuart Banner notes:

> Eighteenth-century Americans saw nothing unseemly about attending an execution. People from all walks of life watched hangings and described them without any hint of embarrassment about having been present. The experience was understood to be spiritually instructive, like attending a sermon, and for that reason parents took their children. In the first few decades of the nineteenth century, however, elite perceptions of mass gatherings shifted. The crowd came to be seen as an unruly, threatening mob.[33]

Banner locates the growing aversion to public executions within a broader shift in sensibility among the middle classes. They began to "see great differences in the realm of taste and manners between themselves and those they considered to be less refined [and] placed a new emphasis on etiquette and gentility, matters that had once been the province of the rich." In particular, the middle class began to pride itself on being "humane and sensitive to the suffering of others," as opposed

32 Gatrell, "The Hanging Tree . . . ," 12.

33 Stuart Banner, The Death Penalty: An American History (Cambridge, MA: Harvard University Press, 2002), 150.

to the crowd, which was "callous to the sight of violence and enjoyed watching the infliction of pain."[34]

Retrenchment and Stabilization

By the second half of the nineteenth century, the discourse of abolitionist elites had reached recognizably modern form. All possible arguments had been marshaled, and most of those who cared about the issue had already taken a position. Opposition to capital punishment as a mark of progressive sympathies and social distinction had established a foothold among the policy and bureaucratic elites of larger European countries: petty officials, civil servants, doctors and apothecaries, lawyers and notaries, and the like. It is important to note, however, that the full abolitionism was still a minority position even among these groups. Mainstream "progressive" opinion about capital punishment held that it should be limited in scope and inflicted humanely, not abolished outright. John Stuart Mill's famous 1868 speech in the British Parliament on capital punishment provides an example.[35] Mill praised the work of "philanthropists" of earlier generations. Thanks to them, "our criminal laws . . . have so greatly relaxed their most revolting and most impolitic ferocity, that aggravated murder is now practically the only crime which is punished with death by any of our lawful tribunals; and we are even now deliberating whether the extreme penalty should be retained in that solitary case." With the troubling abuses of capital punishment now ended, Mill reasoned, it could be retained as the proper response to instances of extreme depravity.

Nevertheless, abolitionism gradually gained popularity among bourgeois elites, and the influence of those groups was growing. In most European countries, the second half of the nineteenth century saw tremendous demographic and structural changes. Social-democratic and other working-class parties emerged. Literacy spread dramatically throughout European populations. In France, for instance, the number of brides and grooms who could not write their names on their marriage registrations, "declined from almost 50% in the middle of the 19th century to near zero at the beginning of World War I."[36] European societies became vastly more complex, as large social-welfare, public works, insurance, banking, and commerce bureaucracies took shape.

Lawyers were needed to coordinate these ambitious modernization projects, and a subset of the legal profession began to be associated with progressive social reform, overseen by an enlightened elite of well-trained jurists of "advanced" views. Eventually, the growing aversion to capital punishment among these increasingly powerful

34 Banner, "The Death Penalty . . . ," 153.

35 John Stuart Mill, Collected Works of John Stuart Mill, vol. XXVIII: Public and Parliamentary Speeches (Toronto: University of Toronto Press, 1988), 266–72.

36 Gillis, "Literacy and the Civilization. . . . "

classes drove serious attempts to end the death penalty. In France, for instance, abolition became a key goal of the French Radical political tendency that emerged in the 1860s. Julie le Quang Sang, the foremost analyst of abolition in France, describes the Radicals thus:

> [T]he party was preferred by the petit and middle-class bourgeoisie, the liberal professions, and, in particular, lawyers.... In the 1870s, the proclamation of the [Third] Republic was associated with a considerable movement of legal professionals into the political sphere.... As a vector of progress and social development, the law, more than ever, constituted an instrument of social regulation, in the service of those in power. Political leadership in social and economic conflicts operated increasingly on the basis of legal dogma, practices, and techniques.[37]

The Radicals emerged as the most powerful force in the legislative elections of 1902. In 1908, the Radical campaign for legislative abolition – ferociously opposed by the yellow press and some judicial officials – culminated in a series of debates and a vote in the French Parliament. Abolition was voted down resoundingly.[38]

Some German states had abolished capital punishment after the 1848 Revolutions, but others had retained it. The German Social Democratic Party, after its unification and refoundation in 1875, gradually became associated with the abolitionist movement. Meanwhile, German lawyers and law professors continued to number among the most prominent opponents of the death penalty. Abolitionists won early victories during the complex parliamentary maneuvers leading up to the unification of Germany in 1870–1871. However, during the third reading of a bill to abolish capital punishment in the new German Reich, Chancellor Otto von Bismarck intervened with a powerful speech in which he warned that attempting to force through the abolition of capital punishment would endanger plans for German national unity. Bismarck's speech caused a critical mass of abolitionist delegates to change their votes, and capital punishment was kept as a punishment for murder in the new *Strafgesetzbuch* (Penal Code) of 1871. In practice, however, the death penalty was increasingly reserved only for the most heinous cases, and from 1877 onward, executions were carried out in private.

England in the late nineteenth century was even farther from abolishing capital punishment. From the sixteenth to the early nineteenth century, death penalty laws had been added haphazardly to England's statute books, generating the so-called "Bloody Code." Writing in the late 1760s, Sir William Blackstone observed: "It is a melancholy truth, that among the variety of actions which men are daily liable to commit, no less than a hundred and sixty have been declared by act of

37 Julie Le Quang Sang, La Loi et la Bourreau: La Peine de Mort in Débats, 1870–1985 (Paris: Editions L'Harmattan, 2001), 37.

38 Julie le Quang Sang, "L'abolition de la peine de mort en France: le rendez-vous manqué de 1906–1908." *Crime, History & Societés/Crime, History & Society* (2002) 6(1): 57–83.

parliament to be felonies without benefit of clergy; or, in words, to be worthy of instant death."[39] During the 1830s, the conviction that the Bloody Code was a disgrace to British justice gradually established itself. The reformist Lord Russell, in the words of historian V.A.C. Gatrell, "presided over the virtual obliteration of the bloody penal code in 1837."[40] By the middle of the nineteenth century, the death penalty was, de facto, only inflicted in Britain for murder. Further progressive reductions in the scope of Britain's capital punishment laws took place, especially in the 1860s. As was so often the case, progressive limitations on capital punishment actually slowed the momentum toward abolition by addressing blatant procedural shortcomings and reserving the death penalty for the most "deserving" group of offenders. Elsewhere, I have called this paradox of capital punishment policy the "stabilization effect."[41]

The Final Push to Abolition

Despite the stabilization effect, capital punishment remained a live issue in England, France, and Germany throughout the early twentieth century. The abolitionist movement grew particularly strong in Great Britain in the 1930s, when the House of Commons passed a Conservative-sponsored bill calling for a five-year moratorium on capital punishment in 1938, only to see it rejected by the House of Lords. A 1919 vote in the Weimar National Assembly calling for the abolition of capital punishment was narrowly defeated. Gustav Radbruch, a liberal jurist and law professor, briefly became Minister of Justice in one of the Weimar Republic's many shifting coalition governments, and proposed a draft criminal code abolishing the death penalty in 1922. The code, however, was never enacted, and Radbruch's two brief terms as Justice Minister were over by the end of 1923. Another near-victory for abolition came in late 1928, when another shift in Weimar power relations brought numerous abolitionists into the legislature. Nevertheless, a series of votes on abolition held by the criminal justice subcommittee in 1928 ended in fourteen-to-fourteen deadlock, and the *Fallbeil* (guillotine) remained in use.[42]

World War II brought abolition initiatives in Europe to a sudden halt. After the war, the political landscape of Western Europe had changed radically. Germany lay in ruins and had to rebuild its political order nearly from scratch. France was also badly divided and unstable. England was able to return to politics as usual the quickest, but not before electing a Labour government that laid the foundation for Britain's modern welfare state. Especially on the European continent, the horrors of World War II had added a decisive new dimension to the distrust of the masses.

39 William Blackstone, Commentaries on the Laws of England, In Four Books (Chicago, IL: Callaghan and Company, 1884), 286.

40 Gatrell, "The Hanging Tree . . . ," 295.

41 Andrew Hammel, Ending the Death Penalty: The European Experience in Global Perspective (Basingstoke: Palgrave MacMillan, 2010), 35–9.

42 Evans, "Rituals of Retribution . . . ," 591–610.

Under National Socialism, the use of capital punishment skyrocketed, and some 30,000 "legal" executions occurred, in addition to the massive, lawless liquidation of politically and ethnically "undesirable" populations. The situation was not as drastic in occupied France, but the behavior of many French citizens during World War II still reflected a latent capacity for brutality and indifference among the ordinary population. In some European narratives, World War II is seen as the spur to final abolition: European elites "discovered" the brutality lurking within the common man's psyche and took action to ensure the state could never kill in the peoples' name again.[43] However, as we have seen, distrust of the masses had *always* been a key component of the abolitionist mindset. The aftermath of World War II simply lent fresh relevance to the critique of public opinion.

Germany was the first country to abolish capital punishment after World War II. Abolition came as a surprise, when a right-wing delegate to Germany's postwar constitutional convention first proposed abolition. The proposal was then taken up by other parties, and abolition was eventually enshrined as Article 102 of the German *Grundgesetz* (Basic Law), which reads "The death penalty is abolished." Radbruch, still a renowned and influential liberal constitutional law professor, was gratified by the outcome of the constitutional convention. Nevertheless, in a 1949 editorial entitled "The Gallows Overthrown," he predicted that the public would soon mobilize to restore capital punishment. Abolitionists "should maintain their standpoint even against occasional public moods in opposition, should not become weak in the face of the bloodlust (*Blutverlangen*) of the unlettered masses, and even more, should prevent the emergence of these instinct-driven demands by an effective popular education campaign (*Volkspädagogik*)."[44]

Radbruch proved prescient. Throughout the 1950s, repeated attempts were made to reintroduce capital punishment. These were skillfully parried by Dr. Thomas Dehler, Germany's first postwar Justice Minister. Dehler, a member of the liberal Free Democratic Party that governed in a coalition with the Christian Democrats, had been persecuted during the National Socialist regime on the grounds of his "mixed" marriage to a Jewish woman. He compounded his problems with the Party by continuing to represent Jewish clients and was even briefly interned in a labor camp. After the war, Dehler's opposition to capital punishment put him at odds with his party and its much larger coalition partner, the center-right Christian Democrats. Konrad Adenauer, the Christian Democrat Chancellor under whom Dehler served, supported reintroducing the death penalty.

43 An official publication of the Council of Europe on capital punishment begins thus: 'In the aftermath of the destruction of the Second World War, the Council of Europe was created to unite Europe around the shared principles of the rule of law, respect for human rights and pluralist democracy.' Directorate General of Human Rights, "Death is not the Answer," (Strasbourg: Council of Europe, 2007), 8.

44 As quoted in Bernhard Düsing, Die Geschichte der Abschaffung der Todesstrafe in der Bundesrepublik Deutschland (Offenbach: Bollwerk-Verlag, 1952), 288.

In a 1952 Parliamentary speech, Dehler bluntly rejected the idea that the popular will should control the question of capital punishment. Comparing the death penalty to witch burning, Dehler continued:

> I say in all clarity: I do not care about the "peoples' conviction," that is, the opinion of the man on the street, when the question on the table is of the highest political and legal order.... The Parliament is not the people in 1:100,000 scale, it must be a select few, an elite; the voter must give his trust to the best among the people, but he must give his trust nonetheless. The parliamentarian is bound by a great responsibility, he is – as the Basic Law requires – beholden only to his conscience, and is not required to carry out any other person's orders, not even those of the voters.[45]

In a later portion of the speech, Dehler even suggested that the majority of the population continued to support capital punishment owing to "genetically inherited" dispositions.[46] Dehler's speech is remarkable for its complete dismissal of nonelite opinion. As an important figure in Germany's fledgling democracy, Dehler obviously feels some pressure to address majority sentiment. Yet his answer is to boldly attack not only the assumption that public opinion should guide Parliament, but public opinion *itself*. His flattery of his fellow delegates as the "best among the people" was, of course, sure to resound with many of his fellow parliamentarians.

In 1954, Dehler's successor as Justice Minister, Fritz Neumayer (a supporter of capital punishment) convened the *Große Strafrechtskommission*, literally the "Large Criminal Law Commission." Its task was to propose a fundamental overhaul of Germany's criminal code. In typical continental European fashion, the Commission was composed exclusively of the prominent and powerful: professors of criminal law, senior civil servants, active and retired judges, psychologists, and criminologists. There were 2 large plenary sessions in which the proposed penal code was read, and 237 individual sessions on subtopics.[47] During the 108th sitting of the Commission, on October 17, 1958, the personnel gathered to debate the question of reintroducing the death penalty.[48] The outcome was never really in question, as most of the Commissions members were declared opponents of capital punishment.

Nevertheless, the Commission's deliberations shed light on the postwar German legal elite's approach to the issue. Opponents of capital punishment set out the usual pragmatic arguments: the impossibility of adequately defining "death-worthiness," the possibility of executing an innocent person, lack of deterrent effect, and capital punishment's inconsistency with enlightened Christian values. However, public

45 Thomas Dehler, Thomas Dehler: Reden und Aufsätze (Köln and Opladen: Westdeutscher Verlag, 1969), 62–3.

46 Bundestagsprotokolle (Stenographische Berichte, 1952), 10613.

47 Tim Busch, Die deutsche Strafrechtsreform: Ein Rückblick auf die sechs Reformen des Deutschen Strafrechts (1969 – 1998), (Kiel: Kieler Rechtswissenschaftliche Abhandlungen, 2005).

48 Große Strafrechtskommission, Niederschrift über die Beratungen zur Todesstrafe am 17. Oktober 1958 (Bonn: Bundesdruckerei, 1959), 1–2.

opinion – still lopsidedly in favor of capital punishment – was also addressed. Professor Eberhard Schmidt from Heidelberg maintained that the "strong cries of support for capital punishment among the general public are nothing more than a scream for vengeance and retribution."[49]

Bundesanwalt (Assistant Attorney General) Wolfgang Fränkel represented the German state in criminal appeals before the highest federal court of general jurisdiction, the *Bundesgerichtshof*. A former Nazi party member with years of experience as a prosecutor, Fränkel argued that since Germans had recently shown an "unmistakable tendency to uncritically follow any state authority, it is simply irresponsible . . . to entrust the state, even through its courts, to decide over the life or death of human beings." The German people's deficiency in "moral self-control" (*sittliche Selbstkontrolle*) was, to Fränkel, evident.[50] Federal Judge Else Koffka, the only woman to submit an opinion to the Commission, rejected the death penalty on the grounds that it "awakens dangerous instincts among the people" and places unacceptable burdens on judges. Almost all other contributors sounded similar antipopulist themes. The only sustained defense of capital punishment was delivered by Richard Lange,[51] a criminal law professor from Cologne. Lange stressed the need for criminal punishments to correspond to the popular will, and asked rhetorically "whether only the most worthless and unreasonable 3/4 or 4/5 of the people register support for capital punishment."

The final vote was nineteen-to-four against capital punishment, and the Commission's proposed penal code thus contained no death penalty. The German case is distinctive in a number of ways. Abolition in Germany was "front-loaded": First came the surprise of the definitive abolition of capital punishment by the Constitution; then, the debate. The debate took place not among public intellectuals, but rather in the rarefied precincts of the Criminal Law Commission. Here, where members of the elite spoke among and to each other, the participants distinguished between the kind of arguments that "should" count among highly educated jurists and civil servants, and those printed in a tabloid or heard in a barroom debate. Dr. Baldus, an appellate judge, argued that the concept of miscarriages of justice should include not only "factual innocence" but also those who have been executed despite doubts as to their mental competency; to do otherwise would be to "fall back on a unacknowledged barbaric assumption: namely, that it is 'not so bad' when a mentally

49 Große Strafrechtskommission, "Niederschrift über die Beratungen zur Todesstrafe," 31–3.

50 Later events show Fränkel's testimony on capital punishment in an ironic light. Shortly after his 1962 appointment as Federal Attorney General it emerged that Fränkel, as an assistant in the prosecutorial office of the *Reich* during the Nazi era, had filed numerous motions requesting harsher penalties – including capital punishment – against persons convicted of theft or ideological 'crimes' such as having an 'anti-German attitude' (*deutschfeindliche Gesinnung*). Fränkel was forced from his post into 'temporary retirement' just months after his appointment. Bundesminister der Justiz, Im Namen des Deutschen Volkes: Justiz und Nationalsozialismus. Katalog zur Ausstellung des Bundesministers der Justiz (Köln: Wissenschaft und Politik, 1989), 373–81.

51 Große Strafrechtskommission, "Niederschrift über die Beratungen zur Todesstrafe," 43–6.

ill lust-murderer is executed."[52] Criminal law professor Paul Bockelmann warned that if we let the "voice of the people" drive policy, we will then have to deal with the "common man's" complaint that keeping someone alive in prison for life costs more than the death penalty. "Of course," Bockelmann assured his distinguished audience, "none of us would ever say something like this, but the voice of the people does."[53]

In contrast to Germany, the debate over capital punishment in other European countries took place in public and was led by public intellectuals. As editor of the influential Resistance journal *Le Combat*, Albert Camus had supported the execution of high-ranking collaborators. Shortly after the liberation of France, however, Camus signed clemency petitions for collaborationist writers such as Robert Brasillach. Finally, in 1948, Camus held a speech at a Dominican convent in Latour-Maubourg in which he told the audience that he had changed his mind and come to recognize that opponents of execution, such as the left-wing Catholic novelist François Mauriac, had been right all along.[54] From that point on, Camus became a convinced abolitionist and advocate of nonviolence. As Hugo had done before him, Camus publicly intervened to request clemency on behalf of death-sentenced prisoners in France and elsewhere.

Camus's change of heart culminated in his 1957 essay *Reflections on the Guillotine*, published the same year he won the Nobel Prize. Camus rehearses familiar arguments for abolition: its failure to deter crime; the physical horror of executions by the guillotine; the fact that executions degrade human life; and society's guilty conscience about the practice, shown in the secrecy with which it is carried out. Camus notes that the state, through its legal processes, inflicts a punishment worse than most murders: an agonizing delay between pronouncement and execution of sentence:

> As the weeks pass, hope and despair increase and become equally unbearable. According to all accounts, the color of the skin changes, fear acting like an acid. . . . Long in advance the condemned man knows that he is going to be killed and that the only thing that can save him is a reprieve, rather similar, for him, to the decrees of heaven. In any case, he cannot intervene, make a plea himself, or convince. He is no longer a man but a thing waiting to be handled by the executioners. He is kept as if he were inert matter, but he still has a consciousness which is his chief enemy.[55]

Camus also invokes France's sordid recent history. If any society has the requisite moral purity to carry out an irrevocable, "perfect" punishment, Camus intones,

52 Große Strafrechtskommission, "Niederschrift über die Beratungen zur Todesstrafe . . . ," 26.
53 Große Strafrechtskommission, "Niederschrift über die Beratungen zur Todesstrafe . . . ," 23.
54 Jean Bloch-Michel, Réflexions sur la peine capitale (Paris: Editions Gallimard, 2002), 247–8.
55 Albert Camus, Resistance, Rebellion, and Death, trans. Justin O'Brien (New York: Alfred A. Knopf, 1960), 200–1.

it is surely not France. The last twenty years, Camus observes, have shown that governments, not individuals, present the greatest threat to human life.

Arthur Koestler joined Camus in making abolition one of his signature issues. Koestler, a Hungarian émigré and former Communist whose novel *Darkness at Noon* had propelled him to world fame, had lived in Britain since the late 1940s. In 1955, he started a "National Campaign" to abolish capital punishment in England and began a series of essays for the *Observer*, later collected into the anti-death penalty polemic *Reflections on Hanging*. In this book, Koestler denounced the British institution of hanging with the rhetorical eagerness associated with Continental – but not necessarily English – political discourse. Koestler described reactionary English judges, for instance, as "Abominable Snowmen" and "wigged fossils," and dismissed mainstream English clergy as feckless servants of the status quo.[56] One contemporary assessed the impact of Koestler's efforts:

> The National Campaign may not have been quite as formidable as its name, but its impact on public opinion was by no means insignificant. By the end of 1955 it had nearly 17000 declared supporters, and by February 1956 the number had risen to 26500. It promoted much active lobbying of MPs and other opinion-formers. But probably its most effective weapons were two books, Gerald Gardiner's *Capital Punishment as a Deterrent, and the Alternative*, and Arthur's *Reflections on Hanging*. In their different ways these two books provided an overwhelming statement of the case for abolition, and though their influence cannot be measured it must have been very considerable.[57]

The parliamentary campaign against capital punishment was led by Gardiner and by Sidney Silverman, a left-wing Labour MP who had represented the Lancashire constituency of Nelson & Colne since 1935. Bills calling for a moratorium on hanging or for outright abolition actually passed the House of Commons in 1948 and 1956, but were rejected in the House of Lords. In the Commons' debate on the 1948 Bill, Silverman denied that one could measure public opinion by "going down to a constituency and counting heads or going into a club or a cinema or a theatre, posing the question, and saying that is the public opinion of this country." Rather, one must gather a cross-section of the population, hold an informed debate, and rely on the "good sense, good judgment and moral integrity" of that cross-section. And where, Silverman asked,

> can we find a better cross-section of the community than this elected House of Commons? We are not delegates; we are not bound to ascertain exactly what a numerical majority of our constituents would wish and then to act accordingly without using our judgment. Edmund Burke long ago destroyed any such theory.

56 Arthur Koestler, Reflections on Hanging (New York: The MacMillan Company, 1957), 40–1.

57 John Grigg, "The Do-Gooder from Seville Gaol," in Astride the Two Cultures: Arthur Koestler at 70 (New York: Random House), 126.

> We are not delegates. We are representatives. Our business is to act according to our consciences, honestly looking at the facts and coming to as right a judgment as we may.[58]

The crucial shift occurred in the late 1950s and early 1960s. The Life Peerages Act of 1958 led to a great influx of Labour peers into the House of Lords. Support for abolition also solidified in a new generation of Labour MPs, who were better educated than their predecessors and thus more likely to take an interest in abstract issues of principle rather than bread-and-butter matters.[59] Finally, and most significantly, growing numbers of Conservative MPs joined the cause. In the decade after 1956, one historian found, the proportion of abolitionists within Conservative ranks doubled from one-eighth of all MPs to one-quarter of them.[60] This shift – as well as a wholesale shift of the English clergy to the abolitionist side – set the stage for the 1965 vote imposing a five-year moratorium on capital punishment and the 1969 vote to make the moratorium permanent. Despite the vote, support for capital punishment remained high, and there were fourteen unsuccessful attempts to reinstate it between 1969 and 1994.[61]

France had to wait longer for abolition. Camus died in a car crash in 1960, but the cause of abolition remained on the progressive agenda. In the 1970s, it was taken up by Robert Badinter, a brilliant lawyer and Socialist politician. After the execution of one of his clients in 1972, Badinter became a public foe of the death penalty, combining legal advocacy for death-eligible defendants with activism against capital punishment. During the 1970s, a spate of crimes against children had galvanized French public opinion, which consistently registered a 60 percent to 65 percent majority in favor of retaining capital punishment. Early in his career as an activist, Badinter realized, by attending public meetings, that a grass-roots campaign against capital punishment was not in the offing:

> The sessions would unfold with little variation. The same arguments provoked the same questions that called for the same answers. Often, supporters of the death penalty questioned me with an air of indignation, sometimes bordering on insults. From their perspective, abolitionists were taking the side of the murderers over their victims. In the fervor that drove these advocates of the death penalty, they wanted quick and summary justice, a kind of permanent Reign of Terror where the guillotine operated without appeal and without delay. To hear them, I realized that it was there, in that obsession with the ritual of death, that lay the core of the irrationality that made abolition so difficult.

58 As quoted in Emrys Hughes, Sydney Silverman: Rebel in Parliament (London and Edinburgh: Charles Skilton Ltd., 1969), 104.

59 Peter Dorey, "The Social Background of Labour MPs Elected in 1964 and 1966," in The Labour Governments, 1964–70, Peter Dorey, ed. (London: Routledge, 2006).

60 Neville Twitchell, "Abolition of the Death Penalty" in The Labour Governments.

61 Roger Hood, The Death Penalty: A Worldwide Perspective (Oxford: Oxford University Press), 26.

> ... To all the arguments that a person could reform, that there was the risk of judicial error, that the lottery of criminal court meant a man's life depended on a thousand imponderable factors, to all the moral, historical, scientific, and political considerations, the supporters of the death penalty had one constant response: the criminals must die because death is the only suitable punishment for such crimes.[62]

To achieve abolition, Badinter turned to his highly placed friends in politics, persuading Socialist Party leader François Mitterrand to make abolition a key plank of Mitterrand's 1981 candidacy for the French Presidency. The outcome of the election was never in doubt; the late 1970s had brought a dramatic leftward shift in public sentiment, and in the legislative elections in 1981, French Socialist and Communist parties were swept into power. Shortly after Mitterrand's election, he appointed Badinter as Justice Minister, and Badinter set about realizing the goal of abolition. Badinter enforced party discipline, wooed the growing ranks of abolitionists in center-right parties, and invoked a quick-vote procedure to secure abolition early in the legislators' terms, so that they would have time to deal with any fallout from the politically unpopular decision. After a stirring address from Badinter, the National Assembly voted out the abolition bill, 333–117, and the Senate followed shortly thereafter by a vote of 160–26.

THE DEATH PENALTY AS CAUSE, MARK OF DISTINCTION, AND POLITICAL STRATEGY

Most commentators approach changing attitudes toward capital punishment as an issue of principle – as a step forward in the march of civilization. Indeed, evidence shows that the movement against capital punishment was guided by the changing sensibilities posited by Elias's civilizing process. Charles Taylor describes a closely related but more inwardly directed change in sensibility. During the Renaissance, Taylor observes, the idea took hold that the enlightened and civilized person is expected to transcend mankind's baser instincts by "constructing [his] own representation of the world" and "tak[ing] charge of the processes by which associations form and shape [his] character and outlook." This change in the structure of the civilized person's *habitus* became even more pronounced during the Enlightenment. The purposeful construction of a "civilized" self requires discipline and a certain amount of self-alienation, "the ability to take an instrumental stance to one's given properties, desires, inclinations, tendencies, habits of thought and feeling, so that they can be worked on, doing away with some and strengthening others, until one meets the desired specifications."[63] The common man might react to descriptions of heinous crimes with an atavistic cry for vengeance (one of his "given properties"),

62 Badinter, "Abolition . . . ," 14.

63 Charles Taylor, Sources of the Self: The Making of the Modern Identity (Cambridge: Cambridge University Press, 1989), 159–60.

but the thinking man showed self-control by distancing himself from his initial emotional reaction and subjecting it to critical analysis.

Yet a change in sensibility is only the first step in a longer-term and more diffuse process of societal transformation. The private, interior change in sensibility must find expression in the public sphere, and attempts to change entrenched social attitudes and practices run into countless unanticipated obstacles. Answering the question why capital punishment became a signature issue for so many public intellectuals and policy elites thus requires sensitivity to historical and social contexts. At different times and among different elite groups, abolition could take on the character of a cause, a mark of social distinction, or a component of a larger political strategy. Of course, these categories are not at all mutually exclusive – in fact, they were almost always present simultaneously in varying degrees.

Abolition as a Cause

Most of the opponents of capital punishment discussed here were sincere opponents of the practice. It is impossible to read Hugo or Thackeray, for instance, without being convinced of their revulsion toward the death penalty. In private correspondence quoted by his biographer, Thomas Dehler cited three main reasons for his rejection of the death penalty. First, the requirement to respect human dignity required the State to value human life in direct proportion to the disrespect shown by the murderer. Second, capital punishment was a "relic" and had no place in a modern justice system. Third, executions treated human beings like "wild animals," which echoed the contempt for human life that had defined National Socialism. Definitively rejecting the death penalty would thus be a symbol of the "renewal" of Germany.[64]

Opponents of capital punishment also took real risks in the political sphere. Dehler's loud denunciations of the death penalty – and of majority opinion – could hardly have sat well with his more conservative party colleagues or, for that matter, with the pro-death penalty Chancellor in whose Cabinet he served. Sydney Silverman, the crusading Labour MP, represented a solidly pro-death penalty constituency. The infamous "Moors Murders" – which involved a British couple abducting, sexually abusing, and murdering children – became a focus of attention in 1965, at the height of Silverman's campaign against hanging. An uncle of one of the victims, Patrick Downey, ran against Silverman in the 1966 general election as a member of the "hanging" party: "I will be fighting on the hanging issue alone. I consider the Bill introduced by Mr Silverman as stupid and idiotic. I intend to fight Mr Silverman in his own constituency and beat him."[65] Silverman won reelection, but only

64 Udo Wengst, Thomas Dehler, 1897–1967: Eine politische Biographie (Munich: R. Oldenbourg Verlag, 1997), 202.

65 Hughes, "Sydney Silverman . . . ," 183.

because his long record of able representation outweighed his death penalty stance. Robert Badinter, by successfully defending notorious French murder defendants in the 1970s, placed himself on the front lines of a rancorous political debate. After securing a life sentence in 1977 for child-killer Patrick Henry, Badinter received letters expressing "hate in its purest form," and he and his family were required to change their daily routines owing to the threats.[66]

Abolition as a Mark of Distinction

Opposition to capital punishment, however, also triggered resonances beyond the scope of straightforward, earnest social reform. In the late eighteenth century, opposing the death penalty fit within a set of commitments common to Enlightenment reformers across Western Europe: calling on monarchs to justify their claims to authority; examining inherited practices and traditions in the light of detached reason; reducing the chaos, brutality, and arbitrariness of state penal policy; and reclaiming the productive potential of offenders by means of work and discipline. As the German jurist Gmelin's reference to the "horde of writers" wishing to be seen as "enlightened thinkers" shows, questioning capital punishment and torture had already, by 1785, become a signature way of demonstrating allegiance to reformist values in the field of penal law. This use of abolition as a synecdoche for humane, enlightened government can still be seen in the Council of Europe's admonition to new EU member states: "A choice whether to abolish or retain the death penalty is also a choice about the kind of society we want to live in and the values it upholds. Abolishing the death penalty is part of a package of values marked human rights, democracy and the rule of law."[67]

The abolitionists' stance also showed the refinement of their moral sensibility. Commenting on capital punishment, Victor Hugo wrote in 1862: "It is by a certain mysterious respect for life that one recognizes the thinking man."[68] The thinking man regards his emotional responses from a distance and subjugates his drives and desires to the scrutiny of reason. He is also able to conceive of human bonds beyond the allegiances of family, tribe, or class. Often, this aspiration took on a Christian tinge. Hugo hopes that "the gentle laws of Christ will penetrate at last" into the legal system, and "[w]e shall look on crime as a disease, and its physicians shall displace the judges, its hospitals displace the galleys."[69] We see here the conflicting imperatives of empathy and detachment: The thinking man shows empathy for outcasts and "mysterious reverence for life," yet at the same time recognizes the need for clinical detachment when addressing the root causes of crime. This dialectic was common

66 Badinter, "Abolition . . . ," 83–4.
67 Directorate General of Human Rights, Death Is Not Justice: The Council of Europe and the Death Penalty, Council of Europe (Strasbourg: Council of Europe, 2001), 10.
68 Smets, "Le Combat Pour L'Abolition . . . ," 7.
69 Hugo, "The Last Day . . . ," 190.

to many works of nineteenth-century social criticism. One scholar, in a study of distance and detachment among nineteenth-century intellectuals, has referred to the "conflicting postures of ethnographic subjectivity" that "attempt to mediate between sympathetic immersion and detached analysis and judgment."[70]

The careful deployments of detachment and empathy that drove the elite worldview of capital punishment signified not only which stratum of society its holder belonged to, but which he or she definitely did *not* belong to. Distrust of the unlettered masses has the very deepest roots in European elite culture, as any study of Plato shows. However, the distance between the elite and the crowds who attended executions began to widen in the early modern era (as Spierenburg shows), and the gap grew significantly in the late eighteenth century. The distance was expressed in one of two ways. The milder, humanitarian expression saw the crowd as vulnerable to the corrupting influence of state killing. Hugo's novels and polemics, for instance, are filled with descriptions of the baleful influence of executions on the crowds who witness them. Writing in 1828, the German penal reformer Paul Anselm von Feuerbach argued against "cruel forms of the death penalty" by arguing that these "barbaric blood-spectacles . . . contribute to blunt people's feelings, feed their coarseness, and drive their spirits wild."[71]

Another expression of social distance was straightforward denunciation. The great Russian critic Vissarion Belinsky, responding to a critique of Voltaire's elitism, admitted in an 1848 letter that the Frenchman had sometimes called the people "'vile,'" but came to Voltaire's defense, justifying this insulting phrase "because the people are uncultivated, superstitious, fanatic, bloodthirsty, and love torture and execution."[72] Of course, there is condescension here: The educated observer, being a person of refined sensibility, is simply presumed to be immune to capital punishment's corrupting influence. The same distancing of the elite from the crowds took place in the United States. As historian Stuart Banner observes:

> Eighteenth-century Americans saw nothing unseemly about attending an execution. People from all walks of life watched hangings and described them without any hint of embarrassment about having been present. The experience was understood to be spiritually instructive, like attending a sermon, and for that reason parents took their children. In the first few decades of the nineteenth century, however, elite perceptions of mass gatherings shifted. The crowd came to be seen as an unruly, threatening mob.[73]

70 Amanda Anderson, The Powers of Distance: Cosmopolitanism and the Cultivation of Detachment (Princeton: Princeton University Press, 2001), 15 (citing Christopher Herbert, Culture and Anomie: Ethnographic Imagination in the Nineteenth Century) (Chicago: University of Chicago Press, 1991).
71 Evans, "Rituals of Retribution . . . ," 247.
72 Joseph Frank, Dostoevsky: A Writer in his Time (Princeton and Oxford: Princeton University Press, 2010), 123.
73 Banner, "The Death Penalty . . . ," 150.

Banner locates the growing aversion to public executions among the elite within a broader shift in sensibility among the American middle classes, which ran almost exactly parallel to the shifts in sensibilities in nineteenth-century Europe.[74]

The use of capital punishment as a touchstone to distinguish "civilized" from the "barbaric" – both in individuals and in society – has lost none of its relevance. As one recent analysis concluded: "Particularly in European abolitionist discourse, the binary opposition between 'civilized' and 'uncivilized' criminal justice systems is conjured up all too often and all too easily."[75] The cultural divide also shows within the upper reaches of the EU bureaucracy in Brussels, in which bureaucratic/policy-making elites from Western European nations – among whom opposition to the death penalty is virtually universal – rub shoulders with their newer colleagues from Eastern Europe. Responding to a recent article about the EU's commitment to human dignity in *Commission en Directe*, an internal newsletter for high-ranking European Commission functionaries, a Hungarian member of the General Directorate for Taxation cited to a recent murder in Hungary, and asked: "by which logic we talk about the human dignity of beings who have obviously none. The esteemed 'goodwill ambassadors' and abolitionist activists would surely not be delighted to meet some of the people they are so eager to save."[76] The first response to Pataki's letter, under the title "Chop Their Heads Off?" registered the writer's "shock" that "views such as Pataki's still exist among educated people." After referring to the fact that Hungary only recently came "*tögether*" with the EU (a mocking reference to the fact that the Hungarian language has no fewer than nine diacritical marks), the author denounces the editors of Commission en Directe for "reproducing" Pataki's "populist views."[77] Other letters from Western European Commission functionaries followed, reminding Pataki of the EU's official abolitionist stance and registering dismay at his views, but often also defending his right to express them.

This exchange of letters recalls the debates in the German criminal law commission. There, members of the elite assembly respected *some* pleas for capital punishment but denounced "populist" arguments such as the cost of maintaining prisoners for life. In the modern situation, the parameters of debate are different – any argument for capital punishment is now out of bounds – but the dynamics are similar. The Western European bureaucrats are less interested in convincing Pataki that his views are *substantively* wrong than they are in conveying the message that retentionist views will "shock" his colleagues, and that the high-prestige government entity for which he works has already taken a public position against capital

74 Banner, "The Death Penalty . . . ," 153.

75 Christian Boulanger and Austin Sarat, "Putting Culture into the Picture: Toward a Comparative Analysis of State Killing" in Boulanger and Sarat, eds., The Cultural Lives of Capital Punishment: Comparative Perspectives (Stanford: Stanford University Press, 2005), 32.

76 Pataki, Z. B. (2007). 'Death Penalty.' Commission en Directe, 448.

77 Vopel, R. (2007). 'Chop Their Heads Off?' Commission en Directe, 449.

punishment. Decades after the last execution in Western Europe, attitudes toward capital punishment continue to be an important way of broadcasting ideological allegiances and signaling membership in elite groups.

As Agata Fijalkowski points out in this volume,[78] the personal conflict between Pataki and his Western European counterparts mirrors developments in former Warsaw Pact nations. Capital punishment is still popular in these countries, and local elites often question the argument that capital punishment is a fundamental violation of human dignity that can never be justified. Capital punishment was practiced in most former Eastern Bloc nations, and the relative insularity of the political culture behind the Iron Curtain limited the impact of human rights discourse there. Many members of the legal and political elite in Eastern Europe were and are convinced that the debate over capital punishment is not over. Further, as Fijalkowski shows, they are keenly aware of the paradox involved in the fact that one of the conditions of joining the "club" of advanced Western European democracies was enforcing a policy rejected by a majority of their own voters. Whether the abolition of capital punishment in Eastern Europe will eventually be embraced by the population (as has occurred in Western Europe) remains to be seen.

Abolition as a Strategic Political Stance

The final aspect of abolition that led to its victory in Western Europe is its use as a means of strategic political positioning. Capital punishment has never been salient enough on its own to serve as the core of a political party or program. Yet it has been used to claim a particular segment of the ideological spectrum. At first, abolition carried risks. Beccaria's *On Crimes and Punishments*, for instance, was originally published under a pseudonym, banned by the Venetian Inquisition, and harshly critiqued by a monk, who used the word "socialist" (to insult Beccaria) apparently for the first time in Italian.[79] Beccaria's friends, philosophers Pietro and Alessandro Verri, countered with an essay in which they noted that the book's author did not contest the sovereign's *right* to exact death as punishment, but maintained only that a wise person would recognize that it is not a "just and necessary" punishment.[80] Even though Austrian jurist von Sonnenfels was not a strict abolitionist, his critique of capital punishment was so controversial that in 1772, he was officially prohibited by Austrian Empress Maria Theresia from addressing his students on this subject.[81]

Abolition's career as a potentially subversive cause was, however, short-lived. Europe's more benevolent rulers soon warmed to the idea of limiting or even

78 Agata Fijalkowski, "European Policy on the Death Penalty," Chapter 10, this volume.
79 Thomas, "On Crimes and Punishments," xxiii–xxiv.
80 Verri and Verri, "On Crimes and Punishments," 70–7.
81 Hermann Conrad, "Joseph von Sonnenfels (1733–1817): Zum 150. Todestag eines Vorkämpfers gegen die Folter," Juristen-Jahrbuch (1967/68) 8: 1–16.

abolishing capital punishment, and in fact began competing among themselves for the services of famous Enlightenment reformers: "Leibniz and Christian Wolff, Voltaire and Diderot, Bentham and Herder, all enjoyed imperial patronage; they were translated and consulted, subsidized and often invited to St. Petersburg by a series of emperors and empresses, climaxing in Catherine the Great, who hoped to construct rational and utilitarian facades for their power."[82] One recent commentator, citing the competition among these rulers for the prestige of hosting Beccaria at court, memorably compared Enlightenment reformers to modern-day football stars.[83]

As of the late eighteenth century, then, supporting abolition was recognized as a reasonable opinion, not a matter for the secret police. Besides its newfound political acceptability, abolition also offered many other advantages. First, unlike more complex reforms, it required no specialized knowledge to understand or articulate. The late eighteenth and early nineteenth centuries saw ambitious reforms of the criminal law. However, weighing the advantages of more specialized reforms often required legal knowledge. Whether to abolish capital punishment, by contrast, was a simple binary issue on which anyone could have an opinion. Further, the salience and simplicity of abolition as an issue enabled abolitionists to form coalitions with prison reformers, church groups, antislavery organizations, and other reformist groups.

These factors also contributed to the vogue for abolition among European center-left intellectuals in the 1950s. Arthur Koestler, Albert Camus, and Manès Sperber – among many others – publicly assailed the death penalty in letters, essays, and books. Their choice of abolition as an issue can best be understood against the unique political background of 1950s Europe. All three of these public intellectuals located themselves on the anti-Communist progressive left. Koestler had written a best-selling critique of Stalinism (*Darkness at Noon*) and, with Hungarian novelist Manès Sperber, was a co-founder of the Congress for Cultural Freedom (CCF), a group founded in 1950. The CCF provided a forum for intellectuals on the non-Communist left to propagate the shared values of Western Europe and the United States, and criticize limits on freedom of thought behind the Iron Curtain. In the volatile atmosphere of the incipient Cold War, the CCF generated controversy. Critics to the left of Koestler alleged that the CCF was funded by the Americans. In 1967, it was discovered that the CCF had, indeed, primarily been funded by the American Central Intelligence Agency. According to his biographer David Cesarani, Koestler knew of this fact (then kept strictly secret) as early as 1951.[84] Fellow-traveling intellectuals also attacked Koestler for permitting his fame to be used for political

82 Marshall Berman, All That Is Solid Melts into Air: The Experience of Modernity (New York: Simon & Schuster, 1983), 178.

83 Dieter Reicher, "Bureaucracy, 'Domesticated' Elites, and the Abolition of Capital Punishment. Processes of State-Formation and Numbers of Executions in England and Habsburg Austria between 1700 and 1914." Crime, Law and Social Change (forthcoming).

84 Cesarani, David. Arthur Koestler: The Homeless Mind (London: Vintage, 1999), 368.

purposes and for downplaying violence and oppression committed by Western colonial powers. Critiquing *Darkness at Noon* in 1947, Maurice Merleau-Ponty wrote:

> [Koestler forgets that] Western liberalism rests upon the forced labor of the colonies and twenty wars, that from an ethical standpoint the death of a Negro lynched in Louisiana, or of a native in Indonesia, Algeria, or Indochina is no less excusable than Rubashov's [a character in the novel] death; he forgets that communism does not invent violence but finds it already institutionalized, that for the moment the question is not to know whether one accepts or rejects violence, but whether the violence with which one is allied is "progressive" and tends toward its own suspension or toward self-perpetuation; and, finally, that in order to decide this question the crime has to be set in the logic of a situation, in the dynamics of a regime and into the historical totality to which it belongs, instead of judging it by itself according to that morality mistakenly called "pure" morality.[85]

Camus did not join the CCF, but decisively broke with Marxism in his 1951 essay *L'Homme Revolté* (usually translated as "The Rebel"). In that series of essays, Camus sketched out a political program of reformist socialism while criticizing the Marxist left for its willingness to be controlled by Moscow and its rationalizations of violence. One commentator wrote of the book:

> Writing it was an act of great political and personal courage. Camus knew what it cost him, knew he would be hailed on the Right and derided on the Left, and knew he was attacking a broad consensus on progress, the Enlightenment, and the French Revolution. . . . Camus also knew that East-West polarization had gone so far in generating its opposing realisms that little space was left for his more idealistic approach.[86]

Camus's stance earned him bitter attacks from his erstwhile friend and supporter, Jean-Paul Sartre, and from other writers at the fellow-traveling journal *Les Temps Modernes*. Like Koestler, Camus was accused of hypocritically overlooking the violence of the West, betraying those who suffered under French colonialism, and, in turn, playing into the hands of the United States' "soft" colonization of Western Europe by means of the Marshall Plan. The attacks greatly disturbed Camus and led to his definitive breach with Sartre.

By the 1950s, Camus and Koestler were already world-famous and thus in a position to choose the political stands they would embrace. Abolition – a traditional cause of the left – set them squarely against reactionaries and even many moderates who saw no reason to question the practice. It also distanced them from the United States, which was important to counter the accusations Camus, Koestler, and their

[85] Maurice Merleau-Ponty, "Koestler's Dilemmas," in Murray Sperber, ed., Arthur Koestler: A Collection of Critical Essays (Englewood Cliffs, NJ: Prentice-Hall, 1977), 69.

[86] Ronald Aronson, Camus & Sartre: The Story of a Friendship and the Quarrel that Ended It (Chicago and London: Chicago University Press, 2004), 125.

colleagues faced from fellow travelers. As Simon Grivet points out in this volume,[87] the American death penalty – in particular, the executions of Julius and Ethel Rosenberg and of Caryl Chessman, a rapist who spent years on California's death row fighting his death sentence – received obsessive attention in 1950s France. Thus, a critique of capital punishment was, necessarily, also a critique of a high-visibility aspect of American society. This critique helped establish the conception of the United States (which survives to this day) as a country with a peculiarly harsh and remorseless brand of justice, meted out by a system in which race and economic resources play a disproportionate role in trial outcomes.

Thus, Camus, Koestler, and others in their camp could stake out a position that burnished their profile as enlightened progressives while distancing them both from the United States *and* from thinkers on the left who justified the violence of "progressive" regimes such as the Soviet Union, or the violence of third-world insurgents. As Tony Judt described Camus's thought: "The moral measure that we bring to bear in condemning the death penalty or the violence of Fascist regimes is indivisible and has the same disqualifying effect upon the actions and regimes of the revolution and its children, however 'progressive.'"[88]

Nor did opposing capital punishment risk too much controversy: By the end of the 1950s, the death penalty seemed to be a withering institution. Parliamentary efforts to restore it in Germany attracted ever-weaker support, Britain's House of Commons had repeatedly voted to abolish hanging, and fundamental social change was in the air. Many conservatives were joining the abolitionist cause, as were representatives of mainstream Christianity. Thus, capital punishment was less fraught than other issues such as the status of European colonies, or the role of former fascist officials or collaborators in postwar society. Of course, Camus and Koestler also addressed these more sensitive issues, but it is not hard to imagine them breathing a sigh of relief at the opportunity to move on from these minefields to the comparatively less dangerous terrain of capital punishment. Taking a public stand against executions placed Camus and Koestler within a grand tradition of European thought, distanced them from the United States, and did so without the risk of deeply alienating ideological allies and potential supporters.

CONCLUSION

Seen in a global context, Europe is somewhat unusual in having abolished capital punishment, and unique in that majorities of ordinary (Western) European citizens now disapprove of the practice. However, large-scale changes in public opinion generally take place only decades after abolition has been enacted. European elites

87 Simon Grivet, "Executions and the Debate about Abolition in France and in the United States," Chapter 6, this volume.

88 Tony Judt, The Burden of Responsibility: Blum, Camus, Aron, and the French Twentieth Century (Chicago: The University of Chicago Press, 1998), 95.

worked in a favorable political environment. First, they operated within a historical and cultural context in which the pronouncements of public intellectuals were taken seriously and debated widely. Second, after the idea of abolition took root among policy/bureaucratic elites, the institutional momentum shifted in favor of abolition. As shown by Dehler and Silverman's speeches on the subject, the notion of Burkean trusteeship – which allows elected representatives to defy their constituents on matters of high principle – is alive and well in continental Europe and in Britain. Third, the policy-making process in continental European civil-law countries fostered elite control. Government law reform commissions are composed exclusively of elites – in fact, their *raison d'être* is to bring elite expertise to bear on penal policy. If a certain point of view becomes subject to unanimous agreement among those elites, the recommendations of these commissions and committees will reflect that.

Finally, the extraordinary centralization of European states played a significant role in the abolition struggle. Criminal law policy is made exclusively at the national level in these countries. To end capital punishment, abolitionists had to convince only the one central lawmaking body, not the representatives of every county in England, every German state, or every *région* in France. These social and structural preconditions also prevail in many countries whose legal and administrative structures are derived from continental European models, and it is these nations that represent the best prospects for future abolition efforts, to the extent that they have not already become abolitionist. In nations with radically different political orders – most prominently the United States – other strategies will have to be developed.

8

The Death of Dignity

Timothy V. Kaufman-Osborn

INTRODUCTION

The executed body is never merely a body, and the method of its execution is never simply a method. Each conspires to construct the other, and together, they participate in the constitution of an executable subject. At some times, and in some places, that subject can become an agent of ethical import, however circumscribed that agency may be, and so a thing that is recognizable as a human being. In other places, at other times, that subject can become an object, and so something that frustrates efforts to recall that this, too, may once have been a being who was human.

One way to chart the difference between these two executable subjects is to ask whether – and if so, how – the category of dignity is employed in characterizing each. The intelligibility of this category turns not on whether the subject in question does or does not possess some antecedent or essential quality that can be accurately represented via this terminology. Instead, the meaningfulness of the category of dignity turns on the existence and exercise of historically contingent as well as fragile practices that regulate bodies in certain ways as opposed to others. Given one set of practices, a body may appear as an agent who can affirm a meaningful claim to dignity as well as the forms of treatment to which an ethical subject is entitled. Given a different set of practices, that body may appear as an object that is not so entitled and, for that reason, is available for incorporation within an apparatus of extermination about which ethical claims are irrelevant and perhaps even incredible.

In contemporary debates within the United State regarding the death penalty, the discourse of dignity has now, in large part, been reduced to the status of the merely rhetorical. That degradation has effectively encouraged friends and foes of the death penalty, within as well as without the courtroom, to construe executions as affairs to be assessed, in considerable measure, by the standards of instrumental efficacy. To show how the category of dignity has come to be largely eviscerated of its substantive import within these debates, in this chapter, I return to a time and place when its sense was less banal. Such a moment can be located in the report issued by the British Royal Commission on Capital Punishment in 1953. Among other recommendations, that report urged that hanging be retained as England's preferred method of execution, and that execution via the administration of a fatal dose of chemicals be rejected as an alternative to this method.

In an argument that cannot help but ring peculiar in most American ears, the Commission justified its defense of hanging in part on the ground that death on the gallows is especially consonant with the dignity and hence the respect owed to the condemned. This recommendation, however, stands in a fraught relationship to others advanced during the testimony given before the Commission, and in particular that offered by one segment of the British medical community. In that testimony, one hears harbingers of a medicalized conception of the executable subject, and that conception is at odds with the appeal to dignity that informs the Commission's recommendation regarding the most felicitous way to execute a death sentence.

As I suggest in this chapter's conclusion, it is a medicalized construction of the executable subject that now dominates much death penalty debate in the United States, especially that concerning how best to kill. When that object is placed within the context of a culture that appears ever more squeamish about the violence required to inflict death sentences, the sensibilities of the living come to take precedence over any concerns that might be registered in the name of the dignity of the condemned. To the extent that this is so, the danger for abolitionists is that the truly urgent question, namely whether to retain or eliminate the death penalty, is ever more swallowed up by the question of whether a living body can be rendered dead without inflicting pain – or, more cynically, can be rendered dead in a way that leaves this question unanswerable because there is no visible evidence that would permit anyone to address it.

THE ROYAL COMMISSION ON CAPITAL PUNISHMENT, 1949–1953

The Commission's Mandate

For the Royal Commission on Capital Punishment, which issued its final report in 1953, five years following its formal constitution, consideration of methods of execution was not an explicit part of its original mandate. Instead, its mandate was to "consider and report whether liability under the criminal law in Great Britain to suffer capital punishment for murder should be limited or modified, and if so, to what extent and by what means, for how long and under what conditions persons who would otherwise have been liable to suffer capital punishment should be detained, and what changes in the existing law and the prison system would be required."[1]

This mandate is well understood as a response to a chronic dilemma posed by the rigidity of British felony law. Prior to the early nineteenth century, with the exception of petty larceny and mayhem, all felonies were punishable by a sentence of death, although the severity of this formal requirement was considerably mitigated by claims to benefit of clergy and by the grant of pardons conditional on transportation. Beginning in 1823, however, British courts were authorized to refrain from pronouncing a death sentence on anyone convicted of a felony other than murder (although these sentences were nonetheless recorded); and, more affirmatively, between 1827 and 1841, a series of acts formally abolished the punishment of death for many offenses other than murder. The trajectory implied in these reforms culminated in 1861 when the death penalty was abolished for all offenses other than murder, with the exception of treason, piracy with violence, and setting fire to dockyards and arsenals.

In that same year, however, the Offenses Against the Person Act reaffirmed the categorical distinguishability of homicide as an offense by mandating that "whosoever shall be convicted of murder shall suffer death as a felon."[2] By 1948, when the Royal Commission was officially constituted (although it did not first meet until 1949), the inflexibility of this requirement had been tempered by exempting from its scope three categories of homicide. First, the Children's Act of 1908 abolished the sentence of death in the case of persons younger than sixteen years of age, providing instead that minors be imprisoned during His Majesty's Pleasure; in 1933, this provision was extended to those younger than eighteen at the time of conviction; and in 1948, to persons younger than eighteen at the time the offense was committed. Second, the Infanticide Act of 1922 provided that a woman who caused the death of her newborn child in circumstances that would otherwise qualify as murder, but who had not yet recovered from childbirth and who for that reason was deemed mentally unbalanced, was to be punished as if she had been found guilty of manslaughter. Finally, the Expectant Mothers Act of 1931 provided that pregnant women convicted

[1] Report of the Royal Commission on Capital Punishment, 1949–53 (London: Her Majesty's Stationery Office, 1953), iii. For an account of the inquiry as well as the recommendations of the Commission, see Ch. 11 in Brian Block and John Hostettler, *Hanging in the Balance* (Winchester: Waterside Press, 1997). Over the course of its four years in existence, the Commission conducted sixty-three meetings, thirty-one of which were principally devoted to oral testimony by individuals as well as representatives of various organizations, including, but not limited to, government agents (e.g., the Home Office, the Prison Officers' Association, and Albert Pierrepoint, England's most experienced hangman); church officials (e.g., the Archbishop of Canterbury); professional associations (e.g., the Society of Labour Lawyers and the British Medical Association); and reform organizations (e.g., the Howard League and the Muir Society). For a complete list of the witnesses who gave evidence before the commission, see Appendix I, Royal Commission, pp. 289–96.

[2] For this brief summary of the history of the English law of homicide prior to 1948, I rely on the Memorandum Submitted by the Home Office, Royal Commission on Capital Punishment, Minutes of Evidence, August 4, 1949 (London: Her Majesty's Stationery Office, 1953) (¶1–5).

of murder were to be sentenced not to death but to penal servitude for life. For all who did not fit into one of these categories, the sole punishment prescribed for anyone convicted of murder was death, and a judge had no discretion to impose any less severe sentence regardless of the circumstances of the offense or the character of the offender.

In the year of the Commission's creation, indicating that at least some found these categorical exceptions insufficient to temper the law's rigor, a proposal was advanced in conjunction with consideration of the Criminal Justice of 1948 to make penal servitude for life the default punishment for homicide.[3] This proposal would have restricted the death penalty to those homicides deemed especially heinous (e.g., murders committed incidental to the commission of other offenses, such as robbery; those involving the use of explosives; and those committed in the course of resisting or avoiding arrest). Although this proposal was eventually rejected by the House of Lords, the question it posed about whether the category of death-eligible homicides should be additionally refined to mitigate the law's indifference to the nuances of murder furnished the proximate context for the mandate of the Royal Commission. As the Commission noted, "there is perhaps no single class of offences that varies so widely in character and in culpability as the class comprising those which may fall within the comprehensive common law definition of murder."[4] Given this variability, the Commission stated, "no one would now dispute that for many of these crimes it would be monstrous to inflict the death penalty," especially

[3] The chair of the Commission, Sir Ernest Arthur Gowers, provides an indication of the positions staked out in the context of this debate: "Amongst our witnesses there have been two different schools of thought. One holds that it is something of a scandal that so many people should be sentenced to death who are eventually reprieved, that it is bringing a ceremony which ought to be a very solemn one and full of meaning into something of the nature of a farce; and that, therefore, if you can so change the law that fewer people are sentenced to death and consequently fewer reprieves will be necessary, it is a thing greatly to be desired. The other school denies altogether that that is an evil. It maintains that anybody who commits what is technically a murder should be sentenced to death, and then the prerogative should be brought into play if necessary, and it regards with indifference the disparity between sentences and executions" (Examination of Witness, Supplementary Memorandum Submitted by the Lord Justice General, Royal Commission on Capital Punishment, Minutes of Evidence, April 5, 1940 (London: Her Majesty's Stationery Office, 1953) (¶5400).

[4] Report of the Royal Commission, p. 6 (¶21). To illustrate this point, the Commission engaged in a detailed review of the facts of fifty cases of murder committed between 1931 and 1951, and, on that basis, concluded the following: "Convicted persons may be men, or they may be women, youths, girls, or hardly older than children. They may be normal or they may be feeble-minded, neurotic, epileptic, borderline cases, or insane; and in each case the mentally abnormal may be differently affected by their abnormality. The crime may be human and understandable, calling more for pity than for censure, or brutal and callous to an almost unbelievable degree. It may have occurred so much in the heat of passion as to rule out the possibility of premeditation, or it may have been well prepared and carried out in cold blood. The crime may be committed in order to carry out another crime or in the course of committing it, or to secure escape after its commission. Murderous intent may be unmistakable, or it may be absent, and death itself may depend on an accident. The motives, springing from weakness as often as from wickedness, show some of the basest and some of the better emotions of mankind, cupidity, revenge, lust, jealousy, anger, fear, pity, despair, duty, self-righteousness, political fanaticism; or there may be no intelligible motive at all" (p. 6, ¶21).

in light of the "widely accepted" view that this punishment "should be reserved for the more heinous cases of murder . . . This rigidity is the outstanding defect of our law of murder."[5]

For many years the Commission proceeded, the problem posed by the tension between the law's rigidity and the idiosyncratic character of acts of murder – and so the specific degree of culpability to be assigned to particular offenders – had been resolved by exercises of the Royal Prerogative of Mercy. Specifically, a recommendation of mercy, about which jury and judge could but were not required to offer an opinion, was advanced to the Home Secretary. The rationale for the ultimate decision of the Home Secretary to commute or not to commute a death sentence in any given case, however, was never disclosed. Defending the discretionary and in principle illimitable character of this authority, the Home Secretary explained to the Commission that such decisions depend in the last analysis "on a full review of a complex combination of circumstances and often on the careful balancing of conflicting considerations."[6] As such, "it would be neither desirable nor possible to lay down hard and fast rules as to the exercise of the prerogative of mercy."[7] To offer a justification in any given case, in other words, would imply the existence of rules that, in principle, can never be articulated.

As the Commission acknowledged, the Crown's appeal to prerogative power as the basis of its acts of clemency, understood as the solution to the incongruity between the law's formal inflexibility and the perceived substantive imperatives of justice, engendered an even more fundamental dilemma. That dilemma was implicit in the Commission's finding that in the period between 1900 and 1948, more than 90 percent of the 126 women sentenced to death were afforded a "respite," as well as more than 40 percent of the 1,052 men. In sum, during these years, nearly 46 percent of those sentenced to death found their punishment commuted to imprisonment for life; and, on average, during this period, only thirteen executions were actually carried out each year.

The situation indicated by these statistics, the Commission worried, jeopardized not just the integrity of the specific law of homicide, but, more broadly, the very authority of the British legal order. To explain, the Commission conceded the validity of a pair of overlapping criticisms often directed at widespread use of the power of royal prerogative in death penalty cases. First, in principle, the Committee affirmed, "the exercise of the Prerogative should be an exceptional measure, interfering with the due process of law only in those rare cases which cannot be foreseen and provided for by the law itself. When, as now, one out of every two capital sentences is commuted, the Prerogative ceases to be an exceptional measure and the Secretary of State becomes in effect an additional Court of Appeals, sitting in private, judging

5 Report of the Royal Commission, p. 6 (¶22).

6 Mr. Herbert Gladstone, quoted in Report of the Royal Commission, p. 12 (¶39).

7 Gladstone, quoted in Memorandum Submitted by the Home Office, Minutes of Evidence, Royal Commission on Capital Punishment, August 4, 1949 (¶10).

on the record only, and giving no reasons for his decisions." Such discretionary authority, which "cannot be effectively questioned about the matter of its exercise, does not fit into the constitutional framework of this country,"[8] presumably because the norms of constitutionalism demand that the exercise of political power provide a reasoned account of itself to ward off the fear that it is merely arbitrary.

The Commission's second but not altogether distinct concern about widespread use of prerogative power to commute death sentences was suggested when it quoted the testimony of the Archbishop of Canterbury as follows:

> It is a very grave thing that the solemn formula of the death sentence should almost as often as not be followed by a reprieve which cancels it . . . It is intolerable that this solemn and deeply significant procedure should be enacted again and again when in almost half the cases the consequence will not follow. . . . If this solemn act is to remain, it must normally mean what it says and carry the consequences which it imposes. Otherwise it is reduced to a mere formula: and in such a matter a mere empty formula is a degradation of the majesty of the law and dangerous to society.[9]

The memorandum submitted by the Home Office put forth much the same point: "It has been widely regarded as shocking to humane feelings and tending to bring the law into contempt that the sentence of death should be solemnly passed in a large number of cases . . . where it is clear to all, except perhaps the prisoner, that it will not in fact be carried out."[10] In short, in the eyes of the public, the law may become little more than a hollow shell if, in the exercise of its supreme power – the power to condemn and execute persons convicted of homicide – its command becomes an idle threat for every second person sentenced to die, especially should it be impossible to discern the reason why one is sent to the gallows whereas another is not.

This, then, is the larger context that explains the Commission's construction of its charge. That charge is "complex and many-sided" because its "terms of reference postulate the retention of capital punishment and at the same time require us to consider how the liability to suffer it might be limited or modified. Our duty then, as we understand it, has been to look for means of confining the scope of that punishment as narrowly as possible without impairing the efficacy attributed to it."[11] Or, more candidly, the Commission's assignment is "to find some practicable half-way house between the present scope of the death penalty and its abolition," acknowledging that "a stage has been reached where there is little room for further limitation short of abolition."[12]

[8] Report of the Royal Commission, p. 15 (¶47).
[9] Archbishop of Canterbury, quoted in Report of the Royal Commission, p. 16 (¶48).
[10] Memorandum Submitted by the Home Office, Report of the Royal Commission, Aug. 4, 1949 (¶55).
[11] Report of the Royal Commission, p. 4 (¶15).
[12] Report of the Royal Commission, p. 212 (¶605).

In pursuit of this end, the specific proposals considered by the Commission can be located in either of two broad categories. The first category included proposals to alter the law that now defines liability to a death sentence – for example, by defining the crime of murder more narrowly and/or by expanding the scope of the definition of manslaughter; or, following the U.S. example, by dividing the crime of murder into two degrees, only one of which would be punishable by death; or, as with the exemption afforded to new mothers and juveniles, by excluding additional categories of persons from those susceptible to a sentence of death. In the last analysis, though, the Commission rejected all but the most incremental of these possibilities. Specifically, it rejected proposals to amend the law of capital punishment by defining more precisely what qualifies as homicide or by distinguishing between different categories of homicide. Echoing the conclusion of the Home Secretary, it did so on the ground that any effort to specify the crimes that are peculiarly death-eligible is "chimerical" because "no legal definition can cover all the multifarious considerations, relating to the offender as well as to his crime, which ought to be taken into account . . . in deciding whether the supreme penalty should be exacted in each individual case."[13]

Quite modestly, however, the Commission did recommend an alteration of the categories of persons who are death-eligible by suggesting that aiding and abetting suicide should no longer be tried as murder; by suggesting that the sentence of death should not be imposed on any person convicted of murder who was younger than age twenty-one at the time the offense was committed; and finally, by proposing certain alterations in the ways certain psychological states, including insanity, mental illness, and mental deficiency, inform the sentencing process. However, even when considered cumulatively, the Commission confessed, these proposals "would go very little way towards solving our general problem as we have defined it. We have considered most carefully whether any more radical solution can be found. We have found none that can be regarded as entirely satisfactory."[14] In sum, to invoke a metaphor that would later be made famous by Justice Harry Blackmun, with respect to efforts to limit the liability to suffer capital punishment, the Commission concluded that it could do little more than tinker with the existing machinery of death.

The second general category of reforms considered by the Commission involved vesting more extensive discretionary authority to impose a punishment other than death in participants in the legal order other than or in addition to that now exercised by the Home Secretary. The Commission declined the possibility of vesting such authority in judges because "the sentence of death differs absolutely, not in degree, from any other sentence," and so "the responsibility of deciding whether a person convinced of murder should be sentenced to death or to a lesser punishment is too

13 Report of the Royal Commission, pp. 190, 189, 173 (¶535, 534, 498).

14 Report of the Royal Commission, p. 213 (¶610).

heavy a burden to impose on any single individual."[15] Instead, the Commission proposed imparting greater discretionary authority to juries on the ground that to do so is to invest this responsibility in a collective body that represents the voice and conscience of the community. More precisely, and anticipating the "bifurcated" capital trial procedures employed in the Unites States, the Commission recommended that "if the jury convict the accused of murder they should then be required, after being given all available relevant information that might justify sentence of death not being passed, to consider whether there are extenuating circumstances, and that, if they find that there are, the Judge should be precluded from passing the sentence of death and required to pass a sentence of imprisonment for life."[16] Even this recommendation, though, was offered with considerable reservation and, more significantly, with an awkward recognition that the question toward which the Commission's four year analysis pressed is precisely that which it is not authorized to address:

> We have reached the conclusion that, if capital punishment is to be retained, and at the same time the defects of the existing law are to be eliminated, this [vesting greater discretionary authority in juries] is the only practicable way of achieving that object. We recognize that it involves a fundamental change in the traditional functions of the jury in Great Britain and is not without practical difficulties. For these reasons its disadvantages may be thought to outweigh its merits. If this view were to prevail, the conclusion to our mind would be inescapable that in this country a stage has been reached where little more can be done effectively to limit the liability to suffer the death penalty, and that the real issue is now whether capital punishment should be retained or abolished.[17]

Assessing Yankee Ingenuity: The Electric Chair and the Gas Chamber

As the Commission acknowledged in this last quotation, absent a momentous change in traditional British legal practice – a modification it has no good reason to believe will be seriously entertained, let alone adopted – the "real issue" toward which its own analysis gravitates is the persistence of capital punishment itself. Yet, in virtue of its mandate, this is a question it cannot consider, and so the best it can do is to offer modest recommendations aimed at adjusting the margins of conventional legal practice. It is within the context of this impasse, I would suggest, that we should consider the Commission's extended flirtation with alternative methods of executions, and especially lethal injection. As noted earlier, consideration of the means of inflicting a death sentence was not part of the initial mandate to the Commission, although a request to add this to its agenda was advanced shortly thereafter by the Prime Minister. Once included, this question became a primary

[15] Report of the Royal Commission, p. 193 (¶549).
[16] Report of the Royal Commission, p. 195 (¶553).
[17] Report of the Royal Commission, p. 214 (¶611)

preoccupation of the Commission's inquiry, eventually comprising one of the final report's three major parts.

The Commission of 1949–1953, it is important to recognize, was not the first to explore the question of possible refinements in execution methods. Almost a century prior, in 1864, the Home Secretary had appointed a commission "to inquire into the existing practice as to carrying out of sentences of death, and the causes which in several recent cases have led either to failure or to unseemly occurrences; and to consider and report what arrangements may be adopted (without altering the existing law) to ensure that all executions may be carried out in a becoming manner without risk of failure of miscarriage in any respect."[18] That commission's work, however, was predicated on the assumption that hanging would remain the sole method of execution, and so it confined its attention to "the adoption of certain improvements in the apparatus and certain tests and precautions before each execution to ensure the apparatus is working properly."[19] Adoption of these improvements in the intervening decades, notes the present Commission, especially calibration of the distance of the drop relative to the weight of the condemned, which "was designed to ensure speedy and painless death by dislocation of the vertebrae without decapitation,"[20] have occasioned salutary results. Indeed, reported the Home Office to the Commission: "(T)here is no record during the present century of any failure or mishap with an execution and as now carried out execution by hanging can be regarded as speedy and certain."[21]

What, then, induces the Commission to consider a wholesale abandonment of hanging?[22] In part, to anticipate a matter to which I will return, the answer is suggested by the fact that, although the "degrading associations" once linked with hanging have been largely overcome as a result of its technical refinement, a certain "stigma" remains associated with the employment of this method.[23] Conceding that the reasons for hanging's initial adoption are "obscure," the Commission speculates that it "may be presumed to have been invented rather for its advertisement value

18 Quoted in Memorandum Submitted by the Home Office, Minutes of Evidence, August 4, 1949, Report of the Royal Commission (¶107).

19 Quoted in the Memorandum Submitted by the Home Office, Minutes of Evidence, August 4, 1949, Report of the Royal Commission (¶108).

20 Report of the Royal Commission, p. 247 (¶703).

21 Memorandum Submitted by the Home Office, Minutes of Evidence, August 4, 1949, Report of the Royal Commission (¶122).

22 This question becomes especially puzzling when we note that, by its own account, the Commission is loath to depart from established practice because of the deep respect of the British for the claims of tradition: "If capital punishment were now being introduced into this country for the first time, we do not think it likely that this way of carrying it out would be chosen. But it is a commonplace that our tenacity of ancient institutions makes us need much stronger arguments to abolish one than would suffice, if it were not there, to persuade us to refrain from setting it up. As a nation we hold, with Francis Bacon, that 'it is good not to try experiments in states except the necessity be urgent, or the utility evident.' This applies with special force to a subject like this, highly charged emotionally and exceptionally controversial." Report of the Royal Commission, p. 248 (¶708).

23 Report of the Royal Commission, pp. 246, 248 (¶701, 707).

than as a more effective way of taking life than other early methods of execution, such as beheading, drowning, stoning, impaling and precipitation from a great height."[24] Leaving unasked the question of why this particular method might once have been considered a peculiarly effective deterrent, the Commission acknowledges that it is not clear that this rationale remains valid in the mid-twentieth century, especially since Parliament, following a recommendation issued by its earlier counterpart, mandated that executions be conducted behind prison walls in 1868. The privatization of execution, in other words, weakens the requirement that executions be conducted as a form of brutal theater and, correlatively, poses the question of whether some alternative method, one that might be unaccompanied by hanging's stigma, could accomplish the task at hand equally well.

The Commission's willingness to entertain alternative methods of execution is also a response to adoption in several of the United States of rival technologies of taking life, especially electrocution and the gas chamber, as well as to advances in the sciences of medicine, especially in pharmacology, which were more or less unknown to the Commission's nineteenth-century predecessor. It is in light of these alternatives that the Commission articulates the three criteria – humanity, certainty, and decency – that it puts to work in conducting its comparison of hanging with other methods of execution. Specifically, by invoking the category of "humanity," the Commission indicates its conviction, first, that "the preliminaries to the act of execution should be as quick and as simple as possible" in order to minimize the "prisoner's apprehension," and second, that "the act of execution should produce immediate unconsciousness passing quickly into death."[25] By "certainty," the Commission announces its intention to ask "which method is most likely to avoid mishaps, due either to the complexity of the machinery or to an error of the executioner."[26] Finally, by invoking "decency," the Commission explains, it has "two things in mind. One is the obligation that obviously rests on every civilized state to conduct its judicial executions with decorum. The other is the regard that should be paid to the feeling . . . that as far as possible judicial execution should be performed without brutality, that it should avoid gross physical violence and should not mutilate or distort the body."[27] Considered together, these three criteria gesture toward the Commission's vision of the normative execution, one that is defined by its rapidity, painlessness, predictability, and tracelessness (in the sense of leaving no enduring mark on the body).

Employing these three criteria, the Commission begins its analysis by dismissing in perfunctory fashion several available methods of execution that, to some, might appear preferable to hanging. Specifically, the Commission rejects the firing squad on the ground that "it does not possess even the first requisite of an efficient method,

[24] Report of the Royal Commission, p. 246 (¶701).
[25] Report of the Royal Commission, p. 253 (¶724).
[26] Report of the Royal Commission, p. 255 (¶729).
[27] Report of the Royal Commission, p. 255 (¶732).

the certainty of causing immediate death," thereby falling short of both of the first two criteria. With equal dispatch, the Commission dismisses the guillotine on the ground that "the mutilation it produces would be shocking to public opinion in this country," thereby violating the third criterion.[28]

The Commission, however, affords more careful attention to two relatively recent American innovations – electrocution and the gas chamber – only to reject these as well. Both, the Commission concludes, fail when assessed by the criterion of humanity, which, recall, essentially reduces to the question of celerity and which is prized principally because any discernible extension in the duration of killing increases the anxiety of the condemned. With respect to electrocution, evidence adduced from several of the United States indicates that the time between removal of the condemned from the holding cell and the administration of the current is typically two to four minutes. With respect to the gas chamber, at best (in California), the time between enclosure within the chamber and the achievement of unconsciousness is 40 seconds, and, at worst (in Nevada), a full seven minutes. By way of contrast, in his testimony, the most famous of British hangmen, Albert Pierrepoint, announces that the "time which elapses between the entry of the executioner into the [holding] cell and the pulling of the lever [in the death chamber] is normally between 9 and 12 seconds but may be 20 to 25 seconds in a few prisons where the condemned cell does not adjoin the execution chamber."[29]

When assessed through reference to the second of the three criteria (certainty), the Commission expresses its concern that the gas chamber "is expensive to install and requires a complicated series of operations to produce the gas and to dispose of it afterwards;" and, for this reason, it anticipates that this method would "give greater scope for mishap than the simpler equipment of the other systems."[30] By way of contrast, the Commission deems the electric chair to be "a simple apparatus." It worries, though, that the "efficacy" of this method "depends upon the supply of electricity, which is usually taken from commercial sources" (in contrast to the British state's unqualified possession of the instrumentalities of hanging); in addition, the provision of this supply, no matter what its source, is subject to interruption caused by a power failure. The "apparatus needed for hanging," however, "does not suffer from disadvantages of complexity or dependence upon outside sources, and mishaps are unlikely to occur through a failure in equipment if it is properly tested before the execution takes place, as it always is."[31] In sum, when assessed by the criterion

28 Report of the Royal Commission, p. 249 (¶710).

29 Report of the Royal Commission, p. 250 (¶713). An invidious comparison between the expertise of British hangmen and the amateurism of their American counterparts is clearly evident when the Commission, in a table comparing these three methods of execution, indicates that in the United States, the time elapsed between the entry of officers into the holding cell and completion of an execution by hanging ranges from an average of two minutes in Washington and Maryland to six in Iowa.

30 Report of the Royal Commission, pp. 252, 255 (¶720, 729).

31 Report of the Royal Commission, p. 255 (¶729).

of certainty, "neither electrocution nor the lethal chamber has, on balance, any advantage over hanging."[32]

Lastly, the Commission assesses hanging against these two American innovations in light of the criterion of decency. Of principal concern to the Commission in this regard are the consequences of employing one method as opposed to another on the surface of the executed body. The Commission begins its analysis by acknowledging that hanging "causes death by a physical shock of extreme violence, and leaves the body with the neck elongated." In comparison (and ignoring the factual accuracy of its belief in this regard), the Commission contends that electrocution "leaves the body unmarked except for slight burning of the flesh," while the gas chamber "causes death without any violence and leaves the body wholly unmarked."[33] For this reason, the Commission concedes, the rival methods currently employed in several but not all of the United States are indeed "preferable."[34]

In the last analysis, though, the Commission deems the absence of bodily mutilation insufficient "to turn the scale,"[35] especially given the evident superiority of hanging with respect to the first two criteria. Moreover, the deficiency of hanging when assessed by the third criterion is "of less practical importance in this country"[36] because, in Great Britain, the body is always buried within the prison walls, whereas in the United States it is often turned over to next-of-kin who are more likely to be disturbed by enduring signs of the violence necessary to kill it. Still more fundamentally, in a claim whose unspecified historical referent cannot help but be clear to the Commission's anticipated audience, the apparent advantage of the gas chamber in this respect is more than offset by the fact that just as "hanging is tainted by the memory of its barbarous history," so too death by means of confinement within an airtight enclosure into which invisible but toxic vapors are pumped is "tainted by more recent but not less barbarous associations."[37]

Assessing Physician Ingenuity: The Lethal Needle

Having dismissed hanging's currently available rivals, more particularly the two recent technical innovations from across the Atlantic, the Commission turns its most sustained analysis to a method of execution – injection into the body of pharmaceutical agents more commonly employed in the practice of medicine – that will not be adopted in any of the United States for more than two decades. "To those who accept our postulate that the only requisites are humanity, certainty and decency, this is likely to be the alternative to hanging that first suggests

[32] Report of the Royal Commission, p. 255 (¶731).
[33] Report of the Royal Commission, p. 255 (¶732).
[34] Report of the Royal Commission, p. 256 (¶734).
[35] Report of the Royal Commission, p. 256 (¶734).
[36] Report of the Royal Commission, p. 255 (¶732).
[37] Report of the Royal Commission, p. 256 (¶732).

itself."[38] As we will see, the Commission ultimately rejects what we now commonly dub "lethal injection" on the basis of these three criteria of assessment. Why this analysis generates not a reluctant call to retain hanging as the least problematic of methods, but instead an affirmation of the peculiar virtue of this way of killing can only be understood through reference to the Commission's appeal to a particular conception of dignity, and of the subject who can credibly affirm a claim to that value. That appeal will in turn suggest the hollowness of much of the contemporary debate in the United States about the best way to execute a death sentence, a debate from which the category of dignity is now largely absent.

In turning its attention from innovations already adopted in several of the United States to as yet untried methods of execution, the Commission states that only two suggestions "were made to us deserving serious consideration. One is the use of lethal gas in a way that does not need a gas-chamber. The other is execution by means of a hypodermic injection of a lethal drug."[39] Of principal import with respect to these two pharmacological options is the testimony provided, first, by members of the Council of the British Medical Association (BMA), and second, by officers of the Association of Anaesthetists of Great Britain and Ireland.

Echoing the position currently held by the American Medical Association, the written memorandum submitted by the representatives of the BMA in January 1950, which was followed a month later by oral examination, begins by disarticulating the *raison d'être* of professional medicine from the task of the Commission. However, in doing so, the BMA is careful not to render its expertise irrelevant to the present inquiry:

> As an organization of persons whose function is to preserve life, the Association, although it could not properly express any view for or against the retention of the death penalty for murder, finds a discussion of methods of taking human life particularly distasteful. Nevertheless, it conceives it to be its duty to offer such observations as it can on this problem, realizing that the Commission, in seeking its advice, is actuated by the humane motive of discovering any possible method of reducing suffering associated with the carrying out of the capital sentence.[40]

Consistent with this principle, the BMA states that it will offer its considered opinion about alternative methods of execution, but that it will also oppose any method that would require the participation of a medical practitioner or, alternatively, that would require a physician's participation in training another to perform this task.

With that stricture in place, the BMA states that "perhaps the most effective and humane method that could be adopted in place of hanging"[41] would be the

38 Report of the Royal Commission, p. 257 (¶737).
39 Report of the Royal Commission, p. 256 (¶735).
40 Memorandum Submitted by the Council of the British Medical Association, Minutes of Evidence, Royal Commission on Capital Punishment, February 3, 1950 (London: His Majesty's Stationery Office, 1950), p. 315 (¶4).
41 Memorandum Submitted by the Council of the British Medical Association, p. 315 (¶31).

introduction of carbon monoxide into a sealed space (which we already know the Commission will reject because of what the Association, too, acknowledges are "historical associations which are not altogether pleasant").[42] As an alternative, the BMA states that "if it were practicable, the intravenous injection of a lethal dose of a narcotic drug would be a speedy and merciful procedure."[43] However, it is quick to dismiss this option in light of the difficulties that physicians often encounter in their daily practice when they seek to administer injections (e.g., in locating a suitable vein), especially should physical abnormalities be present (e.g., significant obesity). Moreover, absent complete cooperation of the person to be injected, a condition that cannot be assumed in the context of an execution, "the slightest struggling would mean that the needle would either slip out of the vein, so that he would not get the injection, or go through the vein and the injection go into the tissue."[44] Granted, a subcutaneous or intramuscular injection might obviate certain of these difficulties. This, though, "would not bring about sudden death or instantaneous loss of consciousness,"[45] and so would entail a protracted period before death occurs (which would violate the Commission's appeal to the criterion of humanity). For these reasons, the BMA concludes, whether intravenous or intramuscular, lethal injection is "quite unsuitable for the purpose of execution," and therefore, all things considered, "hanging is probably as speedy and certain as any other method that could be adopted."[46]

A little less than a year following the testimony offered by the BMA, the chair of the Commission stated: "There are some of us who are reluctant to accept" the BMA's conclusion that "hanging is expeditious and humane," and so "we are pursuing this subject further."[47] To do so, the Commission first considered what it labels "informal evidence" submitted by a certain Dr. Organe, secretary to the Association of Anaesthetists of Great Britain and Ireland, which it then followed by an invitation to several members of the Association to prepare a formal memorandum. That memorandum, which was delivered in December 1951 (although not in the name of the entire Association), was followed by oral examination of its signatories on the final day of the hearings conducted by the Commission prior to submission of its formal report.

What most obviously distinguishes the formal memorandum of the anaesthetists from that offered by the BMA is its unequivocal affirmation that "there are alternative methods of execution which we would regard as more humane than

42 Examination of Witnesses, Minutes of Evidence, Council of the British Medical Association, p. 330 (¶4050).
43 Memorandum Submitted by the Council of the British Medical Association, p. 318 (¶29).
44 Memorandum Submitted by the Council of the British Medical Association, p. 318 (¶4039).
45 Memorandum Submitted by the Council of the British Medical Association, p. 318 (¶29).
46 Memorandum Submitted by the Council of the British Medical Association, p. 318 (¶28, 29).
47 Alternative Methods of Execution, Statement of the Views of Consulting Anaesthetists, Minutes of Evidence, Royal Commission on Capital Punishment, December 6, 1951 (¶8941).

hanging."[48] Specifically, their statement endorses execution by means of an overdose of anaesthesia, whether administered as a gas via a mask or as a fluid via a syringe. Affirming that either would be preferable to current practice, in oral testimony, the participating anaesthetists defend this conclusion by citing the everyday experience of those undergoing surgery: "The sensation of a lethal dose of an intravenous drug like thiopentone, or even an inhalation of nitrous oxide, would be no different from that of going off and becoming unconscious under an ordinary anaesthetic,"[49] an experience routinely described by patients as, at the very least, not unpleasant.

With this general endorsement in place, the Association's members turn to a question that the BMA only touched on in its testimony. Specifically, during its examination by the Commission, representatives of the BMA were asked whether it might be possible to remedy the complications posed by the uncooperative subject by rendering the condemned unconscious, via pharmaceutical means, prior to administration of whatever agent is ultimately employed to kill. Perhaps not surprisingly, given its effort to draw a strict line of demarcation between the practices of medicine and state execution, the BMA members indicate that they cannot endorse this proposal, especially should administration of a powerful sedative be required of a prison medical officer as a mandated part of the execution protocol: "Under the oath we are bound to promote life, if one may put it that way; whereas any action which has as its object the termination of life, even indirectly, we feel is undesirable."[50]

The members of the Association of Anaesthetists, however, are quite willing to entertain this possibility, as indicated by the very organizational structure of its formal memorandum. Following its opening affirmation of the availability of methods of execution that are more humane than hanging, this memorandum is divided into two parts. The first part concerns executions "when the subject is fully conscious,"[51] in which case it recommends the intravenous injection of a short-acting barbiturate. This recommendation is qualified, however, by the memorandum's acknowledgment that such an injection "would be more difficult in a struggling subject," and so should be employed "only when it has been willingly accepted"[52] by the condemned as an alternative to hanging. Such consent, the anaesthetists explain in oral testimony, will reduce the likelihood of resistance at the moment of injection, especially if the condemned understands that the consequence of recalcitrance is recourse to the noose.

48 Alternative Methods of Execution, Statement of the Views of Consulting Anaesthetists, Minutes of Evidence, Royal Commission on Capital Punishment, December 6, 1951 (London: Her Majesty's Stationery Office, 1952) (¶1).

49 Examination of Witnesses, Minutes of Evidence, Association of Anaesthetists of England and Ireland, Royal Commission on Capital Punishment, December 6, 1951 (¶8943).

50 Examination of Witnesses, British Medical Association, Minutes of Evidence, Royal Commission on Capital Punishment, February 3, 1950 (¶4041).

51 Alternative Methods of Execution, Statement of the Views of Consulting Anaesthetists (¶1).

52 Alternative Methods of Execution, Statement of the Views of Consulting Anaesthetists (¶7).

The second part of the memorandum, in contrast, concerns executions conducted "when the subject is already unconscious,"[53] which eliminates the problem posed by the condemned's failure to cooperate. Specifically, if the inmate were to be offered an oral dose of pentobarbital or araldehyde with an alcoholic drink the night before execution, and if that offer were to be accepted, this would "ensure his being deeply asleep in the morning," which in turn would make it "possible to transfer the prisoner on a trolley" to the execution chamber "without waking him."[54] Under these circumstances, the memo concludes, several methods of execution would then prove viable. Such means include the mechanical (by which the memorandum presumably refers to hanging, although it does not say); the administration of lethal gas; or the injection of additional pharmaceutical agents. Of these three possibilities, "apart from consideration of expense," the anaesthetists conclude that because even the unconscious body may respond to an injection with reflexive responses that complicate the matter at hand, in the last analysis, the use of either carbon monoxide or coal gas is "the least objectionable method."[55]

On the Subject of Hanging

In formulating its recommendation about execution methods, the Royal Commission is confronted with competing counsel from different camps of medical experts. On the one hand, the British Medical Association endorses the retention of hanging, whereas the testifying anaesthetists suggest offering the condemned a choice between hanging and intravenous injection; or, alternatively, in order to escape the difficulties posed by the resistant prisoner, the production of an insensate subject who can be dispatched by any number of means, but preferably lethal gas. The Commission ultimately rejects the anaesthetists' recommendation that the condemned be given a choice of execution methods on the ground that "it is the duty of the state that inflicts capital punishment to decide for itself what is the proper method of carrying it out" and "to use that method invariably."[56] It is clear, however, that the Commission is intrigued by the other possibilities advanced by the anaesthetists, in particular by lethal injection:

> If we could have been satisfied that executions could be carried out in this way quickly, painlessly and decently in all cases, we should have recommended its adoption unanimously. But we are bound to conclude from our expert evidence that there is not at present a reasonable certainty of this. We do, however, recommend, unanimously and emphatically, that the question should be periodically examined, especially in light of progress made in the science of anaesthetics.[57]

53 Alternative Methods of Execution, Statement of the Views of Consulting Anaesthetists (¶8).
54 Alternative Methods of Execution, Statement of the Views of Consulting Anaesthetists (¶8.)
55 Alternative Methods of Execution, Statement of the Views of Consulting Anaesthetists (¶12).
56 Report of the Royal Commission, p. 259 (¶746).
57 Report of the Royal Commission, p. 261 (¶749).

On this account, it would appear that only an insufficiency of knowledge now prevents the Commission from commending the adoption of lethal injection – an insufficiency that it seems confident the march of science will one day overcome. Until that day, however, application of its formal criteria of evaluation to various current as well as potential methods of execution leads it to endorse hanging's retention.[58]

The Commission's application of its own formal criteria of evaluation tells but part of the story about why it ultimately concludes in favor of hanging. The Commission's application of these criteria presupposes and is informed by a conception of the executable subject, although that conception is never expressly elaborated as such. However abject the condemned may appear at the moment of execution, this subject is in fact a complex figure, one who incorporates traces of multiple contexts, historical as well as political, not of its own creation. One dimension of this subject's specific character can be presaged by indicating why the Commission ultimately rejects the otherwise tempting possibility of rendering the condemned insensate prior to execution. One reason for doing so is initially posed by a member of the Association of Anaesthetists as follows:

> There is always a risk, and the risk is a very real one, that sooner or later you are going to have a man who is given a dose which should just make him unconscious, but will in fact kill him. If the legal means of execution should be that he should die by means of intravenous barbiturate, I gather that it would be looked upon with disfavour if the drug which was given him the night before should kill him.[59]

Considering this possibility, and bearing in mind the BMA's refusal to authorize its members to participate directly or indirectly in an execution, the Commission concludes: "If the time for giving the dose were the morning of the execution, its administration would become in effect part of the process of execution, in which no doctor would think it right to participate. If the time were the night before, this too would require unprofessional conduct from any doctor asked to give it."[60]

Having rejected this option, the Commission must then consider the employment of a lethal gas, using a mask but not within a sealed chamber, or alternatively, the injection of a lethal chemical on a subject who is conscious at the time of execution. It rejects the former because the condemned would almost certainly avoid inhaling for as long as possible. Given the failure of gas to kill with that first inhalation, execution by this means would prove more protracted than by means of hanging, and that prospect in turn raises troublesome issues in relation to the Commission's

58 See Report of the Royal Commission on Capital Punishment, p. 247 (¶704), for an account of all of the various professional associations, including but not limited to medical experts, who ultimately endorse retention of hanging.

59 Examination of Witnesses, Minutes of Evidence, Association of Anaesthetists of England and Ireland, December 6, 1951 (¶9040).

60 Report of the Royal Commission, p. 259 (¶747).

conviction that "the preliminaries to the act of execution should be as quick and as simple as possible" in order to minimize the "prisoner's apprehension."[61] Even more fundamentally, though, the effort to secure a mask to the face of a "conscious man would invite struggling, involuntary perhaps and certainly ineffective, but distressing and unseemly."[62] A scene of this sort, the Commission notes, "could only be avoided by making the prisoner unconscious first," and "if he were unconscious there would be no point in using gas; he would be dispatched more simply and decently by a lethal injection."[63]

Thus does the logic of the Commission's assessment drive it, finally, to entertain the possibility of administering a lethal injection to a conscious agent. What the Commission finds vexing about this possibility is suggested by a difference of opinion among the testifying anaesthetists. On the one hand, as we have already seen, at least one physician contends that someone who has chosen lethal injection over hanging will submit without struggle: "A prisoner would be more likely to keep still and not struggle if he realized that he was being given the opportunity of this pleasanter method of going out, but that if he did not keep still he would be hanged."[64] On the other hand, the anaesthetist who initially provided the Commission with informal testimony is not nearly so sanguine on this point:

> According to the evidence given previously by Dr. Organe, he said he would have to have the prisoner lying down on some sort of table, he would have to be strapped, his arm would have to be strapped to an armboard, and those are the preliminary stages. It would be quite impossible to say how long that stage would take, I suppose, would it not? . . . The ordeal for the man concerned would start from the moment the strapping commenced, would it not, so we really should not consider the position as from the insertion of the needle, but we should consider it from the time the strapping of the arm commences?[65]

In part, as with lethal gas, the concern implicit in these questions is a function of the indeterminacy of specifying exactly when an execution can be said to commence should strapping become an indispensable element of this procedure. That raises the issue of the temporal duration of an execution by lethal injection, especially if that injection is intramuscular rather than intravenous, and that returns the Commission once again to a potential violation of its criterion of humanity.

What, though, is the conception of the subject that informs the concern about what this commissioner characterizes as an "ordeal"? No doubt, part of the answer concerns an empathetic identification of the condemned subject as a being who,

61 Report of the Royal Commission, p. 253 (¶724).
62 Report of the Royal Commission, p. 257 (¶736).
63 Report of the Royal Commission, p. 257 (¶736).
64 Examination of Witnesses, Minutes of Evidence, Association of Anaesthetists of England and Ireland, Royal Commission on Capital Punishment, December 6, 1951 (¶8998).
65 Alternative Methods of Execution, Statement of the Views of Consulting Anaesthetists, Minutes of Evidence, Royal Commission on Capital Punishment, December 6, 1951, (¶9016–17).

like the executioner, is capable of experiencing terror at the prospect of imminent extermination. But there is more to it than that, as the Commission reveals when it cites a general concern expressed by multiple witnesses about any method of execution that effectively robs the soon-to-be-executed subject of the possibility of affirming a claim to dignity, however modest that claim may be:

> By general consent one of the prime requisites of any form of capital punishment is that it should admit of being so carried out as to minimize the risk of distressing and unseemly scenes of panic and resistance. Those of our witnesses who have the duty of attending executions gave striking and unanimous testimony to the stoicism with which condemned men – and women – almost always face death on the scaffold. . . . The argument that we are now concerned with rests on the belief, supported by this experience, that human nature is so constituted as to make it easier for a condemned man to show courage and composure in his last moments if the final act required of him is a positive one, such as walking to the scaffold, than if it is mere passivity, like awaiting the prick of a needle.[66]

What is noteworthy about this quotation is the way it gestures in two directions simultaneously, each of which anticipates a rather different construction of the subject of hanging. On the one hand, in part, this quotation invites claims framed in terms of the need to respect and sustain the conditions that enable any human being, even the criminal convicted of the most heinous deeds, to confront death with dignity. On the other hand, in part, this quotation invites claims framed in terms of the need to acknowledge and protect the sensibilities of witnesses to an execution. This distinction is fragile; and it is not difficult to see how it might be collapsed via a cynical reading that suggests that cultivating the conditions necessary to the condemned's capacity to "show courage and composure in his last moments" is in the last analysis little more than a means to the end of safeguarding spectators against offense. The tenuousness of this distinction, however, is not a sufficient reason to discard it; and it is this distinction that will inform my remaining remarks in this section as well as my discussion, in the next, of the status of lethal injection in contemporary debates about capital punishment within the United States.

Although framed as a universal claim about "human nature," the subject presupposed by this passage, and in particular that subject's claim to dignity, is a creature of overlapping and not entirely consistent discursive contexts, including those we identify with gender, national identity, religious affiliation, and so forth. In oral testimony, for example, one prison governor relied on a specifically Christian theological explanation to indicate his opposition to the use of sedatives prior to an execution: "The man's brain is not fulfilling its proper function if drugs are administered, and there may be a moral view to take, that he should have all his faculties to realize his position here and hereafter. The point seems to me to be that if you drug a man, you

66 Report of the Royal Commission, pp. 260–61 (¶748).

are denying him his human right of adjusting himself with his God."[67] By the same token, elements of a distinctively British brand of nationalism enter into the makeup of this subject, a form that is given euphemistic expression in the appeal to "keep a stiff upper lip." Such nationalism is evident when one hangman, explaining that the only struggle he ever experienced with a condemned prisoner involved an alien, stated his conviction that as a rule "English people take their punishment better than foreigners."[68] And even though this paragraph expressly cites women, albeit as a category delineated as a hyphenated afterthought, it is clear that gendered elements, including the equation of character with the suppression of emotional expression, enter into the constitution of the subject deemed capable of stoic fortitude in the face of impending doom: "If they are given the proper preparation, they can go to the gallows with their chins right up and face death manfully."[69]

For my purposes, what is important is not whether this conception of the subject is real or unreal in some essentialist sense; it is neither. Rather, for my purposes, what is important is the way in which belief in the meaningful reality of this subject participates in persuading the Commission to reject arguments in favor of methods of execution, such as lethal injection, that would effectively compromise, if not violate altogether, the claim to dignity that it appears to believe is due to each human subject, no matter how vile. Protecting that claim is not chiefly a matter of safeguarding an invisible quality that somehow defines the person, but rather a matter of sustaining the conditions that allow this being to participate in fashioning his or her mode of presentation to others. At minimum, affirmation of that claim appears to require a subject who, in "fac[ing] death on the scaffold," remains cognizant of his or her impending demise until the actual moment of execution; who employs his or her own locomotive power, no matter how circumscribed, in getting from the holding cell to the death chamber; and who, although the end result is preordained, remains vertically rather than horizontally positioned at the moment the instrumentalities of killing are set in motion. In another time, and in another place, perhaps one not unlike our own, these concerns might be dismissed as merely "symbolic," or, alternately, might be treated as merely technical issues that should be taken into account only insofar as they relate to the causation of death in the most efficient manner possible. Should either or both of these claims be made, their affirmation

67 Examination of Witnesses, Minutes of Evidence, Royal Commission on Capital Punishment, October 6, 1949 (¶1315).

68 Examination of Witnesses, Minutes of Evidence, Royal Commission on Capital Punishment, November 2, 1950 (¶8302).

69 Examination of Witnesses, Minutes of Evidence, Royal Commission on Capital Punishment, May 5, 1950 (¶1726). But see also the statement of the under-sheriff of Lancaster County on his experience as an assistant at executions by hanging, including the hanging of one woman: "I have never known a prisoner unable to walk to the scaffold or show any emotion in the shape of tears, hysteria or the like; on the contrary, I consider that the prisoners I have seen have displayed a quite remarkable stoicism." Memorandum Submitted by Mr. J.W. Wilson, Minutes of Evidence, Royal Commission on Capital Punishment, November 2, 1950 (¶3).

will testify not to their truth, but to the reality of a differently constituted executable subject.

An additional element of this subject's discursive complexity can be indicated by recalling that the category of dignity is of aristocratic lineage and as such is uneasily invoked in the context of executing the common criminal. This lineage, which is betokened by the shared etymology of the terms "dignity" and "dignitary," is rooted in hierarchically organized cultures that prize the qualities, encapsulated in the passage's appeal to "stoicism," of nobility, honorability, and high estimation in the eyes of others. In this sense, the claim to dignity is a way of enforcing and commending forms of distinction and, in so doing, elevating one class over another; it achieves this end in part by declaring that certain ways of treating the bodies of those deemed dignified are permissible, whereas others are not (e.g., forms of punishment that involve mutilation). Only with this context in mind can we understand why the Commission concludes that its own defense of hanging's retention entails a "surprising inversion:" "A method of execution whose special merit was formerly thought to be that it was peculiarly degrading is now defended on the ground that it is uniquely humane:"[70]

> Execution by hanging is a practice of great antiquity and obscure origin . . . Hanging inflicted a signal indignity on the victim in a most uniquely conspicuous fashion. It displayed him to the onlookers in the most ignominious and abject of postures, and would thus be likely to enhance the deterrent effect of his punishment on anyone who might be tempted to do what he had done . . . Thus hanging came to be regarded as a peculiarly grim and degrading form of execution, suitable for sordid criminals and crimes. Beheading, among Western peoples, used to be considered a more honourable way of suffering the death penalty, and the firing squad still is.[71]

Conjuring images of spectatorial ceremonials in which humiliated bodies dangle and struggle at rope's end, the durability of this history explains why, according to the Commission, a certain stigma still attaches to this method. (Think in this regard of the media response, especially in Europe, to the hanging of Saddam Hussein, as elaborated in Heard's essay in this volume.) However, as noted earlier, this stigma has dissipated in response to technological improvements in this art, which, for the most part, now render death by hanging expeditious and generally uneventful, as well as in response to the move of executions behind prison walls, which situates them beyond the leering eyes and jeering taunts of an uncouth crowd. In addition, and perhaps more important in this context, these stigmatizing associations have become more problematic by the time the Commission conducts its inquiry in virtue of the democratization of publicly articulated cultural norms of conduct in the nineteenth- and twentieth-century Europe (see Hammel's contribution to this volume for a partial account of the emergence of these norms). Endorsement of

70 Report of the Royal Commission, p. 247 (¶705).
71 Report of the Royal Commission, p. 255 (¶701).

these norms, however qualified and incomplete, now renders vexed any defense of a form of punishment that degrades in virtue of its class-specific history. Such an appeal is "repugnant to modern ideas,"[72] the Commission states; presumably, this is so because it denies the common quality of dignity that is now, at least in principle, equally ascribed to all persons regardless of estate or rank.

The Commission is thus tangled in a web not of its own devising insofar as it defends a method of execution that retains, however faintly, the mark of class distinction during an era when it cannot expressly invoke – indeed, must deny – that import. One of the ways the Commission seeks to negotiate this "surprising inversion," which is not without its own difficulties, is via its appeal to the rhetoric of decency, which is most obviously apparent in its exhortation "to minimize the risk of distressing and unseemly scenes of panic and resistance." The appeal to decency shifts discursive attention away from the condemned's mode of self-representation in the face of others and toward the sensibilities of those who witness this show. This shift, I would suggest, effectively affirms the inegalitarian and specifically bourgeois sensibilities that, in a democratic age, can no longer be framed or justified in the name of dignity. Recall that when the Commission invoked the term "decency" to indicate one of its three criteria of evaluation, it stated that any "civilized state" has an obligation to conduct "its judicial executions with decorum."[73] Appeals to the semantically overlapping terms "decorum" and "decency" are part and parcel of a rhetorical cluster that privileges the norms of what is deemed appropriate in the sense of conforming to the imperatives of good taste (as opposed to what is gauche), of what is deemed polite (as opposed to what is rude), of what is deemed respectable (as opposed to what is crass). In each of these instances, to cite the Oxford English Dictionary, that which is decent and decorous is that which "is in accordance with the standard of good breeding," and that standard enjoins any forms of display that are deemed "unseemly or offensive."

In the last analysis, however, as is suggested by the Commission's ultimate rejection of lethal injection in favor of hanging, the claims of dignity edge out but never entirely displace those of decency. For the most part, more specifically, when the Commission invokes the claims of decency, it frames this issue as a question of whether executions conducted by hanging disturb those who perform them, or other prisoners, or, finally, the public at large. What is perhaps most striking is the way the Commission discounts the gravity of these concerns:

> We heard much about the psychological harm said to be caused indirectly by executions – their distressing, or some say brutalising effect on those who have to carry them out, the nervous strain they impose on other prisoners in the gaol and the morbid interest they arouse in the public. These beliefs are generally adduced as one of the arguments for the abolition of capital punishment altogether, and,

[72] Report of the Royal Commission, p. 255 (¶707).
[73] Report of the Royal Commission, p. 255 (¶732).

> as such, are not our concern. But they would be relevant here if consequences of this sort could be shown to be the result less of the fact of execution than of its method. We shall later consider the question whether, if hanging continues, any changes ought to be made in the way it is done, and we shall then give our opinion on the extent to which the beliefs we have referred to are justified. Here it will be enough to say that we cannot regard them as a factor of any weight in our present comparison.[74]

When the Commission does expressly address this issue, it makes clear its view that any strain caused by executions as currently conducted on prison personnel "is short-lived and has no adverse effect on health;"[75] that their effect on "other prisoners is not marked in present conditions;"[76] and that the interest in decorum might be marginally advanced if, rather than posting a notice outside a prison following completion of an execution, which sometimes attracts a crowd, a press notice were to be issued instead. In short, when the Commission takes up the question of decency (leaving aside its abiding concern, framed in terms of mutilation, about hanging's elongation of the condemned's neck), it finds little reason to recommend any significant alteration in present practice in order to accommodate the sensibilities of persons other than the condemned.

More important, the Commission makes it clear that present practice, precisely *because* it employs the method of hanging, acknowledges the dignity of the condemned in a way that no medicalized alternative can. As we have seen, this is principally so because the condemned, in walking upright from the holding cell to the death chamber, retains some measure of agency; and it is by means of such a practice that a subject capable of constitution in terms of the category of dignity is fashioned. In a way we may be inclined to dismiss as superficial (which would say much about us, but little about the actual practice), creation of much the same subject is fostered when the director of Prison Medical Services testifies that "the officers who are detailed to be with the prisoner during the time between conviction and execution . . . .enter very fully into association with him; they play games with him; they converse with him; and they are on ordinary terms, if one may express it in that way, with him."[77] This appeal to the ordinary makes sense only if we presuppose the tacit ascription of a common humanity to executioner and condemned alike, an ascription that is specifically ethical insofar as it forestalls the temptation to transform the condemned into an alien being, a being whose radical otherness might otherwise invite its construction as an object in preparation for instrumental disposal. By the

74 Report of the Royal Commission, p. 256 (¶733).

75 Report of the Royal Commission, p. 271 (¶781). Indeed, the Commission states that available evidence indicates that "duty in the condemned cell and on the scaffold does not brutalise the prison officers who have to perform it. We are satisfied that those witnesses were nearer the mark who said that it tended to bring out the best in them."

76 Report of the Royal Commission, p. 272 (¶783).

77 Examination of Witnesses, Minutes of Evidence, Report of the Royal Commission, August 4, 1949 (¶466).

same token, only if we presuppose a subject who can affirm a legitimate claim to dignity can we understand why the chair of the Panel of Prison Governors, when asked why prison corridors are emptied of other prisoners when a condemned is escorted to the exercise area, answers not in terms of the imperatives of security, but in terms of respect for the "privacy"[78] of those who are near death. Such practices of dignification, which call a specific subject into being by means of its regulation, are quite unlike those that might be adopted in a penal order that aimed to perfect the condemned's objectification. In the latter order, especially should these practices be reinforced by the conditions outlined in Colin Dayan's account of solitary confinement within supermax facilities, their perfection will be achieved when the condemned, well before the actual moment of execution, is fashioned into a supine being available for and, better still, eager for an anesthetized death.

THE OBJECT OF LETHAL INJECTION

Justifying his belief that "a shot from a hypodermic" should be rejected as an alternative to hanging, a prison chaplain offered the following explanation to the Royal Commission on Capital Punishment: "We do not like this hole-in-the-corner getting rid of the man. If a man is to die, let him walk to his death cleanly . . . Nine out of ten go to their death bravely. I am sure they have some special grace given to them on that morning."[79] At the very moment that the Commission upholds hanging, in large measure on the ground that this practice enables a subject who can be depicted in the language of dignity, the Commission also acknowledges the appeal of emerging pharmacological innovations whose adoption would mock that same subject.[80] As we have seen, in the last analysis, the argument advanced by

78 Examination of Witnesses, Minutes of Evidence, Report of the Royal Commission, October 6, 1949 (¶1231).

79 Examination of Witnesses, Minutes of Evidence, Royal Commission on Capital Punishment, October 6, 1949 (¶1517).

80 At the same time, although I cannot elaborate on this point in this context, the Commission's uneasy embrace of another form of medical expertise, specifically that represented by psychiatric knowledge, undermines the coherence of this subject from another angle. That embrace is apparent, first, in its recommendation that exemption from liability to capital punishment should be expanded to include not only the insane, but also the criminal subject who is determined to be "suffering from disease of the mind or mental deficiency to such a degree that he ought not to be held responsible"; and, second, in its recommendation that "the mental state of every prisoner charged with murder should be examined by two doctors, of whom one at least should be a psychiatrist" (see recommendations 13–38, Report of the Royal Commission, pp. 275–78). The Commission seeks to justify these concessions of law to the claims of psychiatric knowledge by representing them as embodiments of an "ancient and humane principle": specifically, the principle which states that "if a person was, at the time of committing an unlawful act, mentally so disordered that it would be unreasonable to impute guilt to him, he ought not to be held liable to conviction and punishment under the criminal law" (p. 275). Doing so, the Commission seeks to contain its incipient understanding of the ever more problematic character of ascriptions of criminal responsibility, and especially those that presuppose a modernist subject who can be deemed culpable for wrongdoing and so merit punishment. That ascription only

the testifying anaesthetists implies that ideally, the condemned should be rendered insensate at some point, whether the evening prior or the morning of the scheduled execution date, before he or she is killed. Although the condemned will no doubt end up officially dead at some point following the production of unconsciousness, it is less clear what it might mean to say that the cause of that death is an execution. Better, perhaps, to say that he or she has been eased out of existence via a technological process that may perhaps be characterized as "humane," if by this term one means simply that neither conscious suffering nor bodily mutilation is involved. Only with difficulty, however, can that death be characterized as "dignified," if by the term "dignity" one means something akin to preserving whatever minimal modicum of agency is requisite to qualify a being as "human." Better, perhaps, to say that the claims of good taste, whether framed in the language of "decorum" or "decency," effectively trump the claims of dignity.

In the final section of this chapter, my aim is to suggest that in the United States today, we are well along the path indicated by what might well be labeled the "logic of anaesthetization." That this is so can be suggested by noting that in the decades since the Commission issued its recommendations, the progressive medicalization of execution, and in particular the employment of pharmacological means to kill, has now become altogether conventional. This is not to say that this practice is beyond question or contention, but it is to say that the question of moment is no longer whether this method, as opposed to some other, is the appropriate way to execute, but whether this method kills in a way that is truly painless, and if not, what incremental adjustments should be made in order to perfect this procedure.[81] As the presence or absence of pain has become the central issue of legal controversy, it has effectively crowded out all other questions, including those that might be framed in the language of dignity. The subject of execution has come to assume the character of a body exclusively defined by its susceptibility to the experience of intense pain, in sum, as an object.

To illustrate this argument, I explore the way in which the category of dignity does, but for the most part does not participate in the only direct challenge to lethal injection to reach the U.S. Supreme Court: *Baze v. Rees*, which was decided in

makes sense if one still believes in a subject who is autonomous both in the sense that he or she knows right from wrong and in the sense that he or she is deemed capable of acting in accordance with that knowledge. The limit of the Commission's willingness to expand the category of those who are exempt from the death penalty on psychological grounds is indicated by its rejection of category of "diminished responsibility" as the basis of a claim to such exemption (p. 276).

81 To anticipate the discussion of this section, this is clearly the question that Justice Roberts presupposes when, in *Baze v. Rees*, 128 S. Ct. 1520, 1537 (2008) (plurality), he defines a "humane" execution as one that "will result in a painless death," and then goes on to state: "Throughout our history, whenever a method of execution has been challenged in this Court as cruel and unusual, the Court has rejected this challenge. Our society has nonetheless steadily moved to more humane methods of carrying out capital punishment. The firing squad, hanging, the electric chair, and the gas chamber have each in turn given way to more humane methods, culminating in today's consensus on lethal injection" (1538).

2008. In a nutshell, in *Baze*, two persons condemned to death in Kentucky filed suit asserting that the state's lethal injection protocol violates the Eighth Amendment's ban on cruel and unusual punishments. The Kentucky protocol at issue provides for the use of three drugs in order to kill. The first, sodium thiopental, is intended to induce unconsciousness and, in doing so, to ensure that the condemned cannot and will not experience any pain during the execution; the second, pancuronium bromide, is a paralytic, which, according to the state, prevents involuntary convulsions or seizures during the execution and, in addition, hastens death by suppressing respiration; the third, potassium chloride, induces cardiac arrest and so is the chief cause of death.

Among other claims, petitioners contended that because the Kentucky protocol does not ensure adequate expertise on the part of the execution team, there is a significant risk that the injection of sodium thiopental will not be properly administered, leaving the condemned conscious and so susceptible to massive pain when the other two drugs are given. In addition, petitioners claimed that the use of pancuronium bromide is causally unnecessary to the production of death, and that the unacknowledged purpose of this drug is to ensure that any physical suffering that it may cause, or that may be caused by the subsequent injection of potassium chloride, is masked by rendering the condemned incapable of all movement, voluntary or involuntary. On this basis, petitioners argued that the likelihood of a humane death would be significantly enhanced were the state to eliminate the second and third drugs, and, as the Royal Commission had entertained, adopt a protocol that provides for the administration of a lethal dose of a single anesthetic chemical.

On appeal, following an extensive hearing conducted by a state trial court, the supreme court of Kentucky affirmed the lower court's ruling, holding that the protocol in question does not create a substantial risk of wanton and unnecessary infliction of pain, torture, or lingering death. The case was then appealed to the U.S. Supreme Court, which, by a seven-to-two vote, affirmed the ruling of the state supreme court. Doing so, it held that in order to prevail, petitioners must show that the state protocol presents not an "unnecessary risk" of harm, as petitioners had contended, but what it variously phrased as a "substantial risk of serious harm" or "an objectively intolerable risk of harm." Because petitioners had failed to meet this burden, the Court found no reason to accept their contention that the state had a legal obligation to eliminate employment of the paralytic and, more specifically, to shift to a single-drug method of execution. For these reasons, the Supreme Court concluded that Kentucky's present lethal injection protocol satisfies the requirements of the Eighth Amendment.

In the seven opinions filed in *Baze*, the category of dignity is altogether absent, with the exception of a highly abbreviated reference in Chief Justice Roberts' plurality opinion (as well as an equally brief response to this reference by Justice Stevens). Specifically, in Roberts' discussion of the chemicals employed in conjunction with a lethal injection, and more particularly, petitioners' contention that pancuronium bromide should be eliminated because it serves "no therapeutic purpose," he endorses the state's counterargument, concluding that this chemical "prevents involuntary physical movements during unconsciousness that may accompany the injection of potassium chloride. The Commonwealth has an interest in preserving the dignity of the procedure, especially where convulsions or seizures could be misperceived as signs of consciousness or distress."[82]

In order to appreciate what goes unstated but implied in this perfunctory invocation of the category of dignity, a brief word is in order about the more robust work done by this same category in *Furman v. Georgia*, which effectively imposed a temporary moratorium on the death penalty 1972, as well as, albeit less vigorously, in *Gregg v. Georgia*, the 1976 case that reaffirmed the constitutionality of capital punishment just one year prior to the earliest adoption of lethal injection in the United States. In *Furman*, the category of dignity provided the linchpin of Justice Brennan's concurring argument:

> The primary principle is that a punishment must not be so severe as to be degrading to the dignity of human beings. Pain, certainly, may be a factor in the judgment... More than the presence of pain, however, is comprehended in the judgment that the extreme severity of a punishment makes it degrading to the dignity of human beings... The true significance of these punishments is that they treat members of the human race as nonhumans, as objects to be toyed with and discarded. They are thus inconsistent with the fundamental premise of the Clause [the Eighth Amendment's prohibition of cruel and unusual punishments] that even the vilest criminal remains a human being possessed of common dignity.[83]

Here Brennan makes clear that pain's infliction, although relevant to determination of a specific punishment's constitutionality, is not the foremost consideration. Instead, he invokes a conception of dignity that attributes to every human being a timeless quality that, because it is essential to the possibility of being human, cannot be violated without converting a subject into an object, a thing for which the category of dignity is irrelevant. Accordingly, in Brennan's view, in every case involving human subjects, whenever it is a matter of assessing the constitutionality of punishments, all competing considerations must, in the last analysis, give way before this most fundamental imperative.

Just four years later, in *Gregg v. Georgia*, Justice Stewart effects a subtle but important shift in Brennan's reading of the Eighth Amendment's import with regard to the category of dignity. Following a brief indication of the punishments deemed beyond the pale at the time of the Constitution's framing, writing for the seven-to-two majority, Stewart insists that the prohibition on cruel and unusual punishments "must draw its meaning from the evolving standards of decency that mark the progress

82 Baze v. Rees, 128 S. Ct. 1520, 1535 (2008) (plurality).
83 Furman v. Georgia, 408 U.S. 238, 271–73 (1972).

of a maturing society."[84] Acknowledging, however, that the claims of dignity are not rendered irrelevant by an appeal to such standards, Stewart goes on to state:

> (O)ur cases also make clear that public perceptions of standards of decency with respect to criminal sanctions are not conclusive. A penalty also must accord with "the dignity of man," which is the "basic concept underlying the Eight Amendment. This means, at least, that the punishment not be "excessive." When a form of punishment in the abstract (in this case, whether capital punishment may ever be imposed as a sanction for murder), rather than in the particular (the propriety of death as a penalty to be applied to a specific defendant for a specific crime), is under consideration, the inquiry into "excessiveness" has two aspects. First, the punishment must not involve the unnecessary and wanton infliction of pain. Second, the punishment must not be grossly out of proportion to the severity of the crime.[85]

On the one hand, the conception of dignity presupposed by Stewart in *Gregg* is consonant with that invoked by Brennan in *Furman*, as well as by the Royal Commission insofar as its principal concern is with the executable subject. On the other hand, insofar as Stewart's reading defines that subject's dignity through reference to the potential to experience pain, it turns attention to that which can never be known for certain, namely whether a subject is or is not in pain, and hence to the signs that others may (or may not) interpret as evidence that a subject is suffering. In doing so, under cover of an appeal to evolving standards of decency, Stewart effectively encourages the Court to turn its attention away from the condemned and toward an execution's audience.

In *Baze*, Roberts consummates the insidious shift that Stewart initiates in *Gregg*. Specifically, Roberts appropriates a claim about what it means to respect the dignity of the condemned and transmutes it into a constitutional validation of the vulnerable sensibilities of spectators.[86] Granted, at first blush, his contention that the state has "an interest in preserving the dignity of the procedure" might appear to refer to, or at least to encompass, the respect owed to the condemned. That this is not in fact so is made evident when, immediately thereafter, he specifies that this interest arises when "convulsions or seizures could be misperceived as signs of consciousness or distress."[87] This legerdemain, I take it, is what Justice Stevens seeks to expose in his concurring opinion when he states that Roberts offers "a woefully inadequate justification" for the use of pancuronium bromide, because whatever minimal interest the state has in ensuring "that witnesses to the execution are not

84 Gregg v. Georgia, 428 U.S. 153, 172 (1976).

85 Gregg v. Georgia, 428 U.S. 153, 173 (1976).

86 See also Brief of Respondents at 51, Baze v. Rees, 128 S. Ct. 1520 (2008) (No. 07–5439), *available at* http://www.law.berkeley.edu/clinics/dpclinic/LethalInjection/LI/briefs.html: "Petitioners argue that involuntary muscle contractions have no bearing on the dignity of condemned, since the administration of thiopental renders the inmate impervious to pain. However, petitioners' argument ignores the impact on family members and other witnesses who view the involuntary contractions."

87 Baze v. Rees, 128 S. Ct. 1520, 1544 (2008) (plurality).

made uncomfortable by an incorrect belief (which could easily be corrected) that the inmate is in pain, is vastly outweighed by the risk that the inmate is actually experiencing excruciating pain that no one can detect."[88] To put the point more bluntly, in a vexing extension of the victim impact appeals that are now so central to the sentencing phase of capital trials, Roberts effectively represents the inexpert witnesses to an execution as its potential casualties who must be protected from the harm that might be occasioned should the body of the condemned, whether reflexively or deliberately, display any visible signs that might be interpreted, whether correctly or mistakenly, as marks of bodily distress. In short, Roberts relegates the condemned to the role of a silenced body whose inertness must be guaranteed to ensure that these bystanders are not psychologically harmed; and he does so in the name of the state, which, in the last analysis, is regarded as the rightful guardian of the constitutionally protected interest in proper decorum.

That the category of dignity is so readily twisted and/or displaced is perhaps not surprising in a nation where, to cite Pieter Spierenburg, democracy came too soon in the specific sense that its accomplishment did not involve overthrowing the aristocratic regimes whose cultural practices and norms sustained the intelligibility of appeals to dignity in Europe, even as these claims were effectively democratized in the nineteenth and twentieth centuries. Today, in the United States, the dignifying practices that might prop up such appeals are best regarded as relics (consider, for example, the ritual of the last meal and the final words) that appear ever more anachronistic when confronted by the norms of instrumental rationality that govern the conduct of contemporary executions.

It is the ubiquity as well as the authority of such rationality, as well as the practices it informs, that opens up the possibility that the category of dignity may disappear altogether from the debate over execution methods. Absent that category, this debate becomes little more than a matter of tinkering with the machinery of death, and the condemned subject becomes little, if anything, more than a component within this lethal apparatus. Or rather, when the debate over lethal injection is stripped of the ethical reference inherent in an appeal to the category of dignity, even when that appeal reduces to an act of bad faith, as it does in Roberts' opinion, it becomes a purely instrumental affair to be assessed by the criterion of efficacy. Thus defined, the debate lends itself with equal facility to arguments for or against lethal injection, depending on the question of whether one believes the state has or has not succeeded in eliminating from the act of killing all traces of pain, or more cynically, given the inherently unverifiable character of all claims to experience pain, in eliminating from the act of killing any visible sign that might possibly be (mis)interpreted as such.

Such is the character of the argument between Justices Breyer and Ginsburg, which, in the last analysis, I would argue, better reveals the tenor of an era in which

[88] Baze v. Rees, 128 S. Ct. 1520, 1544 (2008) (Stevens, J., concurring).

the claims of instrumental rationality threaten to displace all others than does the disingenuous argument advanced by Roberts. Breyer opens his concurring opinion by indicating his conviction that Ginsburg, in her dissenting opinion, has identified the correct question in assessing the merits of the claims raised by petitioners: "whether the method creates an untoward, readily avoidable risk of inflicting severe and unnecessary suffering."[89] Breyer's search for an answer to this question, he explains, has taken him through various scholarly studies, especially those prepared by medical practitioners, particularly by students of anesthesiology. Not surprisingly, Breyer discovers that there is considerable disagreement among these practitioners on the factual basis for the petitioners' contention that the Kentucky protocol does not adequately alleviate the risk that they may remain conscious and so experience pain at some time during their execution. Because "the legal merits of the kind of claim presented must inevitably turn not so much upon the wording of an intermediate standard of review as upon facts and evidence," Breyer concludes that he "cannot find, either in the record in this case or in the literature on the subject, sufficient evidence that Kentucky's execution method poses the 'significant and unnecessary risk of inflicting severe pain' that the petitioners assert."[90]

For her part, Ginsburg asserts that the "constitutionality of Kentucky's protocol . . . turns on whether inmates are adequately anesthetized by the first drug in the protocol, sodium thiopental."[91] This question, too, is a purely instrumental one, and its answer turns on whether the state has adopted the technical safeguards necessary to ensure that the condemned is unconscious and remains so prior to as well as during injection of the second and third chemicals. Never is the ideal of an anesthetized death subject to critical examination, and never is the congruence of such a death with the dignity of the executable subject posed as a possible question. Instead, and only momentarily, does the pale simulacrum of dignity that takes shape as an appeal to "decency" intrude on what is otherwise an altogether technical analysis: "If readily available measures can materially increase the likelihood that the protocol will cause no pain, a State fails to adhere to contemporary standards of decency if it declines to employ those measures."[92] Just what those standards require becomes clear when Ginsburg closes her dissent by calling on the Court to remand to the trial court with instructions to consider whether the adoption of additional safeguards, such as stroking the inmate's eyelashes, using ammonia tablets to determine responsiveness to a noxious nasal stimulus, and calling the condemned by name, might reduce the risk of "inflicting severe and unnecessary pain."[93]

What one hears in the opinions of Breyer and Ginsburg, one concurring, the other dissenting, is what one should anticipate when the debate about execution has

89 Baze v. Rees, 128 S. Ct. 1520, 1563 (2008) (Breyer, J., concurring).
90 Baze v. Rees, 128 S. Ct. 1520, 1563 (2008) (Breyer, J., concurring).
91 Baze v. Rees, 128 S. Ct. 1520, 1567 (2008) (Ginsburg, J., concurring).
92 Baze v. Rees, 128 S. Ct. 1520, 1569 (2008) (Ginsburg, J., concurring).
93 Baze v. Rees, 128 S. Ct. 1520, 1572 (2008) (Ginsburg, J., concurring).

itself become anaesthetized. That debate is largely immunized from ethical appeals that might render it something other than a technical squabble over the merits of expert claims that no judge is sufficiently equipped to assess. Indeed, when the issue is framed in these terms, it is not clear that any amount of factual evidence, no matter how sophisticated or conclusive, can ever bring this debate to a decisive end. Given the inherent subjectivism of claims to be in pain, even in the absence of administration of a paralytic, it will always be open to defenders of the death penalty to affirm that what appears to be signs of pain are in fact agonal or reflexive responses that signify nothing other than the efficacious accomplishment of an untroubled death.

It is only Justice Thomas, perhaps the Court's most vigorous proponent of the death penalty, who contests the claim that the "Eighth Amendment permits only one mode of execution, or that it requires an anesthetized death."[94] Moreover, and presciently, it is Thomas who predicts that so long as abolitionists find themselves unable to mount a direct assault on the constitutionality of capital punishment, they will continue to "embroil the States in never-ending litigation concerning the adequacy of their execution procedures . . . At what point does a risk become 'substantial'? Which alternative procedures are 'feasible' and 'readily implemented'? When is a reduction in risk 'significant'?"[95] Finally, it is Thomas who correctly complains that the reduction of the death penalty debate to such technical matters requires courts "to resolve medical and scientific controversies that are largely beyond judicial ken":

> Little need be said here, other than to refer to the various opinions filed by my colleagues today. Under the competing risk standards advanced by the plurality opinion and the dissent, for example, the difference between a lethal injection procedure that satisfies the Eighth Amendment and one that does not may well come down to one's judgment with respect to something as hairsplitting as whether an eyelash stroke is necessary to ensure that the inmate is unconscious, or whether instead other measures have already provided sufficient assurance of unconsciousness . . . We have neither the authority nor the expertise to micromanage the States' administration of the death penalty in this manner.[96]

Whatever one thinks of Thomas' stance on capital punishment, or his interpretation of the Eighth Amendment, or his latitudinarian account of permissible methods of punishment, it seems clear that he has correctly identified the cul-de-sac into which courts are pressed when they endorse the ideal of an anesthetized death. And, although clearly not his intent, it seems equally clear that Thomas has indicated the trap into which abolitionists all too quickly enter when they endorse this same ideal and on that basis contest state protocols via technical challenges that are effectively

94 Baze v. Rees, 128 S. Ct. 1520, 1562 (2008) (Thomas, J., concurring).
95 Baze v. Rees, 128 S. Ct. 1520, 1562 (2008) (Thomas, J., concurring).
96 Baze v. Rees, 128 S. Ct. 1520, 1562 (2008) (Thomas, J., concurring).

evacuated of any ethical import. Of greater concern is that when abolitionists endorse this ideal, whether wittingly or not, they also endorse the transformation of the subject of execution into an object.[97] Once deprived of the claim to dignity that is a potential lever of resistance to its objectification, once denied a vocabulary that affirms a limit on the extensiveness of state power in the name of a nonnegotiable moral imperative, that object becomes complicit in consolidation of the very form of state power whose claim to exercise a monopoly over the means of legitimate violence is perhaps most graphically affirmed via the performance of an execution.[98]

What this reading of *Baze* suggests is that the business of capital punishment, to quote Michael Madow, has now become so much "death work . . . The condemned man, previously the central actor in a public theater of justice, ha[s] now become simply the object of medico-bureaucratic techniques – his body read closely for signs of pain, but his voice muffled and barely audible."[99] That work is haunted by the ideal of a death sentence the infliction of which is so imperceptible that it elides the act of killing; and in the world defined by that ideal, there is no place for the discourse of dignity. Or more accurately, as we see in *Baze*, the only place for such discourse is a crooked place, a place where the dignity once ascribed to the hangman's charges is now invoked only to safeguard the sensibilities of those who watch for signs that might betray life's excision but who see nothing.

97 For elaborations of my criticism of contemporary death penalty abolitionism in the United States, see Timothy V. Kaufman-Osborn, "A Critique of Contemporary Death Penalty Abolitionism," Punishment & Society 8:3 (July 2006), pp. 365–83; and "Perfect Execution: Abolitionism and the Challenge of Lethal Injection," *The Road to Abolition*, Charles Ogletree and Austin Sarat, eds. (New York: New York University Press, 2010): pp. 215–51.

98 In his contribution to this volume, Jon Yorke provides a quotation from the former Foreign Minister of France, Robert Badinter, that provides an indication of the sort of claim that, I suspect, has already become and, I fear, is likely to become ever more unintelligible within the context of the death penalty debate in the United States: "In reality, no one is denying the threat posed by terrorism, but not only does the war against terrorism not require the death penalty, it must actually ensure that it does not resort to it. In the face of terrorism, abolition gives democracy an ethical dimension, essential in such a war. The terrorist kills innocent victims in the name of his ideology; democracy defends freedom and recognises all lives as sacred, even that of the terrorist. The conflict is one of values in which, eventually, democracy always triumphs and even more so when it upholds, loud and clear, the principles on which it is founded. Faced with crime and cruelty, a democracy's justice system rejects vengeance and death. It punishes but it does not kill; it prevents the terrorist from harming others but respects his life; by refusing to give him death, democracy guarantees the humanity the terrorist denies through his crimes. Democracy comes out as the moral victor of the test inflicted on it by terrorism. That will not be the least of its victories in the eyes of generations to come."

99 Michael Madow, "Forbidden Spectacle: Executions, the Public and the Press in Nineteenth Century New York," *Buffalo Law Review* 43 (Fall 1995): 465.

9

Sovereignty and the Unnecessary Penalty of Death

European and United States Perspectives

Jon Yorke

INTRODUCTION

José Luis Rodríguez Zapatero, the Prime Minister of Spain,[1] stated in the United Nations' Palace of Nations in Geneva on February 24, 2010, that the Spanish government will take a leading role in promoting the worldwide abolition of the death penalty. It would promote initiatives within the European Union and the United Nations,[2] and also create an International Academic Network Against the Death Penalty.[3] Prime Minister Zapatero's visionary position can be placed within the marked proliferation, most clearly demonstrated since the late 1980s, of sovereign governments accepting the arguments that the death penalty is an ineffective penal

1 Spain held the Presidency of the European Union for the first half of 2010. See the website dedicated to the Spanish Presidency, http://www.eu2010.es/en/. The ratification of the Lisbon Treaty in 2009 has made accession of the European Union to the European Convention on Human Rights legally possible, see Protocol, C306/155 17/12/2007, and also endorsed the Charter of Fundamental Rights of the European Union (2000/C 364/01) 18.12.2000, Article 2 Right to Life, (1) Everyone has the right to life, (2) No one shall be condemned to the death penalty, or executed.

2 Speech at the Palace of Nations, United Nations, Geneva, February 24, 2010, as part of the opening of the World Congress of the Abolition of the Death Penalty, see, http://www.worldcoalition.org/modules/accueil/. The Prime Minister has also outlined his abolitionist strategy in José Luis Rodríguez Zapatero, 'Por la Abolición Universal de la Pena de Muerte,' in Luis Arroyo, Paloma Biglino and William Schabas, (ed) *Hacia la Abolición Universal de la pena capital*, (Valencia: Tirant lo Blanch, 2010), pp. 13–22.

3 See the website of the International Academic Network for the Abolition of the Death Penalty, http://www.academicsforabolition.net/

I am extremely grateful for the conversations with Austin Sarat, Jürgen Martschukat, and other colleagues at our death penalty seminar at Amherst College in April 2010. This chapter has also benefitted from conversations with Roger Hood, Carolyn Hoyle, William Schabas, Sarah Cooper, Julian Killingley, Haydn Davies, Chris King, Will Flavel, Luis Arroyo, Antonio Muñoz Aunion, and Andrew Williams. I am very grateful for the research assistance of Gemma Barnett, Priya Dosanjh, Liam Draper, and Kelly Grainger. Any errors remain my own.

policy, and that it is also a violation of human rights.[4] This statement in the United Nations can be seen as a further political approval, and a strategic continuation, of the first adopted United Nations General Assembly resolution calling for a worldwide moratorium on the death penalty in December 2007,[5] and in 2008 the General Assembly affirmed "the decisions taken by an increasing number of States to apply a moratorium on executions and the global trend towards the abolition of the death penalty."[6] As of March 2010, 139 countries have abolished the death penalty,[7] and since 2000, there have been 23 countries that have abolished this punishment in all circumstances.[8] A minority of 58 countries have the death penalty on their statute

4 For a detailed analysis of the human rights discourse, see William A. Schabas, *The Abolition of the Death Penalty in International Law*, 3rd ed, (Cambridge: Cambridge University Press, 2002); Roger Hood and Carolyn Hoyle, 'Abolishing the Death Penalty Worldwide: The Impact of a "New Dynamic,"' in *Crime and Justice: A Review of Research* (Chicago: University of Chicago Press, 2009); Roger Hood and Carolyn Hoyle, *The Death Penalty: A Worldwide Perspective*, 4th ed, (Oxford: Oxford University Press, 2008);

5 Resolution adopted by the General Assembly, Moratorium on the use of the death penalty, A/res/62/149, 17 December 2007. In the preamble, the General Assembly considers, "that the use of the death penalty undermines human dignity, and convinced that a moratorium on the use of the death penalty contributes to the enhancement and progressive development of human rights, that there is no conclusive evidence of the deterrent value of the death penalty and that any miscarriage or failure of justice in the implementation of the death penalty is irreversible and irreparable."

6 General Assembly, Third Committee, Agenda item 64 (b), Moratorium on the use of the death penalty, A/c.3/63/L.19/Rev.1 7 November 2008.

7 For abolitionist and retentionist country figures, see the Amnesty International website, http://www.amnesty.org/en/death-penalty/abolitionist-and-retentionist-countries. Amnesty International divide the total of 139 as 95 countries as abolitionist for all crimes, which are: Albania, Andorra, Angola, Argentina, Armenia, Australia, Austria, Azerbaijan, Belgium, Bhutan, Bosnia-Herzegovina, Bulgaria, Burundi, Cambodia, Canada, Cape Verde, Colombia, Cook Islands, Costa Rica, Cote D'Ivoire, Croatia, Cyprus, Czech Republic, Denmark, Djibouti, Dominican Republic, Ecuador, Estonia, Finland, France, Georgia, Germany, Greece, Guinea-Bissau, Haiti, Holy See, Honduras, Hungary, Iceland, Ireland, Italy, Kiribati, Kyrgyzstan, Liechtenstein, Lithuania, Luxembourg, Macedonia, Malta, Marshall Islands, Mauritius, Mexico, Micronesia, Moldova, Monaco, Montenegro, Mozambique, Namibia, Nepal, Netherlands, New Zealand, Nicaragua, Niue, Norway, Palau, Panama, Paraguay, Philippines, Poland, Portugal, Romania, Rwanda, Samoa, San Marino, Sao Tome and Principe, Senegal, Serbia (including Kosovo), Seychelles, Slovakia, Slovenia, Solomon Islands, South Africa, Spain, Sweden, Switzerland, Timor-Leste, Togo, Turkey, Turkmenistan, Tuvalu, Ukraine, United Kingdom, Uruguay, Uzbekistan, Vanuatu, and Venezuela. The nine abolitionist countries for ordinary crimes are: Bolivia, Brazil, Chile, El Salvador, Fiji, Israel, Kazakstan, Latvia, and Peru. The thirty-five abolitionist countries in practice are: Algeria, Benin, Brunei, Burkina Faso, Cameroon, Central African Republic, Congo (Republic of), Eritrea, Gabon, Gambia, Ghana, Grenada, Kenya, Laos, Liberia, Madagascar, Malawi, Maldives, Mali, Mauritania, Morocco, Myanmar, Nauru, Niger, Papua New Guinea, Russian Federation, South Korea, Sri Lanka, Suriname, Swaziland, Tajikistan, Tanzania, Tonga, Tunisia, and Zambia.

8 The countries that have abolished the death penalty for all crimes since 2000 are: Albania (2007), Argentina (2008), Armenia (2003), Bhutan (2004), Bosnia-Herzegovina (2001), Burundi (2009), Cook Islands (2007), Cote D'Ivoire (2000), Cyprus (2002), Greece (2004), Kyrgyzstan (2007), Liberia (2005), Malta (2000), Mexico (2005), Montenegro (2002), Philippines (2006), Rwanda (2007), Samoa (2004), Senegal (2004), Serbia (2002), Togo (2009), Turkey (2004), and Uzbekistan (2008).

books,[9] but in 2008, only 25 countries were known to Amnesty International to have administered an execution, and it is notable that "[n]inety three percent of all known executions took place in five countries: China, Iran, Saudi Arabia, Pakistan and the USA."[10]

This chapter engages with a specific issue in the sovereign rejection of the death penalty. The focus for enquiry will be the governmental aim to create effective penal policies in its role of guardian of the mortal choices and decisions within a country. When considering how to punish the worst criminals in a state, or even how to punish those attacking a state from the outside, the question of the legitimacy of the death penalty arises. Max Weber identified that the state holds the "monopoly of the legitimate use of physical force in the enforcement of its order."[11] Historically the death penalty was generally considered to be a legitimate punishment for maintaining public order in society, but over the past thirty years, there has been an almost complete political metamorphosis rejecting this position. As such, it is explored to what extent the *legitimacy* of the death penalty is contingent on it being viewed as a *necessary* punishment for a social and politically valid aim; and alongside this analysis will be a consideration of the impact the internationalization of the abolitionist discourse has had on any isolated, statist, promotion of sovereignty.

The first part of this chapter engages with the theoretical discourse on the question of sovereignty and its relationship with the death penalty. The 2004 dialogue between Jacques Derrida and Elisabeth Roudinesco is offered as a point of departure for the assertion that sovereignty can maintain the death penalty for exceptional cases. To make this argument, Derrida provides a reading of Cesare Beccaria's exception to abolition and Carl Schmitt's sovereignty thesis, which is then critiqued by Roudinesco, and the differences in the two philosopher's positions are considered. Foremost in this section is a theoretical analysis of the political philosophy that attempts to identify that sovereignty and the death penalty are connected, and that death sentences and executions become enacted when threats are visited upon the state. This theory places sovereignty within the statist model and views decisions on punishment being applied through an unfettered monopoly by state governments. A contemporary reading of sovereignty is offered, which moves this political

9 Amnesty International records the remaining fifty-eight retentionist countries as being: Afghanistan, Antigua and Barbuda, Bahamas, Bahrain, Bangladesh, Barbados, Belarus, Belize, Botswana, Chad, China, Comoros, Democratic Republic of Congo, Cuba, Dominica, Egypt, Equatorial Guinea, Ethiopia, Guatemala, Guinea, Guyana, India, Indonesia, Iran, Iraq, Jamaica, Japan, Jordan, Kuwait, Lebanon, Lesotho, Libya, Malaysia, Mongolia, Nigeria, North Korea, Oman, Pakistan, Palestinian Authority, Qatar, Saint Kitts and Nevis, Saint Lucia, Saint Vincent and the Grenadines, Saudi Arabia, Sierra Leone, Singapore, Somalia, Sudan, Syria, Taiwan, Thailand, Trinidad and Tobago, Uganda, United Arab Emirates, United States Of America, Viet Nam, Yemen, and Zimbabwe.

10 See the Amnesty International death penalty webpage, http://www.amnesty.org/en/death-penalty/numbers.

11 Max Weber, *Economy and Society*, vol. 1, (ed: Guenther Roth and Claus Wittich) (Berkeley: University of California Press, 1978), p. 54.

concept outside statism and attempts to place it within a contemporary cosmopolitan construct.

In the second part, the processes for the rejection of the death penalty within the European regions of the Council of Europe and the European Union are considered. By 1981, the geopolitical region of Western Europe had denounced the punishment.[12] It is analysed to what extent individual governments, as part of their own political policy, rejected the death penalty as a useful penological tool for both protecting the lives of individuals from domestic homicides and as an effective penalty for those outside (and inside) attacking the security of the state. Then the various discussions within the Parliamentary Assembly of the Council of Europe which analyzed the necessity of the death penalty in terrorist cases are engaged with. It is investigated to what extent these discussions led to the firm rejection of the death penalty in all circumstances in 2002. The European Union has also developed an abolitionist strategy and has mandated the abolition of the death penalty within its member states, and it seeks to promote global abolition as part of its external human rights project.

In the third part, the extent to which the argument that the death penalty is unnecessary in the United States is analyzed. Hugo Bedau explicitly argued through his theory of the "minimal invasion principle" that the death penalty is unnecessary in the United States, and a political and constitutional history is offered to reveal the cogency of Bedau's position. The debates during the drafting of the Bill of Rights in 1791 are considered, and a U.S. Supreme Court jurisprudential thread is identified to determine whether the U.S. Constitution can be interpreted to reveal that the death penalty is no longer necessary. The question of the necessity of the death penalty is then placed in context with the (in)effectiveness of state capital statutes to render a constitutionally viable sentencing policy, and then the exponential costs of maintaining the capital judicial system is balanced against an adequate alternative punishment through a prison sentence (although not a sentence of life without parole because this is also considered to be a cruel punishment – see the excellent arguments by Marie Gottschalk, this volume).

The Evolution of Sovereignty and the Death Penalty

In her *Foreword* to the "dialogue" with Jacques Derrida, Elisabeth Roudinesco explained that there was a certain level of dissimilarity between the two philosophers' approaches to the questions concerning sources of political power. She reveals that there were "differences . . . stated, points of convergence, discoveries on both sides,

[12] In Western Europe, France was the only country likely to impose executions in the beginning of the 1980s, but it abolished the death penalty in 1981. Belgium still had the death penalty on its statute books but it did not impose an execution after 1953. It had a practice of automatic commutation of death sentences and abolished the punishment in 1998.

surprises, interrogations; in short a complicity without complacency."[13] Roudinesco preselected some of the topics for their discussion, which she discerned as the "great questions that mark our age."[14] Among these was the issue of the "death penalty and its necessary abolition,"[15] and Derrida acquiesced in this selection and identified the special status of the punishment within intellectual enquiry on politics and power as he stated, "what is most hegemonic in philosophy should include a deconstruction of the death penalty, and everything with which it is in solidarity – beginning with a certain concept of sovereignty."[16] Derrida had uncovered this philosophical hegemony during a seminar on the death penalty at Cardozo Law School, and he reveals that he had come to the conclusion that sovereignty and the death penalty were in some sort of symbiotic relationship because the death penalty becomes applicable in "exceptional cases."[17] He provides a history of Western philosophy and a reading of the humanism of Cesare Beccaria and Carl Schmitt's theory of public law. Derrida claimed that no philosopher of the Western tradition had "contested the legitimacy of the death penalty."[18] He interpreted this philosophical tradition (which includes the Enlightenment theory of the social contract and Immanuel Kant's categorical imperatives) as not having adequately solved the problem of how to deal with threats to the life of the sovereign and the life of his citizens. Derrida was of the opinion that there will always be circumstances where the death penalty would be viewed as necessary for the survival of the sovereign and his subjects. A favorite of Derrida's is Jean-Jacques Rousseau's legitimizing of the punishment in

13 Jacques Derrida and Elisabeth Roudinesco, *For What Tomorrow... A Dialogue*, (trans: Jeff Fort) (Stanford: Stanford University Press, 2004), p. ix.

14 Ibid., p. x.

15 Ibid.

16 Ibid., p. 88.

17 Here Derrida is continuing his observation made at his seminar on the death penalty at Cardozo Law School in 2001. Kyron Huigens notes that Derrida stated that "it is impossible to separate political sovereignty from the power over life and death ... [i]n order to maintain an essential aspect of its sovereignty, the state must reserve the right to impose the penalty of death, at least in exceptional cases," 'Derrida on the Death Penalty,' *Cardozo Life*, Winter, 2001, p. 23. Derrida also has engaged with the racism of the death penalty in the United States in *Without Alibi*, (ed: Peggy Kamuf) (Stanford: Stanford University Press, 2002), p. 238; and in his 'Open Letter to Bill Clinton,' Derrida asked President Clinton to show an act of justice in granting Mumi Abu-Jamal a new trial, in *Negotiations, Interventions and Interviews: 1971–2001* (ed: Elizabeth Rottenberg) (Stanford: Stanford University Press, 2002), p. 132.

18 Derrida argued that the "[f]act about the history of Western philosophy: never, *to my knowledge*, has any philosopher *as such, in his or her own, strictly and systematically philosophical discourse*, never has any philosophy *as such* contested the legitimacy of the death penalty" (emphasis in original), in Derrida and Roudinesco, *For What Tomorrow*, p. 146, and this is repeated in Jacques Derrida, 'Capital Punishment: Another "Temptation of Theodicy,"' in Seyla Benhabib and Nancy Fraser (ed), *Pragmatism, Critique, Judgment: Essays for Richard J. Bernstein*, (Cambridge: MIT Press, 2004), pp. 202–3. He further emphasised, "[f]rom Plato to Hegel, from Rousseau to Kant (who was undoubtedly the most rigorous of them all), they expressly, each in his own way, and sometimes without much hand-wringing (Rousseau), took a stand *for* the death penalty" (emphasis in original), p. 203.

the social contract through the execution of the "public enemy"[19] because survival is at stake: either the sovereign or the individual will perish.

In the same way, Derrida claims that the Italian Enlightenment humanist Cesare Beccaria allowed for the death penalty in exceptional circumstances. Beccaria is recognized as one of the main figures promoting the abolitionist discourse in modernity, and within his tract, *An Essay on Crimes and Punishment*, he argued for the general abolition of the death penalty, but conceded that "[t]here are only two grounds on which the death of a citizen might be held to be necessary."[20] The first is when an individual "retains such connections and such power as to endanger the security of the nation, when, that is, his existence may threaten a dangerous revolution in the established form of government."[21] The second was when the death penalty was demonstrated to be a deterrent, but Beccaria argued that "centuries of experience" had revealed that "the ultimate penalty has never dissuaded men from offending against society."[22] Derrida then proposed an extravagant reading of Beccaria's exceptions when he explained:

> If one were to apply to the letter the list of exceptions Beccaria places on the suspension of capital punishment, it would be administered almost every day. As soon as the order of a society is threatened, or every time it is not yet assured, it is admissible to put a citizen to death, according to Beccaria, even if for him the death penalty is not a "right."[23]

Derrida does not engage with the historical context of this Enlightenment position and the evolving techniques of the police force and punishment and the prevalence of crime in eighteenth-century Europe.[24] In particular, it would have been beneficial if he had placed Beccaria in context with the theories of the nineteenth-century

[19] Ibid., p. 153
[20] Ibid., p. 66.
[21] Ibid.
[22] Ibid., p. 67. Beccaria also affirmed this exception in a report to the Austrian Lombardy on the drafting of a new penal code, with Francesco Gallarati Scotti and Paolo Risi, and they stated that, "the death penalty should not be prescribed except in the case of absolute necessity," and that, "in the peaceful circumstances of our society, and with the regular administration of justice, we could not think of any case of absolute necessity other than the situation in which the accused, in plotting the subversion of the state, was capable, either through his external or internal relationships, of disturbing and endangering society even while imprisoned and closely watched," in, 'Opinion of the Undersigned Members of the Committee Charged with the Reform of the Criminal System in Austrian Lombardy for Matters Pertaining to Capital Punishment' (1792), in Aaron Thomas (ed), *Cesare Beccaria, On Crimes and Punishments and Other Writings*, (Ontario: University of Toronto Press, 2008), pp. 153–5.
[23] Derrida and Roudinesco, *For What Tomorrow*, p. 149. See also, Derrida, 'Capital Punishment: Another "Temptation of Theodicy,"' p. 206.
[24] For example see, Pieter Spierenburg, *The Spectacle of Suffering: Executions and the Evolution of Repression: From a Preindustrial Metropolis to the European Experience*, (Cambridge: Cambridge University Press, 2008).

European historian, François Guizot.[25] Through Guizot's reasoning on what are legitimate and necessary punishments, we can see that even Beccaria (and thus Derrida also) was mistaken about the quality of the death penalty for neutralizing threats to the security of the state. Guizot observed that "[c]apital punishment, in spite of appearances, has not, even in a physical sense, the advantage of an immutable efficacy; for in suppressing a known enemy, it does not always suppress danger,"[26] and he further explained, "[w]hat power seeks in the employment of capital punishment is security. I have shown that this it does not find."[27] Guizot demonstrated that in creating mechanisms for the security of the state, the death penalty is impotent and he further explained:

> [p]unishments may destroy men, but they can neither change the interests nor sentiments of the people . . . [the government] may kill one or several individuals, and severely chastise one or several conspiracies, but if it can do no more than this, it will find the same perils and the same enemies always before it. If it is able to do more, let it dispense with killing, for it has no more need of it; less terrible remedies will suffice.[28]

The death penalty has an appearance of being a sophisticated penological tool. But when enemies attack, it is a blunt instrument and is insufficient for dealing with the technical political nuances required to maintain a state's equilibrium. This is against the truncated position of when security is threatened, the only possible outcome is either survival or death; nonexecution leads to the death of the sovereign and his subjects, and an execution leads to the preservation of the life of the sovereign and his subjects. Guizot demonstrated that this is an overly simplified determination, and that even during war, the mortal choices governments make are more complicated, and different political strategies must be thought through for the immediate and long term fostering and flourishing of the populace. In the presence of great violence in society, such as during the French Revolution, Guizot stated, "[w]e live in a society

[25] François Guizot, 'A Treatise on Death Punishments,' in *General History of Civilisation in Europe: From the Fall of the Roman Empire Till the French Revolution* (Edinburgh: William and Robert Chambers Press, 1848).

[26] Ibid., p. 258. Guizot affirmed, '[c]apital punishment . . . has lost its efficacy . . . whatever individual it may fix upon, in destroying him, it by no means neutralises the impending danger,' p. 259.

[27] Ibid., p. 258.

[28] Ibid., p. 327. The French jurist, Marc Ancel, reviewed the French and British abolitionist arguments in the mid-nineteenth century and stated, "[i]n France, Guizot and Charles Lucas represented this movement [arguing against the death penalty for 'reason of state'], which in 1848 ended by removing the death penalty for political crimes . . . the utilitarian current, which, in diverse forms, was evident from Bentham to [John] Stuart Mill or to Spencer, and among jurists to Rossi, affirmed that it was proper to search for happiness and not for pain. In particular, punishment should be 'no more than just, nor more than necessary'; *this led one logically to ask, if it was ever really necessary to punish any offender by death regardless of his crime*" (emphasis added), in Marc Ancel, 'The Problem of the Death Penalty,' p. 3, in Thorsten Sellin (ed), *Capital Punishment* (New York: Harper and Row, 1967).

recently overturned, where legitimate and illegitimate interests, honourable and blameable sentiments, just and false ideas, are so mingled, that it is very difficult to strike hard without striking wrong."[29] Guizot called for governments not to react with death during threats to its security, but for political power to place a more sensitive analysis on political policies and penal techniques, to determine what would be beneficial to the state.

Derrida then placed his reading of Beccaria's legitimizing of the death penalty in exceptional cases in juxtaposition with the Weimar Constitutional public law theory of Carl Schmitt. Derrida makes an attempt to identify the cogency of Schmitt for a theory against legal and political "limitations of sovereignty," and for proposing the ever-present possibility of the death penalty he engages with Schmitt's theory on "the right to suspend the law, or the rule of law, the constitutional state."[30] Article 48 of the Weimar Constitution enabled the president of the Reich to suspend the provisions of the constitution in times of public emergency, and to "suspend for the time being, either wholly or in part, the fundamental rights described [in the Constitution]" in an attempt to restore order, and Schmitt explains that what materializes is a "state of exception" in which the political and legal process create, "unlimited authority, which means the suspension of the existing legal order."[31] This authority is exercised in moments of political reaction against internal and external threats to public order, and consequently in the use of emergency law, the "state suspends the law in the exception on the basis of its right of self-preservation," and that the sovereign "has the monopoly over this last decision."[32] Schmitt explains that the ultimate questions of life and death are dealt with in the exception because "a philosophy of concrete life must not withdraw from the exception and the extreme case, but must be interested in it to the highest degree," and this is because in "the exception the power of real life breaks through."[33]

This political decisionism depicts a pre–World War II statist conception of sovereignty within a "borderline concept," where the sovereign is able to oscillate *inside* and *outside* of constitutional norms; as Andrew Norris observes this, for Schmitt, "sovereignty decides upon its own limits."[34] The mechanisms provided by Article 48 was utilized by Hitler to instigate the Holocaust, where Jews, gypsies, and the disabled were killed for the mere fact of *who* they were; their crime was their

[29] Ibid., p. 277.

[30] Derrida and Roudinesco, *For What Tomorrow*, p. 91.

[31] Carl Schmitt, *Political Theology: Four Chapters on the Concept of Sovereignty* (trans: George Schwab) (Cambridge: MIT Press, 1998), p. 12.

[32] Ibid., pp. 12–13.

[33] Ibid., p. 15.

[34] Andrew Norris, 'The Exemplary Exception: Philosophical and Political Decisions in Giorgio Agamben's *Homo Sacer*,' p. 268, in Andrew Norris (ed), *Politics, Metaphysics and Death: Essays in Giorgio Agamben's* Homo Sacer (Durham: Duke University Press, 2005).

existence. Such repugnant eugenicism was denounced in 1949–1950 by the drafters of the European Convention on Human Rights. To prevent such illegitimate *thanatos* in the future, the Council of Europe created the framework for a supranational region to protect human rights, which elevates these rights over absolutist political considerations of the individual states. During the drafting debates, Henri-Pierre Teitgen, the *rapporteur* to the Committee for Legal and Administrative Affairs, stated, "[i]t is necessary . . . to create in advance a conscience in Europe which will sound the alarm,"[35] and this is because, "the reason of state" is a "permanent temptation," and "Fascism and Hitlerism have unfortunately tainted European public opinion. These doctrines of death have infiltrated into our countries."[36] The drafters understood that the formulation of the European Convention on Human Rights would limit "state sovereignty on behalf of the law, and for that purpose all restrictions are permitted."[37] Hence the mechanisms for repudiating the state of exception, and Schmitt's theory on sovereignty, were set in motion.

Roudinesco recognized the evolution of European human rights principles and firmly disagreed with Derrida's position. It appears that Roudinesco had more appropriately considered the policies of the Council of Europe[38] and the European Union[39] for the internal removal of the death penalty and the prerequisite requirement that new member states abolish the death penalty, when she stated "it seems impossible to me that the death penalty could be reinstated in Europe."[40] Derrida, in recalling Schmitt, replied, "Oh, of course it could!"[41] and he further argued that:

> [a]s long as an abolitionist discourse has not been elaborated and effectively accredited (and this has not yet been done) at the level of unconditional principles, beyond the problems of purpose, exemplarity, and even the "right to life," we will not be shielded from a return of the death penalty.[42]

35 Council of Europe, *Collected Edition of the "Travaux Préparatoires," of the European Convention on Human Rights*, volume 2 (The Hague: Martinus Nijhoff, 1975), p. 174.

36 Ibid., volume 1, p. 40.

37 Ibid., volume 1, p. 294.

38 For further discussion of the Council of Europe policies on the death penalty, see Jon Yorke, "Inhuman Punishment and Abolition of the Death Penalty in the Council of Europe," *European Public Law*, vol. 16, no. 1, 2010; Jon Yorke, 'The right to life and the abolition of the death penalty in the Council of Europe, European Law Review, vol. 34, no. 2, 2009; Council of Europe, *Death Penalty: Beyond Abolition* (Strasbourg: Council of Europe Publishing, 2004).

39 For a discussion of the general European Union policies for the abolition of the death penalty, see Jon Yorke, "Part One: The Evolving European Union Strategy Against the Death Penalty: From Internal Renunciation to a Global Ideology," 16 *Amicus Journal* (2006) 25, and "Part Two," 17 *Amicus Journal* (2007) 26; Evi Girling, 'European Identity and the Mission Against the Death Penalty in the United States,' in Austin Sarat and Christian Boulanger (eds), *The Cultural Lives of Capital Punishment: Comparative Perspectives* (Stanford: Stanford University Press, 2005).

40 Derrida and Roudinesco, *For What Tomorrow*, p. 91.

41 Ibid.

42 Ibid., p. 137.

Then Roudinesco replied:

> I am among those who think that this is not possible. The abolition is inscribed into European law. It has become, in a way, *outside the law*, out of the reach of law, since it falls under a higher order, that of international treaties (emphasis in original).[43]

Roudinesco correctly articulated the supranational nature of sovereignty within the Council of Europe and the role of legislation that provides for abolition. Roudinesco understood that through regional law, the Beccarian exception and Schmitt's public law theory are now denounced and neutralized. This is what Roudinesco means when she thinks that the return of the death penalty is "not possible" – it is a practical impossibility in our current times. There would be insurmountable obstacles at each stage of a recreation of a capital judicial system; from the training of lawyers and judges, to the formulation of fair trial and appellate review processes, to the construction of death rows, the execution chamber and the execution machine. The Council of Europe has built up a wealth of political statements, legislation, and court judgments detailing how the right to life and the prohibition of inhuman punishment can be used to denounce the capital trial process, and in 2005 (so after the dialogue), the European Union adopted a Council Regulation on the prohibition of trading in equipment that may be used in the administration of the death penalty;[44] it is the first regional instrument of its kind. The Regulation Article 3(1) prohibits EU member states from the export of "goods" that have "no practical use other than for the purpose of capital punishment," and Article 4(1) prohibits the import of such "goods" into Europe. In Annex II of the Regulation, "goods designed for the execution of human beings" include the gallows and guillotines, electric chairs, airtight vaults for the purpose of execution by the administration of lethal gas, and automatic drug injections systems. This Regulation is important for the European policies that guard against the return of the death penalty, because as is explained in paragraph 7 of the introductory note, "[t]hese rules are instrumental in promoting respect for human life and for fundamental human rights and thus serve the purpose of protecting public morals."

Roudinesco was interpreting the maintenance of the *now*, for a hopeful *future*. Derrida could not pull his gaze from the possibility of the return of war and disorder, and did not adequately consider the cogency of the hegemonic provisions created by the Council of Europe and the European Union. For the member states of the Council of Europe, Protocol No. 6 provides for the abolition of the death penalty in

43 Ibid.

44 Council regulation concerning trade in certain goods which could be used for capital punishment, torture, or other cruel, inhuman, or degrading treatment or punishment (EC) No. 1236/2005, 27 June 2005; OJ, L 200/1, 30 July 2005.

peacetime,[45] and Protocol No. 13 provides for abolition of the death penalty in all circumstances.[46] Following the adoption of the Lisbon Treaty in December 2009, the European Union member states have the EU Charter of Fundamental Rights endorsed within their domestic law, and Article 2 mandates the right to life and provides for the abolition of the death penalty. Furthermore, through the Treaty, the European Union has made legally possible the incorporation of the European Convention on Human Rights and Protocol No. 6 and No. 13.

This model for the severing of the death penalty from European sovereignty does not easily fit with the principle of sovereignty in the United States, and neither Derrida nor Roudinesco make an explicit attempt to frame the issue concerning the United States. The federal constitutional system, with the sovereignty of the federal government in relational existence with the sovereignty of the governments of the individual fifty states, provides variable processes for the removal of the death penalty within the United States. This is not to be viewed as a hindrance but as providing numerous possibilities for engaging sovereignty at both the federal and state levels. If at the federal level, the United States Supreme Court is of the opinion that it cannot strike down retentionist state statutes through holding that, once and for all, the death penalty is a violation of the Eighth Amendment (see discussions on this issue further in this chapter), we can evaluate the individual state's implementation or rejection of the punishment and engage in political dialogue with individual states. Indeed, the United States is a Council of Europe "observer state,"[47] and its following of the development of human rights principles within the region will provide U.S. abolitionists with comparative materials for political discussions. Renate Wohlwend, the *rapporteur* to the Parliamentary Assembly of the Council of Europe's Legal Affairs and Human Rights Committee, has attempted to create a "transatlantic parliamentary dialogue" with U.S. federal and state governments and the Parliamentary Assembly:

> [a]sks the United States Congress and Government, at federal and state level to enter into a more constructive dialogue with the Council of Europe on this issue. It encourages American politicians to create abolitionist 'caucuses' in their respective parliamentary assemblies, and to continue to engage opponents in informed debate.[48]

45 Protocol No. 6 to the Convention for the Protection of Human Rights and Fundamental Freedoms concerning the abolition of the death penalty, 28 March 1983, Strasbourg, CETS No. 114.

46 Protocol No. 13 to the Convention for the Protection of Human Rights and Fundamental Freedoms concerning the abolition of the death penalty in all circumstances, 3 May 2002, Vilnius, CETS No. 187.

47 See, Abolition of the death penalty in Council of Europe observer states, Doc. 9115, Parliamentary Assembly, 7 June 2001.

48 Abolition of the death penalty in Council of Europe observer states, text adopted by the Parliamentary Assembly on 1 October 2003, (30th sitting), para. 10.

Furthermore, the United States is also a participating state of the Organization for Security and Co-operation in Europe (OSCE), and out of the fifty-six participating states, the United States is one of only two states that impose the death penalty; the other one is Belarus.[49] The OSCE is a regional security organization, and it is cogent that the vast majority of governments in the OSCE do not consider the death penalty to be an essential component of global security. The OSCE encourages transparency in all participating state's capital judicial systems, and the monitoring of the death penalty by this organization is helpful for the continual strategies for removing the death penalty from sovereignty; in the 2009 edition of the annual report on the death penalty, Janez Lenarčič stated the it was a "useful resource for governments and civil society alike in the further discussion of issues relating to capital punishment and its abolition."[50]

The impact of the international abolitionist discourse on the United States did not go unnoticed by Derrida and Roudinesco. Roudinesco had argued that the death penalty was connected to a "sort of social pathology,"[51] and Derrida responded that in "the question of pathology," the "symptoms of a veritable crisis have begun to multiply in the American consciousness and conscience, notably because of international pressures."[52] The introduction to this chapter detailed the world abolitionist picture which reveals that the United States is the final liberal democracy to implement the death penalty. What this demonstrates is that there has been a change in the consciousness of sovereignty. Firstly, individual sovereigns removed the punishment, which produced a marked change in the right of punishment, and then there was a collective assimilation at various regional levels, and in the United Nations, with the majority of sovereign states voting for the first General Assembly resolution against the death penalty in December 2007. What has taken place is a demonstrable shift in the sovereign relationship with the death penalty; it has changed because of the realization that the death penalty is no longer to be viewed as an integral component of sovereign power. This change in political discourse by abolitionist governments from all continents is a statement to individual retentionist governments that they

[49] The participating states of the OSCE are: Albania, Andorra, Armenia, Austria, Azerbaijan, Belarus, Belgium, Bosnia and Herzegovina, Bulgaria, Canada, Croatia, Cyprus, Czech Republic, Denmark, Estonia, Finland, France, Georgia, Germany, Greece, Holy See, Hungary, Iceland, Ireland, Italy, Kazakhstan, Kyrgyzstan, Latvia, Liechtenstein, Lithuania, Luxembourg, Malta, Moldova, Monaco, Montenegro, Netherlands, Norway, Poland, Portugal, Romania, Russian Federation, San Marino, Serbia, Slovakia, Slovenia, Spain, Sweden, Switzerland, Tajikistan, the former Yugoslav, Republic of, Macedonia, Turkey, Turkmenistan, Ukraine, United Kingdom, United States, and Uzbekistan. See the OSCE website on the death penalty at http://www.osce.org/odihr/13453.html. The OSCE produces annual reports on the death penalty, see *The Death Penalty in the OSCE Area: Background Paper 2009* (OSCE: ODIHR, 2009).

[50] Ibid., p. ix.

[51] Derrida and Roudinesco, *For What Tomorrow*, p. 155.

[52] Ibid., p. 157.

should reconsider this penal policy. Indeed, the internationalizing of the abolitionist position has revealed the penetrability of the individual sovereign monopoly to implement the death penalty.

The global communication network, through the Internet and the mobilization of NGOs and civil society, constantly exposes the repugnance of the application of the death penalty. The retentionist Leviathans of our contemporary times (notably China and the United States) will not be able to maintain the death penalty in perpetuity. International pressures will eventually cause the fall of the death penalty, and these countries will, perhaps, be the most significant dominoes in the global downfall of the punishment. Hence, the key to the understanding of the severability of the death penalty from sovereignty is to look to the future through the sentiment of the need to repudiate the sanguinary past and visualize the falling of the dominoes. Derrida states, "[b]eginning with the word 'life.' It would be necessary to think of life on the basis of heritage," and he explains that this heritage:

> demands reinterpretation, critique, displacement, that is, an active intervention, so that a transformation worthy of the name might take place: so that something might happen, an event, some history, an unforeseeable future-to-come.[53]

We aim for a future without the death penalty. Whereas this was once an unforeseeable future, it is becoming more and more believable and possible as one country after another abolishes it. We reject the past heritage of the death penalty in a "responding to a heritage."[54] We are the "heirs," the *receivers* and *choosers* of the abolitionist discourse (the fathers of abolitionism in Enlightenment Europe were Beccaria and Voltaire, and in the United States, it was perhaps Benjamin Rush), and we can further understand this as Derrida explained:

> the idea of heritage implies not only a reaffirmation . . . but at every moment, in a different context, a filtering, a choice, a strategy. An heir is not only someone who receives, he or she is someone who chooses, and who takes the risk of deciding.[55]

Since the 1980s, there has been a proliferation of sovereign governments that have taken the risk of deciding and rejecting the claim that sovereignty has a right of the death penalty. We have reviewed our past heritage by filtering the law, and the residue – or in Walter Benjamin's terms, the "rotten element of law"[56] – that is discarded is capital punishment. However, this political decision needs to be a resolute conviction, because even a severed principle can be realigned, and it is possible for the sovereign to seek to reintroduce the punishment. Michel Foucault

53 Ibid., p. 4.
54 Ibid., p. 6.
55 Ibid., p. 8.
56 Walter Benjamin, "Critique of Violence," in Marcus Bullock and Michael Jennings (eds), *Walter Benjamin, Selected Writings vol. 1, 1913–1926* (Belknap: Harvard University Press, 1997), p. 239.

had argued, "the way in which the death penalty is done away with is at least as important as the doing away. The roots are deep. And many things will depend on how they are cleared out."[57] So the maintenance of the separation of sovereignty from the death penalty is the "infinite task of deconstruction,"[58] an ongoing political project of the abolitionist movement because *the roots can grow back*. Consequently, it is necessary to "draw on the heritage and its memory for the conceptual tools that allow one to challenge the limits that this heritage has imposed up to now,"[59] because:

> [a]t the heart of international law, there are sites where it is necessary to pass beyond or to displace limits. Human rights are perfectible; they are ceaselessly transformed. So it is better to define these rights by pulling them out of their limits.[60]

The right to life and the prohibition against cruel and inhuman punishments, as deontological expressions, are diluting and neutralizing the sovereign claim to a right of the death penalty and is contributing to a monolithic structure within international law. These international law provisions are perfectible and will be when there is a *jus cogens* principle that the death penalty is a violation of international human rights law. This is the infinite task of deconstruction; first in the attaining of the *jus cogens* principle, and second in the maintenance of this principle. On the road to achieving this, we look to the future of the removal of the death penalty from all of the member states of the United Nations.

EUROPEAN PERSPECTIVES ON THE UNNECESSARY PUNISHMENT

The Mid-Twentieth Century European Abolitionist Movement

Following the atrocities of World War II, the Council of Europe was founded in 1949 for the promotion of peace, the rule of law, and pluralist democracy in Europe. The question arose as to whether the death penalty could be reconciled with these political aims. Although the European Convention on Human Rights included the possibility of the death penalty within Article 2(1),[61] there was dissatisfaction concerning the legitimacy of the death penalty following the atrocities of the war. The vast history of the sanguine sovereign had accumulated in the Holocaust, and as a consequence, the old arguments on retribution, deterrence, and the protection

57 Michel Foucault, "Against Replacement Penalties," in *Michel Foucault: Power: Essential Works of Foucault 1954–1984*. In James D. Faubion (ed), (London: Penguin, 2000), p. 459.
58 Derrida and Roudinesco, *For What Tomorrow*, p. 19.
59 Ibid.
60 Ibid.
61 The Convention for the Protection of Human Rights and Fundamental Freedoms, (1953), Article 2(1) states, "Everyone's right to life shall be protected by law. No one shall be deprived of his life intentionally save in the execution of a sentence of a court following his conviction of a crime for which this penalty is provided by law."

of the state were no longer as easily accepted as in the past. The fractures in these theories were becoming more receptive in European political and legal circles, and there was a growing governmental rejection of the death penalty.[62]

These political opinions had been gestating before World War II, as in 1928, the Howard League for Penal Reform compiled comparative municipal data from Denmark, Sweden, Norway, the Netherlands, and England, which indicated that the evidence collated could not by itself "prove either the utility or futility of Capital Punishment as a deterrent," but that "we can obtain evidence of probability, almost amounting to proof, that its abolition does not permanently raise [the murder rate]."[63] The Select Committee on Capital Punishment in 1930 conducted a wide-ranging comparative analysis of European perspectives,[64] and the Belgium Minister of Justice prepared written evidence for the Committee and stated, "[i]t seems inconceivable that a Minister of Justice should ever think it possible to re-establish a penalty the uselessness of which, to put it no higher, has been amply demonstrated."[65] The Danish government stated, "it seems unnecessary to propose

62 James Megivern noted that the "old argument used to justify the theoretical legitimacy of the state's right to execute continued to be repeated by defenders of capital punishment, but it would never sound the same after Hitler," in *The Death Penalty: An Historical and Theological Survey* (New York: Paulist Press, 1997), p. 282. Christopher Hollis, the British Member of Parliament, argued that "the whole case stands or falls on whether the death penalty was a deterrent or not," in 'Epilogue,' in R.T. Paget and S.S. Silverman, *Hanged-And Innocent?* (London: Victor Gollancz Ltd, 1953), p. 259. H.L.A. Hart affirmed, "[i]n any public discussion of this subject the question that is likely to be the central one is 'What is the character and weight of the evidence that the death penalty is required for the protection of society?'" in "Murder and the Principles of Punishment: England and the United States," in H.L.A. Hart, *Punishment and Responsibility: Essays in the Philosophy of Law* (Oxford: Clarendon Press, 1968), p. 71.

63 S. Margery Fry (ed), *The Abolition of the Death Penalty in Holland and Scandinavia*, 2nd ed, (London: The Howard League for Penal Reform, 1928), p. 4. Carl Torp, Professor of Penal Law at the University of Copenhagen, succinctly stated that in Denmark, the absence of the death penalty had "not in any way contributed to an increase in the number of such crimes which were formerly punished by death," in 'The Abolition of Capital Punishment in Denmark,' ibid., Fry, p. 5. In Holland, Dr. J. Simon Van der Aa, pointed out that "since the abolition of capital punishment, the number of life sentences passed has shown a tendency to diminish," in 'The Abolition of Capital Punishment in Holland, p. 8, in ibid. Victor Almquist, the Head of the Swedish Prison Administration, argued that "[t]he reduction in the number of capital sentences and the final abolition of the penalty so far from leading to an increase of offences of this kind was actually followed by a noticeable decrease in crimes legally punishable by death," in 'The Abolition of Capital Punishment in Sweden,' p. 15, in ibid. Previously, in 1831, Jeremy Bentham had argued that the death penalty was "inefficient" and questioned its deterrent value, see *Jeremy Bentham To His Fellow Citizens of France on Death Punishment* (London: Robert Heward, 1831).

64 *Report from the Select Committee on Capital Punishment* (London: HMSO, 1931), In giving testimony to the Select Committee, Professor Herbert Speyer of the University of Brussels stated, "in Belgium the infliction of the death penalty is not necessary for the protection of society and the reduction of crime," p. 257. For a review of the findings of the Select Committee, see E. Roy Calvert, *The Death Penalty Enquiry: The Evidence Reviewed* (London: Victor Golancz Ltd, 1931).

65 Ibid., Appendix: Belgium, Note prepared by the Belgium Ministry of Justice, Supplied by the Belgian Embassy in London, p. 577.

the retention of capital punishment for the sake of public security."[66] The Select Committee reviewed this evidence and concluded that "capital punishment may be abolished in [England] without endangering life or property, or impairing the security of society."[67] Then between 1949 and 1953, the British Royal Commission on Capital Punishment undertook a further comparative study, and the findings were essentially the same as those of the Select Committee, although more cautiously expressed (for a further discussion on the Royal Commission on Capital Punishment, see Timothy Kaufman-Osborn in this volume). Professor Thorsten Sellin from the University of Pennsylvania gave evidence to the Royal Commission and stated that "it is impossible to arrive confidently at firm conclusions about the deterrent effect of the death penalty."[68] Lord Templewood reviewed the evidence presented by the various foreign governments and scholars to the Royal Commission, and stated more firmly that the "conclusion seems to be inescapable that, whatever may be argued to the contrary, the existence of the death penalty makes little or no difference to the security of life."[69]

Then in 1961, the question of the necessity of the death penalty arose in an exchange between Jean Graven, Judge of the Court of Appeal of Geneva, and his fellow abolitionists, Albert Camus and Arthur Koestler, at their symposium on the death penalty in Paris. The symposium proceedings were published as *Reflection on the Death Penalty*, and Camus presented his arguments from his text, *Reflections on the Guillotine*,[70] and Koestler from his *Reflections on Hanging*.[71] In *New Reflections on the Death Penalty*,[72] Graven argued that his fellow abolitionists had missed the "*true* problem [concerning] the protection of the organized, civilized community."[73] In echoing the Beccarian exception, Graven was of the opinion that the death penalty should be reserved for "those antisocial elements which can be stopped only

66 Ibid., Appendix: Denmark, p. 584. Viktor Almquist, the Head of the Swedish Prison Administration, confirmed, "the state did not require the death penalty for its protection," and that this "hitherto had not been contradicted by experience," at Appendix: The Abolition of Capital Punishment in Sweden, p. 613.

67 Ibid., p. xcvi.

68 *Royal Commission on Capital Punishment* (1949–1953) (London: HMSO, 1953), pp. iii–iv, 24. Arthur Koestler argued "[t]o give it a fair hearing, we must set all humanitarian considerations and charitable feelings aside, and examine the effectiveness of the gallows as a deterrent to potential murderers from a coldly practical, purely utilitarian point of view . . . it will be seen that the theory of hanging as the best deterrent can be refuted on its own purely utilitarian grounds, without calling ethics and charity to aid," in *Reflections on Hanging* (London: Gollancz Publishing, 1956), p. 53.

69 Viscount Templewood, *The Shadow of the Gallows: The Case Against Capital Punishment* (London: Victor Gollancz, 1951), p. 85

70 Albert Camus, "Reflections on the Guillotine," in *Resistance, Rebellion and Death* (New York: Vintage Books, 1998).

71 Koestler, *Reflections on Hanging*.

72 This book was published by the Institute of Comparative Law of the University of Paris in 1961, as referred to by James Avery Joyce, *The Right to Life: A Worldview of Capital Punishment* (London: Victor Gollancz Ltd, 1962), in his 'Appendix B, Postscript in Reply, pp. 268–73.

73 Ibid., p. 268.

by being eliminated, in the 'last resort,'"[74] and he asked "[w]hat then should be done with those individuals who have always been considered proper subjects for elimination? . . . Society has not the right to kill even these 'monsters'!"[75]

Graven was presenting a legal phenomenology and did not demonstrate *how* such monsters were to be classified. He did not adequately identify *who* was to decide this point of legal fact, and he did not provide for the elimination of the danger that any created classification of a capital crime may be widened in the future with the possibility of arbitrary executions being reintroduced. Writing at the same time as the symposium, the French criminologist Marc Ancel agreed that these vicissitudes of the capital judicial system were irresolvable:

> assuming [such human 'monsters'] did exist, who would decide it? The jury on the basis of an impression? The special judges on the basis of the particular conception they would have of their duties? Experts? Whether or not one wants it, does not the taking of this road mean the admission that some human beings do not have the right to live or may have the right withdrawn from them? Here one approaches some of the worst ideas of totalitarian eugenicism . . . In such a system, an all powerful state arrogates to itself the ultimate power to decide, under the cover of pseudoscientific claims, what persons will have the right to live . . . In a world pretending to be humane and to believe in universal human rights, the first right of a person is the right to life that society should guarantee him. Therefore, the first duty of the state is to abstain from killing.[76]

Through his studies on criminology and the death penalty, Ancel rejected the idea that juries could adequately identify who the "worst of the worst" were, and he was also not confident that individual judges could make consistently correct identifications. Furthermore, Ancel was of the opinion that the scientific methods that would include a mental health evaluation of the defendant by health care professionals were inadequate for identifying who should live and who should die. Consequently, the state cannot adopt the necessary fact-finding procedures to administer a fair capital judicial system. James Avery Joyce similarly critiqued Graven's argument and claimed that the judge had not adequately considered the wider picture of the fallacy of the death penalty as a *cure* for the criminal elements within society, and pointed to sociological reasons for the creation of "social monsters." Joyce asked, "[h]ow did we get these "monsters" anyway – national and international ones"?[77] He then identified that in 1960s Europe, more should be done politically and legally to

74 Ibid.

75 Translated by James Avery Joyce, ibid., p. 270. Marc Ancel affirmed the prominence of this retentionist argument in 1960s Europe, pp. 20–2, in Sellin, *Capital Punishment*.

76 Ibid., pp. 20–1. Ancel stated, "people talk of keeping the death penalty at least for social monsters or for crimes against humanity. Society would then act in self defense and remove these persons as it would dangerous beasts," p. 20.

77 Joyce, *The Right to Life*, p. 270.

understand the motivations behind attacks and learn effective policies for the future. Joyce understood that it is the administration of the death penalty that may create human "monsters" in the first place. The perpetuation of violence through a death penalty was not going to solve the problem.

The Council of Europe's Position against the Death Penalty

The last execution in Western Europe was in France in 1977. Denmark[78] had removed the death penalty from its statutes for ordinary crimes in peacetime in 1933, and so had (West) Germany (which abolished the punishment for all crimes in 1949; East Germany had done so in 1978), Italy (1947), the Netherlands (1870), Norway (1905), Portugal (1978), Spain (1976), Sweden (1921), the United Kingdom (suspended in 1965 and confirmed in 1969), and France (1981).[79] These Western European states were taking the first steps in the complete rejection of the death penalty, and it was this fertile political circumstance in which the Parliamentary Assembly was able to begin to formulate a regional position.

The Council of Europe replicated the arguments that had first become politically accepted by Western European governments. However, the debates revealed some dissenting voices in the Parliamentary Assembly of the Council of Europe. This was primarily due to fears raised by terrorist violence in some European countries in the 1960s to 1970s, and although France had not executed anyone since 1977, it still retained the death penalty and did not abolish it until 1981 (for a consideration of the abolition of the death penalty in France, see Simon Grivet in this volume).[80] In 1980, the Parliamentary Assembly considered the evolving positions against the death penalty – including the governmental acceptance that the death penalty does not effectively contribute to the security of the state; that it is not an effective

[78] Denmark had administered the death penalty for wartime offenses in 1950.

[79] Belgium had retained the death penalty but did not impose it during this time and was considered de facto abolitionist. The last execution in Belgium was in 1950, and it finally abolished the punishment in 1998.

[80] See Debate on the Report on the abolition of capital punishment, by the Legal Affairs Committee, Doc. 4509, Parliamentary Assembly, 2nd Sitting, 22 April 1980. In the debates, Mr. Mercier of France observed the pressures surrounding the debates, "I should like to underline the paradox of the situation: a resolution calling for the abolition of capital punishment is submitted to the Council of Europe at the very time when death holds sway and human life is treated with contempt all over the world. Hatred and violence are rampant everywhere," p. 55, and Mr. Smith of the United Kingdom, "the world is now a more dangerous place than it ever was, that we face increased terrorism . . . Surely it is amazing at this time that we should be discussing the total abolition of capital punishment throughout the European area. It must bring great comfort to those who indulge in the trade of terrorism and armed robbery to know that so many are prepared to turn to one side in the face of this war against civilised society," p. 58, and Mr Michel of Belgium similarly argued, "[i]t would be absurd at a time when international terrorism is displaying great imagination in devising new methods, to do away with a penalty which enables present-day highwaymen to be taught a lesson," p. 59.

deterrent; that innocent people could be – and have been – executed; that the punishment brutalizes society; and that it is an uncivilized punishment.[81] Carl Lidbom, the *rapporteur* of the Legal Affairs Committee, argued that the "[*l*]*ex talionis* is obsolete,"[82] and Mr. Flanagan of Ireland argued that European society must accept "certain essential limits on the power of the state to coerce or to condemn . . . we must consider what response will be most useful for society in the long run."[83] Flanagan's argument for the curtailing of state power was extended by Mr. Stoffelen of the Netherlands to the terrorist context when he stated:

> the practical reason not to maintain or reintroduce the death penalty for terrorists is that terrorists often commit acts of terrorism as a revenge for the death of one of them, who by his death becomes a martyr.[84]

These arguments are essentially the same as Guizot's position in the eighteenth century, in that the death penalty should not be imposed during terrorist violence, and that the political powers should engage a more nuanced consideration for adopting policies to curtail violence in society. A more complex political reflection would lead to the conclusion of the counterproductive nature of the label of the "monster," "terrorist," or "worst criminal" for the legitimizing of the death penalty. Following the 1980 debates, the Parliamentary Assembly drafted regional legislation to denounce the use of the death penalty in peacetime, and in 1983, Protocol No. 6 was adopted that removed the death penalty but provided an exception in war or during imminent threats of war.[85] Any claim that an individual was a "social monster" could not result in a death penalty in the domestic criminal law.

Since the atrocities inflicted upon the United States on September 11, 2001 (hereinafter "9/11"), there has been a heightened global concern about terrorist violence and an increased claim that terrorism is an act of war. The Council of Europe revisited the threshold of punishment for convicted terrorists within the borders of its member states.[86] In effect, the events of 9/11 were an opportune moment for the Council of Europe to affirm that the human rights organization wanted to keep the wartime exception within Protocol No. 6. However, the Council was of the

81 For a more detailed consideration of the debates in the Parliamentary Assembly, see Yorke 2009 and 2010.

82 Mr. Lidbom of Sweden, Debate on the Report on the abolition of capital punishment, by the Legal Affairs Committee, Doc. 4509, Parliamentary Assembly, 2nd Sitting, 22 April 1980, p. 53.

83 Ibid., Mr. Flanagan of Ireland, pp. 56–7.

84 Ibid., Mr Stoffelen of the Netherlands p. 60.

85 Protocol No. 6 to the Convention for the Protection of Human Rights and Fundamental Freedoms concerning the abolition of the death penalty, 28 March 1983, Strasbourg, CETS No. 114.

86 Guidelines on Human Rights and the Fight Against Terrorism, adopted on 11 July 2002, at the 804th meeting of the Minister's Deputies. See also, Council of Europe, *The Fight Against Terrorism: Council of Europe Standards*, 3rd ed, (Strasbourg: Council of Europe Press, 2005).

opinion that Protocol No. 6 was outdated, and that the wartime exception should not remain. Only nine months after the 9/11 attacks, and in the shadow of existing terrorist violence within some member states, the Parliamentary Assembly and the Committee of Ministers drafted Protocol No. 13 to abolish the death penalty under all circumstances.[87]

The Council was not merely making theoretical arguments against the death penalty for terrorists; it was creating legislation to solidify this rhetoric. The effect of Protocol No. 13 was to create not only an elevated position of human rights against any sovereign imposition of punishment, but it also dismantled any utilitarian notion of the benefit of the death penalty for governments and European society. However, the question remained as to whether member states would accept this evolved position. Indeed, it was a *prima facie* ideal moment for member states to reiterate the wartime exception and keep the death penalty as a sovereign state issue under Protocol No. 6. But the vast majority of member state governments have accepted the arguments revealing the punishment to be inutile and therefore unnecessary, and, with the exception of Armenia, Azerbaijan, Latvia, Poland, and Russia, have embraced Protocol No. 13. It is now a hegemonic principle in the Council of Europe that the death penalty is abolished in all circumstances, even for the most serious crimes committed by terrorists.[88] The Parliamentary Assembly considers that the retention of the death penalty in terrorist cases is based upon "hollow arguments,"[89] and the French jurist and former Minister of Justice Robert Badinter rejected the utility of the death penalty for terrorists and argued that democracy "comes out as the moral victor" against terrorists when the death penalty is not imposed.[90]

There is still the dark shadow of terrorism looming and so those advocating the position of liberal democracy need to keep on promoting the absolute nature of the

87 Protocol No. 13 to the Convention for the Protection of Human Rights and Fundamental Freedoms concerning the abolition of the death penalty in all circumstances, 3 May 2002, Vilnius, CETS No. 187.

88 See Jon Yorke, "The Evolving Human Rights Discourse of the Council of Europe: Renouncing the Sovereign Right of the Death Penalty," in Jon Yorke (ed), *Against the Death Penalty: International Initiatives and Implications* (Farnham: Ashgate Publishing, 2008), pp. 65–6.

89 Recent initiative in France to reintroduce the death penalty for the perpetrators of terrorist acts, Doc. 10211, June 17, 2004.

90 Robert Badinter stated "[f]aced with crime and cruelty, a democracy's justice system rejects vengeance and death. It punishes but it does not kill; it prevents the terrorist from harming others but respects his life; by refusing to give him death, democracy guarantees the humanity the terrorist denies through his crimes. Democracy comes out as the moral victor of the test inflicted on it by terrorism. That will not be the least of its victories in the eyes of generations to come," in "The OSCE and the Death Penalty," in *The Death Penalty in the OSCE Area* (Warsaw: OSCE Office for Democratic Institutions and Human Rights, 2006), p. 8. Badinter also noted that "[e]ach execution would only breed more terrorists in search of vengeance and that infernal cycle – terrorist attack, execution, terrorist attack – would never be stopped," in *Abolition: One Man's Battle Against the Death Penalty*, (trans: Jeremy Mercer) (Boston: Northeastern University Press, 2008), p. 92.

right to life for everyone, including that of the terrorist, in order to contribute to neutralising the power of terrorism.[91] Fátima Aburto Baselga of the Political Affairs Committee of the Parliamentary Assembly stated in 2007: "I am afraid that there is a real risk that in our times, in the context of the fight against terrorism, our societies lose sight of their principles and values and take steps backwards, driven by fear,"[92] and she warned of the "risk that in the context created by the fight against terrorism," recourse to the death penalty can become "more acceptable."[93] Although the fear remains, it has not become a legal and political reality. William Schabas identified at a conference on the death penalty in Madrid in December 2009 that the increase in terrorist activity had not led to an increase in retentionist use of the death penalty worldwide.[94] Terrorist violence has continued in Europe post–9/11, including the PKK attacks in Turkey,[95] the ETA attacks in Spain,[96] the London tube and bus bombings,[97] and the attack on the school in Beslan in South Ossetia, Russia.[98] In none of these cases was the death penalty used, and it is significant that Russia did not discontinue its moratorium on the death penalty[99] by sentencing Nur-Pashi Kulayev to life imprisonment for his part in the 330 deaths in the school siege (for a wider consideration of the death penalty in Central and Eastern Europe, see Fijalkowski and Girling, this collection). On November 19, 2009, the Constitutional Court of the Russian Federation stated that due to Russia's signing of Protocol No. 6, the death penalty cannot be implemented,[100] and Svetlana Paramonova argues that because the Court determined that the nonapplication of the death penalty was part of the "legitimate constitutional regime," the decision points to an "irreversible process towards a definite abolition of the death penalty."[101]

91 See also, Jean Baudrillard, *The Spirit of Terrorism*, (trans: Chris Turner) (London: Verso, 2003).

92 Promotion by the Council of Europe Member States of an International Moratorium on the Death Penalty, Parliamentary Assembly, Doc. 11321, 25 June 2007. Sigmund Freud reminded us that consciences can change and emotional shifts occur when questions of life and death are confronted, see, *On Murder, Mourning and Melancholia* (London: Penguin, 2005), pp. 167–194, 219–232.

93 Promotion by the Council of Europe Member States of an International Moratorium on the Death Penalty, Parliamentary Assembly, Doc. 11321, 25 June 2007.

94 William Schabas, Roundtable discussion: Strategies Against the Death Penalty in a Time Horizon of 2015, International Symposium on the Universal Abolition of the Death Penalty, Centre for Political and Constitutional Studies and the Institute for European and International Criminal Law, Madrid, December 9–11, 2009.

95 See, *Öcalan v. Turkey*, (2003) 37 E.H.R.R. 10; (2005) 41 E.H.R.R. 45.

96 For a timeline of the ETA attacks, see http://news.bbc.co.uk/1/hi/world/europe/545452.stm.

97 For a timeline of the London bombings, see http://news.bbc.co.uk/1/hi/uk/4694069.stm.

98 See http://news.bbc.co.uk/1/shared/spl/hi/world/04/russian_s/html/1.stm.

99 Presidential Decree No. 724 of May 16, 1996.

100 See, Bill Bowring, "The Death Penalty and Russia," in Jon Yorke (ed), *The Right to Life and the Value of Life: Orientations in Law, Politics and Ethics* (Farnham: Ashgate Publishing, 2010), p. 284.

101 Svetlana Paramonova, "The Death Penalty in Russia: Decision of the Constitutional Court of the Russian Federation from November 19, 2009," conference paper, International Symposium on the Universal Abolition of the Death Penalty, Centre for Political and Constitutional Studies and the Institute for European and International Criminal Law, Madrid, December 9–11, 2009.

THE UNNECESSARY PUNISHMENT IN THE UNITED STATES

The Drafting and Early Interpretation of the Bill of Rights

In 1791, the Bill of Rights became part of the U.S. Constitution, and the Grand Jury Clause of the Fifth Amendment expressly allowed for the application of the death penalty, stating that "[n]o person shall be held to answer for a capital, or otherwise infamous crime, unless on a presentment or indictment of a Grand Jury." At the same time, the Due Process Clause states, "[n]o person shall . . . be deprived of life, liberty or property, without due process of law." This is repeated in the Fourteenth Amendment with the addition of the Equal Protection Clause that states, "nor deny any person within its jurisdiction the equal protection of the laws." The Cruel and Unusual Punishments Clause of the Eighth Amendment prohibits the infliction of "cruel and unusual punishments." These Amendments demonstrate that the death penalty is preserved only on a contingent basis. Before a constitutionally permissible sentence of death, there must be a "presentment or indictment of a Grand Jury," "due process of law," "equal protection of the laws," and along with these determinations, the capital judicial system must not violate the prohibition of "cruel and unusual punishments." Without this legal scrutiny, the punishment cannot be imposed.

The Annals of Congress reveal very little of any debates on the Cruel and Unusual Punishments Clause. Justice Douglas affirmed that the published records "throw little light on its intended meaning,"[102] and Meghan Ryan has reviewed the Annals and the documentations of the state ratifying conventions, and has observed that they only reveal "unclear origins of the Eighth Amendment."[103] There are two recorded observations on the Eighth Amendment in the Annals. William Smith of South Carolina objected to the words "nor cruel and unusual punishments," because he thought them "too indefinite."[104] Smith was not satisfied with the concise textual *enumeration*, and it appears that he would have favored a more encompassing *definition* for establishing specific examples that were thought to be cruel and unusual. Samuel

[102] Per Justice Douglas, in *Furman v. Georgia*, 408 U.S. 238, 244 (1972). In *Furman*, Justice Brennan considered the drafting debates and stated, "Livermore, Holmes and Henry agreed that the Cruel and Unusual Punishments Clause imposed a limitation upon the legislative power to prescribe punishments," and that "we cannot now know exactly what the Framers thought 'cruel and unusual punishments' were . . . nor did they intend simply to forbid punishments considered 'cruel and unusual' at the time. The 'import' of the Clause is, indeed, 'indefinite' and for good reasons." Justice Scalia outlined the influence of the English Bill of Rights on the Clause when he stated, in *Harmelin v. Michigan*, 501 U.S. 957 (1991), "the entire text of the Eighth Amendment is taken from the English Declaration of Rights, which provided, 'that excessive Baile ought not to be required nor excessive Fines imposed nor cruell and unusuall Punishment inflicted.'" 966. See also, Robert J. McWhirter, "Baby, Don't Be Cruel: What's So 'Cruel and Unusual' about the Eighth Amendment?" *Arizona Attorney*, 46 (December 2009), p. 12.

[103] Meghan J. Ryan, "Does the Eighth Amendment Punishments Clause Prohibit Only Punishments That Are Both Cruel and Unusual?" 87 *Wash. U. L. Rev.* 567 (2010), p. 573.

[104] Annals of Congress, 1, 754 (1789), cited in *Furman*, p. 244.

Livermore of New Hampshire stated "[t]he Clause seems to express a great deal of humanity, on which account I have no objection to it; but as it seems to have no meaning in it, I do not think it necessary."[105] But Livermore developed the issue further when he argued:

> [n]o cruel and unusual punishment is to be inflicted; it is sometimes necessary to hang a man, villains often deserve whipping, and perhaps having their ears cut off; but are we in the future to be prevented from inflicting these punishments because they are cruel? If a more lenient mode of correcting vice and deterring others from the commission of it could be invented, it would be very prudent in the Legislature to adopt it; but until we have some security that this will be done, we ought not to be restrained from making necessary laws by any declaration of this kind.[106]

Livermore's statement reveals that the Eighth Amendment should be interpreted as a guiding standard not to be viewed as static, but reflexive (because it can look "in the future"), to encompass new penological techniques and technologies as they are "invented." Furthermore, these techniques in the future were not to become more severe, or even allow state sanctioned violence imposed by corporal and capital punishment to remain at a constant level of severity; instead, governments should identify "a more lenient mode of correcting vice." During the Revolutionary era, there were those advocating humanitarian sentiments and more humane methods of punishment, and concerning the question of the death penalty, Louis Mazur noted that "a diverse group of Americans considered the death penalty morally and politically repugnant."[107] One of the founders of the American abolitionist movement was Benjamin Rush, who lectured against public executions in 1787[108] and published a pamphlet against the death penalty in 1797, entitled *Considerations on the Injustice and Impolicy of Punishing Murderers by Death*, in which he argued that the death penalty "is contrary to reason."[109]

Livermore's statements in Congress called for an application of "reason" in the quest for legitimate penology. He placed together the death penalty, whipping, and cutting off ears, which in 1791 were perceived as necessary punishments in certain circumstances, but he then acknowledged the possibility that each punishment may be repealed in the future. When American experts in penal law invent new "lenient," more humane methods, then "it would be very prudent" for the legislature to adopt

[105] Ibid.

[106] Ibid.

[107] Louis P. Masur, *Rites of Execution: Capital Punishment and the Transformation of American Culture, 1776–1865* (New York: Oxford University Press, 1989), p. 61. See also Austin Sarat, *When the State Kills*, p. 17.

[108] Hugo Bedau notes that, "as early as 1787 Dr. Benjamin Rush . . . lectured and wrote against public executions," in Hugo Adam Bedau, *The Death Penalty in America: Current Controversies* (New York: Oxford University Press, 1997), p. 5.

[109] Cited in Hugo Adam Bedau, "An Abolitionist's Survey of the Death Penalty in America Today," in Hugo Bedau and Paul Cassell (eds), *Debating the Death Penalty: Should America Have Capital Punishment?* (New York: Oxford University Press, 2004), p. 16.

these measures. Livermore concluded by focussing on "making necessary laws." Livermore's contemporary, Thomas Paine, made a similar argument in *Rights of Man* that was dedicated to George Washington and President Andrew Jackson, and in his pamphlet calling for France to spare the life of Louis Capet, he stated: "[I]t is our duty as legislators not to spill a drop of blood when our purpose may be effectually accomplished without it."[110]

It is clear that Livermore (along with Rush and Paine) wanted American opinions on penology to advance within the framework of humanism and utilitarianism. The Eighth Amendment's Cruel and Unusual Punishments Clause was established as a barometer of legal and societal sentiment, to be used to check the power to punish. An appropriate interpretation of the original drafting opinions on the Clause is that it does not preserve the death penalty in perpetuity. It provides for the possibility, along with the abolition of whipping and cutting off ears, for the abolition of the death penalty. In support of the early thoughts of the future evolution of the interpretation of the Clause, the U.S. Supreme Court stated in *Weems v. United States*:

> [l]egislation, both statutory and constitutional, is enacted, it is true from an experience of evils but its general language should not, therefore, be necessarily confined to the form that evil had therefore taken. Time works changes, brings into existence new conditions and purposes. Therefore a principle, to be vital, must be capable of wider application than the mischief which gave it birth . . . [i]n the application of a constitution, therefore, our contemplation cannot be only of what has been, but of what may be.[111]

The *Weems* court interpreted the constitution as providing a governing standard that at its heart fights against "evil" in society. This "evil" can be both derived from the actions of individuals – through the committing of crimes – and so criminal law is instituted to combat this, and following the Eighth and, Fourteenth Amendments, a check is placed against any "experience of evils" that the federal and state government may impose upon individuals and groups within the jurisdiction of the United States. Any unjustified actions of both the federal and state governments can be counteracted with an evolved understanding of what constitutes 'legitimate'

[110] In 1791–1792, Thomas Paine published *Rights of Man*, and Part One was dedicated to George Washington. President Andrew Jackson was greatly influenced by the text. Regarding the death penalty, Paine stated, "[l]ay the axe at the root, and teach governments humanity. It is their sanguinary punishments which corrupt mankind," p. 213. In 1793, Paine made a similar argument in France for the preservation of the life of Louis Capet in, "Reasons for preserving the life of Louis Capet" (1793), p. 397, both texts are found in, Michael Foot and Isaac Kramnick (eds), *Thomas Paine Reader* (London: Penguin Books, 1987).

[111] *Weems v. United States*, 217 U.S. 349, 373 (1910); applied in *Furman v. Georgia*, at 420, *Robinson v. California*, at 666. See also, Pressly Millen, "Interpretation of the Eighth Amendment: Rummel, Solem, and the Venerable Case of Weems v. United States," *Duke L. J.* 784 (1984); William C. Hefferman, "Constitutional Historicism: An Examination of the Eighth Amendment Standards of Decency Test," 54 *Am. U. L. Rev.* 1355 (2005); Celia Rumann, "Tortured History: Finding Our Way Back to the Lost Origins of the Eighth Amendment," 31 *Pepp. L. Rev.* 661 (2004).

penological policies, and to help formulate this principle, the U.S. Supreme Court has observed that the Eighth Amendment "is not fastened to the obsolete but may acquire meaning as public opinion becomes enlightened by a humane justice."[112] In *Trop v. Dulles*, Chief Justice Warren stated that the Eighth Amendment "must draw its meaning from the evolving standards of decency that mark the progress of a maturing society,"[113] and this evolutionary principle was also expressed by Justice Stewart in *Robinson v. California*, as "in the light of contemporary human knowledge."[114] Consequently, the meaning of the U.S. Constitution is not merely frozen in the past to be applied in the present, but it also reveals the possibilities of the future in "what may be."

Producing a Legal Classification of the Worst of the Worst

Following the early cases considering the constitutionality of the death penalty,[115] in *Furman v. Georgia* (1972), the U.S. Supreme Court held that state capital statutes as they were then applied did not provide the adequate guiding standards demanded by the Eighth Amendment.[116] Within a plurality decision, the court held that the death penalty was applied in an arbitrary way and was therefore capricious. Four years later, following the modification of state capital statutes, the U.S. Supreme Court held, in *Gregg v. Georgia*, that the death penalty was constitutional as long as it followed a bifurcated process of firstly establishing the guilt or innocence of an individual and then, if found guilty, a sentencing phase, which would determine the appropriate sentence, including the possibility of a death penalty.[117] In the sentencing phase, the prosecution presents "aggravating factors" as to why an individual should be sentenced to death (these include *inter alia*, multiple homicide, homicide committed during other felonies, and contract killings[118]), and the defense presents "mitigating factors" to demonstrate the appropriateness of a lesser sentence (these include *inter alia*, mental and emotional disorders[119]). In *Gregg*, the U.S. Supreme Court thought that a constitutionally permissible capital judicial system could be created by state legislatures. However, over the following thirty-five years, the U.S. Supreme Court has reduced the class of persons for which the death penalty may be implemented,

[112] *Weems*, 378.

[113] *Trop v. Dulles*, 356 U.S. 86, 101 (1958).

[114] *Robinson v. California*, 370 U.S. 660, 666 (1962).

[115] See *Wilkerson v. Utah*, 99 U.S. 130 (1878), where death by firing squad was held to not violate the Eighth Amendment; *In re Kemmler* 136 U.S. 436 (1890), electrocution as a method of execution did not violate the Eighth Amendment; *McElvaine v. Brush* 142 U.S. 155 (1891) and *Trezza v. Brush* 142 U.S. 160 (1891), it was not a violation of the Eighth Amendment to isolate an inmate while awaiting execution.

[116] *Furman v. Georgia*, 408 U.S. 238 (1972).

[117] *Gregg v. Georgia*, 428 U.S. 153, 164 (1976).

[118] See, Franklin Zimring, *The Contradictions of American Capital Punishment* (New York: Oxford University Press, 2003), p. 9.

[119] Ibid.

and the punishment should now only be "limited to those offenders who commit a 'narrow category of the most serious crimes' and whose extreme culpability makes them the most deserving of execution."[120] Hence the death penalty is viewed as only being *necessary* for such criminals.

There are serious questions as to the clarity and workability of the aggravating and mitigating circumstances established since *Gregg*, and if the jury cannot adequately understand the meaning of the two circumstances in the sentencing phase, there is a real possibility of arbitrary executions being administered again. The American Bar Association, which issues reports assessing state capital judicial systems, has identified various flaws in the statutory definitions of capital murder and concluded that states "cannot ensure that fairness and accuracy are the hallmark of every case in which the death penalty is sought and imposed."[121] On April 15, 2009, the American Law Institute identified that there is real concern as to whether state capital statutes "meet or are likely ever to meet basic concerns of fairness in process and outcome," and significantly that there was an inherent problem with regards to "the tension between clear statutory identification of which murders should command the death penalty and the constitutional requirement of individualized determination," and the "difficulty of limiting the list of aggravating factors so that they do not cover . . . a large percentage of murderers."[122]

Consequently, a relevant analogy can be drawn from First Amendment freedom of speech cases and the Equal Protection Clause of the Fourteenth Amendment.[123] In *Winters v. People of State of New York*,[124] the clarity of the statutory definition for public policy considerations concerning the dissemination of published materials that were "sanguinary or salacious publications with their stimulation of juvenile delinquency"[125] was considered. The court held that if statutes are drafted using imprecise language, the text may be a "denial of due process for uncertainty,"[126] and if a "statute uses words of no determinative meaning," it is "void for uncertainty."[127] There is now gathering a hegemonic school of thought rebutting the claim that the state capital judicial systems provide clear sentencing guidance, and thus the statutes may be viewed as "void for uncertainty."

[120] *Atkins v. Virginia* 536 U.S. 304 (2002), affirmed in *Roper v. Simmons*, 543 U.S. 551, 568 (2005), and *Kennedy v. Louisiana*, 128 S.Ct. 2641, 2650 (2008).

[121] American Bar Association, Evaluating Fairness and Accuracy in State Death Penalty Systems: the Georgia Death Penalty Assessment Report, 2006, Executive Summary, p. v. See the American Bar Association website for the reports are www.aba.net, and the evaluation of the reports in Hood and Hoyle, *The Death Penalty*, pp. 121–2.

[122] The American Law Institute, Report of the Council to the Membership of The American Law Institute on the Matter of the Death Penalty, (April 15, 2009), p. 5.

[123] For example, see the cases concerned with the freedom of the press; *Stromberg v. People of State of California*, 283 U.S. 359 (1931); *Herndon v. Lowry*, 301 U.S. 242 (1937).

[124] *Winters v. People of State of New York*, 333 U.S. 507 (1948).

[125] Ibid., 510.

[126] Ibid., 512.

[127] Ibid., 616–617, citing *State v. Diamond*, 27 N.Mex 477 (1921).

Such uncertainty is inherent within the qualitative observations for identifying who is the 'worst of the worst' criminal who commits the most serious crimes. The boundaries of the worst of the worst become blurred, and different people will have different opinions because the classification of this person is inherently a value judgment. There will thus be a possibility of inconsistency within the jury deliberations. Katherine Polzer and Kimberly Kempf-Leonard, having interviewed jurors in capital cases, conclude that, on the whole, jurors do not understand the definitions of the various aggravating and mitigating circumstances, and that the "penalty phase decision making process is complex and riddled with errors, incorrect assumptions and difficult and lengthy instructions."[128] Polzer and Kempf-Leonard argue that there is inconsistency in jury consideration of aggravating and mitigating circumstances, and that "there is no measure for how humans' perceive and process certain information."[129]

There will be a possibility that the jury thinks that the aggravating and mitigating circumstances are evenly balanced. In such a case, the logical conclusion is that this individual cannot fall into the 'worst of the worst' category because there are substantial reasons for demonstrating a lower moral culpability for the crime. However, the U.S. Supreme Court thought otherwise in *Kansas v. Marsh*. The jury imposed a death sentence after finding that the aggravating and mitigating circumstances were balanced, but the court allowed the decision to stand. The dissenting opinion of Justice Souter, joined by Justices Stevens, Ginsberg, and Breyer, reveals the injustice in such a case when he stated:

> the jury does not see the evidence as showing the worst sort of crime committed by the worst sort of criminal, in a combination heinous enough to demand death. It operates, that is, when a jury has applied the state's chosen standards of culpability and mitigation and reached nothing more than what the Supreme Court of Kansas calls a "tie."[130]

Justice Souter also affirmed this principle in *Atkins v. Virginia* and *Roper v. Simmons*, that "within the category of capital crimes, the death penalty must be reserved for 'the worst of the worst,'"[131] but he held that the current evidence was that the United States capital judicial system continued the "kaleidoscope of life and death verdicts that made no sense in fact or morality in the random sentencing before *Furman* was decided in 1972."[132] The research by Jonathan Simon and Christina Spaulding supports this view as they note that the extent to which defendants are identified

[128] Katherine Polzer and Kimberly Kempf-Leonard, "Social Construction of Aggravating and Mitigating Factors: How Capital Jurors Attribute Blame," 45 No. 6 *Crim. Law Bulletin* ART 4.

[129] Ibid.

[130] *Kansas v. Marsh* 548 U.S. 163, 206 (2006).

[131] *Kansas v. Marsh*, at 206, citing *Roper v. Simmons* at 568, affirming Justice Stevens in *Atkins v. Virginia*, "[c]apital punishment must be limited to those offenders who commit 'a narrow category of the most serious crimes' and whose extreme culpability makes them 'the most deserving of execution,'" at 319.

[132] Per Justice Souter, *Kansas v. Marsh*, 207.

as "death eligible," both pre- and post-*Furman*, is almost indistinguishable.[133] If it is only necessary to execute the 'worst of the worst,' it will always be an impossible quest because it signifies a search for an elusive individual. The U.S. capital judicial system provides a heightened scrutiny of capital cases, because 'death is different,' yet it cannot provide a foolproof class of criminals for whom the penalty should be reserved, and so the system constantly has the shadow of arbitrary executions hanging over it. Justice Blackmun was illuminating in his famous dissent against the denial of *certiorari* in *Callins v. Collins*, when he stated:

> [i]t is virtually self evident to me now that no combination of procedural rules or substantive regulations ever can save the death penalty from its inherent constitutional deficiencies. The basic question – does the system accurately and consistently determine which defendants "deserve" to die? – cannot be answered in the affirmative.[134]

In extending this damning observation, Justice Stevens in *Baze v. Rees* claimed:

> that current decisions by state legislatures, by the Congress of the United States, and by this Court to retain the death penalty as a part of our law are the product of habit and inattention rather than an acceptable deliberative process that weighs the cost and risks of administering that penalty against its identifiable benefits.[135]

Allowing the death penalty to remain merely because it is the product of "habit" and "inattention" is unacceptable. It does not adhere to the calls of those, from Samuel Livermore through to the present American voices of reason, who have adequately demonstrated the ineffectiveness and inhumanity of the punishment. In effect, it may be observed that the U.S. capital judicial system has failed under the severe interpretive and adjudicative pressures that capital cases bring to bear. It is perhaps true that the United States has developed the most technical capital judicial system ever created, and even though the death penalty is one of the most litigated issues within U.S. constitutional law, what remains, according to Justice Stevens, are "faulty assumptions" and an unacceptable "deliberative process." Robert Cover argued that it is:

> [b]ecause in capital punishment the action or *deed* is extreme and irrevocable, there is pressure placed on the *word*... the fact that capital punishment constitutes the

[133] See Jonathan Simon and Christina Spaulding, "Tokens of Our Esteem: Aggravating Factors in the Era of Deregulated Death Penalties," in Austin Sarat (ed), *The Killing State: Capital Punishment in Law, Politics, and Culture* (New York: Oxford University Press, 1999), p. 87.

[134] *Callins v. Collins*, 510 U.S. 1141 (1994).

[135] *Baze v. Rees*, 128 S.Ct. 1520, 1546 (2008). Justice Stevens then cited *Gregg* and stated, "we explained that unless a criminal sanction serves a legitimate penological function, it constitutes 'gratuitous infliction of suffering' in violation of the Eighth Amendment," at 1547, and Justice Stevens affirmed this principle in *Thompson v. McNeil*, 129 S.Ct. 1299, 1300–1301 (2009).

most pain, the most deliberate, and the most thoughtful manifestation of legal interpretation as violence makes the imposition of the sentence an especially powerful test of the faith and commitment of the interpreters.[136]

Justice Blackmun and then Justice Stevens had lost *faith*, and there is further evidence of a growing apostasy. The commitment of the judiciary and indeed state legislatures to the capital judicial system is waning. Currently, thirty-five states retain the death penalty as a possible criminal punishment,[137] and although there is a minority of fifteen states that abolished it, there is a recognizable unease with the punishment.[138] The Death Penalty Information Center records that both death sentences and execution rates in the United States have been diminishing over the past decade. In 2005, there were 138 death sentences across the country, and this number continued to decline in 2006 (122), 2007 (119), 2008 (111), and 2009 (106).[139] In 1999, there were 98 executions, with a steady decrease afterward in 2005 (60 executions), 2006 (53), 2007 (42), and 2008 (37). The year 2009, however, witnessed an increase to 52.[140] Most executions are confined to a select few states with Texas at the apex. Since 1976, there have been 1,212 executions in the United States, but Texas has accounted for 458 of these state-sanctioned deaths. American exceptionalism appears to have been replaced with Texas' exceptionalism, although this may be unfair to Texas as a whole, because Adam Gershowitz has demonstrated that it is only a few of the 254 counties in Texas that impose the death penalty.[141]

The punishment is becoming increasingly expensive. Both the findings of state commissions on the death penalty and independent research have revealed the spiralling costs of the capital judicial system. When Governor Richardson of New Mexico signed the law to abolish the death penalty in this state in 2009, he noted

136 Robert M. Cover, 'Violence and the Word,' 95 Yale L.J. 1601 (1986), pp. 1601, 1622. See also, Austin Sarat (ed), *Pain, Death and the Law* (Ann Arbor: The University of Michigan Press, 2001). See also *Gregg v. Georgia*, at 226, "Imposition of the death penalty is surely an awesome responsibility for any system of justice and those who participate in it. Mistakes will be made and discriminations will occur which will be difficult to explain. However, one of society's most basic tasks is that of protecting the lives of its citizens and one of the most basic ways in which it achieves the task is through criminal laws against murder." This cannot be satisfactory.

137 The thirty-five retentionist states are: Alabama, Arizona, Arkansas, California, Colorado, Connecticut Delaware, Florida, Georgia, Idaho, Illinois, Indiana, Kansas, Kentucky, Louisiana, Maryland, Mississippi, Missouri, Montana, Nebraska, Nevada, New Hampshire, North Carolina, Ohio, Oklahoma Oregon, Pennsylvania, South Carolina, South Dakota, Tennessee, Texas, Utah, Virginia, Washington and Wyoming. The death penalty is also included within the U.S. government's federal jurisdiction and under military law.

138 The fifteen abolitionist states are: Alaska, Hawaii, Iowa, Maine, Massachusetts, Michigan, Minnesota New Jersey, New Mexico, New York, North Dakota, Rhode Island, Vermont, West Virginia, Wisconsin, and also the District of Columbia.

139 Source – Death Penalty Information Center, Facts about the Death Penalty, May 28, 2010.

140 Ibid.

141 See, Adam M. Gershowitz, "Statewide Capital Punishment: The Case for Eliminating Counties' Role in the Death Penalty," 63 *Vand. L. Rev.* 307 (2010), pp. 308–9.

the exponential costs of the death penalty and stated that the fiscal issue was "a valid reason" for the removal of the death penalty;[142] he was also concerned about the possibility of innocent people being executed.[143] In California, the cost of the death penalty is becoming an increasingly contentious issue. Since the reinstating of the death penalty in California in 1976, there have been 13 executions, and this state currently houses the largest state death row population of more than 670 inmates.[144] *The New York Times* has reported that the California capital judicial system and death row costs $114 million per year more than it would cost if these 670 were imprisoned.[145] The Death Penalty Information Center is collating information on the fiscal issues and affirms that in Kansas, "the costs of capital cases are 70% more expensive than comparable non-capital cases, including the costs of incarceration"; in North Carolina, the death penalty amounts to "$2.16 million per execution *over* the costs of sentencing murderers to life imprisonment." In Florida, the death penalty is "$51 million a year above what it would cost to punish all first-degree murders with life in prison without parole," and in Texas, "a death penalty case costs an average of $2.3 million, about three times the cost of imprisoning someone in a single cell at the highest security level for 40 years."[146] It is clear that the death penalty is placing an unnecessary financial burden on state budgets.

Hugo Bedau and the "Minimal Invasion Principle"

We may recognize a significant congruence of intellectual opinion between Samuel Livermore and Hugo Bedau – or perhaps it may be more accurate to state that Bedau has continued and improved Livermore's opinions recorded in the Annals of Congress. At the drafting of the Eighth Amendment, Samuel Livermore recognized the role of necessity in punishment; he conceded that "it is sometimes necessary to hang a man,"[147] but then went on to indicate that the existence of the death penalty should only be contingent on there not being the invention of "a more lenient mode of correcting vice and deterring others from the commission of it." Once such penological mechanisms had been created, the death penalty could be done away with because it would be "very prudent in the Legislature to adopt" these more lenient measures.

[142] See, Ian Urbina, "Citing Costs, States Consider the End of the Death Penalty," *The New York Times*, February 24, 2009, at A1.

[143] Scherzer, "The Abolition of the Death Penalty," p. 254. For a detailed analysis of actual innocence claims, and the complex judicial hurdles needed surmounting in order to bring an innocence claim, see Jonathan Aminoff, 'Something Very Wrong Is Taking Place Tonight: The Diminishing Impact of the Actual Innocence Exception for the Death Penalty," 46 No. 1 *Crim Law Bulletin* Art 4 (2010).

[144] Death Penalty Information Center, Facts about the Death Penalty, May 28, 2010.

[145] See, Editorial, "High Cost of Death Row," *The New York Times*, September 27, 2009, at A22.

[146] These figures are found in, Death Penalty Information Center, Facts about the Death Penalty, May 28, 2010.

[147] Annals of Congress, 1, 754, (1789), cited in *Furman v. Georgia*, 244.

Hugo Bedau has revealed that this evolution in criminal justice and penology has now happened. Imprisonment is now an adequate punishment for the imposition of retribution, and the incarceration mechanisms are an adequate means of deterrence. Hence, a fair and humane prison system can be viewed as a more lenient and thus legitimate means of punishment, and the death penalty becomes merely a "gratuitous infliction of suffering."[148] Bedau has articulated this assessment of legitimacy through a measurement of the interference in a criminal's life necessary to achieve the aims of penology and the governmental policies for the protection of society. He terms this measurement the "minimal invasion principle."[149] Bedau argues that if governments are democratic, they must justify their punishment practices and that the "only justification available is that it is a necessary means to a fundamental social goal"[150] as:

> [g]iven a compelling state interest in some goal or purpose, the government in a constitutional democracy built on the principle of equal freedom and human rights for all must use the least restrictive means sufficient to achieve that goal or purpose.[151]

Hence a specific punishment practice is justified only if there are no alternatives that are "less invasive." In applying this principle to the death penalty, Bedau sets it out as:

1. Punishment is justified only if it is necessary as a means to some socially valid end.
2. The death penalty is more severe – more invasive – than long-term imprisonment.
3. Long-term imprisonment is sufficient as an invasion of individual liberty, privacy, and autonomy (and other fundamental values) to achieve valid social goals.

[148] In *Gregg v. Georgia*, it was held that "the sanction imposed cannot be so totally without penological justification that it results in the gratuitous infliction of suffering," at 183. Justice Stevens affirmed this principle in *Thomson v. McNeil*, when he held, "[i]t would therefore be appropriate to conclude that a punishment of death after significant delay is "so totally without penological justification that it results in the gratuitous infliction of suffering," *Thomas v. McNeil*, 129 S.Ct. 1299 (2009), p. 1300. See also *Johnson v. Bredensen*, 130 S.Ct. 541 (2009).

[149] See, Hugo Adam Bedau, The Minimal Invasion Argument Against the Death Penalty, Criminal Justice Ethics, June 22, 2002; Hugo A. Bedau, "An Abolitionist's Survey of the Death Penalty in America Today," in Hugo Bedau and Paul Cassell (eds), *Debating the Death Penalty: Should America Have Capital Punishment?* (New York: Oxford University Press, 2004), p. 32. See also Hugo A. Bedau, *Killing as Punishment: Reflections on the Death Penalty in America* (Boston: Northeastern University Press, 2004), pp. 142–58.

[150] Bedau, An Abolitionist's Survey of the Death penalty in America Today, p. 35.

[151] Ibid., p. 32.

4. Society ought to abolish any lawful practice that imposes more violation of individual liberty, privacy, or autonomy (or other fundamental value) when it is known that a less invasive practice is available and is sufficient.[152]

Bedau concluded with the words: "Society ought to abolish the death penalty." He has most effectively demonstrated that Livermore's observation that the death penalty becomes unnecessary once more lenient (but also effective) methods of punishment are created is now fulfilled because of the availability of imprisonment. A fixed term of imprisonment that does not extend to life without parole is a sufficient and effective punishment. A humane incarceration system makes the death penalty unnecessary and renders it a gratuitous infliction of violence on the human body. In addition, the arguments presented in this chapter have attempted to demonstrate that because the death penalty is not necessary for the preservation of the security of the state, it should be viewed as serving no "socially valid end," as expressed in Bedau's point 1 presented earlier. Furthermore, if the death penalty is becoming too expensive, it may also become an illegitimate financial drain because this money could be redistributed for "socially valid ends," such as healthcare.

CONCLUSION

Along with the human rights rationale for the abolition of the death penalty, it is seen that globally, a vast majority of governments do not view the death penalty as a necessary tool for the protection of its citizens from ordinary crimes; it is also ineffective as a means of state security in war and terrorist attacks. Following 9/11 and the continued terrorist attacks around the world, instead of there being a global embrace of the death penalty, there has been a clear absence of this punishment. The OSCE focuses on maintaining security within its participating states and has witnessed the rejection of the death penalty as an integral tool for its fundamental aim; thus the death penalty is not necessary for the maintenance of global security. As such, we can see that there is a growing governmental expression at the United Nations, the Council of Europe, the European Union, and the OSCE that the death penalty is no longer a legitimate manifestation of sovereign power. The United States should join the abolitionist community and take part in the global movement for the eradication of this repugnant punishment. Indeed, the United States' membership in this most noble club would be a significant event for a world free of the death penalty, and would represent the closing of the final act in the *severing* from sovereignty the right to impose this outdated punishment.

[152] Ibid., pp. 33–4.

10

European Policy on the Death Penalty

Agata Fijalkowski

INTRODUCTION

As Europe moves in the direction of absolute abolitionism, it is easy to miss the fact that these developments are fraught with tensions. The European policy on the abolition of the death penalty has come to be presented, above all, as a human rights issue. The drafting of the European Convention on Human Rights, key judgments of the European Court of Human Rights, and initiatives of the Council of Europe contribute to this policy. In 1989, this European policy was reinvigorated with the prospect of European enlargement and new members to the Council of Europe. Comprising key mechanisms to facilitate implementation, the policy reflects a uniform approach to the death penalty, one that is particularly European. 'New' European states, although pleased to be back in the fold of Europe, have expressed problems with this policy, and some proactively support a pro-death penalty stance that is largely ignored by the Council of Europe and European Union (EU) member states.

This chapter critically examines these European transformations. It is organized in the following way. The chapter first sets out European policy on the abolition of the death penalty, providing a general survey of its mechanisms and procedures. Western European states have traditionally been afforded a margin of appreciation on certain human rights issues. This also applied to the imposition of the capital sentence. The position on the death penalty has reflected a certain unity on the matter. The unity on abolition, it is argued, has transformed itself into an unyielding and firm objective, resulting in apprehension in some quarters. The chapter continues to consider the tension that has emerged between the 'older' and 'newer' members of the Council of Europe and EU on the abolition of the death penalty. The discussion considers the common features that characterize the debates, common to

The author would like to thank David Seymour at Lancaster University Law School and colleagues who participated in the Amherst College workshop for valuable comments. Any remaining errors are my own

the sphere of punishment, namely obedience, deterrence, public opinion, and state sovereignty. Reference to 'newer' member states concerns those European countries that were formerly under Communist rule. These regimes underwent massive political changes in 1989, which is generally seen as the endpoint of Communism. A number of these states have entered the EU in 2004[1] and 2007,[2] respectively. Because the literature in this area tends to focus on the technical aspects of abolition from a regional or international institutional perspective, the chapter moves beyond these examinations to consider the way in which European policy accommodates the peculiar history and context of states on this issue. It asks how we can find a space between these positions, setting these questions within the framework and broader role of the EU. The chapter argues that addressing this space is critical, and not only as an important addition to the American debate on the subject. By offering a constructive approach to the discussion concerning abolition, we also can gain further understanding on the significance of European identity and values.

EUROPEAN POLICY

Protocol No. 6

European politics views the death penalty as an issue that is firmly placed in international human rights. In other words, it is a matter that is not for states to govern themselves. In that vein, European policy is one that aims to end all executions, and it boldly asks that all nations who proclaim they are civilized to do the same. It is an objective that is pursued eagerly, led by the Council of Europe. It is also a momentum that has its origins in the not-so-recent past.

The Council of Europe has created some 165 international agreements, treaties, and conventions. The Council of Europe has long campaigned for the abolition of the death penalty. And it has achieved an amazing feat, namely to draw boundaries on the way states exercise their powers. This is done through the Council of Europe's greatest contribution to the development of regional human rights in the form of the European Convention on Human Rights (ECHR) of 1950. The ECHR exemplifies the core of the Council of Europe's mission, namely:

> the achievement of greater unity between its Members and . . . one of the methods by which the aim is to be pursued is the maintenance and further realization of Human Rights and Freedoms.[3]

The unity in relation to the question on the death penalty between member states has been piecemeal. The circumstances on this question were different when discussions

[1] The Czech Republic, Estonia, Hungary, Latvia, Lithuania, Poland, Slovak Republic, and Slovenia.
[2] Bulgaria and Romania.
[3] Preamble, European Convention on Human Rights, at http://www.hri.org/docs/ECHR50.html (accessed June 14, 2010).

were initiated in relation to the ECHR.[4] The 'right to life' had much narrower boundaries and was never absolute, albeit the state now had to be clear with respect to the circumstances in which the capital sentence was to be imposed. In other words, the international community felt compelled to respond to horrors of the capital sentence that was applied arbitrarily. In its jurisprudence, the European Court of Human Rights confirms this – state interference cannot be arbitrary.[5] It was not until later that proposals based on human rights' justifications were presented. At that time, states that were undergoing political transformations could more readily adopt an abolitionist approach than those states that could boast a stable democracy. Until then, the position was one that was cautious in protecting the legality of the death penalty in defined circumstances.[6] The position of the Council has been described as 'an initiation of *catch-up* with Western European state renunciation of the punishment', which began an 'experiment' to test its longevity.[7]

In 1973, the Parliamentary Assembly of the Council of Europe (PACE) passed a motion for the resolution on the abolition of the death penalty, which did not, however, lead to any particular movement. It was not until 1980 that a more concrete move was made; the ECHR was the first instrument to treat the abolition of the death penalty. This was introduced in 1983, in the form of Protocol No. 6 to the ECHR. This Protocol was opened for signature and ratification. It came into force in 1985. The Protocol, which is now ratified by forty-five European countries, prohibits death sentences generally, but it does permit states to retain capital punishment "in time of war or imminent threat of war."[8]

The next step in firming up the policy comprised the decision of the First Summit of Heads of State and Government. This meeting was held in Vienna in 1993, and it agreed that applicant states should undertake to sign and ratify the ECHR. Because the membership extended to former Communist states, where capital punishment was imposed, the position was made stronger and urgent as concerns the signing and ratification of Protocol No. 6. The Council of Europe argued that the "death penalty has no place in a civilized democracy. Abolition of the death penalty is the mark of civilised society and a civilised Europe."[9]

4 See, for example, Jon Yorke, "The Evolving Human Rights Discourse of the Council of Europe," in *Against the Death Penalty: International Initiatives and Implications*, ed. J. Yorke (Farnham: Ashgate, 2008), 43–73.

5 As confirmed in *Tomasi* v. *France* [1992] 15 EHRR 1, a case that is celebrated by both scholars and the European Court of Human Rights for the dynamic interpretation of the ECHR.

6 See Jon Yorke, "The Right to Life and Abolition of the Death Penalty in the Council of Europe," *European Law Review* 34 (2009): 205–29.

7 Jon Yorke, "The Evolving Human Rights Discourse of the Council of Europe," in *Against the Death Penalty: International Initiatives and Implications*, ed. J. Yorke (Farnham: Ashgate, 2008), 53.

8 See http://conventions.coe.int/Treaty/Commun/ChercheSig.asp?NT=114&CM=7&DF=07/10/2005&CL=ENG (accessed June 14, 2010).

9 Council of Europe, "Resolution 1179 (1999): Honouring of Obligations and Commitments by the Ukraine" at http://assembly.coe.int/Main.asp?link=/Documents/AdoptedText/ta99/ERES1179.htm (accessed June 14, 2010).

The year 1989 provided a perfect opportunity to unify on the issue. The Council of Europe has assisted the states in the region in the complex, post-Communist democratization process. Constitution making, drafting legal codes, and reforming political systems are matters on which the Council of Europe offers advice. The programs are extensive and available to all of its new member states.

Articles III and IV of the 1949 Statute of Council of Europe ensure that member states agree to promote human rights and fundamental freedoms in their respective states and to cooperate in realizing the Council's objectives.[10] This is a reciprocal arrangement and significantly it includes steps toward the abolition of the death penalty. The relevant political actors of the new member states agreed, in principle, and a new framework of human rights was ushered in, to the dismay and bewilderment of many people.[11] Zimring's contention that the abolition movement is more a 'trend in government policy' is to a certain extent true of the manner in which abolition was delivered and concluded in post-Communist Europe.[12] This is considered further in this chapter.

Worthwhile to note, at this juncture, is Garland's observation about punishment. He aptly notes that it is a reflection of our comprehension of other people and at the same time it reveals an understanding about ourselves.[13] For Europeans, Protocol No. 6 indicated the shift in regional thinking about killing – no longer was toleration an option. This would become a foundation of European identity and European core values.[14] It was European in the sense that the human rights discourse that underpins the European Convention is *evolving*.[15] The unified front is the product of a protracted process where different forces and actors finally meet.[16] A European policy started to emerge, one that could be characterized as having a purpose, a vision, and it embraced the values that were identified early on in the Council of Europe's history as espousing tolerance, pluralism, and a view to protect human dignity. Although the period demonstrated an evolving discourse, it was not yet universal, nor regional, as "the dark shadow of state sovereignty lingered as some states were reluctant to sign and ratify a document which would symbolise an acceptance that this anti-death penalty position was evolving into a regional public

[10] ETS no. 001 (5 May 1949), at http://conventions.coe.int/Treaty/en/Treaties/html/001.htm (accessed June 11, 2010).

[11] See Agata Fijalkowski, "The Abolition of the Death Penalty in Central and Eastern Europe," 9 *Tilburg Foreign Law Review* (2001), 62–83, and Sangmin Bae, *When the State No Longer Kills: International Human Rights Norms and Abolition of Capital Punishment* (Albany, NY: SUNY Press, 2007).

[12] Franklin E. Zimring, *The Contradictions of American Capital Punishment* (Oxford University Press, 2003), 17.

[13] David Garland, *Punishment and Modern Society* (Oxford: Oxford University Press, 1990), 268.

[14] Council of Europe Press Service, "Protocol No. 6 to the Convention for the Protection of Human Rights and Fundamental Freedoms Concerning the Abolition of the Death Penalty: The Turning Point," 1999.

[15] Yorke, "The Right to Life and Abolition," supra n. 6.

[16] Here Elias's work on civilization is demonstrated.

law norm."[17] In fact, the diffusion of the sovereign right of the death penalty was ensuing as it became both a right to life *and* inhuman and degrading treatment and punishment issue.[18]

Protocol No. 13

In early 2000, PACE recommended that a further protocol to the ECHR be created to provide for total abolition of capital punishment with no reservations. Protocol No. 13 demonstrates how this norm has grown stronger. In February 2002, the Committee of Ministers of the Council of Europe took a bold step to sign Protocol No. 13 to the ECHR. This Protocol provides for the total abolition of the death penalty in all circumstances, allowing for no exceptions. There are thirty-three state ratifications, and eleven other states have signed the protocol.[19] The Protocol is much more specific and linked to efforts at monitoring and enforcing the norm against capital punishment. The mechanisms are discussed further in this chapter. Scholars in the area aptly note that this instrument is the "most important political decision" for the European human rights regime.[20]

These developments need to be considered alongside the Second Optional Protocol to the International Covenant on Civil and Political Rights (ICCPR) that declares that "[n]o one within the jurisdiction of a State Party to the present Protocol shall be executed" (Article 1[1]). Reservations to the Optional Protocol are permitted and, not surprisingly, taken advantage of by the United States. Seventy-two states have ratified the protocol, and three other states have signed it.[21] Protocol No. 13 is interesting in that is has given substance to the European position on abolition. This is especially so as concerns the right to life. Although found in Article 2 of the ECHR, the right is not "absolute," outlining qualifications that does not sit well with the growing voices for abolition. The sanctity and quality of life is arguably represented in Protocol No. 13. In fact, Protocol No. 6 already started to give substance to Article 2 of the ECHR, with the landmark case of *Soering* v. *United Kingdom*, where the European Court of Human Rights held that the risk of torture facing an individual being extradited to the United States – a state where the capital sentence could be imposed – runs counter to Convention values embracing the sanctity of life.[22] The jurisprudence in the area has clearly gone beyond *Soering*. In this area, Article 2 sets out the boundaries between the protection of the right to life and refraining from

17 Yorke, "The Right to Life and Abolition," supra n. 6, 212.

18 Yorke, "The Evolving Human Rights Discourse," supra n. 7, 43–73.

19 See http://conventions.coe.int/Treaty/Commun/ChercheSig.asp?NT=187&CM=7&DF=07/10/2005&CL=ENG (accessed June 14, 2010).

20 Roger Hood, "Introduction: The Importance of Abolishing the Death Penalty," in Council of Europe, *The Death Penalty – Beyond Abolition* (2004), 16.

21 See http://treaties.un.org/Pages/ViewDetails.aspx?src=TREATY&mtdsg_no=IV-12&chapter=4&lang=en (accessed June 14, 2010).

22 [1989] 1 EHRR 439.

taking life. Moreover, and as noted earlier, the overlap between Articles 2 and 3 of the European Convention on Human Rights is confirmed in key cases in the area. To recall, Article 3 is a nonderogable right stating that "[n]o one shall be subjected to torture or to inhumane or degrading treatment and punishment." Commentators, such as Yorke who also looks at sovereignty in greater depth in this volume, have considered how this article has evolved to contribute to the dismantling of the death penalty in the Council of Europe, which is beyond the mandate of this chapter.[23] Protocol No. 13 is yet another added element to extradition cases – the most recent being, *inter alia*, *Aylor-Davis* v. *France*, *G.B.* v. *Bulgaria*, *Mamatkulov and Askarov* v. *Turkey*, *Shamayev* v. *Georgia and Russia*, and *Bader* v. *Sweden*.[24] The Grand Chamber decision in *Öcalan* v. *Turkey* is important to this discussion – it stopped short of confirming that a "penological revolution" has taken place in regional human rights.[25] Both Protocol No. 13 and developing case law on the part of the European Court of Human Rights provides further support for the abolition movement, solidifying a zone that is "death-free." The boundaries are fixed but ready to include new members and expand.

Elsewhere, scholars have documented the different approaches taken by PACE and the Committee of Ministers.[26] The point rested with "legality of the death penalty" in Article 2(1) and Protocol No. 6, which meant that both had to be ratified as a prerequisite for membership of the Council of Europe. This was highlighted in the Council of Europe Resolution 1097 from 1996. A further requirement calling upon states to respect a moratorium was stated in paragraph 4 of the Declaration for a European Death Penalty-Free Area, adopted by the Committee of Ministers in November 2000. This is significant in that the European policy has suddenly been given an identity and a stronger position vis-à-vis those states that do not share this view. Its policy becomes one that is hard to reject. It also indicates a policy that has become formalized through institutions and procedures that also aim to reeducate the population about the death penalty. This trajectory differs from the one considered by Gottschalk in this volume, as concerns U.S. developments.

CIVILISED NATIONS – ABOLISH!

We have seen how caution has dictated the discussions concerning abolition in Europe, and how this piecemeal process has evolved within the human rights discourse. The underpinning idea that the European human rights discourse is one

[23] See Jon Yorke, "Inhuman Punishment and Abolition of the Death Penalty in the Council of Europe," 16 *European Public Law* (2010): 77–103, and *idem*, 'Sovereignty, State Security and the Unnecessary Penalty of Death: European and United States Perspectives', this volume.

[24] [1994] European Commission of Human Rights 76-B164, 172; App no. 42346/98, 11 March 2004; [2005] 20 EHRR 7; [2005] 41 EHRR 25; App no. 36378/02, 12 April 2005; [2008] 46 EHRR 13.

[25] Grand Chamber, Application No. 46221/99 (12 May 2005). See Yorke, "The Evolving Human Rights Discourse," supra n. 7, 59–60.

[26] Yorke, "The Right to Life and Abolition," supra n. 6.

that evolves has resonance with Elias's contention that "civilisation is never completed and constantly endangered."[27] Civilization, or the continuation of it, is also dynamic. The reason for this fragility is because of the requirements needed to maintain it – namely discipline. As a consequence, stress arises between the proactive and reactive camps; the tension that Elias identifies between aggression and pacification is where the state's role comes to the fore. It is a question of organization and who has control over punishment. In other words, whatever the technology or form employed in punishment, the critical issue rests with power, not necessarily with its implementation.[28]

This experience is usually considered in relation to the American experience. It is with great consternation that abolitionists view the American retention of the capital sentence. The Council of Europe has attempted to put pressure on the United States, calling on arguments that indicate the great significance the region places on human dignity. The contention that civilized nations do not impose capital punishment is set out for the United States to respond to; the United States, which has Observer Status within the Council of Europe, is at risk of losing it if significant progress is not made with respect to a move toward abolition. The importance of this sentiment is conveyed in the following statement issued in 2003 by the Council of Europe at a conference in Springfield, Illinois, namely "if any Council of Europe member state arrested Osama bin Laden, for example, it would not be able to extradite him to the United States unless it was given assurance that the death penalty would not be sought."[29] To the Council's dismay, the United States prefers to retain sovereignty and control over matters that justify retributive measures in dealing with criminals, especially those guilty of horrific crimes and identified as "monsters."[30] Furthermore, the views echoed by the U.S. Secretary of State to the EU foreign leaders finds sympathy on the part of newer states to the Council of Europe and EU.[31]

As noted earlier, abolition is also a process that has taken Western Europe a while to achieve. The United Kingdom abolished the death penalty in 1969 and conducted its last execution in 1964. In fact, the question of reinstatement of the

27 Norbert Elias, "Violence and Civilization," in *Civil Society and the State: New European Perspectives*, ed. J. Keane (London: Verso, 1988), 177.

28 See Carol S. Steiker and Jordan M. Steiker, "A Tale of Two Nations: Implementation of the Death Penalty in 'Executing' Versus 'Symbolic' States in the United States," 84 *Texas Law Review* (2006): 1869–1927.

29 Council of Europe, "An Assembly Conference on the Death Penalty Opens in Springfield, Illinois" (April 2003). See also Bae, *When the State No Longer Kills*, supra n. 11, 29.

30 Austin Sarat, *When the State Kills: Capital Punishment and the American Condition* (Princeton, NJ: Princeton University Press, 2001), 37. See also EU Action in U.S. cases at http://www.eurunion.org/eu/index.php?option=com_content&task=view&id=1783#ActiononUSDeathRowCases (accessed June 14, 2010).

31 Roger Hood, "Abolition and Retention," in *The Death Penalty: A Worldwide Perspective* (Oxford: Oxford University Press, 2002), 73.

sentence was a matter that came before the parliament on several occasions.[32] The last time this occurred in the United Kingdom was in 1994, when the then-Home Secretary led the move to reintroduce the death penalty when the public mood indicated strong, relatively enduring support for the death penalty.[33] The same occurred in France and Germany,[34] as well as Italy, where a passionate campaign against capital punishment started in 2000 with the Italian-owned clothing store Benetton (concerning an advertising drive that featured pictures of twenty-six U.S. death-row inmates). The World Day Against the Death Penalty has been celebrated ever since.[35] It was during this time that a pattern can be identified in which Europeans started to identify with fellow Europeans facing the capital sentence in the United States.[36] The American approach was criticized, with abolitionists pointing to an attitude and practice that is out of place with other states that have evolved and developed in terms of their commitment to maintain human rights. Whereas the Europe of the 1970s and 1980s might have felt that it was being "'infiltrated' by [. . .] US and American values, which has resulted in some kind of uncertainty and forced (Western) Europeans to adopt a defensive position,"[37] the position of the 1990s was critical of the American inability to call on historical origins in a close scrutiny of its own social attitudes. As Americans have often exaggerated the differences between their country and Europe, the death penalty discourse provided Europeans an opportunity to transform this defensive position into a more concrete European position and identity.[38] As Girling demonstrates, time has assisted Europeans in shaping a European identity that makes a compelling case for abolition – such barbarous practices as the death penalty being rooted in a past that no longer characterizes the death-free zone of today's Europe – so any states that continue to impose the death sentence are frozen in a time warp.[39] Civilization is explained as a particular account of social development and organization.[40] Recent political changes have not only meant that European states return to the European fold, but also provided Europe the opportunity to set itself apart from other states and regions locked in outdated and barbaric practices. It was now a question of how to increase the membership of the abolition movement. But the movement would meet resistance, not only on the part of the United States, but, to its surprise, on

32 Hood, "Introduction," supra n. 20, 26.

33 *Ibid.*

34 *Ibid.*

35 See http://www.worldcoalition.org/modules/news/article.php?storyid=276 (accessed June 14, 2010).

36 Such as the German-born LaGrand brothers. See also Evi Girling, "European Identity and the Mission Against the Death Penalty in the United States," in *The Cultural Lives of Capital Punishment*, eds. A. Sarat and C. Boulanger (Stanford: Stanford University Press, 2005), 112–28.

37 Mihály Vajda, "East-Central European Perspectives," in *Civil Society and the State: New European Perspectives*, ed. J. Keane (London: Verso, 1988), 335.

38 See Stephen Mennell, *The American Civilizing Process* (Cambridge: Polity, 2007).

39 Girling, "European Identity," supra n. 36.

40 Garland, *Punishment and Modern Society*, *supra* n. 13, 213–47.

the part of its European neighbors. So, whereas Zimring has observed that "the changing of governments can itself precipitate legal reforms that might take much longer to accomplish in stable governments," this does not seem to tally concerning "new Europe."[41]

European identity, like the European human rights discourse, is an ongoing and complex process. To become a member of the EU, states enter a complex negotiation process. As noted earlier, a key part of these negotiations entails advice on democratization. The setting up of a rule-of-law state also depends on the clarification of what the democracy means for the state – in other words, its political legitimacy. The negation talks are also discussed as accession talks; these are characterized by discussions driven by the practicalities of achieving institutional and structural foundations of the democratic state, market economy, and human rights – a formidable task, considering the legacy of Communist rule and the moribund legal framework that was left in its wake.[42] The job of setting up a rule-of-law state should not be underestimated. Even though the respective Communist histories differ, there are common obstacles in the form of weak judiciaries and protection afforded to human rights. If anything, these new European states have an affinity toward a strong state, accompanied by a belief in the deterrent effect of punishment.[43] This usually comes as some surprise, because the death sentence was applied arbitrarily – on the other hand, such beliefs do not work in isolation and are usually accompanied by strong institutional support that more often than not refers to the church, as discussed further in the chapter. One quickly realizes that the notion of identity, which includes a European and national one, emerged at the forefront of post-1989 Europe. As one commentator notes:

> The integration process was part of the post-Communist state-building and constitution-making both because of its symbolic power (symbolic rationality) to re-unite the region with the rest of liberal democratic and prosperous Europe and its pragmatic effect on political, economic and constitutional transformations (purposive rationality). The European Union was a main external 'focal point', which profoundly affected the quality of the political process and the self reflection of collective political identity in those countries.[44]

The symbolic power of reunification with the EU and the notion of a collective European identity will be considered later. At this juncture, it is important to note that Přibán's idea of dual rationalities (symbolic and purposive) augments the bold

41 Zimring, *The Contradictions of American Capital Punishment*, supra n. 12, 19.

42 See, for example, Maria Łoś, *Communist Ideology, Law and Crime: A Comparative View of the USSR and Poland* (New York: St Martin's Press, 1988).

43 See Agata Fijalkowski, "Capital Punishment in Poland: An Aspect of the 'Cultural Life' of the Death Penalty Discourse," in *The Cultural Lives of Capital Punishment*, eds. A. Sarat and C. Boulanger (Stanford: Stanford University Press, 2005), 147–68.

44 Jiří Přibán, "European Union Constitution-Making, Political Identity and Central European Reflections," 11 *European Law Journal* (2005): 136.

European effort that both reunites and acknowledges national identities (of which support for the death penalty is a part) that is also very much a constitution-making effort.[45] In other words, this return to Europe went far beyond the original expectation of post-Communist states. From their point of view, entry into the EU is a restorative question – the mere restoration of Europe.

From a practical perspective, it is important to note that the process of integration is assisted by the European Commission for Democracy, or the Venice Commission. Created in 1990, this body – Europe's 'think tank' – is the Council of Europe's advisory body on constitutional matters.[46] The Venice Commission's mandate is far-reaching, including guidance with respect to judicial opinions concerning capital punishment, as seen in the Albanian context, and warnings when issues of compliance arise, as demonstrated in the Ukrainian context (see *infra*). The Venice Commission unquestionably promotes Protocol No. 13 as part of upholding the European constitutional heritage comprising democracy, human rights, and the rule of law.[47] Of the four key areas of assistance, two – namely constitutional assistance and cooperation with constitutional courts – are significant to this discussion.

To summarize, the original vision for Europe, namely the one presented by its founding fathers, saw this process of Europeanization as ongoing. Looked at this way, one can forgive the original members the lack of foresight with respect to the complexities of an enlarged union, which included a Communist experience that had its own peculiar effect on punishment.[48] This affects the symbolic rationale of the European policy. As concerns the purposive rationale, the Venice Commission has faced challenges in the form of local sensibilities. Examining these local sensibilities requires us to revisit several classic themes that underpin punishment, namely obedience, deterrence, public opinion, and sovereignty. In his work on punishment, Garland considers the essential ingredients of culture as "all those conceptions and values, categories and distinctions, frameworks of ideas and systems of belief which human beings use to construe their world and render it orderly and meaningful."[49] Garland does not see culture as underlying a country's choice to retain capital punishment. Instead, "the structures in question [are] political and legal ones, and [have] little to do with any peculiarly [in this case American] value-system or distinctive underlying culture."[50] Political and legal factors guide our choices – culture, on the other hand, is defined by mainstream ways of thinking, or mentalities, which are in turn influenced by the prevailing sentiments and feelings, or sensibilities. Undoubtedly, and inevitably, mentalities and sensibilities change with time, as practices evolve and grow to be more or less acceptable to society.

45 *Ibid.*

46 See http://www.venice.coe.int/site/main/Presentation_E.asp (accessed June 11, 2010).

47 Yorke, "Inhuman Punishment and Abolition of the Death Penalty," supra n. 6.

48 Přibán, "European Union Constitution-Making," supra n. 44.

49 David Garland, *Punishment and Modern Society*, supra n. 13, 195

50 David Garland, "Capital Punishment and American Culture" 7 *Punishment and Society* (2005): 350.

In this way, complete abolition, in the form of Protocol No. 13, became a key objective to the Council. The quickness with which this was adopted varied from country to country and depended in large part on the manner that the transition to democracy was followed. As noted at the outset, the resistance to this unified stance comprised the post-Communist states.

The manner of the transition refers to the regime change, from Communism to democracy, through negotiation (such as in Poland and Hungary at the well-known Round Table Talks) or more violent means (such as the former Czechoslovakia and Romania). The road to abolition in the region is outlined elsewhere.[51] The nature of the transition might lend clues as to the question of consensus. Concerning post-Communist countries, most of these states have become abolitionist, citing "political will, official inquiry, and the influence of the United Nations policy" as the most important reasons for choosing this course.[52] As noted earlier, the majority of the countries are state parties to the relevant international legal instruments, namely Protocol No. 6 of the ECHR and the Second Optional Protocol to the ICCPR; those which have not yet ratified these agreements are signatories. Equally significant, these states have substantially amended or adopted new criminal codes in which the death penalty has been eliminated as a form of punishment, or have imposed a moratorium. Other countries, such as Romania, have gone so far as to amend their constitutions to prohibit the reinstatement of capital punishment. Despite the fact that several states had eliminated the capital sentence through legislation – such as the Czech Republic, Slovakia, Slovenia, Croatia, and Romania – the law has not captured the societal view.[53]

Consensus within the international community was a factor that, early on, was viewed realistically. In 1986, Kaiser observed that "there appears to be little hope that international bodies, whether private or official, will be able to achieve unanimity [among] the majority of countries concerning the restriction or abolition of capital punishment."[54] The opportunity to make abolition a condition of membership (to the EU, for example), was an incredible development. It also is an event that requires the adoption of certain values that run counter to shared values.

Obedience

Obedience, for example, was not an issue for the original member states. Of course, the timeframe, and discourse, was different. There was no specific momentum for the

51 See Fijalkowski, "The Abolition of the Death Penalty," supra n. 11.

52 Such was the response of Poland. See "Crime Prevention and Criminal Justice," (March 2000), UN Doc/E/2000/3.

53 See Fijalkowski, "The Abolition of the Death Penalty," supra n. 11.

54 Quoted in Hood, "Introduction," supra n. 20, 11.

states to reply to, and in certain cases charismatic leaders, such as the former French Prime Minister François Mitterrand, stepped in to play an integral role in obtaining support.[55] This was in 1981, at a time when 63 percent of the French population supported capital punishment. This peculiar French experience is considered in this volume in contributions by Grivet and also by Hammel.

Obeying international norms and rules can be a contentious area.[56] On the surface, obedience means that rewards are allocated. These can be in the important form of beneficial economic agreements. These can also address more pragmatic considerations, such as the facilitation of cooperation agreements and coordination. What makes compliance with these norms especially interesting is that in more cases than not, they do not share local concerns on the issues. In other words, state decisions have not complied with societal calls for a certain form of punishment. The Venice Commission, for example, considered the application of the death penalty in Albania twice, in 1994 and 1999, respectively. Despite an amended criminal code, [57] in 1998, the Albanian authorities approached the Council of Europe to temporarily reinstate the death penalty.[58] Prosecutors were asking for capital sentences, even with a moratorium on executions. The 1999 consultation was urgently initiated by PACE, who requested the Venice Commission to examine the compatibility of the death penalty with the 1998 Albanian constitution.[59] The opinion, written by the Swiss and Polish representatives, critiqued the lack of an express provision prohibiting the death penalty. It did, however, carefully note the protection afforded the right to life in the document that, in conjunction with other provisions, would leave 'no room, in practice, for imposing and carrying out the death penalty'.[60] The opinion points out that:

> [the] death penalty is now no longer and acceptable punishment in the European legal field, except within the strict confines of the logic of transition [in other words, a moratorium on executions], and that its execution is no longer tolerated.[61]

Albanian appeals to retain capital punishment were based on the instability and mass corruption that has tragically characterized most of its post-Communist period.[62] This did not impress the Council of Europe. In December 1999, the Albanian Constitutional Court, in what appears to be a decision guided by the 1999 Commission

55 Hood, *ibid.*, 25.

56 Bae, *When the State No Longer Kills*, supra n. 11.

57 See "Constitutional Watch," 4 *East European Constitutional Review* 2 (1996): 4.

58 See 9 *Survey of East European Legislation* 1 (1998): 11.

59 Opinion on the Compatibility of the Death Penalty with the Constitution of Albania (February 11, 1999) at http://www.venice.coe.int/docs/1999/CDL(1999)001-e.asp (accessed June 14, 2010).

60 The Polish representative was former Polish Prime Minister Hanna Suchocka from 1992–1993. Suchocka was a member of the Democratic Union, a center-right political party. She also was Minister of Justice from 1997–2000. As a constitutional lawyer Suchocka appreciated the wider European context and sought to introduce key institutional reforms to facilitate Poland's entry into the EU. *Ibid.*

61 *Ibid.*

62 See 2 *Survey of East European Legislation* 2 (2000): 8.

opinion, ruled that capital punishment is unconstitutional.[63] In 2007, Protocol No. 13 was ratified. Research in the area has pointed out that compliance is not something to be taken for granted.[64] Deference cannot be expected when laws restrict behavior against the wishes of individuals; further, those who defer can change their minds.[65]

Legitimacy is an important quality. As noted earlier, in the French example, if an authority and/or law possess this quality, then people will feel more compelled to follow. Furthermore, a strong intellectual tradition is arguably important; it bolsters the preservation of positive social values toward cultural, political, and legal authorities. These supportive attitudes rely on a system that is successful in achieving "voluntary deference."[66]

Most of the post-Communist states also have been members of the Council of Europe since the mid-1990s. This is a cherished membership. For most states, membership meant integration with Europe and eventual membership in the EU. In speeches across new members, leaders would proclaim this dedication. Indeed, the states saw this as a return to their 'rightful' place in Europe.[67] In other words, this includes common values shared by European states; values that comprise the protection of human rights, democracy, and the rule of law. This also is reflected in national positions, as seen in constitutional documents promulgated and amended. This is an important aspect of the democratization process that is led by Europe. Elsewhere, commentators have expanded on the criticism faced by Europe as concerns European politics and the deficit of legitimacy as it seeks to realize a unified Europe, where the shift of power is gradually allocated to the European level and its respective institutions. This is the point of harmonization, the success of which necessitates legitimacy. On this point, Přibán correctly singles out identity as the key to successful integration. The European integration process "accommodates the notion of cosmopolitan citizenship."[68] This notion works as a channel for Europeans that relates to common values and adherence to the "principles of democratic government."[69] Přibán divides these principles into *ethnos* and *demos* – two important components regarding power in the protracted process of integration and incorporation of new Member states. The first aspect refers to the notion of cosmopolitan citizenship, whereas the second aspect constitutes the bridge between the national level and the supranational institution, namely the EU. Above all, a political identity is one that

63 The decision of the Albanian Constitutional Court can be found (in English) on http://www.gjk.gov.al/ (accessed June 14, 2010).

64 S.D. Mastrofski, J.B. Snipes, and A.E. Supina, "Compliance on Demand: the Public's Responses to Specific Police Requests," 33 *Journal of Crime and Delinquency* (1996): 272.

65 *Ibid.*, 283.

66 Tom R. Tyler, "Psychology and the Law," in *The Oxford Handbook of Law and Politics*, eds. K Whittington, R. Daniel Kelemen, and G. A. Caldeira (Oxford: Oxford University Press, 2008), 716.

67 See, for example, Tony Judt, *Postwar: A History of Europe Since 1945* (London: Penguin, 2005).

68 Přibán, "European Union Constitution-Making," supra n. 44, 138.

69 *Ibid.*

is symbolic and essential if this bridge is to work; the EU political identity "has been symbolically constructed as a civil alternative to the ethnically burdened nation state."[70] The European approach should come as no surprise:

> The 'Europeanization' of the Central and East European countries was perceived as the best scenario for the region because the post-Communist political reconstruction of democratic institutions and economic reforms could be backed by the 'grand design' of the European Union.[71]

The troubling developments that were occurring in the region in the 1990s could be answered by the "strong involvement of [the] 'patron power'."[72] Interestingly, all member states to the Council of Europe unanimously agreed to the procedures concerning full compliance. This includes a comprehensive education package, offering:

> freedom of expression and information, implementation and protection of democratic institutions, and adherence to the ideals of human rights in the functioning of the judicial system, local democracy, the rejection of capital punishment, and the operation of police and security forces.[73]

Capital punishment appeared often in the monitoring reports that include information on the law and legal reforms, statistics concerning executions, and policy issues and attitudes.[74]

In additional to the educational aspect, there is a law enforcement side too. PACE also issues a series of warnings, as well as resolutions and threats against a state that disregards its obligations. The warnings are usually accompanied by the statement that "all necessary steps to ensure compliance" will be taken, that might include "non-ratification of the credentials," which can be carried out under its Rules of Procedure.

Deterrence

The deterrence position proved to be a weak position. Deterrence is very much alive in certain segments of the post-Communist world, where capital punishment having a place in deterring crime captures a common societal view.[75] Furthermore, the political change was accompanied by a rise in crime rates that left respective societies helpless as to an alternate solution, and abolition was not it. The political campaigns in the region promised to be tough on crime, which meant that law and order would be achieved by any means possible. Thus, several states referred to American

70 Přibán, "European Union Constitution-Making," supra n. 44, 140.
71 Přibán, "European Union Constitution-Making," supra n. 44, 140.
72 *Ibid.*
73 See Bae, *When the State No Longer Kills*, supra n. 11, 25–6.
74 *Ibid.*, 26.
75 Fijalkowski, "Capital Punishment in Poland," supra n. 43.

approaches and separated criminal justice from human rights as being mutually exclusive matters.[76] The arguments pointed to the fact that in the United States – a democracy – federal and state criminal regimes included the capital sentence. These positions, however, arguably had more to do with the symbolic retention of decision making, critical to a nascent democracy like the post-Communist one, rather than deterrence. According to Melucci, "[d]emocracy in complex societies requires conditions which enable individuals and social groups to affirm themselves and to be recognized for what they are or wish to be."[77] Importantly, "belonging is not identical with being represented – it is in a certain sense its opposite."[78] Melucci elaborates on the process that occurs in a democracy:

> [a] non-authoritarian democracy in complex societies presupposes the capacity of foreseeing and supporting the double possibility: the right to make one's voice heard by means of representation or by modifying the conditions of listening, as well as the right to belong or to withdraw from belonging in order to produce new meanings.[79]

Since the collapse of Communism, disillusionment with the moribund and inefficient nature of the criminal justice system, in particular the inability to combat crime, was evidenced in the post-Communist states. The crisis was further exacerbated when politicians chose to manipulate discussions concerning the ineffective nature of the criminal law, leading to threats that capital punishment would be reinstated or abolition postponed.[80]

A fascinating example of resisting and attempting to control the process of abolishing the death penalty is Latvia. This Baltic state signed and ratified Protocol No. 6 to the ECHR. Although a new Latvian criminal code was adopted by Parliament in 1998, political leaders argued at the time that abolition could not be envisaged before 2001, when certain prison reforms would be concluded.[81] More recently, in 2008, the Latvian parliament's human rights committee called for an EU-wide debate on the reinstatement of the death penalty, following the brutal murder of an eleven-year-old girl.[82] The move was led by the Christian right-wing group, as well as the Latvian Minister of Justice, and was closely followed by Polish leaders whose conservative government, at least in this debate, has proved to be a thorn

76 Hood, "Introduction," supra n. 20, 17.

77 Alberto Melucci, "Social Movements and the Democratization of Everyday Life," *Civil Society and the State: New European Perspectives*, ed. J. Keane (London: Verso, 1988), 258.

78 *Ibid.*

79 *Ibid.*

80 Since 1989, the crime rate in CEE countries has been on the rise, and crimes previously unknown under the former Communist structure have emerged. For a brief overview, see Wojciech Cebulak, "Rising Crime Rates Amidst Transformations in Eastern Europe: Socio-Political Transition and Societal Response," 20 *International Journal of Comparative and Applied Criminal Justice*, 20 (1996): 77–82.

81 See "Constitutional Watch," *East European Constitutional Review*, 7 (1998): 18.

82 Philippa Runner, "Latvian Death Penalty Debate Rumbles On," in euro.oberserver.com (September 25, 2008), at http://euobserver.com/9/26807 (accessed June 14, 2010).

in the common European side. Similar to Albania, the prohibition of the death penalty as such is not mentioned in the Polish Constitution from 1997 (in contrast to, for example, the Romanian case). This certainly can be attributed to the debates that centered around the drafting of the document and the subsequent referendum on the Constitution, which included the strong position of the Catholic Church.[83] Alongside this, the role of ratified international agreements was considered, as well as what should guide the mode of interpretation of domestic legal provisions. On April 14, 2000, Poland adopted legislation approving ratification of the Protocol No. 6 to the ECHR, amid a fair amount of controversy.[84]

The involvement of key institutions needs to be addressed. Concerning Poland, the role of the Catholic Church is interesting and unavoidable in the debate on the abolition of the death penalty. The stance of the Catholic Church is quite significant in a country that is predominantly Catholic. This has been identified and used in the political platforms of the government, such as the Law and Justice . The former Polish president, Lech Kaczyński, and his brother, Jarosław Kaczyński, when he served as Prime Minister, have paved the way for undermining the European role and European politics in the country, questioning its legitimate influence on Polish affairs during the period 2005–2007. In 2007, Poland astonished the EU justice experts by rejecting the proposal for establishing a European Day Against the Death Penalty. Polish representatives in Brussels argued that the issue was one that forms a broader discussion on life and death that includes abortion and euthanasia. Poland resisted the idea that the right to life be strictly viewed as 'death penalty' matter. Around this time as well, the Polish government sought to reopen the debate on the death penalty and explore the question of its reinstatement.[85] It is worthwhile to note that throughout Communist rule, the church was a safe haven for free expression and the promotion of human rights.[86] In fact, starting in the 1970s, a strong abolitionist movement operated in the country. In 1995, the former Polish pope John Paul II indicated support for abolition. However, as Borowik observes:

> [i]n Polish mentality as well as the opinion of the Church, Catholicism is entirely connected with Polishness. Religious and national identity are characterised by a feeling of belonging to Polishness and Catholicism.[87]

[83] *Ibid.* See also Paweł Sarnecki, "Opinie: Dopuśczalność kary śmierci w świetle obowiązujących przepisów konstytucyjnych" (Opinion: Retention of the Death Penalty in Light of Constitutional Provisions), 3 *Przegląd Sejmowy* (2000): 77–85.

[84] See http://www.europa.eu.int/comm/enlargement/poland/index.htm. See also "Zniesienie przypieczętowane" (A Sealed Abolition), *Rzeczpospolita*, April 15, 2000 (online at http://www.rzeczpospolita.pl).

[85] See Mark Beunderman, "Poland Opposes EU Day Against the Death Penalty" (September 5, 2007), at http://euobserver.com/9/24704 (accessed June 14, 2010).

[86] See Irena Borowik, "The Roman Catholic Church in the Process of Democratic Transformation: The Case of Poland," 49 *Social Compass* (2002): 239–52.

[87] *Ibid.*

The same author also notes the manner in which the Catholic Church coped with challenges to its authority in the post-Communist period – not well – an attitude based on an obstinate belief in its own infallibility and the use of language struggle that aims to construct a "fortress mentality" or unified front, clearly not willing to accommodate change.[88] In a similar vein, when Ukraine failed to ratify Protocol No. 6 on October 6, 1997[89] it was up to the Ukrainian Constitutional Court to rule that the death penalty is unconstitutional and recall the obligations that Ukraine bound itself with in 1995 upon joining the Council of Europe.[90] Bulgaria too has struggled with the question of retention of capital punishment as a means to control the increasing crime rate.[91]

The Committee of Ministers has been known to be more sympathetic, using persuasive language, stressing that it is not criticizing but *identifying with* the post-Communist states and their problems, and is keen to assist in organizing the resolution of these difficulties.[92] The language characterizing European policy is also firm and forward-looking. Those who question the reasons for eventual compliance point try to show that society is not ready psychologically, culturally, and institutionally to accept the reforms.[93] The approach adopted toward the new states is one that is followed along procedural lines and ensuring compliance. Such an approach seems to assume that certain features and attitudes on punishment in post-Communist states are being indigenous. This fails to bring into relief the complex social and political underpinnings of what is taken first hand as a natural phenomenon. In response, newer states will renege or resist. From the European perspective, extending the policy to new members should be celebrated as a commitment to human rights.

To reiterate, the European position can be summarized as follows. The events of World War II had motivated the movement that led to the Council of Europe and the European Convention. The abolition movement has become focused, including fixing an identity of Europe to abolition. It is a reassuring tale and in this way it allows a sterner approach to be used against the 'culprits' who have not adopted the European project. As noted by Girling, the European position is very much focused on the 'punisher'; this position shapes the policy and sustains the momentum.[94] The European project is argued as being civilized, the embodiment of values, the protector of these liberties and freedoms. The attitude is depicted as a natural position, with "roots [that] are deeply buried in West European political culture."[95] Once again, it is identity that is at stake, and for the European position,

88 See Agata Fijalkowski, "The Paradoxical Nature of Crime Control in Post-Communist Europe," 15 *European Journal of Crime, Criminal Law and Criminal Justice* (2007): 155–72.

89 See "Constitutional Watch," 7 *East European Constitutional Review*, 1 (1998): 42.

90 See "Constitutional Watch," 9 *East European Constitutional Review*, 1–2 (2000): 43.

91 Stanislaw Frankowski, "Post-Communist Europe," in *Capital Punishment: Global Issues and* Prospects, eds. P. Hodgkinson and A. Rutherford (Winchester, 1996), 228.

92 See Bae, *When the State No Longer Kills*, supra n. 11, 25–6.

93 See Bae, *When the State No Longer Kills, supra n.* 11, 36.

94 Girling, supra n. 39.

95 Hood, supra n. 20, 25.

this was only clarified vis-à-vis the new European states. In other words, a process of self-reflection for the 'original' European states was imminent.

Public Opinion

The final area that is inevitably treated in the debate on capital punishment is public opinion. Like deterrence, public opinion is put forward by states as having a critical role in abolition or retention. A common claim contends that the fact that there is majority support counters the call for abolition. Hood indicates the deeper contention that abolition without support would destroy confidence in the law and result in "mob justice."[96] The American experience demonstrates the importance of public opinion, and the U.S. Supreme Court has reinforced this position in allowing states to decide on the matter of the reinstatement of capital punishment.[97] However, support for the death penalty does not mean support for executions, where often information is also not available as concerns alternate sentences. And, of course, public opinion can change, too. The well-known Marshall Hypothesis, for example, contends that it is imperative for constitutional purposes to attempt to discern the probable opinion of an informed electorate.[98] In other words, with informed opinion, most would find capital punishment immoral and therefore unconstitutional. Although it is too early to see this development in post-Communist states, respective constitutional court case law, in particular the advisory opinion, is paramount.[99] Having the competence to give advisory opinions allows for the judicial review of legal rules prior to and after enactment. This can have a profound effect on the protection of human dignity and can contribute to the debate on the existence of the capital sentence in the national criminal law. Of course, it can be highly politicized owing to the matter that is contested.[100]

For some states, membership in the Council of Europe was immediately followed by an intense and heated debate about the future of capital punishment. In Ukraine, for example, in a 1994 survey, 67 percent of those polled wanted the death penalty retained and expanded.[101] This view was supported by people even when presented with the risk of losing the support of European countries. Retention meant that the crime rates could be controlled, at least, as some states argued, until law and order was stabilized. It had, if anything, symbolic value. An abolitionist policy could,

[96] Hood, supra n. 18, 223.

[97] Consider the American context and *Gregg* v. *Georgia* 428 US 153 [1976].

[98] Roger Hood, "A Question of Opinion or a Question of Principle?" in *The Death Penalty: A Worldwide Perspective* (Oxford: Oxford University Press, 2002), 239.

[99] See Wojciech Sadurski, *Rights Before Courts: A Study of Constitutional Courts in Postcommunist States of Central and Eastern Europe* (Budapest: Central European University Press, 1999).

[100] For the Hungarian context see László Sólyom and Georg Brunner, *Constitutional Judiciary in a New Democracy: The Hungarian Constitutional Court* (Ann Arbor: The University of Michigan Press, 2000).

[101] See Bae, *When the State No Longer Kills, supra n.* 11, 29–40.

however, eventually lead to a change in the domestic consciousness, despite a potential increase in the crime rate.

Elsewhere, there is little national debate to speak of. The absence of a discussion on the relevance of the punishment has been noted in the Russian experience, where one campaigner noted:

> '[i]n order to satisfy the West's political demands and despite the people's will, a moratoria on the death penalty for particularly serious crimes against the person has been introduced in Russia . . . the decision to impose a moratoria on the death penalty was not simply mistaken, but pernicious. It has turned out to be a major tragedy for society . . . '[102]

Moreover, one of the greatest Russian intellectuals, Aleksander Solzhenitsyn, supported the death penalty, finding it the only effective solution against terrorism. The position of the Russian Orthodox Church is ambivalent. In terms of political leadership, the current president expressed alliance with the Council of Europe on the matter, whereas the former president elaborated in detail. Putin's responded:

> If the hypothesis that we suffer most from the evil existing within ourselves is true, then we can say that by making punishment harsher – and the death penalty is in fact not punishment, but rather vengeance on the part of the state – then, by increasing the severity of punishments, the state is not eliminating cruelty but merely reproducing it again and again. The state ought not to assume a right that can belong to the Almighty alone – taking life from a human being. As a result, I can firmly state that I am against restoration of the death penalty in Russia.[103]

The lack of national debate might be correct. Polls show that the death penalty as a societal concern does not rank high. "It sometimes seems that is there is one thing on which a moratorium must be placed, then it is on this debate, which has no practical import whatsoever in our particular social conditions."[104]

In November 2009, the Russian Constitutional Court ruled the punishment unconstitutional.[105] Chief Justice Zorkin (who returns to the Court after a hiatus and controversial exit) referred to the application of the death sentence as impossible in light of the country's international obligations. Indeed, the current Russian president has expressed unity with the Council of Europe on this matter. Interestingly, the Court only insisted that the moratorium on executions be extended; it is still for the Russian parliament to ban capital punishment. In 1999, the Russian Constitutional Court held that the death penalty could not be used until jury trials were introduced in all eighty-nine regions of the country. The Russian experience resonates with the

102 Anatoly Pristavkin, "The Russian Federation and the Death Penalty," in *Death Penalty: Beyond Abolition*, ed. R. Hood (Strasbourg: Council of Europe Publishing, 2004), 200.

103 *Ibid.*, 203.

104 *Ibid.*, 204.

105 "Russian enshrines ban on death penalty," BBC News (November 19, 2010) at http://news.bbc.co.uk 1/hi/8367831.stm (accessed March 14, 2010).

Latvian one. For some, it represents the kind of situation over which the Council of Europe despairs as a position that challenges the European policy at its very core. Further to the Federal Constitutional Court judgment, the representative of the Federation Council of the Russian parliament issued a public statement, wanting "to *assure the Russian public that the ban on the death penalty is the duty to its citizens, not international commitments* [emphasis is mine]."[106] It is interesting to note another important development in Europe, namely in Turkey, a country that retained the death penalty within its criminal law for a long period after imposing a moratorium, and which eventually joined the European movement in removing the capital sentence from its books by ratifying Protocol No. 13 in 2006.

In the end, public opinion is only a sentiment, and one that cannot override serious human rights concerns and questions. For Europe, education is the key to making informed decisions. This is delivered in its package of accession talks. For the national perspective, political will is important. Not to be ignored, respective constitutional courts have reiterated, one by one, throughout post-Communist Europe, that the death penalty is untenable alongside constitutional norms and/or international obligations; outside the scope of this chapter, this is shared among these courts, whether 'dictated' by the Venice Commission or the result creative judicial reasoning.[107] In many ways the European abolition movement is also an epic judicial movement within the recent histories of European constitutional courts.[108]

European Project and Identity

We have seen the challenges that are presented in the form of local sensibilities, indicating that European policy is not wholeheartedly embraced. The local sensibilities reveal a shared experience between post-Communist states of repressive, for the most part imposed Communist rule and limited experiences with democracy. An appreciation of this point is necessary with respect to the position of the Council of Europe and the EU.

As noted earlier, the European position is presented as an identity. This is complemented by the EU project that is driven by the idea of a common identity. Both are premised on forward-looking thinking:

> Unlike the historical future, the future in process is not primarily legitimated by the past experiences and therefore must be modelled in a more abstract way.[109]

[106] *Ibid.*

[107] The interesting case, as highlighted by Schabas, is *Pratt et al* v. *Attorney General for Jamaica* [1994] 2 AC 1 that set out an opinion that made that shift from administrative regulation to a human rights issue.

[108] See C. Neal Tate and Torbjörn Vallinder, eds., *The Global Expansion of Judicial Power* (New York: New York University Press, 1995).

[109] Přibán, "European Union Constitution-Making," supra n. 44, 143.

This is also reflected in the 1973 Declaration on the European Identity.[110] The European position is afforded little legitimacy when used by populist campaigns and Eurosceptics, such as in Poland, as another 'imposed' regime where analogies between 'us and them' is revived in political platforms.

Despite this symbolic value of membership, many states struggled to meet the demands of abolition. The main dilemma was posed by a newly formed state relinquishing its sovereignty. This was a common sentiment that suggests some doubt as to the close association with the Council of Europe.[111] States are normally loath to let go of control over its criminal law framework and policies. This is an issue that has been explored elsewhere[112] and questions the idea that a state should have the last word about punishment, and whether punishment is a reflection of societal norm that only the state has the competence to fulfill. As noted earlier, many states embarked on intense campaigns to resist international expectations to abolish capital punishment. Strong political arguments were put forward, grounding the capital sentence as part of the social, cultural, and religious fabric of society. This was not a human rights argument, and it involved key institutions within the state. The matter of compliance came to raise questions about the European policy that is viewed by some states as control over areas that the European policy cannot fully appreciate. The matter of sovereignty challenges European policy – strong institutions, such as the organized church in some states, do this quite forcefully.

In this area, it is apparent that promoting national compliance with international procedures and norms is not just a balance between incentives and warnings. It is a process of social interaction that can promote state compliance through "policy dialogues, jawboning, learning, persuasion, and the like."[113] In the end, the Council is viewed as a 'gatekeeper' to the organization for integration in the European Union; this is supported by various decisions on the part of respective constitutional courts in the region.[114]

It is important not to forget that "Europe's search of its people and constitution-making are examples of a historically unique and paradoxical situation in which the 'constitutive power' is desperate to constitute the 'constituent power'."[115] Within the death penalty debate, it would seem that an answer has been found as concerns the so-called destructive force of the supranational, European process on the national level. This can be achieved by focusing on the benefits of Přibán's purposive rationale.

110 See http://www.ena.lu/declaration-european-identity-copenhagen-14-december-1973–020002278.html (accessed 14 June 14, 2010).

111 Bae, *When the State No Longer Kills*, *supra* n. 11.

112 See, Christopher Harding et al., eds, *Criminal Justice in Europe: A Comparative Study* (Oxford: Clarendon, 1995).

113 Bae, *When the State No Longer Kills*, supra n. 11, p. 36.

114 See, in particular, Sadurski's discussion about the Hungarian experience in *Rights Before Courts*, supra n. 98.

115 Přibán, "European Union Constitution-Making," supra n. 44, 147.

To the realist, this is a recent phenomenon best expressed in the notion of the judicialization of politics, where there is a noted reliance on courts and judicial means for addressing critical issues comprising moral predicaments, public policy questions, and political controversies. Hirschl's work in this area points to a global shift toward judicial empowerment based on what he sees as self-interested behavior of strategic actors.[116] According to his theory of hegemonic preservation, when a ruling party foresees its replacement, it is willing to transfer power to the courts and to enact constitutional reforms that will constrain those who will replace it, adding another dimension to the relationship between key European institutions and member states and ways in which to view post-Communist legal transformations.[117] So, as the group of threatened politicians sees their support begin to disappear, they attempt to fix their policy preferences by transferring policy-making power to the courts, including those decisions addressing a state's *raison d'etre*. For some, penality comprises that very core essence, if not a key part. For the majority of the systems in question, the hierarchical nature of the centralized state makes political decision making easier, which can be both a headache and welcome feature.[118]

The way that European policy is implemented in the 'new' European states is perceived by some as another form of imposed rule. The "us and them" analogy noted earlier gives way to a "good versus bad" analogy. Whereas we may appreciate Western Europe as an example where eventually abolition has become part of its identity and broader European position, it is a position that is not entirely accurate because there never was a thread of continuity that has existed in the area of penality and the support for capital punishment in Western European states. For the most part, a response to the death penalty was a defensive position until recently. This is not to say that abolition is a bad or misplaced goal. What this does highlight is the ongoing debate concerning the common European identity. This dimension of the identity needs to be included in a discussion of national histories that are part of the Western and new states' experiences that have a "unifying role of negative historical experience [that] should work as a mechanism of enhancing the unification process."[119] To do otherwise misses the point of this European policy's place in the wider European project and what this reveals in terms of statehood and common values. The linkages between certain types of pathologies need to be appreciated, as well as the fact that Western Europe and its policy on the death penalty cannot be a substitute to the histories of the European states, both old and new.[120] In other words, Europe needs to be clearer when selecting "its positive past" in its commitment to

[116] Ran Hirschl, "The Judicialization of Politics," in *The Oxford Handbook of Law and Politics*, eds. K. Whittington, R. Daniel Kelemen, and G. A. Caldeira (Oxford: Oxford University Press, 2008), 119–41.

[117] *Ibid.*

[118] Bae, supra n. 11, p. 39.

[119] Přibán, "European Union Constitution-Making," supra n. 44, 148

[120] See Hannah Arendt's discussion on the Europeanist way of thinking and approach to European heritage in *The Origins of Totalitarianism* (New York: World Publishing Co., 1958).

its, *inter alia*, treaty objectives.[121] Moreover, there are concrete achievements to be cited. In the end, Europe is perceived as a refuge, which is significant for certain regions of the new Europe. Alongside this, the new European states have had the benefit of being "treated as equals" and "not forced to renounce too much of their recently re-established sovereignty."[122] One can forgive these newly established democracies for wanting to retain sovereignty. In the end, European policy has not resulted in destroying internal national policies. The firm language in terms of the criteria that had to be met before membership to the Council of Europe and the EU means a serious consideration of human rights. Not to say that European policy cannot accommodate diverse interests and views that are debated in political and legal spheres. The fact that the issue remains so hotly contested in certain post-Communist states must be acknowledged by Europe. It is important to recognize that the European idea of civilization can be challenged as not being the 'natural' common position, but an evolving one:

> [The p]ost-Communist experience of the accession countries show that the identity dilemma had an enormous impact on constitution-making and political processes, which could be stabilised externally by the symbolic power of the European Union as a supranational structure representing the political virtues of civility.[123]

The symbolic rationale will gain more substance and support with evolving case law that comprises part of the European human rights framework that is expanding and is no longer ignored by foreign jurisdictions throughout the world.[124] European policy "need not be conflictual . . . but may be synergistic, producing an outcome which is greater than the sum of its parts."[125]

CONCLUSIONS

European policy on the death penalty has been formalized institutionally. Because the power is allocated to the Council of Europe, it is a position that is difficult to ignore – a convincing case has been made that the capital sentence violates human dignity. The campaign includes a variety of mechanisms that aim to inculcate a populace through education, advertising, and other ways of mobilization. 'New' European states, while pleased to be back in Europe, have expressed problems with this policy, and some proactively support a pro-death penalty stance that is largely ignored by the Council of Europe and EU member states.

[121] Přibán, "European Union Constitution-Making," supra n. 44, 148

[122] *Ibid.*

[123] Přibán, "European Union Constitution-Making," supra n. 44, 151.

[124] An important example of the recognition of international law and practice by the U.S. Supreme Court is found in *Roper* v. *Simmons* 543 US 551 [2005].

[125] Laura Cram, "Introduction: Banal Europeanism: European Union Identity and National Identities in Synergy," 15 *Nations and Nationalism* (2009): 101, and *idem*, 'Identity and European Integration: Diversity as a Source of Integration', 15 *Nations and Nationalism* (2009): 109–28.

This chapter critically examined these European transformations. Although the position on the death penalty has reflected a certain unity on the matter, it has resulted in anxiety on the part of the 'newer' members of the Council of Europe and the EU. The discussion considered the common features that characterize the debates, common to the sphere of punishment, namely obedience, deterrence, public opinion, and state sovereignty. The chapter then examined the way in which European policy has accommodated the peculiar history and context of states on this issue. This seemed to be addressed superficially by the European movement. Whereas solutions could be found to address arguments related to compliance, deterrence, and public opinion, the question of sovereignty proved more contentious as an issue that is more symbolic and linked to a wider notion of identity. It is not disputed that the new states do not believe in a Europe – in fact, in their view, the European project is restorative. The EU and its mandate were explored; similarities were found between the Council of Europe and EU projects on forging a common position and identity. Although there is no European identity per se, and neither project can be said to reflect "natural positions," both are evolving and very much forward-looking and identify with a commitment to human rights that is becoming more tangible with a growing body of case law. Because European policy is open-ended it, can accommodate diverse positions without undermining the main objective, that of upholding the common values of and commitment to human rights and democracy, of which abolition of capital punishment is an integral part.

11

The Long Shadow of the Death Penalty

Mass Incarceration, Capital Punishment, and Penal Policy in the United States

Marie Gottschalk

The death penalty has cast a long, often dark shadow over the U.S. penal system and the politics of punishment. The contentious politics surrounding efforts to abolish and reinstate the death penalty in the United States in the twentieth century helped transform the broader politics associated with criminal justice and law enforcement. In an exceptional outcome, the political and judicial debate over capital punishment facilitated the construction of a vast penal system in the United States.

Over the past four decades, the United States has embarked on a prison-building boom without precedent here or elsewhere. The number of inmates increased dramatically, rising more than sixfold since the early 1970s. Today a higher proportion of the adult population is behind bars than anywhere else in the world. The U.S. incarceration rate of 754 per 100,000 is 5 to 12 times the rate of the Western European countries and Japan.[1] About one of every one hundred adults in the United States is behind bars today, and one in thirty-one is under some form of state supervision, including jail, prison, parole, probation, and other sanctions.[2]

The exceptional political and institutional trajectory of capital punishment is not the sole or even the primary explanation for the turn toward more punitive policies and mass incarceration in the United States. Rather, it is an important contributing factor alongside the social, political, racial, institutional, and economic factors identified by Garland, Beckett, Alexander, Wacquant, Simon, Tonry, and

1 William J. Sabol, Heather C. West, and Matthew Cooper, "Prisoners in 2008," *Bureau of Justice Statistics Bulletin*, December 2009; and International Centre for Prison Studies, "World Prison Brief," http://www.kcl.ac.uk/depsta/law/research/icps/worldbrief/ (accessed January 30, 2010).

2 Pew Center on the States, "One in 100: Behind Bars in America 2008," Washington, DC: Pew Center on the States, 2008; and Pew Center on the States, "One in 31: The Long Reach of American Corrections," Washington, DC: Pew Center on the States, 2009.

A special thanks to Jürgen Martschukat, Austin Sarat, and all the other contributors to this volume for their constructive suggestions to revise this chapter.

others.[3] By the late twentieth century, capital punishment and the carceral state had become firmly entrenched, mutually reinforcing institutions. The death penalty insinuated itself in complex ways into the national debate over crime and punishment. Capital punishment became more than just a convenient shorthand way for U.S. politicians and public officials to signal their commitment to hardline penal policies. The regulation of capital punishment through the judiciary had powerful spillover effects. It shaped how proponents and opponents of the death penalty organized themselves. But it also helped to legitimize the conservative, zero-sum view of victims and offenders.

Capital punishment as practiced in the United States contributed to an erosion of the separation between state and society in the making of penal policy, allowing blunt measures of public passions, such as opinion polls, to be accorded a central role. This helped render the passions of the public a central and legitimate consideration in the formation of penal policy. It also drew public attention away from extensive social scientific evidence showing that the death penalty has no deterrent effect. Moreover, it deflected attention away from the larger issue of what are the limits, if any, on the state's power to punish and kill, which was central to discussions of capital punishment and penal policy in Europe.

This is an exceptional outcome in other respects. As Andrew Hammel argues elsewhere in this volume, successful movements to attack capital punishment in Western Europe were conceived and led almost exclusively by elites in the face of strong, often massive public support for retaining the death penalty. Nonetheless, the abolition of capital punishment in Europe and Canada – unlike in the United States – did not ignite a powerful countermovement that succeeded in bringing back executions in the name of defending law and order that bolstered the carceral state.

Most accounts of the courts and capital punishment focus on the legal strategies and landmark court decisions involving the death penalty in the 1960s and 1970s that brought about and then ended the decade-long moratorium on executions. But capital punishment was deeply lodged in the judicial process long before it became a national issue with the 1972 *Furman* decision that suspended the death penalty

[3] David Garland, *The Culture of Control: Crime and Social Order in Contemporary Society*. (Chicago: University of Chicago Press, 2001); Katherine Beckett, *Making Crime Pay: Law and Order in Contemporary American Politics* (New York: Oxford University Press, 1997); Ruth Wilson Gilmore, *The Golden Gulag: Prisons, Surplus, Crisis and Opposition in Globalizing California* (Berkeley: University of California, 2007); Loïc Wacquant, "Deadly Symbiosis: When Ghetto and Prison Meet and Mesh," in David Garland, ed., *Mass Imprisonment: Social Causes and Consequences* (London: Sage Publications, 2001); Michelle Alexander, *The New Jim Crow: Mass Incarceration in the Age of Colorblindness* (New York: The New Press, 2010); Jonathan Simon, *Governing Through Crime: How the War on Crime Transformed American Democracy and Created a Culture of Fear* (New York: Oxford University Press, 2007); Michael Tonry, "Determinants of Penal Policies," in *Crime, Punishment, and Politics in Comparative Perspective*, ed. Michael Tonry (Chicago: University of Chicago Press, 2007): 1–48; and Marie Gottschalk, *The Prison and the Gallows: The Politics of Mass Incarceration in America* (New York: Cambridge University Press, 2006).

and the 1976 *Gregg* decision that reinstated it. As will be shown, the legal framing of the death penalty and the evolving strategies of opponents and proponents helped fortify the U.S. penal system. In keeping with some of the other contributors to this volume, notably Colin Dayan and Pieter Spierenburg, I argue that we cannot compartmentalize analyses of capital punishment. Rather, in the words of Spierenburg, we need to widen the scope of the discussion to take in the penal system as a whole, in particular imprisonment.

My analysis begins by highlighting the importance of the muted rights revolution that began in the United States in the late 1920s and set an important context for the subsequent development of capital punishment. I then examine the institutional, political, and judicial factors that account for the waning of capital punishment from the 1930s to the early 1960s, prior to the emergence of the contemporary anti-death penalty movement. I focus on the role of the courts and the legal process in framing the political debate over capital punishment. I then examine the emergence of the contemporary anti-death penalty movement in mid-1960s and the enduring marks that the *Furman* and *Gregg* decisions left on the development of penal policy. The chapter concludes with a brief analysis of what impact the most recent efforts to abolish the death penalty – especially the new "innocence movement" – are likely to have on the U.S. penal system more broadly.

THE COURTS AND CAPITAL PUNISHMENT FROM THE 1920S TO THE 1960S

In the mid-1960s, an elite-led anti-death penalty movement began to take shape in the United States. The conventional understanding of the history of anti-death penalty activism is that the earlier waves of reform in the antebellum period and Progressive era were premised primarily on moral and legislative strategies for challenging capital punishment. This changed decisively around the mid-1960s, so the argument goes, because public-interest groups, notably the Legal and Educational Defense Fund (LDF) of the National Association for the Advancement of Colored People (NAACP) and the American Civil Liberties Union (ACLU) made a key decision – some would say a fateful decision – to launch an all-out assault on capital punishment through the courts by challenging its fundamental constitutionality rather than by attempting to abolish it through legislative means. As a consequence, the main arena to battle the death penalty shifted from state legislatures to the courts.

Yet capital punishment was already lodged in the judicial process, which set it on a particular developmental path, long before the LDF and ACLU brought about a de facto moratorium on capital punishment in 1967 and prodded the Supreme Court to address its fundamental constitutionality. Prior to the emergence of the contemporary anti-death penalty movement, capital punishment was entangled with the development of the courts and criminal law procedures in ways not seen in Western Europe and Canada. From the 1930s to the mid-1960s, it was anchored almost exclusively in the judicial process. This set important parameters for the way it could be challenged and defended not just in the courts but also in the wider political arena once it became a high-profile political issue after the *Furman* decision.

In the decades since the *Furman* and *Gregg* decisions, capital punishment cases have comprised the most frequent business of the Supreme Court. In the century prior to the *Furman* decision, the Supreme Court rarely reviewed death penalty cases. However, the Court did make several important decisions in the decades immediately prior to *Furman* that were critical to the development of capital punishment and to shaping the national debate over crime and punishment.

Prior to the Progressive era, the only organized litigants who regularly succeeded in getting the Supreme Court to hear their claims were those with economic or property disputes. During the Progressive era, a number of new rights organizations were founded. In the 1920s, a rights-advocacy network centered on the ACLU, the NAACP, and the American Jewish Congress was consolidated. It had the resources, expertise, and political savvy to eventually compel the Supreme Court to take up more rights-based claims.[4] As a result, criminal procedures became a new arena of Supreme Court action from the 1930s onward and thus were critical to the development of the national state.

Largely unknown and unappreciated "is the fact that the most complex and time-consuming litigation the NAACP undertook in its early years was not concerned with the constitutional right of equality as such but rather with criminal procedure requirements."[5] The most striking victories for civil rights groups in the interwar years involved Southern criminal cases marred by Jim Crow.[6] Thanks to the efforts of the NAACP in the late 1920s and 1930s, the national government, through several landmark Supreme Court decisions, put federal restrictions on capital punishment for the first time since the ratification of the Constitution a century and a half earlier. The Court established important procedural safeguards for capital defendants under the Fourteenth Amendment's due process clause. In *Moore v. Dempsey*, the Court ruled in 1923 that state trials dominated by mob pressures violated the due process protections of the Fourteenth Amendment.[7] Prior to *Moore*, virtually no precedent existed for the intervention of federal courts in state criminal proceedings.[8] In *Powell v. Alabama*, the Court ordered a retrial in 1932 for the "Scottsboro boys" on the grounds that poor defendants in capital cases were entitled to adequate

4 Charles R. Epp, *The Rights Revolution: Lawyers, Activists, and Supreme Courts in Comparative Perspective* (Chicago: University of Chicago Press, 1998), 44–52.

5 Richard C. Cortner, *A Mob Intent on Death: The NAACP and the Arkansas Race Riot Cases* (Middletown, CT: Wesleyan University Press, 1988), 3.

6 Michael J. Klarman, *From Jim Crow to Civil Rights: The Supreme Court and the Struggle for Racial Equality* (New York: Oxford University Press, 2004), 117–35.

7 Hugo Adam Bedau, *Death Is Different: Studies in the Morality, Law, and Politics of Capital Punishment* (Boston: Northeastern University Press, 1987), 13; and Cortner, *A Mob Intent on Death*, 154–5.

8 Klarman, *From Jim Crow to Civil Rights*, 117.

legal counsel. The 1936 ruling in *Brown v. Mississippi* vacated the convictions and death sentences of three black tenant farmers accused of murdering a white planter whose confessions were extracted under torture by deputy sheriffs.[9] Other decisions prohibited discrimination in jury selection and "generally clarified the procedural rights of criminal defendants."[10] The expansion of federal habeas corpus in the early 1960s opened up additional legal vistas for prisoners on death row to challenge their sentences.[11] Taken together, these decisions gave defendants in capital cases and prisoners on death row new means and opportunities to whittle away at capital punishment on a case-by-case basis and help explain the steep drop in executions between the 1930s and the early 1960s.[12]

This precocious development of a comparatively expansive network of advocacy organizations that succeeded in prevailing on the Supreme Court to address rights-based claims set capital punishment in the United States on a distinctive track. The fate of the death penalty was to be battled out on judicial rather than legislative terrain. The considerable success these groups had beginning in the 1930s in extending the rights of defendants appeared to confirm the wisdom of this strategy. Unlike in Britain and elsewhere, important parameters for attacking and defending capital punishment were forged in the courts in the decades prior to the emergence of a pronounced death penalty movement (either for or against).

The NAACP was a central player in the emerging network of rights-advocacy groups that litigated these landmark capital cases. In 1939, it created a new corporation officially known as its Legal and Educational Defense Fund. The LDF's primary goal, in the words of longtime staff attorney Michael Meltsner, was "to pursue equality for blacks by bringing test cases in the courts challenging the laws and customs on which racial segregation rested."[13] The LDF was at the forefront of the major civil rights cases of the 1940s and 1950s, including equal access to higher education, challenges to restrictive covenants and white primaries, and, of course, the 1954 *Brown v. Board of Education* decision calling for desegregation in public schools. The LDF was also at the forefront of some of the major capital punishment cases during this time. As Jack Greenberg of the LDF once said: "Any organization that concerns itself with America's racial problems and their relationship to the law soon confronts the grim fact of capital punishment."[14]

9 Jerome H. Skolnick, "On Controlling Torture," in *Punishment and Social Control*, 2nd ed., ed. Thomas G. Blomberg and Stanley Cohen (New York: Aldine de Gruyter, 2003), 218.

10 William J. Bowers, Glenn L. Pierce, and John F. McDevitt, *Legal Homicide: Death as Punishment in America, 1864–1982* (Boston: Northeastern University Press, 1984), 63–4; and Franklin E. Zimring, *The Contradictions of American Capital Punishment* (Oxford: Oxford University Press, 2003), 69.

11 Herbert H. Haines, *Against Capital Punishment: The Anti-Death Penalty Movement in America, 1972–1994* (New York: Oxford University Press, 1996), 24.

12 Stuart Banner, *The Death Penalty: An American History* (Cambridge, MA: Harvard University Press, 2002), 246.

13 Michael Meltsner, *Cruel and Unusual: The Supreme Court and Capital Punishment* (New York: Random House, 1973), 5–6.

14 Jack Greenberg and Jack Himmelstein, "Varieties of Attack on the Death Penalty," *Crime and Delinquency* 15.1 (January 1969), 113.

Capital punishment was in many ways a natural issue for the LDF because it appeared so starkly discriminatory. Blacks were executed in disproportionate numbers. It was virtually unheard of to execute a white for crimes committed against a black. Blacks convicted of killing whites ran the greatest risk of being killed by the state. Whites convicted of rape were seldom executed whereas blacks risked death for this offense, especially in the South. Sophisticated statistical analyses of racial disparities in the exercise of capital punishment carried out in earnest from the late 1960s onward merely confirmed and quantified patterns that had been readily apparent for decades to anyone involved in the exercise of the death penalty.

Even though blacks bore a disproportionate burden of the death penalty, the LDF and other rights groups were slow to launch a broad challenge to the constitutionality of capital punishment. Instead, until the early 1960s, the LDF fought capital punishment primarily on procedural grounds on a case-by-case basis. Most of these cases involved black men charged with raping white women. Occasionally, the LDF raised questions about the validity of capital punishment based on patterns of racial discrimination, but time and again the courts rejected such challenges.

As the number of capital cases accumulated, the LDF considered attacking the death penalty on more sweeping constitutional grounds. But LDF lawyers did not begin to map out such a campaign until Supreme Court Justice Arthur Goldberg issued a dissenting opinion in an obscure Alabama rape case that the Court refused to hear in 1963. In his dissent from the Court's denial of certiorari in *Rudolph v. Alabama*, Goldberg urged the Court to take up the case and address several questions regarding the constitutionality of the death penalty that had not been raised by the defendant's lawyers, who had focused on procedural issues in this interracial capital rape case. Goldberg questioned whether imposition of the death penalty for rape violated "evolving standards of decency that mark the progress of [our] maturing society." He also questioned whether "the taking of a human life to protect a value other than human life" was an excessive punishment and whether punishing rape with death constituted "unnecessary cruelty."[15]

This was a highly calculated and premeditated dissent.[16] Coming as it did and when it did, Goldberg's dissent laid down certain parameters for the debate over capital punishment that opponents of the death penalty in other countries did not have to contend with. Ironically, it helped channel the national debate on capital punishment in ways that helped build the carceral state on the back of capital punishment. First, the Goldberg dissent provided a tantalizing opening to pursue the end of capital punishment through the courts. This helped solidify the legal arena, not the political arena, as the main stage of action to abolish the death penalty. Second, the dissent did not cite racial discrimination "as relevant and, apparently, worthy of argument," even though Rudolph was black, and nine out of

15 *Rudolph v. Alabama*, 375 U.S. 889, 84 S. Ct. 155, 11 L.Ed.2d 119, quoted in Jack Greenberg, *Cases and Materials on Judicial Process and Social Change: Constitutional Litigation* (St. Paul, MN: West Publishing Co., 1977), 429–30.

16 Ian Gray and Moira Stanley, *A Punishment in Search of a Crime* (New York: Avon Books, 1989), 331.

ten men executed for this crime since 1930 had been black.[17] Ironically the dissent served to spur the LDF, a group whose *raison d'etat* was race-based claims, into taking greater action against capital punishment in the face of a Supreme Court that still appeared to be denying that racial concerns were relevant to the exercise of the death penalty. Thus, capital punishment was to become even more tightly associated with civil rights issues even though the courts appeared unreceptive to claims that race mattered in the imposition of the death penalty. Most significantly, Goldberg's dissent inserted public opinion considerations into the national debate on capital punishment. Whether public sentiment for the death penalty was waxing or waning became a relevant factor in the debates over abolition in the United States. In Europe, this was not a central issue in the debate over abolition that unfolded at about the same time, as discussed later.

THE BROADER CAMPAIGN AGAINST CAPITAL PUNISHMENT

Goldberg's dissent "jolted Fund lawyers into action."[18] Roughly around 1965, the LDF embarked on a wider legal campaign aimed primarily at abolishing the death penalty for rape. Capital punishment and race were to be explicitly linked for the first time in a national campaign. The LDF sought to postpone all capital rape cases on appeal as sociologist Marvin Wolfgang collected the statistical data necessary to prove racial discrimination in rape sentencing. LDF attorneys used Wolfgang's research to argue for outright abolition of the death penalty in capital rape cases or creation of new procedural safeguards to prevent racial discrimination in sentencing.[19]

Propelled along by the logic of its legal arguments, the LDF soon decided to expand its campaign to cover all capital punishment defendants, not just blacks convicted of rape. After all, other capital cases lacked many of the same procedural safeguards found wanting in capital rape cases and were vexed with discriminatory sentencing patterns (though they were not as stark as in capital rape cases). The LDF also decided to launch a broader assault because the courts appeared unreceptive to Wolfgang's sophisticated statistical analyses that demonstrated widespread racial discrimination in capital rape cases. A major turning point for the LDF was *Maxwell v. Bishop*, in which a U.S. District Court in 1966 was not persuaded by the statistical evidence and refused to vacate the death sentence of William L. Maxwell, a young black man convicted of raping a white woman in Alabama. Two years later, the U.S. Court of Appeals for the Eighth Circuit also rejected Maxwell's appeal.

The Fund had a political as well as legal rationale for expanding its capital campaign. It hoped to make capital punishment a high-profile political issue by creating a huge backlog of cases in the courts and risk a "bloodbath" should executions

17 Greenberg, *Cases and Materials on Judicial Process and Social Change*, 431.

18 Meltsner, *Cruel and Unusual*, 28.

19 Eric L. Muller, "The Legal Defense Fund's Capital Punishment Campaign: The Distorting Influence of Death," *Yale Law and Policy Review* 4 (1985), 165–66.

resume again. Under its new strategy, the Fund sought to block all executions nationwide. This was a massive undertaking without precedent. It required the LDF to be involved with potentially hundreds of cases nationwide.[20]

The LDF was constrained in its attempt to take full advantage of the opening that Goldberg's dissent appeared to present. The Fund's resources had expanded considerably since its inception in 1939, but so also had its broad litigation responsibilities. Its staff was "still small, spread dangerously thin, and plagued by almost daily civil rights movement crises that required immediate action."[21] Furthermore, it was primarily a law office, not a political organization, and its tax-exempt status precluded political lobbying. Also, unlike the ACLU and the NAACP, it did not have local branches that could put pressure on and educate the public and state legislators.[22] Moreover, two decades of major civil rights triumphs in the courts had biased the LDF toward legal solutions.[23] Once it expanded its campaign to challenge all death sentences, this civil rights organization found itself in the awkward position of defending numerous marginal, violent members of society, many of whom were "drawn from the most racist segment of white society."[24] As the Fund sought stays of execution for all rapists and murderers, it also drew national attention to heinous crimes that reinforced white stereotypes about black criminality.[25] The Fund sought to make capital punishment a high-profile political issue, yet it eschewed the public relations and public education aspects of its advocacy.[26] Even though the LDF had a larger political rationale for its legal strategy, it concentrated primarily on its legal campaign.

The ACLU was tagged with the responsibility of educating the wider public and legislators about capital punishment. But at a time when public support for the death penalty was falling to record lows in the mid-1960s, the ACLU was poorly positioned to take advantage of the public's change of heart or the political opening presented by the Goldberg dissent and the LDF's new strategy. Internal dissent about whether the death penalty constituted a civil liberties violation, regardless of how it was administered by the criminal justice system, prohibited the ACLU from officially taking a stance against capital punishment until 1965.[27] Even after the

20 Meltsner, *Cruel and Unusual*, 107–10.

21 Jack Greenberg, *Crusaders in the Courts: How a Dedicated Band of Lawyers Fought for the Civil Rights Revolution* (New York: Basic Books, 1994), 284. See also the remarks by Anthony Amsterdam in Bertram H. Wolfe, *Pileup on Death Row* (Garden City, NY: Doubleday, 1973), 244–5.

22 Aryeh Neier, *Only Judgment: The Limits of Litigation in Social Change* (Middletown, CT: Wesleyan University Press, 1982), 197.

23 Muller, "The Legal Defense Fund's Capital Punishment Campaign," 166–7.

24 Michael Meltsner, quoted in Muller, "The Legal Defense Fund's Capital Punishment Campaign," 181. See also Neier, *Only Judgment*, 209.

25 Muller, "The Legal Defense Fund's Capital Punishment Campaign," 178.

26 Muller, "The Legal Defense Fund's Capital Punishment Campaign," 177–9.

27 Norman Dorsen, *Frontiers of Civil Liberties* (New York: Pantheon Books, 1968), 278; and Roger E. Schwed, *Abolition and Capital Punishment: The United States' Judicial, Political and Moral Barometer* (New York: AMS Press, Inc., 1983), 113.

rights organization formally repudiated the death penalty, some disgruntled affiliates remained unreliable allies.[28] Moreover, from the mid-1960s to the mid-1970s, the ACLU was preoccupied with other civil liberties issues stemming from the civil rights movement, the Vietnam War, and Watergate.[29] And from the early- to mid-1970s, a financial crisis and organizational disarray gripped the ACLU.[30] Lawyers active in the ACLU played critical legal roles in certain capital cases, but the ACLU did not enter the battle against the death penalty in a politically significant way until much later. Neither did the NAACP, which was permitted to engage in lobbying (unlike the tax-exempt LDF).[31]

If measured by the number of executions and some of the early judicial decisions, the legal campaign appeared to be having great success. This further reduced pressure on the Fund and ACLU to develop an effective political campaign. The number of executions dwindled from twenty-one in 1963 to seven in 1965 to just two in 1967.[32] In 1968, for the first time in U.S. history, not a single person was executed. For nearly a decade thereafter, no more executions took place as the constitutionality of capital punishment was tested in the courts and hundreds of prisoners piled up on death row. In 1968, abolitionists won what appeared at the time to be a major victory when the Supreme Court ruled in *Witherspoon v. Illinois* that death-qualified juries were unconstitutional.[33]

Whereas the LDF and the ACLU succeeded in raising the political profile of capital punishment, they were less successful in reframing the issue so as to shore up public opposition to the death penalty at a time when public sentiment on capital punishment was quite fluid. The absence of an organized pro-death penalty movement or organized public sentiment in favor of capital punishment reduced pressure on the LDF and the ACLU to develop a politically significant abolitionist movement that stretched beyond the courtroom. Although a number of public officials and politicians certainly favored capital punishment, their support was muted. They did not utter bloodthirsty statements advocating more executions, nor did they promote the death penalty as a panacea for society's ills.[34]

Indeed, at the time, there were some notable retreats among leading conservative hardliners and proponents of the death penalty, and in some surprising parts of the country. J. Edgar Hoover, the longtime director of the FBI and for years one of the most forceful proponents of capital punishment, appeared to be abandoning

28 Dorsen, *Frontiers of Civil Liberties*, 270–8; and Schwed, *Abolition and Capital Punishment*, 113.

29 Samuel Walker, *In Defense of American Liberties: A History of the ACLU*, 2nd ed. (Carbondale, IL: Southern Illinois University Press, 1999), chaps. 12, 13, and 14.

30 Walker, *In Defense of American Liberties*, 327–40.

31 Haines, *Against Capital Punishment*, 49–50; and Neier, *Only Judgment*, 198, 207, and 212.

32 *National Prisoner Statistics Report: Capital Punishment, 1984* (Washington, DC: Bureau of Justice Statistics, n.d.), 12, in Haines, *Against Capital Punishment*, Table 2, 12.

33 State trial courts subsequently learned how to circumvent this decision, which appeared to prohibit excluding potential jurors from serving who expressed any qualms about the death penalty.

34 Meltsner, *Cruel and Unusual*, 55–6.

the deterrence argument for the first time. In the FBI's annual report in 1968, Hoover conceded that murder is basically a "social problem" that is not affected by punishment.[35] Governors and other state officials became increasingly reluctant to carry out executions, even in the South and in capital punishment strongholds in the North like Pennsylvania. In the most notable example, segregationist Governor Lester Maddox of Georgia went through semantic contortions to justify commuting the death sentence of William Patrick Clark, a twenty-nine-year-old man scheduled to be executed in April 1967.[36]

Views about capital punishment had not ossified even among some of its most outspoken proponents. Ronald Reagan ran for governor of California on a strident pro-death penalty platform in 1966. True to his promise, shortly after taking office, he was determined to carry out the April 1967 execution of Aaron Mitchell, California's first execution in four years. Yet even after the LDF and other abolitionists suffered a major legal setback in May 1971 with the Supreme Court's decisions in *McGautha v. California* and *Crampton v. Ohio*, Reagan followed the lead of other governors and vowed to take a wait-and-see approach to resuming executions in California as the constitutionality of the death penalty continued to hang in the balance.[37] No one else was executed in California during his tenure as governor. Even the Nixon administration appeared hesitant to jump into the fray about capital punishment. President Richard Nixon's first solicitor general, Erwin Griswold, defended the constitutionality of the death penalty in oral arguments as an *amicus curiae* in *McGautha* and *Crampton*, but only after being invited to participate by the Court.[38]

The *McGautha* and *Crampton* decisions were major defeats for the LDF and other abolitionists. The Court was not persuaded by claims that capital punishment violated the Fourteenth Amendment's due process protections. It ruled that juries and judges should have absolute discretion to impose the death penalty in capital cases and could be trusted to act responsibly.[39] It also determined that juries were not required to decide the punishment at a separate proceeding after the trial that determined guilt or innocence, thus giving its blessing to so-called unitary trials.[40]

The *McGautha* and *Crampton* defeats prompted the LDF, ACLU, and other abolitionists to reaffirm their legal strategy of blocking all executions. They also supported a bill in Congress imposing a two-year moratorium on executions and agreed to put more pressure on state executives to grant more commutations.[41] But these organizations were either unwilling or unable to put considerable resources

35 Wolfe, *Pileup on Death Row*, 67–8 and 301.

36 Wolfe, *Pileup on Death Row*, 29–30.

37 Meltsner, *Cruel and Unusual*, 245.

38 Lee Epstein and Joseph F. Kobylka, *The Supreme Court and Legal Change: Abortion and the Death Penalty* (Chapel Hill, NC: The University of North Carolina Press, 1992), 67 and 131.

39 James R. Acker, "The Death Penalty: A 25-Year Retrospective and a Perspective on the Future," *Criminal Justice Review* 21.2 (Autumn 1996), 143.

40 Acker, "The Death Penalty," 142–4.

41 Epstein and Kobylka, *The Supreme Court and Legal Change*, 69.

into the political leg of this strategy, for the reasons discussed earlier. A month after the *McGautha* and *Crampton* decisions, the Supreme Court announced it would review several cases involving the constitutionality of capital punishment that became collectively known as *Furman v. Georgia*. It also signaled that the Constitution's ban on cruel and unusual punishment would be the primary entre point to decide the constitutionality of capital punishment.

To sum up, as late as 1971, capital punishment was not a signature issue for law-and-order conservatives. Thus the political arena offered abolitionists some leeway to frame the issue. But accustomed to fighting and winning in the courts and bereft of the resources necessary to wage a wider political campaign, the abolitionists focused, as they had for decades, on the legal arena instead. Although they did not face intense organized opposition, they were constrained by how the courts had framed issues related to the death penalty and crime and punishment in the past. The courts repeatedly had rejected arguments that the death penalty was imposed in a racially discriminatory manner. They also were not persuaded by data challenging the alleged deterrent value of capital punishment. In short, the Supreme Court established important parameters for attacking and defending capital punishment in these earlier years that would subsequently help lock in the carceral state, as discussed further.

FURMAN V. GEORGIA AND PUBLIC SENTIMENT

After the *Furman* decision in 1972, the death penalty catapulted to the center of debates over crime and punishment in the United States and remained stubbornly lodged there, deforming U.S. penal policies and disfiguring U.S. society in ways not seen in other developed countries.[42] Select politicians and public officials began in earnest to exploit this issue for electoral or ideological reasons. They made their moves at a time when capital punishment was already firmly anchored in the judicial process. Groups and organizations likely to oppose the death penalty remained focused on the courts. This impeded the development of a wider political movement against the death penalty that could effectively exploit the mid-1960s trough in public support for capital punishment. But it did more than that.

The legal debate over the death penalty developed in ways that bolstered the vast expansion of the penal system. It helped conservative forces capture the debate over the death penalty and penal policy, unimpeded by popular political resistance. It was not just that the Supreme Court did not close the door once and for all on capital punishment with its *Furman* decision in 1972, or that it cleared the way

42 Michael A. Mello, *Dead Wrong: A Death Row Lawyer Speaks Out Against Capital Punishment* (Madison, WI: University of Wisconsin Press, 1997), 12; and Franklin E. Zimring and Gordon Hawkins, *Capital Punishment and the American Agenda* (Cambridge: Cambridge University Press), 164.

for the resumption of executions with the *Gregg* decision in 1976. A whole host of subsequent legal decisions related to capital punishment bolstered the carceral state in subtle but profound ways. They created a discourse around capital punishment that reinforced wider punitive tendencies that were then surfacing and helped them take root. Specifically, the battle over capital punishment, initially confined to the courts, helped enshrine in society a view that popular sentiments and passions were paramount in the formulation of penal policy. Furthermore, the judicial decisions and legal arguments involving capital punishment over the last three decades or so helped transform the death penalty into "the ultimate form of public victim recognition," something it had never been in U.S. history.[43]

From an immediate legal and legislative perspective, the most noteworthy aspects of *Furman* were how it vacated more than 600 death sentences and spurred a mad dash by dozens of state legislatures to rewrite their capital punishment statutes to meet the objections the Court had raised to standardless sentencing. From a political point of view, the ruling is significant in how the fiercest opponents and proponents of capital punishment reframed the issue in similar terms. The dissenting justices denied that the American public had repudiated the death penalty. The LDF and other abolitionists contended that it had. In doing so, both proponents and opponents ended up legitimizing popular sentiment as an important factor in the making of penal policy. The battle then began to hinge on how to measure, shape, and interpret public sentiment on capital punishment and other penal policies.

This was a dramatic reframing of the death penalty issue, which had wider political repercussions. It essentially legitimized public sentiment as the main political terrain on which capital punishment would be contested and on which the carceral state would be constructed and legitimized over the coming decades. It contributed to a collapse between the state and society in the making of penal policy not seen in Western Europe or Canada. Furthermore, by failing to close the door once and for all on the death penalty by declaring it unconstitutional under all circumstances, the Supreme Court ensured that the courts would remain an important battleground for capital punishment. Judicial decisions involving the death penalty would continue to have wider repercussions for the development of penal policy and the politics of punishment.

Even though the *Furman* decision was quite muddled, the fiercest opponents and proponents of capital punishment did agree on one thing: Public sentiment was critical in determining the constitutionality of capital punishment. Events unfolding in California in the months leading up to the *Furman* decision bolstered this view and set an important context for how *Furman* would be interpreted. A month after

43 Jonathan Simon, "Violence, Vengeance and Risk: Capital Punishment in the Near-Liberal State," unpublished manuscript, 1997, quoted in Austin Sarat, *When the State Kills: Capital Punishment and the American Condition* (Princeton, NJ: Princeton University Press, 2001), 19.

oral arguments in *Furman*, the California Supreme Court ruled in a decisive and surprising six-to-one verdict in February 1972 that capital punishment violated the state constitution's ban on "cruel or unusual punishment." The California court then vacated the death sentences of the 107 prisoners on the state's death row. In *People v. Anderson*, Chief Justice Donald R. Wright, a Reagan appointee, argued for the majority that "evolving standards of decency" were the yardstick by which to measure cruel or unusual punishment under the California constitution. He singled out the infrequency of executions as evidence that an informed public, when confronted with the reality of capital punishment, repudiates it.[44]

The California decision likely did not change any minds on the U.S. Supreme Court, but it did alter the political context in which *Furman* would be received and interpreted four months later.[45] The peculiarities of California's initiative and referendum process assured that the death penalty would not die with the California Supreme Court. In May 1972, the California State Senate rejected a proposal by Republican State Senator George Deukmejian for legislation authorizing a referendum on a constitutional amendment to reinstate the death penalty. After this defeat, California's attorney general Evelle Younger, backed by the correctional officers and other law enforcement groups, set out with the blessing of Governor Reagan to collect the necessary 500,000-plus signatures to put the issue of a constitutional amendment on the November 1972 ballot. Under Younger's leadership, police stations, sheriffs' offices, fire stations, correctional facilities, and even city halls were turned into headquarters for the massive petition drive in a remarkable use of public resources for political ends.[46] That November, voters approved by a two-to-one margin the proposal to amend the state constitution to restore to the California legislature the power to enact death penalty statutes.[47]

California's institutional environment with its initiative and referendum option gave the death penalty new life and set an important context for the political and popular interpretation of *Furman*. This institutional context, together with the specific way capital punishment had developed largely in the courts over the years, provided combustible fuel for penal populism. As a result, pro-death penalty sentiment ignited among political elites after *Furman*, and President Nixon became a key national instigator of it. Up until then, Nixon had run hot and cold on capital punishment. He pushed successfully in 1970 for a federal death penalty statute in cases of bombings that resulted in death, and in March 1972 made a speech in which he advocated death for drug pushers.[48] Yet he absented his administration from some

44 Meltsner, *Cruel and Unusual*, 281–2.

45 Epstein and Kobylka, *The Supreme Court and Legal Change*, 77; and Banner, *The Death Penalty*, 260–4.

46 Peter Petrakis, "The Death Penalty Initiative," *San Francisco Bay Guardian*, October 4, 1972, in Wolfe, *Pileup on Death Row*, 409.

47 Meltsner, *Cruel and Unusual*, 281–7 and 306; Wolfe, *Pileup on Death Row*, 390–2 and 408–9.

48 Wolfe, *Pileup on Death Row*, 392; Meltsner, *Cruel and Unusual*, 212.

of the key death penalty cases to come before the Supreme Court. Remarkably, the Nixon administration was not involved in litigating *Furman*.[49]

Even after the Supreme Court announced its intentions in June 1971 to rule on the constitutionality of capital punishment in *Furman*, pro-death penalty sentiment remained muted. No organized groups filed *amicus curiae* briefs in favor of retention. Of the twelve *amicus* briefs submitted during the litigation of the group of cases consolidated under *Furman v. Georgia*, all were in support of abolition.[50] The few organizations that were outspoken proponents of the death penalty were marginal groups whose national stature paled compared with abolitionist organizations like the LDF and the ACLU.[51] The main organized support for the death penalty consisted of state attorneys from California, Texas, and Georgia, the states at the forefront of litigating these cases.

The five-to-four *Furman* decision has been described as "precarious, vague, and temporizing."[52] Comprised of nine separate opinions totaling 243 pages in length, it was the longest decision to date in the history of the Supreme Court.[53] Whereas two of the justices viewed the death penalty as unconstitutional under all circumstances, the three others who comprised the majority only agreed that capital punishment as then imposed violated the Constitution. In an apparent reversal of *McGautha* and *Crampton*, they suggested that the unbounded discretion that juries exercised in capital trials was unconstitutional. In their view, standardless juries violated the Eighth Amendment prohibition on cruel and unusual punishment. In the famous words of Justice Potter Stewart, death sentences are "cruel and unusual" because they are "wantonly and freakishly" imposed in a way that is no more meaningful or rational than the random striking of lightning.[54]

The four dissenters were more united in their views. They argued that the Court's decision severely encroached on legislative prerogatives. Chief Justice Warren Burger suggested that state legislators might successfully write new statutes to satisfy the Court's objections, but in private conceded later that "[t]here will never be another execution in this country."[55] Taking direct aim at the central argument of the LDF, the lead counsel in the case, the dissenting justices denied that the American public had repudiated capital punishment. They disputed the LDF's claim that the death penalty "is a cruel and unusual punishment because it affronts the

49 Epstein and Kobylka, *The Supreme Court and Legal Change*, 131.

50 Bedau, *Death Is Different*, 142.

51 Bedau, *Death Is Different*, 142.

52 Bedau, *Death Is Different*, 166.

53 Mark Costanzo, *Just Revenge: Costs and Consequences of the Death Penalty* (New York: St. Martin's Press, 1997), 20.

54 *Furman v. Georgia*, 408 U.S. 238 1972, 309–10, in Raymond Paternoster, *Capital Punishment in America* (New York: Lexington Books, 1991), 55.

55 Bob Woodward and Scott Armstrong, *The Brethren* (New York: Simon and Schuster, 1979), 219, quoted in Epstein and Kobylka, *The Supreme Court and Legal Change*, 80.

basic standards of decency of contemporary society" and is at odds with "enlightened public opinion."[56]

The day after the *Furman* verdict was handed down, Nixon took the lead in denouncing it at a press conference. Reiterating what Burger suggested in his dissent, Nixon declared "the holding of the Court must not be taken . . . to rule out capital punishment."[57] Nixon did not provide any details on what types of new state or federal death penalty statutes might satisfy the objections the Court had raised in *Furman*. His comments were significant nonetheless because he was the first major public figure to claim publicly that *Furman* had not abolished capital punishment once and for all.[58]

The political and legislative response to *Furman* was "fast, furious," and "bordered on hysteria."[59] Lester Maddox, then Georgia's lieutenant governor, characterized the decision as "a license for anarchy, rape, murder."[60] Governor Nelson Rockefeller, who in 1965 signed legislation repealing capital punishment for most offenses in New York State, announced in 1973 that he was seriously considering bringing back the death penalty for major drug dealers.[61] Ten states quickly enacted mandatory death penalty statutes, and twenty-five others adopted some form of "guided discretion" death penalty legislation.[62]

The *Furman* decision galvanized such a powerful political backlash not merely because the Supreme Court ruled that the death penalty (as then practiced) was unconstitutional, nor because the abolitionists were ill-prepared to battle a political backlash they did not see coming. Rather, over the years, capital punishment had gotten lodged in the judicial process and framed in a way that made public sentiment a central issue. California's *People v. Anderson* seared public sentiment into the capital punishment debate in the months preceding the *Furman* decision. Reagan, Nixon, and other hardliners who chose to seize this moment to make an issue of capital punishment were so successful because abolitionists in the United States ended up having to tread a very slippery slope of public opinion that their counterparts elsewhere did not have to contend with. Capital punishment was abolished in Canada and Western Europe in spite of public opinion, not because of public opinion, as Andrew Hammel shows in his contribution to this volume. In the U.S. case, abolitionists had to prove that public sentiment had turned decisively against capital punishment – a very tall order.

56 Brief for Petitioner, *Aiken* [sic] v. *California* (1971), in Greenberg, *Cases and Materials on Judicial Process and Social Change*, 478 and 480–1.

57 "Transcript of President's News Conference Emphasizing Foreign Affairs," June 30, 1972, quoted in Epstein and Kobylka, *The Supreme Court and Legal Change*, 84.

58 Epstein and Kobylka, *The Supreme Court and Legal Change*, 84.

59 Acker, "The Death Penalty," 145; and Zimring and Hawkins, *Capital Punishment and the American Agenda*, 38.

60 Meltsner, *Cruel and Unusual*, 290.

61 Jerry M. Flint, "States on the Move," *The New York Times*, March 11, 1973, 1.

62 Acker, "The Death Penalty," 145.

GREGG, DETERRENCE, AND PUBLIC OPINION

The post-*Furman* strategy of the abolitionists consisted of three parts: a lobbying campaign led by the ACLU, LDF challenges to the new death penalty statutes in the courts, and the incorporation of new social scientific data on deterrence, discrimination, and public opinion into their legal briefs.[63] For the reasons discussed earlier, this was treacherous terrain to battle capital punishment. The ACLU was ill-equipped to lead the campaign. The LDF risked becoming overloaded by the number of new cases. The Supreme Court had a history of not being receptive to racial discrimination claims regarding the death penalty. As state legislatures briskly passed dozens of new death penalty statutes, as the number of defendants receiving the death penalty increased to record levels, and as public opinion polls showed that support for capital punishment was the highest in two decades, it was hard to make a convincing case that the public had rejected the death penalty.

Opponents of the death penalty were also handicapped because another weapon that had proved so powerful elsewhere – challenges to the deterrence argument – was neutralized. Capital punishment, after simmering as an issue for decades, emerged as a national issue in the early 1970s at just the moment when the number of homicides was escalating in the United States. Thus it became easy for supporters of capital punishment to blame the de facto moratorium on executions for the rising homicide rate that was a source of growing public angst. This view held great sway, despite enormous social scientific evidence to the contrary. Testimony contending that *Furman* had to be neutralized or else the country risked sinking deeper into a morass of violent crime dominated U.S. Senate hearings in 1973 on a bill to reintroduce the federal death penalty.[64] Studies showing the death penalty had no real deterrent effect on murder or other serious offenses did not take center stage the way they did in Britain or Canada because they did not have the imprimatur of the state, among other reasons. In the United States, no major public or private funding was made available to study capital punishment's deterrence effect.[65] Moreover, although most expert opinion agreed that the death penalty was not a deterrent, most major crime-related scholarly and academic organizations in the United States did not invest significant resources in pushing for abolition.[66] By contrast, nearly every criminologist in Britain joined the abolitionist campaign and put his or her expert credentials in the service of liberal reform.[67]

63 Epstein and Kobylka, *The Supreme Court and Legal Change*, 91.
64 Hugo Adam Bedau, *The Courts, the Constitution, and Capital Punishment* (Lexington, MA: Lexington Books, 1977), 98.
65 Bedau, *Death Is Different*, 143.
66 Bedau, *Death Is Different*, 142.
67 David Garland and Richard Sparks, "Criminology, Social Theory, and the Challenge of Our Times," in *Criminology and Social Theory*, ed. David Garland and Richard Sparks (Oxford: Oxford University Press, 2000), 11.

In the United States, private studies showing that the death penalty had no real deterrent value had to compete with a cacophony of other arguments about the death penalty and public sentiment. For the first time in many decades, the anti-death penalty movement had to contend with growing elite and organized support for capital punishment. As mentioned earlier, law enforcement organizations were on the front lines of California's ballot referendum in 1972. Later that same year, the National Association of Attorneys General voted thirty-two-to-one in support of federal capital punishment legislation to address the defects identified in the *Furman* decision so that executions could resume.[68] The death penalty was also starting to become an issue for some victims' rights advocates. Frank G. Carrington, a leading spokesperson for the nascent victims' movement, charged abolitionists with having "an utter disregard for the victims of crime."[69] New York Mayor Ed Koch declared: "When the killer lives, the victim dies twice."[70]

Although some organized support for the death penalty was emerging, there was still no "grand mobilization" by interest groups "to change the context of litigation on this issue."[71] The most significant shift toward active support of capital punishment in the years immediately after *Furman* came from elites, in particular the White House, as the new death penalty statutes were challenged in the courts. Attorney general designate Edward Levi extolled the deterrent value of the death penalty in January 1975.[72] Two months later, Robert H. Bork, solicitor general under Nixon and then President Gerald Ford, filed a lengthy *amicus curiae* brief supportive of capital punishment. In a sharp reversal, the federal government was now asserting that it had a "federal" interest in capital punishment, where previously it had viewed the death penalty as largely a state concern.[73]

In January 1976, the Supreme Court issued an order to review five capital punishment cases based on the new death penalty statutes. As in 1972, the main legal proponents of the new statutes were state attorneys, but this time the White House aggressively sided with them. Instead of refuting the LDF point by point as they had in the past, the state attorneys went on the offensive and took various approaches in each of the cases, with little overlap between them. One exception was that they and Bork all denied that "evolving standards of decency" had turned against the death penalty. They presented evidence that, in their view, proved that public sentiment resoundingly supported capital punishment. In his brief, Bork affirmed the deterrent value of the death penalty, relying on an unpublished study that has since been

68 Meltsner, *Cruel and Unusual*, 308.

69 Frank G. Carrington, *The Victims* (New Rochelle, NY: Arlington House, 1975), 182.

70 Ian Gray and Moira Stanley, "Introduction," in *A Punishment in Search of a Crime: Americans Speak Out Against the Death Penalty*, ed. Ian Gray and Moira Stanley (New York: Avon Books, 1989), 16.

71 Epstein and Kobylka, *The Supreme Court and Legal Change*, 307.

72 Linda Charlton, "Attorney General Designate Asserts Death Penalty, If Enforced, Is Deterrent," *The New York Times*, January 28, 1975, in Epstein and Kobylka, *The Supreme Court and Legal Challenge*, 97.

73 Epstein and Kobylka, *The Supreme Court and Legal Challenge*, 97.

widely discredited. The deterrence issue appeared to have great sway with some of the justices. After presenting statistics from a 1973 FBI report documenting the escalating murder rate in the United States, Justice Lewis Powell suggested during oral arguments for *Gregg* in March 1976, "It is perfectly obvious from these figures that we need some way to deter the slaughter of Americans." Powell then awarded Bork five extra minutes to make his points about deterrence.[74]

On July 2, 1976, in a seven-to-two decision in the three cases grouped together as *Gregg v. Georgia*, the Supreme Court essentially reinstated capital punishment. The *Gregg* decision affirmed that the new "guided discretion" statutes enacted by the states in the wake of *Furman* were constitutional.[75] The majority ruled that imposition of the death penalty under these new statutes did not constitute cruel and unusual punishment and was not an affront to evolving standards of decency.[76] It also took the controversial position that the death penalty served a legitimate government function of deterrence and retribution. That same day, in a five-to-four decision in two other cases, the Court struck down "mandatory" death penalty statutes in *Woodson v. North Carolina* and *Roberts v. Louisiana*.

The *Gregg* case reaffirmed the centrality of public opinion in the making of penal policy. It also drew public attention to the deterrence issue at an inauspicious movement – when escalating homicide rates coincided with the nation's de facto moratorium on executions. Sophisticated statistical studies proving the absence of any deterrent effect had great difficulty competing with these compelling facts on the ground and, as a result, were less effective in restraining penal populism. As in a number of capital punishment cases before and since, the justices demonstrated in *Gregg* that they paid close attention to public opinion polls, to the dismay of Justice Thurgood Marshall. In his dissent in *Gregg*, Marshall argued that the proper yardstick should be "the opinions of an *informed* citizenry."[77]

LIFE, DEATH, VICTIMS, AND OFFENDERS AFTER GREGG

After *Gregg*, executions resumed, first hesitantly and then with matter-of-fact regularity. U.S. politicians and public officials increasingly expressed their enthusiasm for executing their own citizens, including juvenile offenders (something done almost nowhere else in the world) and the mentally retarded. The *Gregg* decision spurred abolitionist groups to mobilize. Several new groups dedicated to battling the death penalty were born immediately in its wake, and the human rights organization

74 Epstein and Kobylka, *The Supreme Court and Legal Change*, 109.

75 Although these statutes were not identical, they generally shared some essential features, including standards to narrow the range of offenses punishable by death, creation of bifurcated guilt and penalty trials, and mandated review of capital convictions by appellate courts. Acker, "The Death Penalty," 145.

76 Epstein and Kobylka, *The Supreme Court and Legal Change*, 113.

77 Marshall dissent in *Gregg v. Georgia*, as excerpted in Greenberg, *Cases and Materials on Judicial Process and Social Change*, 628. Emphasis in the original.

Amnesty International launched a major initiative against capital punishment in the United States.

As executions resumed with the killing of Gary Gilmore in 1977, the growing backlog of prisoners on death row "created a serious crisis in legal representation, overwhelming the resources of the ACLU and the LDF, the only two organizations providing any regular assistance."[78] But the *Gregg* decision did not immediately prompt the expected "bloodbath." Executions resumed with a trickle, not a gush. Over the next half-dozen years, the Supreme Court upheld death sentences in just two cases while vacating capital punishment sentences in fourteen others as it put some important restrictions on the exercise of the death penalty.

From around 1983 onward, however, the Supreme Court began a hasty retreat from involvement in many of the procedural details of the administration of the death penalty. The number of executions began to escalate rapidly, going from two in 1979 to five in 1983 to almost one hundred in 1999.[79] In the mid-1980s, Chief Justice Warren Burger began publicly complaining that the appeals process in capital cases was too protracted, making it virtually impossible to execute anyone. This prompted other justices and prominent public officials to comment publicly on capital punishment and drew public attention to the growing backlog of prisoners on death row and the big increase in the average time from sentencing to execution.[80] At the same time, the unfounded idea that imposition of the death penalty would bring about "closure" and thus provide some psychological comfort to victims' families was gaining ground.[81] All this fueled public concern that the courts were bending over backwards for capital defendants while denying victims and their families justice.

A series of decisions involving victim impact statements bolstered this concern. In the immediate aftermath of *Gregg*, the courts accorded defendants in capital cases expansive rights to present mitigating evidence. As a consequence, many defense attorneys in capital cases sought to portray the defendant as a sympathetic or tragic figure, which had the effect of overshadowing the grief and grievances of victims' families.[82] The 1976 *Woodson* decision was particularly important for this reframing of capital punishment. In vacating North Carolina's mandatory death penalty statute, the justices had affirmed that capital punishment proceedings must

78 Walker, *In Defense of American Liberties*, 359.

79 "Executions by Year," Death Penalty Information Center, http://www.deathpenaltyinfo.org/executions-year (accessed January 30, 2010).

80 Epstein and Kobylka, *The Supreme Court and Legal Change*, 122. For example, in 1991, President H. W. Bush lamented the lack of "a workable death penalty – which is to say a real death penalty." George H. W. Bush, "Remarks at Attorney General's Crime Summit: President Bush: 'Take Back the Streets,'" *The NOVA Newsletter* 15.3 (1991): 1–2.

81 Susan Bandes, "When Victims Seek Closure: Forgiveness, Vengeance, and the Role of Government," *Fordham Urban Law Journal* 27.5 (June 2000): 1599–606; and Margaret Vandiver, "The Impact of the Death Penalty on the Families of Homicide Victims and of Condemned Prisoners," in *America's Experiment with Capital Punishment*: 613–45.

82 Austin Sarat, "Narrative Strategy and Death Penalty Advocacy," *Harvard Civil Rights-Civil Liberties Law Review* 31 (1996): 353–81.

be "individualized" so as to permit capital defendants to present mitigating evidence. This provided a platform for the *Lockett v. Ohio* decision two years later in which the Court insisted that capital defendants be permitted to present as mitigating factors almost "any aspect" of their "character or record and any circumstances of the offense" that might serve as a "basis for a sentence less than death."[83]

In response, prosecutors and other state officials pushed to permit the introduction of victim impact evidence in the sentencing phase of capital trials. In *Booth v. Maryland* (1987) and *South Carolina v. Gathers* (1989), the Supreme Court ruled that victim impact statements were inadmissible. But in 1991, the Court reversed itself in *Payne v. Tennessee* and provided an opening for a dramatic reframing of capital punishment.[84] In the *Payne* decision, the court tried to put victims and defendants on a more equal footing, which served to reinforce the zero-sum view of victims and offenders that provides such powerful fuel for penal populism and that undergirded the ascendant victim rights' movement in the United States.[85]

Since *Payne*, at least twelve states have authorized victim impact statements in capital cases, creating the opportunity for the capital courtroom to be turned into a morality play that pits the good and virtuous victim against the evil, morally bankrupt or tragically flawed defendant, depending on whether you were for the prosecution or the defense.[86] The grief and grievances of victims' families soon became central to capital and noncapital criminal cases. The courtroom was not just a site to determine guilt and innocence in a particular case. It was transformed into a dramatic stage to magnify the suffering of all victims, the immorality that taints all offenders, and the fundamental antagonism between victims and offenders. In 1980, only a few jurisdictions permitted consideration of the impact of a crime on the victim in noncapital cases. By the late 1990s, nearly every state allowed victims to have input at sentencing and in parole decisions, and many permitted written and oral victim impact statements in noncapital cases.[87] In short, the constitutional politics of the death penalty and the politics of penal policy more broadly were transformed into "a contest to claim the status of victim," unlike in Canada and Western Europe.[88]

83 *Lockett v. Ohio* 438 U.S. 586 (1978), 606, quoted in Bedau, *Death Is Different*, 178.

84 Vivian Berger, "*Payne* and Suffering – A Personal Reflection and a Victim-Centered Critique," *Florida State University Law Review* 20 (1992): 21–65; and Sharon English, "It's Time for a Cam*Payne*," *The NOVA Newsletter* 15.9 (1991), 2.

85 For more on the development of the victims' rights movement, see Gottschalk, *The Prison and the Gallows*, chap. 4.

86 Charles F. Baird and Elizabeth E. McGinn, "Re-Victimizing the Victim: How Prosecutorial and Judicial Discretion Are Being Exercised to Silence Victims Who Oppose Capital Punishment," *Stanford Law and Policy Review* 15 (2004), 463.

87 National Organization for Victim Assistance, "NOVA's Mission, Purposes, Accomplishments, and Organizational Structure," http://www.trynova.org/victims/mission.html (accessed August 30, 2004).

88 Austin Sarat, "Capital Punishment as a Legal, Political, and Cultural Fact: An Introduction," in *The Killing State: Capital Punishment in Law, Politics, and Culture*, ed. Austin Sarat (New York: Oxford University Press, 1999), 14.

As a consequence, the death penalty was repersonalized. This was "a stark departure from the efforts begun with the privatization of executions in the 1830s to depersonalize the execution and to purify it from the polluting influences of individual emotion and desires."[89] This helped solidify a view of capital punishment and penal punishment more broadly as primarily a contest between victims and offenders in which the state's power to punish was an incidental issue, as were issues about how capital punishment discriminated against the poor and people of color. In such an atmosphere, it is not so surprising that the courts and legislators dismissed sophisticated studies demonstrating the racially discriminatory manner in which the death penalty is imposed and the absence of any deterrence effect. In the 1987 *McCleskey v. Kemp* decision, the Supreme Court rejected arguments based on social scientific evidence demonstrating how capital punishment is imposed in a racially discriminatory manner. Seven years later, in another major defeat for abolitionists, the U.S. Congress spurned the Racial Justice Act, which proposed that defendants in capital cases be allowed to use statistical evidence to demonstrate whether race was a major factor in the decision to invoke capital punishment.

THE COMPARATIVE POLITICS OF CAPITAL PUNISHMENT

Over the past few decades, the death penalty has undergone a transformation not only in the United States but in Europe and Canada as well. Whereas in the United States it has become more tightly tethered to the criminal justice process, in Europe it has been transformed from a national issue to an international human rights issue and has become a penetrating symbol of unbridled state power. In the immediate postwar decades, abolition of the death penalty in many Western European countries and Canada was largely a matter of the internal politics of individual countries. International or bilateral pressure was largely nonexistent. Over the past four decades or so, capital punishment has been transformed into a fundamental human rights issue in Europe. Even though tensions are rising between the newer and older member states of the Council of Europe and European Union over capital punishment, as Agata Fijalkowski elaborates in her chapter in this volume, these leading multilateral organizations still officially consider the death penalty an affront to international human rights standards. This great transformation obscures a startling and revealing fact about the successful wave of abolition that washed over Western Europe and Canada after World War II: Leading West European countries and Canada abolished the death penalty in the face of strong, sometimes overwhelming public support for its retention.[90]

89 Annulla Linders, "The Execution Spectacle and State Legitimacy: The Changing Nature of the American Execution Audience, 1833–1937," *Law & Society Review* 36.3 (2002), 647.

90 Richard J. Evans, *Rituals of Retribution: Capital Punishment in Germany, 1600–1987* (Oxford: Oxford University Press, 1996), 775–804; M. Mohrenschlager, "The Abolition of Capital Punishment in the Federal Republic of Germany: German Experiences," *Revue Internationale de Droit Pe'nal* 58

The very different institutional and political contexts help explain why Europe and Canada were able to abolish the death penalty in the face of considerable public support for its retention and why in the U.S. case the death penalty was reinstated and became a key building block of the carceral state. By the early 1960s, capital punishment was on a very different trajectory in the United States than elsewhere. On the surface, the United States appeared to be moving toward abolition, along with Britain and other European countries, as the number of executions fell and U.S. politicians did not perceive a substantial political risk to opposing capital punishment. Yet in the United States, the main assault on capital punishment in these years came as an outgrowth of the civil rights movement, as discussed earlier. The LDF got involved in capital punishment because blacks were disproportionately sentenced to death and killed by the state. Discussions of capital punishment thus naturally focused on the fairness of the criminal justice system to administer capital cases and, secondarily, on the apparent patterns of racial discrimination. As U.S. courts became more receptive to rights-based claims, they appeared to be a more promising venue to challenge the death penalty.

Western Europe was reckoning with a starkly different debate over capital punishment at this time. In the British case, the parameters for the brewing debate over capital punishment were set outside the judiciary because the courts did not emerge as a promising venue to challenge the death penalty based on procedural or other grounds. Differences in the British legal system and the absence of a highly developed network of rights-based groups or a powerful civil rights movement help explain why. Higher courts in Britain and elsewhere did not have to contend with a comparable rights revolution during the interwar years and after. In Britain, the appeals system continued to manifest "a marked reluctance to make itself too available" to criminal defendants.[91]

The final report of Britain's Royal Commission on Capital Punishment in 1953 was pivotal in defining the contours of the death penalty debate in Britain, as Timothy Kaufman-Osborn elaborates in this volume.[92] Arguably the most systematic study of capital punishment up to that point, the 500-plus-page report did not directly recommended abolition. However, it marshaled an impressive array of evidence

(1987): 509–19; Robert Jay Lifton and Greg Mitchell, *Who Owns Death? Capital Punishment, the American Conscience, and the End of Executions* (New York: HarperCollins, 2000), 247; Zimring, *The Contradictions of American Capital Punishment*, 16–17; David Chandler, *Capital Punishment in Canada: A Sociological Study of Repressive Law* (Toronto: McClelland and Stewart, 1976), chap. 2; Paul A. Rock, *A View From the Shadows: The Ministry of the Solicitor General of Canada and the Making of the Justice for Victims of Crime Initiative* (Clarendon Press: Oxford, 1986), 118–39; and Joshua Micah Marshall, "Death in Venice: Europe's Death-Penalty Elitism," *The New Republic*, July 31, 2000, 14.

91 Michael Zander, *Cases and Materials of the English Legal System*, 5th ed. (London: Weidenfeld & Nicolson, 1988), 559, cited in Epp, *The Rights Revolution*, 122.

92 Ernest Gowers, *A Life For a Life? The Problem of Capital Punishment* (London: Chatto and Windus, 1956), 42; and Bedau, *The Courts, the Constitution, and Capital Punishment*, 101.

against the death penalty. Doubts about the deterrent value of the death penalty were a major theme of the report, as were concerns about how capital punishment might violate notions of human dignity, as Kaufman-Osborn shows.[93] The report set up the terms of the debate over capital punishment in Britain for the next decade and a half, until the death penalty was formally abolished in 1969. It drew public attention to the weak evidence in support of the deterrence argument at a fortuitous time in Britain in the early 1950s, when public alarm about crime was not at a high pitch.[94] The report analyzed capital punishment primarily from the vantage point of its utility in public policy, thus anchoring it in the political rather than judicial realm. As such, capital punishment was defined as an issue for public servants other than judges to be the final arbiters of.

Canada underwent a similar effort. About the same time that *Furman* was being decided, Canada's Solicitor General's Office published a special report on the death penalty and deterrence that dismissed claims that the suspension of the death penalty in Canada in 1967 caused any increase in the homicide rate. This study was a successor to a mid-1950s study by a special parliamentary commission to investigate the death penalty that initiated some of the best research on capital punishment.[95]

In contrast to the United States, the national governments in Canada and Britain made considerable investments in publicly financed empirical research centering on disputed areas of fact in the administration of capital punishment, in particular the question of whether the death penalty deters homicide. Britain and Canada were more at liberty to focus single-mindedly on the deterrence issue and make that a central feature of the national debate because they did not have to contend with claims about how the death penalty was imposed in a racially discriminatory manner. Furthermore, concerns about crime were not yet on the rise in Britain when the deterrence question became prominent. As a consequence, the deterrence question took center stage in a more dispassionate context.

When Britain formally abolished capital punishment in 1969 after a five-year moratorium imposed in 1965, the public strongly disapproved of Parliament's actions.[96] Subsequently, public support for the death penalty did not diminish and may have

93 Royal Commission on Capital Punishment 1949–1953, *Report* (London: Her Majesty's Stationery Office, September 1953), 24. See also James B. Christoph, *Capital Punishment and British Politics: The British Movement to Abolish the Death Penalty, 1945–57* (Chicago: University of Chicago Press, 1962); and Gowers, *A Life For a Life?*, chap. 5.

94 Likewise in Germany, capital punishment was introduced at a time when concerns about crime were low. Thus it was harder to make a compelling argument that the death penalty was needed to stem violent crime. Indeed, the murder rate actually fell after promulgation of Germany's Basic Law, which abolished the death penalty. Evans, *Rituals of Retribution*, 798.

95 Chandler, *Capital Punishment in Canada*, 21–2 and 26–9; and Bedau, *The Courts, the Constitution, and Capital Punishment*, 101.

96 Lord Windlesham, *Responses to Crime: Penal Policy in the Making*, v. 2 (Oxford: Clarendon Press, 1993), 53–64, 82–90; and Christoph, *Capital Punishment and British Politics*.

hardened in the 1980s.[97] Although members of the Conservative Party, notably Margaret Thatcher, proclaimed their support for capital punishment, they did not expend much energy or political capital to get it restored even though the public strongly favored reinstatement, and the Police Federation pushed for it.[98] This sharply contrasts with the stampede by U.S. politicians and public officials in the 1980s and early 1990s to make more crimes punishable by death. As Sen. Joseph Biden (D-DE) grimly joked in 1992, Democratic get-tough proposals did "everything but hang people for jaywalking."[99]

CAPITAL PUNISHMENT AND THE FUTURE OF THE CARCERAL STATE

Over the past decade or so, the political and legal terrain surrounding capital punishment has shifted markedly. As more and more legal avenues were closed in the 1980s and 1990s, U.S. opponents of the death penalty were forced to pursue other strategies, spurring "political abolitionism." The emergence of the "innocence movement," with its dramatic focus on people wrongly condemned to death, has profoundly reframed the debate over capital punishment and arguably transformed public policy.[100] This may result in a final retreat for capital punishment but perhaps at the cost of bolstering the carceral state.

After numerous setbacks, abolitionists recently got the upper hand in the debate for the first time in more than a generation. More than a dozen states considered moratorium legislation. In 2000, Illinois became the first state to impose a moratorium, prompted by fears of executing the innocent. Two years later, Maryland followed suit. In June 2002, the Supreme Court surprised many foes of the death penalty by declaring that the execution of mentally handicapped offenders was unconstitutional, reversing the stance it took in 1989. Public support for the death penalty as measured by public opinion polls fell to its lowest point in decades, as did the number of people sentenced to death each year. The annual number of executions continued to plummet after hitting a high of ninety-eight in 1999. In early 2003, Republican Governor George Ryan decided to spare the lives of all 167 men and women on death row in Illinois in the wake of a steady stream of exonerations of innocent prisoners. Two years later, the Supreme Court declared it was unconstitutional to execute offenders who committed their crimes when they were younger

97 Windlesham, *Responses to Crime*, 417–18; and N. C. M. Elder, "Conclusion," in *Law and Order and British Politics*, ed. Philip Norton (Aldershot, England: Gower, 1984), 198.

98 Elder, "Conclusion," 198; Marshall, "Death in Venice"; and David Downes, *Contrasts in Tolerance: Post-War Penal Policy in The Netherlands and England and Wales* (Oxford: Clarendon Press, 1988), 70–71; and Windlesham, *Responses to Crime*, 89–90 and 417–19.

99 Guy Gugliotta, "Crime Bill a Hostage of Politics," *Washington Post*, August 5, 1992, A1.

100 Frank R. Baumgartner, Suzanna L. De Boef, and Amber E. Boydstun, *The Decline of the Death Penalty and the Discovery of Innocence* (Cambridge: Cambridge University Press, 2008).

than eighteen years of age. Recently, New Jersey and New Mexico abolished the death penalty, the first states to do so in more than two decades.

Based on these and other recent developments, many analysts predict that we may see the de jure – or even the de facto – abolition of capital punishment in the United States in this generation or the next.[101] But even as executions dwindle and public enthusiasm for meting out the ultimate sanction wanes, capital punishment will likely continue to cast a long shadow over U.S. penal policy and will remain inseparable from the broader politics of punishment.

By focusing so intently recently on the injustice of sending innocent people to death, abolitionists have illuminated just how fallible and unfair the criminal justice system is more generally. In this respect, the latest wave of abolitionism may be complementary to brewing efforts to roll back the carceral state. But as Carolyn S. Steiker and Jordan M. Steiker warn, recent legislative reforms, such as mandatory DNA preservation and testing and improved legal representation for capital offenders, could help legitimize the death penalty. These reforms offer "the appearance of much greater procedural regularity than they actually produce, thus inducing a false or exaggerated belief in the fairness of the entire system of capital punishment."[102] By extension, this could help bolster public confidence in the criminal justice system more widely.

The innocence movement has contributed – no doubt unwittingly – to rendering DNA results as the unimpeachable gold standard in determining guilt or innocence. This has helped forestall a wider public debate on the scientific limitations and problems with DNA testing.[103] Furthermore, civil rights objections to amassing huge DNA databases are not gaining much traction. Federal law now requires that DNA be collected from all federal convicts and arrestees, regardless of crime, and from anyone detained by a federal agency, including immigrants stopped by the Border Patrol. At least fifteen states now collect DNA upon arrest, and dozens of states require people convicted of certain misdemeanors, including shoplifting, to surrender a DNA sample.[104] Law enforcement officials are increasingly using DNA databases not just to search for "perfect matches" but also to look for partial matches that implicate family members. DNA databases are likely to magnify existing

[101] This is the consensus of most of the contributors to Charles J. Ogletree, Jr., and Austin Sarat, eds., *The Road to Abolition? The Future of Capital Punishment in the United States* (New York: New York University Press, 2009). For one of the exceptions, see Michael McCann and David T. Johnson, "Rocked but Still Rolling: The Enduring Institution of Capital Punishment in Historical and Comparative Perspective": 139–80.

[102] Carol S. Steiker and Jordan M. Steiker, "Should Abolitionists Support Legislative 'Reform' of the Death Penalty?" *Ohio State Law Journal* 63 (2002), 422.

[103] Simon A. Cole and Jay D. Aronson, "Blinded by Science on the Road to Abolition?" in *The Road to Abolition?*: 46–71.

[104] Ben Protess, "The DNA Debacle: How the Federal Government Botched the DNA Backlog Crisis," *Propublica*, May 5, 2009, http://www.propublica.org/special/dna-tracker-crime-labs-and-their-dna-backlog-724 (accessed January 29, 2010).

racial disparities in the criminal justice and penal systems because of the enormous racial disparities in how particular crimes are classified and punished (the crack-powder cocaine disparity being the best known example), expansive policing and prosecutorial discretion about which crimes to pursue (white-collar crimes versus street-corner drug sales), and racial profiling by individual police officers.[105]

Today's "obsessive focus" on the innocent, estimated to comprise anywhere from 1 percent to one-third of the death-row population, has overshadowed the wider question of what constitutes justice for the guilty housed on death row and elsewhere in the carceral state.[106] The number of people sentenced to death and executed has fallen sharply but at the cost of a huge spike in life sentences, also known as "the other death penalty." The promotion of life in prison without the possibility of parole (LWOP) as an alternative to capital punishment by leading abolitionists, most notably Sister Helen Prejean, author of *Dead Man Walking*, and former New York governor Mario Cuomo, appears to have legitimized the greater use of life sentences, even for noncapital crimes. Prior to 1974, LWOP was used sparingly. Today, forty-nine states have some form of LWOP on the books, up from sixteen in the mid-1990s.[107] One out of eleven people in prison in the United States is serving a life sentence, and about one-third of these lifers have LWOP sentences.[108] The total life sentenced population in the United States is about 141,000 people – about twice the size of the *entire* incarcerated population in Japan. Some abolitionists helped normalize a sanction that, like the death penalty, is way out of line with human rights and sentencing norms in other developed countries. Many European countries do not permit LWOP, and those that do use it sparingly. In much of Western Europe, a "life" sentence typically amounts to a dozen years or so, as it once did in practice in many U.S. states.

Life sentences are like a death in slow motion for many prisoners, causing great mental and sometimes great physical distress. Offenders sentenced to life often have fewer legal resources to challenge their sentences because they are not entitled to

105 Michael T. Risher, "Racial Disparities in Databanking of DNA Profiles," GeneWatch, http://www.councilforresponsiblegenetics.org/GeneWatch/GeneWatchPage.aspx?pageId=204 (accessed January 30, 2010); and Jeffrey Rosen, "Genetic Surveillance for All," *Slate*, http://www.slate.com/id/2213958/pagenum/all/ (accessed January 29, 2010), March 17, 2009.

106 David Feige, "The Dark Side of Innocence," *The New York Times Magazine*, June 15, 2003, 15. The 1 percent figure comes from David R. Dow, "The Problem of 'Innocence'," in *Machinery of Death: The Reality of America's Death Penalty Regime*, ed. David R. Dow and Mark Dow (New York: Routledge, 2002), 5. For higher estimates, see Gordon P. Waldo and Raymond Paternoster, "Tinkering With the Machinery of Death: The Failure of a Social Experiment," in *Punishment and Social Control*, 312.

107 Robert M. Bohm, "The Economic Costs of Capital Punishment: Past, Present, and Future," in *America's Experiment with Capital Punishment*, 591; and Ashley Nellis and Ryan S. King, "No Exit: The Expanding Use of Life Sentences in America (Washington, DC: The Sentencing Project, July 2009).

108 This is a very conservative estimate of the number of people who will spend the rest of their lives in prison. It does not include so-called basketball sentences that exceed a natural life span (for example, a sentence requiring 90 years served before becoming eligible for parole). Nellis and King, "No Exit," 2–3.

the automatic appeals process available to prisoners on death row. Generally, the Supreme Court has been very supportive of life sentences. In *Schick v. Reed* (1974), it dismissed any notion that LWOP was unconstitutional.[109] In *Harmelin v. Michigan*, it ruled that LWOP sentences do not require the same "super due process" procedures mandated in capital punishment cases.[110] Thus, LWOP has become cheaper and easier to mete out than a death sentence.[111] This has become an acceptable sentence not only for murder, but also for a wide variety of other crimes, some of them quite trivial, as evidenced by the popularity of "three strikes" legislation. In *Lockyer v. Andrade* (2003), the Court affirmed two twenty-five-years-to-life sentences for a man in California whose third strike was the theft of $153 worth of videotapes intended as Christmas gifts for his nieces.

Over the past decade or so, what counts as evidence of "evolving standards of decency" in capital punishment cases has become a more contested issue on the Supreme Court. Some of the justices still hold to the blunt *Gregg*-era measures of public sentiment, notably state statutes and jury determinations.[112] But in two recent landmark decisions, *Atkins v. Virginia* in 2002 and *Roper v. Simmons* three years later, which banned the execution of mentally retarded individuals and juvenile offenders, respectively, some members of the Court appeared receptive to more refined measures of public sentiment in determining "evolving standards of decency." In *Atkins*, the majority acknowledged that although most states retained the death penalty for mentally retarded offenders, the "direction of change" among state legislatures was toward prohibition of the practice. In an important footnote, the majority also highlighted important nonlegislative barometers of public sentiment, including expert opinion from relevant professional organizations, the views of religious organizations, world opinion, and domestic public opinion polls.[113] In *Roper*, these alternative gauges of public sentiment were front and center in the majority opinion and not relegated to a footnote as the Court "invalidated a death penalty practice notwithstanding its authorization by a majority of death penalty states."[114] The introduction of these new barometers to gauge public sentiment in capital punishment cases could pry open new legal avenues to challenge disproportionate sentences in noncapital cases. It also might open up some political space for a more nuanced

[109] Julian H. Wright, Jr., "Life-without-parole: An Alternative to Death or Not Much of a Life at All?" *Vanderbilt Law Review* 43 (March 1990), 535–7; and Paternoster, *Capital Punishment in America*, 279.

[110] J. Mark Lane, "'Is There Life Without Parole?' A Capital Defendant's Right to a Meaningful Alternative Sentence," *Loyola (Los Angeles) Law Review* 26 (1992–93), 351–3.

[111] Bohm, "The Economic Costs of Capital Punishment," 591–2. In Texas, each death penalty case costs taxpayers on average $2.3 million, about three times the lifetime cost of imprisoning someone at the highest level of security. Richard C. Dieter, "Millions Misspent: What Politicians Don't Say about the High Costs of the Death Penalty," in *The Death Penalty in America: Current Controversies*, ed. Hugo Adam Bedau (New York: Oxford University Press, 1997), 402.

[112] Carol S. Steiker and Jordan M. Steiker, "The Beginning of the End?" in The Road to *Abolition?* 112.

[113] Steiker and Steiker, "The Beginning of the End?" 117.

[114] Steiker and Steiker, "The Beginning of the End?" 120.

discussion of what role public sentiment should play in the making of penal policy more generally. Both of these developments could foster a political climate more conducive to rolling back the carceral state.

CONCLUSION: THE POWER TO PUNISH

The enthusiasm with which U.S. politicians and public officials began embracing the death penalty in the 1970s so as to demonstrate their law-and-order credentials is nothing short of remarkable. By the 1990s, it was hard to find prominent candidates for national or statewide office who publicly opposed capital punishment. The death penalty also became a major factor in judicial elections, especially in states that retained capital punishment and ones that permitted judges to override a jury's sentence of life imprisonment and impose the death penalty.[115] Candidates who did not support the death penalty were vilified by their political opponents and in the press. Politicians regularly boasted about their willingness and indeed eagerness to carry out executions. As Florida's Attorney General Bob Butterworth warned after a series of botched executions in his state's electric chair, most notoriously the macabre 1997 death of Pedro Medina, whose head burst into flames: "People who wish to commit murder better not do it in the state of Florida, because we may have a problem with our electric chair."[116]

The central place capital punishment once again assumed in American politics and the enthusiasm politicians and public officials displayed for the ultimate penalty represented a marked change from the 1950s and much of the 1960s. At that time, elected officials and their political rivals generally did not view opposition to the death penalty as a major political liability. Indeed some politicians and public officials were outspoken foes of capital punishment.

A number of analysts emphasize the symbolic value of capital punishment in American politics. This begs the question, however, of why capital punishment became such a powerful symbol to express society's fear of crime and revulsion at criminals in the United States[117] but not elsewhere. The institution of capital punishment in the United States has been stubbornly impervious to rational or scientific arguments that have been its undoing elsewhere. Moreover, in the United States, but not Western Europe and Canada, efforts to abolish capital punishment sparked a powerful countermovement that succeeded not only in bringing back executions in the name of law and order, but also contributed to the construction of the carceral state.

[115] Stephen B. Bright and Patrick J. Keenan, "Judges and the Politics of Death: Deciding Between the Bill of Rights and the Next Election in Capital Cases," *Boston University Law Review* 75 (May 1995). This practice was successfully challenged in 2002 in *Ring v. Arizona*.

[116] Lifton and Mitchell, *Who Owns Death?* 56.

[117] Paternoster, *Capital Punishment in America*, 286. See also Zimring and Hawkins, *Capital Punishment and the American Agenda*, 11; and Bedau, *Death is Different*, 8.

Looking back on the 1960s from the vantage point of nearly four decades of massive, almost continuous growth in the carceral state, it is tempting to single out the actions of key politicians like Goldwater, Nixon, and Reagan as decisive turning points that set the United States firmly on its punitive path. Yet what is remarkable about the 1960s, for all the political and violent unrest, is that views on crime and punishment were still in great flux. This was particularly so in the case of capital punishment. At the start of the 1960s and for much of that decade, capital punishment was not a leading issue. Politicians and public officials perceived the political costs of opposing the death penalty as low, or ones they were willing to pay. Even some public officials who became notorious hardliners, notably Nixon and Georgia's Lester Maddox, did not immediately embrace death as the answer even amid the rising calls for law and order. Indeed, until the mid-1970s, one would be hard-pressed to talk about the existence of a pro-death penalty movement.

This chapter examined the wider political context in which capital punishment developed and was transformed as an institution. It challenges the view that the country's apartheid inheritance is the prime reason why the death penalty has persisted as such a potent symbol. Certainly the South's historical "culture of vengeance" and its triple legacies of slavery, Jim Crow, and lynchings set an important context for the resurrection and transformation of capital punishment in contemporary American politics.[118] But the country's apartheid history is only the starting point for explaining how race mattered in the political development of capital punishment. As shown in this chapter, race got refracted through particular institutions at specific points in time – in this instance, the courts and certain civil and human rights organizations. My account also casts doubt on claims that a monolithic, well-organized, richly endowed conservative movement emerged to trounce the abolitionists and drown out their arguments once leading politicians decided to play the law-and-order card beginning in the 1960s.

Instead, I demonstrate how through an exceptional set of institutions and circumstances, capital punishment got lodged in the judicial process long before the contemporary anti-death penalty movement congealed and well before the death penalty became a cause célèbre among conservative leaders and their followers. Lodged in the courts, its fiercest opponents became public-interest lawyers bereft of a wider political movement to make the case for abolishing capital punishment. Initially, these public interest lawyers did not have to contend with any organized movement dedicated to preserving the death penalty. As a consequence, the debate

[118] On the South's "culture of vengeance" and Southern exceptionalism in penal policy, see Edward L. Ayers, *Vengeance and Justice: Crime and Punishment in the 19th-Century American South* (New York: Oxford University Press, 1984); Richard E. Nisbett and Dov Cohen, *Culture of Honor: The Psychology of Violence in the South* (Boulder, CO: Westview Press, 1996); Zimring, *The Contradictions of American Capital Punishment*; and James W. Marquart, Sheldon Ekland-Olson, and Jonathan R. Sorensen, *The Rope, the Chair, and the Needle: Capital Punishment in Texas, 1923–1990* (Austin, TX: University of Texas Press, 1994), 4.

over the death penalty was channeled in certain directions that ultimately helped preserve capital punishment and lock in the carceral state. In short, capital punishment helped launch U.S. penal policy on a very different trajectory well before law-and-order politicians discovered the electoral votes to be harvested by promising to pull the switch early and often. Even as the number of death sentences and executions dwindle in the United States today, capital punishment is likely to continue casting a lengthy shadow over the future development of penal policy.

Index